中国-阿拉伯国家博览会
معرض الصين والدول العربية
CHINA-ARAB STATES EXPO

The Development Process of China-Arab States Economic and Trade Relations Annual Report

2021

CCPIT Ningxia /Edit
Wang Guangda /Editor in Chief

中阿经贸关系发展进程
2021年度报告

社会科学文献出版社
SOCIAL SCIENCES ACADEMIC PRESS (CHINA)

Acknowledgments

This report was organized and completed by the Shanghai International Studies University and China-Arab Research Center on Reform and Development under the guidance of CCPIT Ningxia. Relying on their long-term accumulation of knowledge in China-Arab states economic and trade relations, the members of the research group used appropriate analytical tools to describe the annual process, characteristics and development trends of China-Arab states economic and trade relations.

Professor Wang Guangda served as the editor-in-chief of this report, and Ms. Ding Liping reviewed the Chinese version. Ms Jin Rui, Wang Yihan and others managed the English translation of the manuscript.

We want to express our sincere gratitude to all who worked so hard to produce this report. The team's professionalism and fortitude were evident throughout the process. The team's exceptional collective efforts reflect in the quality and substance contained therein. We thank CCPIT Ningxia for its support and assistance in producing this report with admiration and respect.

"The Development Process of China-Arab States Economic and Trade Relations 2021 Annual Report"Research Group Members

Consultant

Zhu Weilie（Professor of Shanghai International Studies University, Director of the Expert Committee of China-Arab Research Center on Reform and Development）

Editor-in-chief

Wang Guangda（Professor of Shanghai International Studies University, Executive Director of China-Arab Research Center on Reform and Development）

Chief Compiler

Ding Liping（Editor of Sunshine Publishing House, Yellow River Publishing and Media Group）

Chapter writer

Sun Degang/Wu Tongyu（Researcher of Middle East Research Center, Institute of International Studies, Fudan University/Ph.D. student of Middle East Institute, Shanghai International Studies University）

Yang Shaoyan（Professor of School of Economics and Management, Ningxia University）

Jiang Yingmei（Associate Researcher of Institute of West Asian and African Studies, Chinese Academy of Social Sciences）

Zhang Shuai（Lecturer of Shanghai University of Political Science and Law）

Qian Xuming/Zhang Yisen（Associate Researcher, Middle East Institute, Shanghai International Studies University/Ph.D. student of Middle East Studies, Shanghai International Studies University）

Wang Xiaoyu（Lecturer and postdoctoral teacher of Shanghai International

Studies University, China-Arab Research Center on Reform and Development）

Zhou Fang （Associate Professor of School of Oriental Languages, Shanghai International Studies University）

Wang Guangda/Li Xueting （Professor of Shanghai International Studies University/Associate Researcher of China-Arab Research Center on Reform and Development）

Yang Zishi/Ding Liping （Ph.D. of Ningxia University/Editor of Sunshine Publishing House, Yellow River Publishing and Media Group）

CONTENTS

Chapter 1 Overall Situation of China-Arab States Economic and Trade Cooperation during the COVID-19 Pandemic / 001

1.1 Overall Developments of China-Arab States Economic and Trade Cooperation during the COVID-19 Pandemic / 002

1.2 Developments and Trends in Sectors Involved in China-Arab States Economic and Trade Cooperation during the COVID-19 Pandemic / 006

1.3 Progress of China-Arab States Economic and Trade Cooperation during the COVID-19 Pandemic / 011

1.4 Outlook of China-Arab States Economic and Trade Cooperation Trends / 017

Chapter 2 Report on China-Arab States Trade Cooperation / 021

2.1 Situation of China's Trade with the Arab States / 022

2.2 Situation of the Arab States' Trade with China / 028

2.3 China's Trade Relations with the Arab States / 037

Chapter 3 Report on China-Arab States Investment Cooperation / 048

3.1 Scale and Characteristics of China's and the Arab States' Direct Investments / 048

3.2 New Trends of China-Arab States Investments / 055

3.3 New Opportunities and Challenges for China-Arab States Investment

Cooperation / 060

Chapter 4　Report on China-Arab States Agricultural Cooperation / 067

4.1　Current Situation of Agricultural Development in the Arab States / 068

4.2　Situation of China-Arab States Agricultural Cooperation / 073

4.3　Future Prospects of China-Arab States Agricultural Cooperation / 081

Chapter 5　Report on China-Arab States Energy Cooperation / 086

5.1　Overview of Energy Resources in the Arab States / 086

5.2　China-Arab States Cooperation in Traditional Energy / 091

5.3　China-Arab States Cooperation in New Energy / 098

5.4　The Future of China-Arab States Energy Cooperation / 104

Chapter 6　Report on China-Arab States Digital Economy Cooperation / 108

6.1　The Digital Economy Development in the Arab States / 108

6.2　China-Arab States Cooperation in Digital Economy / 117

6.3　The Future of China-Arab States Cooperation in the Digital Economy / 123

Chapter 7　Report on China-Arab States Cooperation in Science, Technology, and Eco-environmental Governance / 127

7.1　The China-Arab States Science and Technology Cooperation Framework and Traditional Cooperation Field / 127

7.2　Key Fields of China-Arab States Science and Technology Cooperation / 130

7.3　The Current Status and Future Development of China-Arab States Cooperation in Eco-environmental Governance / 137

7.4　The Future of China-Arab States Science and Technology Cooperation / 144

Chapter 8　Report on China-Arab States Healthcare and Pandemic Containment Cooperation / 149

8.1　The Overall Status of China-Arab States Pandemic Containment Cooperation / 149

CONTENTS

8.2　The Characteristics and Meaning of China-Arab States Pandemic
　　　Containment Cooperation　　　　　　　　　　　　　　　／ 162

8.3　The Outlook of China-Arab States Healthcare Cooperation　／ 165

Chapter 9 Report on the Opening up of Ningxia　　　　　　／ 170

9.1　General Situation of Economic and Trade Cooperation between
　　　Ningxia and the Arab States　　　　　　　　　　　　　／ 170

9.2　Report on the First Five Sessions of China-Arab States Expo　／ 176

Chapter 1 Overall Situation of China-Arab States Economic and Trade Cooperation during the COVID-19 Pandemic

2020 was an unusual year in the history of mankind, during which the COVID-19 outbreak profoundly affected the international landscape and economic order, thus making the international and regional situations more complicated. Under the auspices of the Chinese President and Arab leaders, China-Arab States relations have been further consolidated with frequent high-level interactions. The pragmatic cooperation between China and the Arab States to fight against COVID-19 was exceptional, and has yielded remarkable achievements in various sectors. China and the Arab States issued a joint statement on solidarity against COVID-19, in which both sides reaffirmed their commitment to strengthen solidarity, promote cooperation, and support each other to fight against COVID-19 and address common threats and challenges. Furthermore, China and the Arab States have been dedicating themselves to post-COVID-19 economic recovery and development to safeguard their citizens' well-being and sustainable growth. Chinese Foreign Minister Wang Yi commended China-Arab States relations in the face of the pandemic: "China and the Arab States have stood by each other, fought in solidarity and extended a helping hand to each other. Our relations have been further strengthened and elevated."[1]

---

[1] Wang Yi: "Strengthening cooperation against COVID-19 to build a community with shared future for China, Arab states", *People's Daily*, July 3, 2020, p. 6.

The Development Process of China-Arab States Economic and Trade Relations
Annual Report 2021

1.1 Overall Developments of China-Arab States Economic and Trade Cooperation during the COVID-19 Pandemic

In 2020, the economic and trade cooperation between China and the Arab States suffered impacts of the adverse events resulting from the COVID-19 pandemic and the global economic downturn. Despite such challenges, the China-Arab States strategic partnership stood strong. In particular, the two sides forged a China-Arab States health community with a shared future. Thanks to their shared efforts, China and the Arab States successfully contained the COVID-19 outbreaks, so demand and opportunities for China-Arab States cooperation gradually started increasing. China-Arab States strategic partnership became stronger during the pandemic. This demonstrated to the world developing countries' solidarity and paved the way for China and the Arab States to build a community with a shared future.

1.1.1 Steady Progress of China-Arab States Economic and Trade Cooperation during the COVID-19 Pandemic

In addition to preventing and controlling the coronavirus, China and the Arab States continued to promote the high-quality development of the Belt and Road initiative, strengthen macroeconomic policy coordination, coordinate economic and social development, and keep the trade and investment markets open. In 2020, the total volume of trade between China and the Arab States reached USD 239.343 billion. The value of China's exports to the Arab countries amounted to USD 127.799 billion, achieving a year-on-year increase of 6.15% despite the impacts of the pandemic. Of the total export value, the value of electromechanical and high-tech products accounted for 67.4%, up 6.1% and 3.3% respectively. China steadily remained the top trading partner of Arab countries. By the end of 2020, China's FDI stock in Arab countries amounted to USD 20.1 billion, and the accumulated investments from Arab countries to China arrived at USD 3.8 billion. The two sides' investments covered sectors such as crude oil, gas, construction, manufacturing, logistics, and electricity.

002

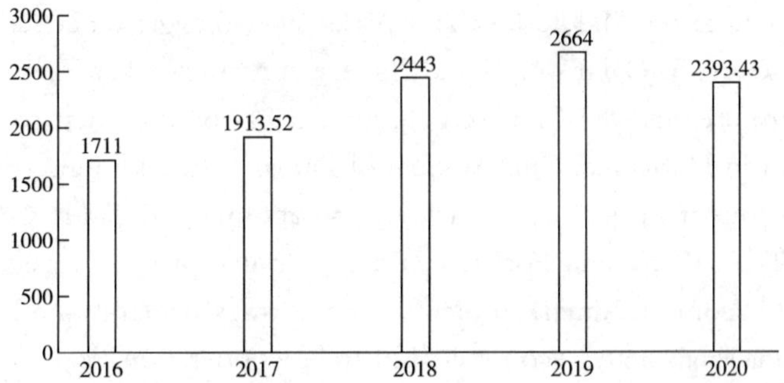

Chapter 1   Overall Situation of China-Arab States Economic and Trade Cooperation
during the COVID-19 Pandemic

Total volume of trade between China and the Arab States,2016-2020(USD 100 million)

Source: Ministry of Commerce of the People's Republic of China.

On July 6, 2020, the ninth Ministerial Conference of the China-Arab States Cooperation Forum was successfully convened via video conferencing. The two sides concluded and signed the China-Arab States Joint Statement on Solidarity against COVID-19, the Amman Declaration of the 9th Ministerial Meeting of CASCF, and the CASCF Execution Plan for 2020-2022. At the conference, the two sides agreed to hold the China-Arab Summit and reached an important consensus on building a China-Arab States community with a shared future, supporting each other on core interests issues, promoting the joint development of the Belt and Road Initiative, and strengthening cooperation in COVID-19 responses and how businesses get back to work and production after lockdowns. This laid the foundation for the China-Arab States comprehensive strategic partnership in the context of the current situation.

1.1.2   Notable Highlights of China-Arab States Economic and Trade Cooperation

Despite continued COVID-19 outbreaks across the world, China and the Arab States never balk at difficulties and have been steadily conducting economic and trade exchanges and cooperation. As a result of COVID-19 and strict disease prevention and control measures, many China-Arab States projects were affected. However, as the epidemic eased, China and the Arab countries resumed work and production, and their cooperation made substantial progress. For example, the first phase of the school project in Ramallah, Palestine aided by the Chinese government has been successfully completed; Shenzhen has opened an

003

all-cargo route to the Middle East and Africa; the strategic water security mega reservoir project in Qatar built by a Chinese constructor has been completed and put into use; and the Chinese government has built its first overseas full-time school in Dubai, i.e. Chinese School Dubai.[1] In addition, a number of major investment projects, such as Suez Economic and Trade Cooperation Zone (SETC) and Khalifa Port Container Terminal project (Phase II) in the UAE have become landmark projects for the transformation and upgrading of the China-Arab States economic and trade cooperation in the new era. In the context of the global economic downturn, China and the Arab States have been promoting cooperation in a number of new projects in the sectors such as solar energy, railroads, and locomotives, in order to boost the China-Arab States comprehensive strategic partnership.

China and the GCC countries have been forging ahead with their economic and trade cooperation through active interactions despite adverse conditions. This testifies to the mutual benefits for their economy and resilience of their pragmatic cooperation. Specifically, the trading volume of crude oil grew by more than 30%, reaching nearly 100 million tons; and the total value of newly executed construction projects increased by 14.5% to over USD 10 billion. Meanwhile, China fully supported the UAE to host the Expo 2020 Dubai, and helped with building the main stadium for the FIFA World Cup Qatar. China Railway International Group (CRIG) won the contract for the main stadium construction project for FIFA World Cup Qatar 2022. The company completed placing the stadium's final steel structural beam in 2020, which marked CRIG's completion of the main steel structure of the stadium for FIFA World Cup Qatar 2022.

In the context of the global pandemic, China-Arab States cooperation in digital economy was particularly eye-catching. The e-commerce industry became not only a new growth pole of the two sides' economic and trade cooperation, but also an opportunity for them to jointly advance the Belt and Road Initiative. At the Ministerial Conference of the CASCF in July 2020, China and the Arab States decided to strengthen cooperation and learn from each other in the field

---

[1] "Foreign Ministry Spokesperson Hua Chunying's Regular Press Conference on December 10, 2020", Ministry of Foreign Affairs of the People's Republic of China, December 10, 2020, https://www.mfa.gov.cn/web/wjdt_674879/fyrbt_674889/202012/t20201210_7816953.shtml.

Chapter 1   Overall Situation of China-Arab States Economic and Trade Cooperation
during the COVID-19 Pandemic

of Internet and digital economy. After the initial COVID-19 outbreak ended, Chinese e-commerce companies actively shared with the Arab States their technology and experience in platform development and logistics management, making their contributions to help Arab countries resume work and production. The penetration rate of Chinese e-commerce platforms in the GCC countries among their Internet users has reached 80%.[1] The Internet + cross-border e-commerce model has the benefit of being complementary, allowing great potential for development of the e-commerce industry in the Arab States.

1.1.3   Continued Optimization of China-Arab States Economic and Trade Cooperation Mechanism

In the context of the global pandemic, the China-Arab States economic and trade cooperation mechanism acted as an essential platform for businesses on both sides to conduct cooperation, which is of considerable significance in promoting trade between China and the Arab States. China and the Arab States actively participate in expos, investment and trade fairs, and other activities held by each other. Arab countries actively participated in the 3rd China International Import Expo in 2020. On July 15, 2020, the China-UAE Economic and Trade Digital Expo was successfully held online. More than 1,000 companies from China and the UAE participated in the Expo, and their exhibits involved in various categories such as smart city, medical products, textile fashion, cultural and creative products, new agriculture, and food. On October 20, 2020, Ni Jian, Chinese Ambassador to the UAE, was invited to the online roadshow for China's participation in the Expo 2020 Dubai. In November 2020, the Ninth Session of the China-Oman Joint Committee on Economics and Trade and the Ministry of Commerce, Industry and Investment Promotion of Oman was successfully convened via video conferencing.[2] On March 4, 2020, China and the Syrian government signed the Economic and Technical Cooperation Agreement between the Government of the People's Republic of China and the Government of the Syrian Arab Republic.

---

[1]   "Opening a new chapter for global digital governance (Heyin)", People's Daily, March 30, 2021, p. 3.

[2]   "The Ninth Session of China-Oman Joint Committee on Economics and Trade was successfully convened", China-Arab States Cooperation Forum, November 27, 2020, http://www.chinaarabcf. org/chn/zagx/zajw/t1836073.htm.

005

1.1.4 China-Arab States Economic and Trade Cooperation Empowered by Emerging Technologies

China and the Arab States have been actively sharing and using digital trading and innovative technologies to promote a technology-based approach to overcoming COVID-19. In terms of the energy sector, China continues to promote China-Arab States cooperation in renewable energy such as photovoltaic energy, solar thermal energy, and wind energy. Moreover, their cooperation in artificial intelligence and big data has become a highlight. The Saudi SOE Saudi Telecommunication Company (STC), Alibaba Cloud Intelligence, and eWTP Arabia Capital Fund will establish a partnership to provide high-performance public cloud services for Saudi Arabia.[1]

1.2 Developments and Trends in Sectors Involved in China-Arab States Economic and Trade Cooperation during the COVID-19 Pandemic

China and the Arab States have been using CASCF as an opportunity to increase cooperation and share experience in COVID-19 prevention and control. At the beginning of the global pandemic on April 9, 2020, China held a video conference with the Arab League where Chinese health experts shared their practices in dealing with and overcoming COVID-19. More than 100 people attended the conference online, including the heads of ministries of health and experts from the Arab League General Secretariat and 12 Arab countries, as well as WHO Special Envoys on COVID-19 Preparedness and Response. After confirmed cases started decreasing in the second half of 2020, the Arab countries became poised to resume work in various sectors. On September 23, 2020, China and the Arab League held a video seminar on "China's Experience in Coping with the Economic Impacts of COVID-19." Nearly 100 participants from the Arab League General Secretariat, the Arab Labor Organization, and the Arab Organization for Agricultural Development, the Arab Federation

---

[1] "Alibaba Cloud Intelligence to provide cloud services for Saudi Arabia", Economic and Commercial Office of the Consulate General of the People's Republic of China in Jeddah, December 31, 2020, http://jedda.mofcom.gov.cn/article/zxhz/202012/20201203027788.shtml, access date: January 12, 2021.

Chapter 1　Overall Situation of China-Arab States Economic and Trade Cooperation during the COVID-19 Pandemic

for Digital Economy, and UNCTAD Investment and Enterprise Division attended this seminar. China sincerely shared with the Arab States its experience in coordinating COVID-19 prevention and control and economic and social development. On September 29, the Ministry of Foreign Affairs of the People's Republic of China, together with the National Health Commission and the Ministry of Science and Technology, held a video conference with the Arab League. Officials and health experts from the Arab League General Secretariat and ten Arab States health agencies attended this conference. The two sides focused on topics such as "risk assessment and graded prevention and control of COVID-19 outbreaks under new situations", "vaccine development," and "evolution of the virulence of COVID-19."

1.2.1　Further Enhancement of Economic and Industry Cooperation

Currently, China-Arab States relations are in the golden age, and China-Arab States infrastructure construction projects have been flourishing. Chinese companies in Egypt worked hard to both follow COVID-19 protocols and ensure regular operations. As a result, their construction projects were not significantly affected. The main structure of the Iconic Tower of the first phase of the Central Business District project in Egypt's New Administrative Capital built by CSCEC Egypt has exceeded 53 floors (around 260 meters), and the main structures of eight single stand-alone buildings have completed topping out. The first phase of the 10th of Ramadan Railway (LRT) project constructed by a Chinese company is progressing smoothly and will become the first electric rail line in Egypt. Moreover, the 500-kV electric transmission line project is near completion and will become a critical artery of Egypt's national electricity grid.[1] By the end of 2020, China-Egypt TEDA Suez Economic and Trade Cooperation Zone attracted 96 companies, with actual investment amounting to more than USD 1.25 billion, accumulated sales more than USD 2.5 billion, and paid taxes nearly USD 176 million. These companies directly provided around 4,000 jobs and indirectly provided more than 36,000 jobs, making the zone became the

---

[1]　"The pragmatic economic and trade cooperation between China and Egypt enhancing steadily in the face of COVID-19", Xinhua News Agency, January 18, 2021, http://www.xinhuanet.com/silkroad/2021-01/14/c_1126981548.htm.

"economic engine in the desert."[1] The underground tunnels in Saudi Arabia, built by a Chinese company, were completed and opened to traffic on December 31, 2020. The agreement for the first large-scale infrastructure project RABT after the State Grid Corporation of China successfully took a stake in OETC was signed.[2] China-UAE Industrial Capacity Cooperation Demonstration Zone, Khalifa Port Container Terminal, Dubai 700 MW CSP, and other Belt and Road Initiative projects are steadily progressing.

China and the Arab States have aligned their green economy strategies and have been jointly practicing green development. In November 2020, China Yutong Bus and Mowasalat signed an agreement, where the parties agreed that Yutong Bus would provide 1,002 vehicles dedicated to FIFA World Cup Qatar and other public transport support.[3] The two companies signed a framework agreement to build an electric bus assembly plant in the Qatar Free Zones, so as to improve Qatar's industrial technology, serve the country's environmental protection and vehicle transformation strategies, enhance the supporting capacity of its auto industry, promote the development of auto industry clusters, and serve the country's bus electrification strategies. On another note, in 2020, sales of Chinese car companies in Saudi Arabia continued to grow. Specifically, Changan Automobile exported nearly 20,000 vehicles to Saudi Arabia, up nearly 100% year-on-year, with end-user sales reaching more than 19,000. Bestune exported 2,500 vehicles, up more than 200% year-on-year. SAIC MG sold 18,000 vehicles, up 80% year-on-year.[4]

---

[1] "The "new town in the desert" further upgraded after five years", Middle East Watch Official Account, January 26, 2021.

[2] "Oman OETC held a collective signing ceremony for North-South networking project", Economic and Commercial Office of the Embassy of the People's Republic of China in the Sultanate of Oman, October 26, 2020, http://om.mofcom.gov.cn/article/jmxw/202010/20201003010814.shtml.

[3] "Chinese Ambassador to Qatar Zhou Jian attended the opening ceremony for the pilot operation of electric buses and charging stations in Qatar", Embassy of the People's Republic of China in the State of Qatar, June 30, 2021. http://qa.china-embassy.org/chn/zkgx/jmhz/202106/t20210630_8941420.htm.

[4] "Chinese passenger cars making remarkable progress in developing the Saudi market", Chinese Consulate-General in Jeddah Official Account, May 24, 2021.

Chapter 1   Overall Situation of China-Arab States Economic and Trade Cooperation during the COVID-19 Pandemic

1.2.2   Close-up of Technical Cooperation in Green Energy

Energy cooperation, a key area of the Belt and Road Initiative, is the buttress of China-Arab States cooperation. Despite the spread of coronavirus across the globe, which exerted enormous impact on global energy production and demand, China-Arab States energy cooperation continued to advance steadily. Arab countries' proven crude oil reserves in 2020 remained the same as in 2019, i.e. 715.8 billion barrels, of which Saudi Arabia accounted for 37.3%, followed by Iraq (20.7%), Kuwait (14.2%), the UAE (13.7%), and Libya (6.8%).[1] China's crude oil imports from Arab countries accounted for half of its imports in the same period. Therefore, Arab countries are China's top source of crude oil imports. According to the General Administration of Customs of China, China's crude oil imports from Saudi Arabia in 2020 totaled about 84.93 million tons, or about 1.69 million barrels per day, an increase of 1.92% over the same period in 2019. Saudi Arabia remained China's largest crude oil supplier.[2] Energy cooperation as the buttress of the China-Arab States cooperation has become the major direction. China-Arab States energy cooperation should be strengthened in all aspects and energy security under open conditions should be achieved.

Under the double carbon goals, China and the Arab States have been focusing on the renewable energy industry, where they have been accelerating the optimization of energy supply structures to achieve breakthroughs. Relying on their respective advantages, China State Shipbuilding Corporation and QatarEnergy have been cooperating extensively in the fields of energy transportation, equipment manufacturing and globalization services. In order to stabilize the development of the global energy industry and boost the global economy, China State Shipbuilding Corporation Limited and QatarEnergy jointly signed the agreement for CSSC-QatarEnergy LNG Vessel Construction Project in Beijing (China), Shanghai (China), and Doha (Qatar) on April 22, 2020 via

---

[1]   "Arab countries account for 11% of global gas consumption", Economic and Commercial Counselor's Office of the Embassy of the People's Republic of China in Kingdom of Saudi Arabia, January 17, 2022, http://sa.mofcom.gov.cn/article/jmxw/202201/20220103237389.shtml.

[2]   In 2019, China imported 83.33 million tons of crude oil from Saudi Arabia. In 2018, China imported 56.73 million tons of crude oil from Saudi Arabia. In 2017, China imported 52.18 million tons of crude oil from Saudi Arabia. (Source: General Administration of Customs of the People's Republic of China, http://dzs.customs.gov.cn/customs/index/index.html).

The Development Process of China-Arab States Economic and Trade Relations
Annual Report 2021

cloud signing. The total value of the agreement exceeded RMB 20 billion. This agreement was the first order from Qatar gas projects, and is by far the largest export shipbuilding order undertaken by a Chinese shipbuilding company.

Promote clean energy, share benefits of green development, and steadily accelerate industrial transformation and upgrading. China and Saudi Arabia have been building smart cities together, and funding is leading China-Saudi cooperation. For example, a number of Chinese companies made significant contributions to the continued development of Yanbu, the first smart city in Saudi Arabia. In 2020, China and Saudi Arabia jointly announced plans to invest USD 5.6 billion to co-build a petrochemical plant in Yanbu Industrial City, Saudi Arabia. So far, Yanbu has become the third largest refining hub in the world. Moreover, China has discussed with the UAE and Egypt cooperation in crude oil, gas, renewable energy, and nuclear energy, and a number of consensuses have been reached.

1.2.3 Strengthening Cooperation in Medical and Healthcare

Solidarity against COVID-19 is another highlight of China-Arab States cooperation, and vaccine R&D has become the core of China-Arab States cooperation against COVID-19. China and the Arab States have been jointly promoting bilateral cooperation in health and medical care, including vaccine research and development, to build a China-Arab States health community with a shared future. They have been continuously deepening the China-Arab States comprehensive strategic partnership. In addition, China and the Arab States have communicated frequently strengthening international cooperation in the procurement of supplies for COVID-19 prevention and control. Taking the cooperation in vaccine R&D and clinical trials as an opportunity, China and the Arab States have been further deepening their cooperation in the field of medicine and health. China has been deepening its cooperation with the Arab States in the prevention and control of infectious diseases, medical institutions, and technology research by introducing the Internet + medical health model.

Working hand in hand, the two sides have announced the Joint Statement by China and the Arab States on Solidarity against COVID-19 and implemented the China-Arab States Health Cooperation 2019 Beijing Initiative. They are committed to making public health a new highlight in China-Arab States cooperation, and to fostering the development of China-Arab States Alliance for

010

Chapter 1   Overall Situation of China-Arab States Economic and Trade Cooperation
during the COVID-19 Pandemic

Medical and Health Cooperation.

1.2.4   Innovative and Integrated Development of Digital Economy

In response to the impacts of COVID-19 outbreaks, the Arab States have started to focus on formulating effective mitigation measures. Some Arab States have begun to actively encourage increased investment in digital economy, with a focus on the development of advanced technologies such as 5G, artificial intelligence, biotechnology, and green economy, so as to promote economic recovery, transformation, and upgrading. In light of current trends of digital economy in the world, digital economy, which can be integrated with various industries, plays an important role in driving transformation and upgrading of traditional industries in China and the Arab States, optimizing resource allocation, and adjusting industrial structures. China and the Arab States have been solidifying the foundation for digital economy through digital infrastructure development. In 2020, Huawei collaborated with Orange Egypt to build Orange Business Cloud, an advanced data center for cloud computing services in Egypt. In June 2020, Huawei and Saudi Smart City Solutions signed an agreement on smart city cooperation.

The deepening cooperation between China and the Arab States in the digitization field gives rise to the two sides' alignment of digital economy development strategies. Such alignment has added momentum to the economic recovery of countries involved. In particular, the experience shared by China has played a positive role in accelerating the digital transformation of the Arab States.

1.3   Progress of China-Arab States Economic and Trade Cooperation during the COVID-19 Pandemic

1.3.1   Exemplary Vaccine Cooperation

In the face of challenges from COVID-19, China and the Arab States have been standing together through thick and thin, demonstrating their deep friendship and strategic partnership. Since the beginning of the global COVID-19 outbreak, Chinese embassies in the Arab States have established close connections with the ministries of health, foreign affairs and other agencies of respective host countries to help prevent and control the disease. To this end,

011

The Development Process of China-Arab States Economic and Trade Relations
Annual Report 2021

China proactively shared with the Arab States available COVID-19 data and prevention and control materials. Moreover, the Chinese business associations in the Arab States also called on its members to donate medical supplies to local communities at the beginning of COVID-19 outbreaks. Chinese embassies convened a video conference with representatives from Chinese institutions, overseas Chinese organizations, and Chinese students in the Arab States to establish a joint prevention and control mechanism for COVID-19 outbreaks.

China and the Arab States share the same principles in addressing COVID-19 and have been working together to overcome challenges. China-Arab States cooperation in vaccines underscores their mutual trust and reflects fairness and inclusiveness. It has become a highlight of the China-Arab States comprehensive strategic partnership. China has actively implemented national leaders' commitments to making vaccines a global public good, and has donated and exported more than 72 million doses of vaccines to 17 Arab countries and the Arab League.[1]

The UAE was the first Arab country to accept a Phase III clinical trial of COVID-19 vaccine developed by China. On June 23, 2020, China National Biotec Group (CNBG) held a launch ceremony via video conferencing for Phase III clinical trial of Sinopharm attenuated COVID-19 vaccine in the UAE. Such cooperation between China and the UAE has set an example of international solidarity and cooperation against the disease. Currently, the UAE's vaccine-filling production lines in collaboration with China have been put into operation. As such, Chinese State Councilor and Foreign Minister Wang Yi commented: "The cooperation between China and the UAE created a global record of multi-national, large-scale clinical trials, helped Chinese vaccines gain international recognition, and made important contributions to global cooperation against COVID-19."[2] To help regions and countries improve their capabilities to independently prevent and control COVID-19 and achieve herd immunity

---

[1] "Wang Yi, China donated and exported over 72 million doses of vaccine to 17 Arab countries and Arab League", China News Service Website, July 22, 2021, https://www.chinanews.com.cn/gn/2021/07-22/9525868.shtml.

[2] "Wang Yi: Collaborative filling of Chinese vaccines between China and the Arab States making new contributions to regional and global communities in overcoming COVID-19", Embassy of the People's Republic of China in the United Arab Emirates, March 29, 2021, http://ae.china-embassy.org/chn/xwdt/202103/t20210329_8910579.htm.

Chapter 1   Overall Situation of China-Arab States Economic and Trade Cooperation during the COVID-19 Pandemic

through mass vaccination, China and Egypt jointly completed the first stable vaccine production line in Africa, which would manufacture one million doses of vaccine as the first batch. The two countries signed the Letter of Intent for Cooperation on COVID-19 Vaccine Production on January 1, 2021. On August 20, 2020, CNBG signed cooperation agreements with Morocco on COVID-19 vaccine, which promoted the cooperation between China and the Maghreb region to fight against the disease. In addition, China and Algeria have been actively discussing issues related to building collaborative vaccine-filling production lines.

Apart from donating COVID-19 vaccines, the Chinese government shared its experience with and provided medical supplies to Algeria, Syria, and other Arab countries to help them overcome COVID-19. Meanwhile, many of the Arab States supported China's "Spring Sprout" campaign, which enabled China to smoothly implement the campaign. For example, Saudi Arabia, the UAE, Egypt, and Oman actively participated in the campaign and assisted China in promoting vaccination.

China's practical actions such as vaccine assistance and donation to the Arab States helped mitigate the Arab people's cognitive bias and aversion to China's investment, increased their understanding and knowledge of China, and laid a solid foundation for positive impression towards future cooperation and project implementation in Arab communities. In the future, China and the Arab States will continue to play an exemplary role of solidarity against COVID-19. China plans to provide vaccines to developing countries by various means, including through donations and non-reimbursable assistance.

1.3.2   Multi-field Cooperation for Synergistic Development

China-Arab States economic and trade cooperation is welcomed in multiple fields, and all stakeholders have been actively responding to the Belt and Road Initiative and supporting their cooperation through different platforms. On November 24, 2020, the 4th China-Arab Media Cooperation Forum was successfully held via video conferencing. Nearly 60 representatives from the media agencies of China and Arab League members and chiefs of mainstream media organizations attended the forum, where they had in-depth discussions on "media responsibility in strengthening coordinated development of China and the Arab States under COVID-19." The two sides reached a wide consensus on

013

The Development Process of China-Arab States Economic and Trade Relations
Annual Report 2021

strengthening pragmatic cooperation in journalism and issued the "Communiqué of the 4th China-Arab Media Cooperation Forum."

On December 3, 2020, CCPIT Chairperson Gao Yan met with Arab envoys to China in Beijing to exchange views on further deepening China-Arab States business interactions and promoting mutually beneficial and win-win relationships between China and the Arab States.[1] Chinese companies carried forward the spirit of China. They kept their promises and overcame difficulties such as environmental adversities, lack of materials, traffic problems, and COVID-19 outbreaks. They rose to the occasion and spared no effort to build FIFA World Cup Qatar venues, ports, airports, and other major construction projects in the Arab States, which was highly acclaimed by the governments and counterparts. This laid a solid foundation for China's future construction projects in the Arab States.

In the communications technology field, China encourages Chinese companies to actively participate in the economic and social development of the Arab States and to contribute to their digital economy and high-tech development. Moreover, it further supports increasing interactions and cooperation in implementation of communications technologies and talent training, thus continuously expanding the areas of pragmatic China-Arab States cooperation. For example, Huawei has been focusing on developing non-profit training programs such as Huawei ICT Academy, Huawei ICT Competition, Huawei Seeds for the Future Program in the Middle East, which have cultivated numerous ICT talents and fostered ICT development. In October 2020, the 2nd Algeria Huawei ICT Competition Awards Ceremony & 5th Algeria Huawei Seeds for the Future Program Launch Ceremony was successfully held.

In the financial field, China and the Arab States have been stepping up cooperation in fin-tech and innovative investments, and the outcomes of the Belt and Road Initiative such as the China-Arab Cooperation Development Fund and cross-border encrypted digital financial payments drew much attention from the world. The China International Fair for Trade in Services in September 2020 acted as a bridge for China and the Arab States to get to know each other. For

---

[1] "CCPIT Chairperson Gao Yan meets with Arab envoys to China," China Council for the Promotion of International Trade, December 4, 2020, https://www.ccpit.org/a/20201204/20201204qcu3.html.

Chapter 1   Overall Situation of China-Arab States Economic and Trade Cooperation
during the COVID-19 Pandemic

example, the information of a number of large Abu Dhabi companies, financial institutions, innovative institutions, and industrial institutions information was displayed on the Abu Dhabi Global Market (ADGM) booth exhibition board. Many of them started exploring Chinese markets and targeted investments with ADGM's assistance. Furthermore, the 2020 Forum on Industrial Investment and International Financial Cooperation also served as a platform for China-Arab States financial cooperation.[1] The Arab States expressed that they are fully capable of supporting financial cooperation for the Belt and Road Initiative, and they are dedicated to exploring new financial ecosystems with the help with new technologies to achieve sustainable development goals.

1.3.3　Fruitful China-Arab States Cooperation in Science and Technology

The cooperation between China and the Arab States in artificial intelligence and big data has become a highlight. On October 21-22, 2020, the Saudi Data and Artificial Intelligence Authority hosted the Global AI Summit, and established a partnership with Huawei to promote the Saudi National AI Capability Development Program and to help Saudi Arabia achieve digital transformation.[2]

In the science and technology field, the cooperation in the field of drones has been a highlight of China-Arab States science and technology cooperation. The King Abdulaziz City for Science and Technology showcased the Al EQAB-1, a large three-engine reconnaissance and strike UAV that is jointly developed with Sichuan-based Tenguen Technology, at the IDEX-2021 defense exhibition in the UAE.

1.3.4　Steady Advancement of China-Arab States Agricultural Cooperation

Agriculture is an important area of economic and trade cooperation between China and the Arab States. Taking advantage of platforms such as China-Arab

---

[1]　"2020 Forum on Industrial Investment and International Financial Cooperation held in Shanghai", China's Foreign Trade Website, November 16, 2020, http://www.ccpitcft.com/newsinfo/864438. html.

[2]　"Alibaba Cloud Intelligence to provide cloud services for Saudi Arabia", Economic and Commercial Office of the Consulate General of the People's Republic of China in Jeddah, December 31, 2020, http://jedda.mofcom.gov.cn/article/zxhz/202012/20201203027788.shtml.

Cooperation Forum, China-Arab States Expo, and the Belt and Road Initiative, China and the Arab States have been increasing agricultural trade interactions, deepening agricultural and technical cooperation, and jointly driving economic and social development. In particular, the agricultural cooperation under the CASCF framework is an important path to deepening China-Arab States cooperation in multiple fields, as it showcases efforts at different levels, extensive topics for cooperation, interactions between the whole and individual, different stages during implementation, and balanced distribution of partner regions.[1]

China-Arab States cooperation in agricultural technology has been deepening. China's self-developed intelligent landscape water-saving irrigation technology has achieved considerable economic and social gains. Since 2015 after becoming the China-Arab States Technology Transfer Center, Ningxia in China has completed a plan for opening up its agriculture to the outside world based on its agricultural development characteristics and its needs for opening up. The Chinese province has established an inter-departmental joint conference mechanism comprising 16 departments for international agricultural cooperation and has formulated the "Measures for the Management and Development of Overseas Sub-centers of China-Arab States Agricultural Technology Transfer Center (for Trial Implementation)." It has been continuously consolidating and improving the development of overseas sub-centers of agricultural technology transfer centers and has established 8 overseas sub-centers. Furthermore, it is committed to building a platform for promoting international agricultural exchanges and cooperation in Ningxia and even China, and to accelerating the pace of "going out" of Chinese-style agriculture.[2]

From December 21 to 25, 2020, the sub-forums of the 16th Belt and Road Forum of China-Arab States Technology Transfer & Innovation Cooperation series of sub-forums were held both online and offline. The Chinese technologies and Chinese solutions are expected to revitalize agriculture in the Arab States.

---

[1] Zhang Shuai, "Agricultural cooperation under the CASCF framework: Characteristics, motives, and challenges", West Asia and Africa, No. 6, 2020.

[2] Jing Chunmei: "How does Ningxia boost agriculture "going out"?", China Agriculture for Trade and Economy, December 7, 2020, http://www.mczx.agri.cn/mybw/202012/t20201207_7572403.htm.

Chapter 1   Overall Situation of China-Arab States Economic and Trade Cooperation during the COVID-19 Pandemic

1.4   Outlook of China-Arab States Economic and Trade Cooperation Trends

The COVID-19 pandemic is both a challenge and an opportunity for the China-Arab States strategic partnership. China-Arab States relations, moving forward against the impacts of COVID-19, continue to be vibrant and dynamic. Chinese and Arab companies have been working together to get back to business, fight against COVID-19, and overcome difficulties. In the future, China and the Arab States need to trust and benefit each other, continue to enhance friendly exchanges and mutually beneficial cooperation in various fields, jointly promote international cooperation against COVID-19, support global economic recovery, promote sustainable development, jointly uphold multilateralism, and bring China-Arab States relations to a new level.

1.4.1   Implementing the Economic and Trade Consensus and Consolidating the Foundation for Cooperation

China and the Arab States should continue to firmly uphold the multilateral trading system, promote free trade, oppose unilateralism and protectionism, and safeguard fair competition. Moreover, under the Belt and Road Initiative framework, they should take advantage of multilateral dialogue and cooperation platforms such as the CASCF and the China-Gulf Cooperation Council Strategic Dialogue, in order to further normalize China-Arab States communication mechanisms and ensure mutual trust in each other's strategies. They should also continue to implement the Belt and Road Initiative, actively promote the integration of the Belt and Road Initiative with Arab States' strategies, share each other's practical economic achievements, reach the consensus to reduce political risks, and enhance cooperation to achieve mutual benefits. In addition, China and the Arab States should, through building more platforms, develop an all-around mechanism to serve companies, encourage them to develop and expand their business by utilizing national activities, and help more companies achieve faster and better development.

They should also implement the Execution Plan for 2020-2022 of the CASCF, accelerate the construction of the China-Palestine Free Trade Area, and complete the China-GCC Free Trade Area negotiations as early as possible, so as to facilitate China-Arab States trade exchanges and provide more trade

017

The Development Process of China-Arab States Economic and Trade Relations
Annual Report 2021

opportunities for companies on both sides. By the end of 2020, the China-Oman (Duqm) Industrial Park had attracted investments of USD 80 million from six companies.[①]

1.4.2 Increased Efforts on Promoting High-quality China-Arab States Economic and Trade and Cooperation

The global digital economic transformation is an inevitable trend. China and the Arab States should strengthen their integration of and cooperation in green infrastructure, green energy, and green finance with digital technologies, and strive to conduct more environment-friendly projects. For example, cooperation in digital energy technologies will significantly improve the quality of China-Arab States economic and trade cooperation. Specifically, clean energy generation, energy digitalization, transportation electrification, green ICT infrastructure, and integrated intelligent energy will help green, low-carbon, and high-quality development.

China-Arab States investment projects are comprehensive, specialized, large-scale, innovative, and high-end. Such characteristics give rise to high requirements for Chinese companies' capabilities in product innovation, resource integration, efficient management, and comprehensive coordination. In the future, as the quality of China-Arab States economic and trade cooperation continues to improve, companies need to continuously improve their competitiveness in international cooperation to match the high requirements of the China-Arab States strategic partnership.

1.4.3 Deepening and Expanding New Areas of China-Arab States Economic and Trade Cooperation

It is a long-term development process for China and the Arab States to transition from cooperation in just energy and economic fields to all-around and multi-faceted cooperation. Both sides should continue to consolidate their foundation of cooperation in energy and economic fields while exploring cooperation in other fields. In addition, they should pay attention to the long-term development, stability, and multi-level nature of China-Arab States cooperation. In recent years, in order to change the single economic structure

---

① Source: China-Arab States Expo, https://cn.cas-expo.org.cn/index.html.

018

Chapter 1　Overall Situation of China-Arab States Economic and Trade Cooperation
during the COVID-19 Pandemic

which is overly dependent on oil and gas industry, the Arab States have been comprehensively promoting economic diversification strategy, vigorously attracting investments, striving to develop infrastructure, manufacturing, logistics, tourism, fisheries and other non-oil and gas industries, and encouraging and supporting the private sector, especially SMEs, to play a greater role in economic development. In the future, China and the Arab States should dig deeper into their potential for cooperation, broaden the areas of cooperation, and cultivate new products, technologies, modes, and business models. Both sides should help companies identify their appropriate market positions to find their starting point, and help them carry out promotion and marketing per local conditions to raise Chinese companies' brand awareness and influence in local communities. For example, they should help companies improve their soft power, including conducting flexible industrial cooperation, holding cross-border e-commerce conferences, hosting forums, and expanding open-up policies.

The China-Arab States strategic partnership stands stronger and closer after going through and fighting against the COVID-19 pandemic. In the future, they should make full use of existing cooperation mechanisms, such as conducting anti-COVID-19 cooperation under the CASCF framework, deepening the consultation and sharing mechanism, maintaining close communication and cooperation, and implementing the China-Arab Countries Health Cooperation 2019 Beijing Initiative to build the Health Silk Road. They should also innovate their methods and contents of cooperation, such as by holding health and medicine forums, and increase their interactions and deepen their pragmatic cooperation in various fields such as public health, traditional medicine, and health. Moreover, they should promote the development of the China-Arab States Alliance for Medical and Health Cooperation, and work together to safeguard the lives and health of the Chinese and Arab peoples, achieve their common welfare, and build a health community with a shared future for mankind.

1.4.4　Jointly Ushering in the New Era of China-Arab States Economic and Trade Cooperation

The subject of climate change and sustainable development has become the most important topic in global socio-economic development. In the future, the way to deal with energy challenges of green transformation requires joint

019

response and cooperation between China and the Arab States. Additionally, to make digital economy a driving force, China and the Arab States should create growth momentum with technological innovations and digital transformation, reach consensus on expanding cooperation in digital economy, clean energy and, other emerging areas, and address the challenges posed by digital economy to employment, taxation, and vulnerable groups to bridge the digital divide. This will create new opportunities for China and the Arab States to seek cooperation and development, achieve a win-win situation, and advance high-quality Belt and Road cooperation.

China will continue to align its Belt and Road Initiative with the Arab States' vision and development plans. They will jointly advance high-quality Belt and Road cooperation, and consolidate cooperation in energy, investment, fisheries, high-tech, and human resources to make use of each other's advantages and achieve common development. China has been vigorously establishing a "dual circulation" development pattern in which domestic economic cycle plays a leading role while international economic cycle remains its extension and supplement, striving to cultivate the domestic market and comprehensively expanding its opening-up to the international market. In its future economic and trade cooperation with the Arab States, China will, on the one hand, continue to increase imports to deepen economic and trade cooperation; and will, on the other hand, encourage more Chinese companies to invest in the Arab States to contribute to their diversified economic development. In the COVID-19 era, development and livelihood issues have become the top priority in China-Arab States cooperation. China and the Arab States should jointly develop the Belt and Road Initiative through consultation to meet the interests of all, consolidate existing cooperation projects, expand cooperation in new areas, carry out fruitful economic and trade cooperation, and further enrich their strategic partnership to form a closer China-Arab States community with a shared future.

Chapter 2 Report on China-Arab States Trade Cooperation

The year 2020 is a watershed in the course of human history. The sudden COVID-19 outbreak triggered a global crisis, pressing a pause button on international travel, returning the global economy to reverse gear, and giving rise to power politics and Cold War thinking. As unilateralism and protectionism rise, China's foreign trade confronts many risks and challenges.

In recent years, China's trade development risks and challenges have risen significantly. Outside China, trade friction between China and the US has been continuing. In China, the market drivers for its consumer demand increase in urban and rural areas are insufficient. As major changes unfold in our world, China has always been dedicated to upholding the fundamental state policy of opening up, building a global community with a shared future, and pursuing a mutually beneficial strategy of opening up. With the implementation of measures for stabilizing foreign trade, China has introduced a set of policies to expand opening-up and promote the stable growth of foreign trade. China has been continuously optimizing its foreign trade structure and speeding up its transformation of growth drivers, and has achieved steady improvement in both quantity and quality of trading volume. In 2020, China's foreign trade remained stable and even made progress.

In 2020, the situation in the Middle East was tumultuous. In order to divert attention away from their domestic COVID-19 outbreak conflicts and fill the strategic vacuum left by the US, some countries in the region started to compete for dominance of regional affairs and to expand their influence to increase their discourse power. Against this backdrop, the cards have been reshuffled in the Middle East, with the emergence of political camps, pluralism, fragmentation,

021

and menu-driven cooperation. Meanwhile, in order to promote economic development, the Arab States have been taking a series of measures to expand their single economic model, promoting economic reform and diversified development to seek a path of transformation, and encouraging the private sector to play a greater role. Specifically, they have been implementing fiscal and tax incentives to attract foreign direct investments, increase infrastructure investments and financing, and optimize their business environment. These measures have contributed significantly to the economic development of the Arab States.

Additionally, the Arab States have been seeking more diversified foreign relations. For example, they have joined the implementation of the Belt and Road Initiative, and have made fruitful progress in foreign investments and foreign trade. Despite the severe impacts of COVID-19 and the global economic downturn, China-Arab States cooperation has still been progressing steadily for mutual benefit. Through advancing high-quality Belt and Road development, the two sides have been working together to promote a global community with a shared future for mankind. China-Arab States cooperation has successively involved getting companies back to business, media sector, reform and development, and in-depth exchange of experience in governance. The two sides have been continuously enriching the development of China-Arab States cooperation.

2.1 Situation of China's Trade with the Arab States

2.1.1 Basic Situation of China's Foreign Trade

The global economic uncertainties, risks, and challenges increased significantly in 2020, and the external environment for China's foreign trade was severe and complex. As a result, its economic growth continued to slow down. Statistics show that China's total value of imports and exports in 2020 reached USD 4,646.2 billion, up 1.72% compared to 2019. Of the total value, export value reached USD 2,590.601 billion, an increase of 3.68% over 2019; and import value reached USD 2,055.591 billion, a decrease of 0.65% over 2019. The trade surplus grew to USD 535.01 billion, up 24.53% compared to 2019. By 2020, China's foreign trade achieved four consecutive years of growth in the total value of imports and exports; however, its total import value dropped for the first time

Chapter 2   Report on China–Arab States Trade Cooperation

in nearly three years (see Table 2.1).

In 2021, China's foreign trade still faced serious and complex situations both at home and abroad. Fortunately, however, due to the export substitution effect resulting from recurring COVID-19 waves and import and export price increases, China's import and export value exceeded USD 6 trillion for the first time, setting a record high. According to statistics from the UN Comtrade Database, China's total value of imports and exports in 2021 reached USD 6,046.7 billion, up 30.14% compared to 2020. Of the total value, export value reached USD 3,362.302 billion, an increase of 29.79% over 2020; and import value reached USD 2,684.363 billion, an increase of 30.59% over 2019. The trade surplus grew to USD 677.939 billion, up 26.72% compared to 2020 (see Table 2.1). The above data reflects the strong toughness of our country's exports, but we must also see that export growth in 2021 has greatly affected the increased external demand and price factors. At present, due to the continuity of the epidemic, the difficulty of recovery of the world economy, coupled with logistics interruption and other reasons, the challenges facing our country's exports are still large.

Table 2.1   Volume and growth rate of China's foreign trade, 2011-2021

Indicator / Year	Imports and exports		Export value		Import value		Balance of trade	
	Total amount (USD 100 million)	YoY (%)	Amount (USD 100 million)	YoY (%)	Amount (USD 100 million)	YoY (%)	Amount (USD 100 million)	YoY (%)
2011	35,191	22.75	18,983.88	20.32	16207.80	25.73	2776.08	-3.82
2012	37240	5.82	20487.82	7.92	16752.69	3.36	3735.13	34.55
2013	40014	7.45	22090.07	7.82	17924.51	6.99	4165.56	11.52
2014	41566	3.88	23422.93	6.03	18143.54	1.22	5279.39	26.74
2015	38096	-8.35	22734.68	-2.94	15361.95	-15.33	7,372.73	39.65
2016	36855	-3.26	20976.37	-7.73	15879.21	3.37	5097.16	-30.86
2017	39747	7.85	22633.71	7.90	17114.24	7.78	5519.47	8.29
2018	44828	12.78	24942.30	10.20	19886.01	16.20	5056.29	-8.39
2019	45675	1.89	24985.78	0.17	20689.50	4.04	4296.20	-15.03
2020	46462	1.72	25906.01	3.68	20555.91	-0.65	5350.10	24.53

The Development Process of China-Arab States Economic and Trade Relations
Annual Report 2021

Continued

Indicator / Year	Imports and exports		Export value		Import value		Balance of trade	
	Total amount (USD 100 million)	YoY (%)	Amount (USD 100 million)	YoY (%)	Amount (USD 100 million)	YoY (%)	Amount (USD 100 million)	YoY (%)
2021	60467	30.14	33623.02	29.79	26843.63	30.59	6779.39	26.72

Source: Organized and calculated per statistics from the UN Comtrade Database
Note: China is the reporting economy for the above statistics.
Classification: HS3.

In 2020, China's top four trading partners were the EU, ASEAN, the US, and Japan, accounting for 16.42%, 15.14%, 13.02%, and 7.02% of total imports and exports respectively, and a combined total of 51.60% of total imports and exports (see Figure 2.1). Compared with 2019, China's top four trading partners remained unchanged, but the percentage of their total value of imports and exports increased.

As shown in Figure 2.1, in 2021, China's top four trading partners were the EU, the US, Japan, and South Korea, accounting for 13.70%, 12.54%, 6.14%, and 5.99% of total imports and exports respectively, and a combined total of 38.37% of total imports and exports. Despite the complex evolving international situation and recurring COVID-19 outbreaks since 2020, China's foreign trade business demonstrated remarkable resilience.

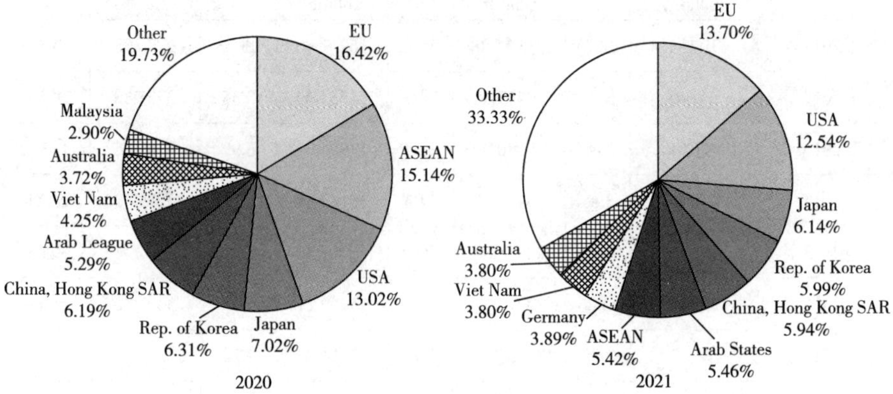

Figure 2.1 Percentage of total import and export value of China's top ten trading partners, 2020-2021

Source: Organized and calculated per statistics from the UN Comtrade Database.
Note: China is the reporting economy for the above statistics.
Classification: HS3.

024

Chapter 2   Report on China–Arab States Trade Cooperation

2.1.2   Situation of China's Foreign Trade in Services

In 2020, the Chinese economy was generally stable and even achieved growth. Nonetheless, due to the impacts of COVID-19 and other factors, trade in services shrank for the first time since 2011, with both imports and exports demonstrating a downturn. Meanwhile, the balance of services narrowed, the structure of trade in services continued to improve, and progress was made in terms of high-quality development.

According to statistics from the WTO, China's total value of service imports and exports amounted to USD 667.1 billion in 2020, down 14.9%. Of the total value, exports amounted to USD 280.6 billion, a decrease of 0.9%; and imports reached USD 381.1 billion, a year-on-year decrease of 23.9%.

As shown in Table 2.2, China's trade in services demonstrated a deficit. The deficit was USD 46.8 billion in 2011, and reached a maximum of USD 255 billion in 2018 after continuous increases. However, the deficit dropped in both 2019 and 2020, and the deficit was USD 100.5 billion in 2020. Since the 18th National Congress of the CPC, China's imported services have reached USD 3.8 trillion, with an average annual growth rate of 4.6%, which is higher than the global average of 3.7% during the same period. China has contributed 17.1% of global service import growth and acted as a leader in the world in terms of contribution to global service import growth.

Table 2.2   Value of China's imported and exported services, 2011-2020

Year	China's imports and exports		China's exports		China's imports		Balance of trade (USD 100 million)
	Amount (USD 100 million)	YoY (%)	Amount (USD 100 million)	YoY (%)	Amount (USD 100 million)	YoY (%)	
2011	4489	20.8	2010	12.7	2478	28.2	-468
2012	4829	7.6	2016	0.3	2813	13.5	-797
2013	5376	11.3	2070	2.7	3306	17.5	-1236
2014	6520	21.3	2191	5.9	4329	30.9	-2137
2015	6542	0.3	2186	-0.2	4355	0.6	-2169
2016	6616	1.1	2095	-4.2	4521	3.8	-2426
2017	6957	5	2281	8.9	4676	3.4	-2395
2018	7821	12.4	2636	15.5	5186	10.9	-2550
2019	7839	0.2	2832	7.4	5007	-3.5	-2175
2020	6671	-14.9	2806	-0.9	3811	-23.9	-1005

Source: WTO.

025

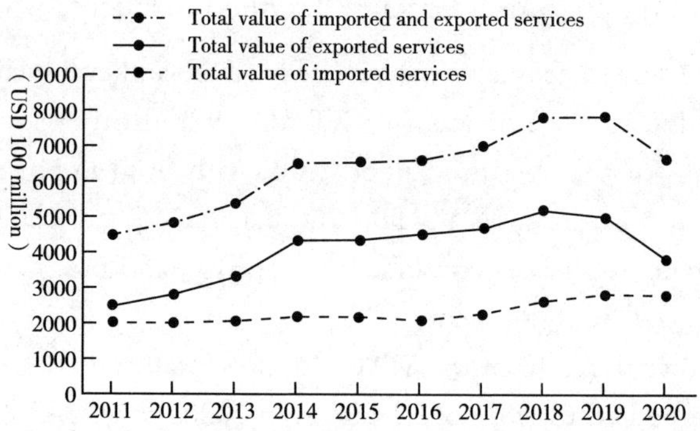

The Development Process of China-Arab States Economic and Trade Relations
Annual Report 2021

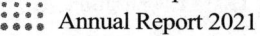

Figure 2.2 Trends of China's trade in services, 2011-2020

Source: WTO.

As shown in Figure 2.2, China's total value of imported and exported services, the total value of exported services, and the total value of imported services fluctuated between 2011 and 2020 in general, and the scale of its trade in services as a whole kept expanding. Meanwhile, Figure 2.2 depicts directly the deficits in China's trade in services from 2011 to 2020. The value of its exported services was much higher than that of its imported services. Thankfully, the trade deficit narrowed over the past two years.

2.1.3 Basic Situation of China's Exports to the Arab States

Despite the impacts of COVID-19 which hit both China's and the Arab States' economies hard in 2020, the two sides' bilateral economic and trade cooperation remained relatively solid.

In 2020, China's total value of imports and exports to the Arab States reached USD 239.343 billion, a decrease of 10.09% compared to 2019. Of the total value, China's total value of imports to the Arab States reached USD 116.544 billion, a decrease of 20% compared to 2019; and its total value of exports to the Arab States reached USD 122.799 billion, a decrease of 1.89% compared to 2019; Its trade surplus amounted to USD 6.255 billion, up 124.86% compared to 2019. (See Table 2.3.) China's total value of imports and exports, import value, and export value to the Arab States all achieved fluctuating growth. The ties between China and the Arab States in terms of trade became closer (see Figure 2.3).

026

Chapter 2　Report on China–Arab States Trade Cooperation

Table 2.3　Overall situation of China's trade with the Arab States, 2011-2021

Indicator / Year	Imports and exports		Export value		Import value		Balance of trade	
	Total amount (USD 100 million)	YoY (%)	Amount (USD 100 million)(%)	YoY (%)	Amount (USD 100 million)	YoY (%)	Amount (USD 100 million)	YoY (%)
2011	1843.58	34.71	758.61	20.53	1084.96	46.77	-326.35	197.14
2012	2224.20	20.65	912.79	20.32	1311.41	20.87	-398.62	22.14
2013	2388.97	7.41	1013.52	11.03	1375.45	4.88	-361.93	-9.20
2014	2510.51	5.09	1138.21	12.30	1372.30	-0.23	-234.09	-35.32
2015	2025.41	-19.32	1150.40	1.07	875.01	-36.24	275.38	117.64
2016	1710.29	-15.56	1006.74	-12.49	703.56	-19.59	303.18	10.10
2017	1917.57	12.12	986.73	-1.99	930.84	32.30	55.89	-181.57
2018	2445.67	27.57	1053.10	6.7	1392.57	49.60	-339.47	-807.39
2019	2662.01	8.85	1205.21	14.44	1456.82	4.61	-251.61	-25.88
2020	2393.43	-10.09	1227.99	1.89	1165.44	-20	62.55	124.86
2021	3301.90	37.96	1473.12	19.96	1828.78	56.92	-355.66	-668.60

Source: Organized and calculated per statistics from the UN Comtrade Database.

Note: China is the reporting economy for the above statistics.

Classification: HS3.

In 2021, China's total value of imports and exports to the Arab States reached USD 330.190 billion, up 37.96% compared to 2020. Of the total value, China's total value of imports to the Arab States reached USD 182.878 billion, up 56.92% compared to 2020; and its total value of exports to the Arab States reached USD 147.312 billion, up 19.96% compared to 2020. Its trade deficit was USD -35.566 billion, a decrease of 668.60% compared to 2020. As shown in Table 2.3, China's total value of imports and exports, import value, and export value to the Arab States all achieved significant increases. The trade relations between China and the Arab States became strong.

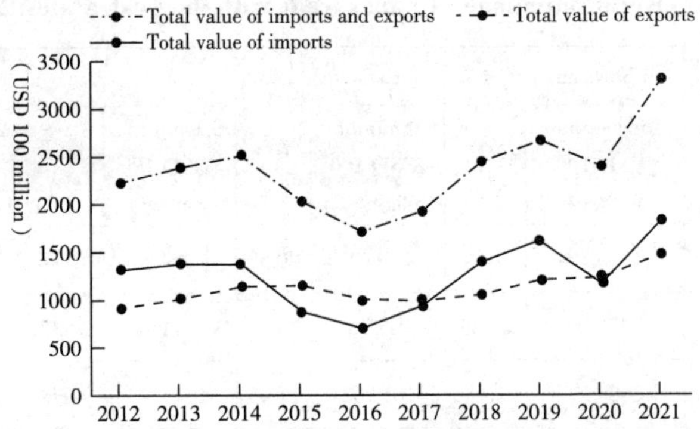

The Development Process of China-Arab States Economic and Trade Relations
Annual Report 2021

Figure 2.3   Trends of China's trade with the Arab States, 2012-2021

Source: Organized and calculated per statistics from the UN Comtrade Database.

Note: China is the reporting economy for the above statistics.

Classification: HS3.

2.2   Situation of the Arab States' Trade with China

2.2.1   Basic Situation of the Arab States' Foreign Trade

In 2020, the Arab States' total value of imports and exports reached USD 1,139.847 billion, a substantial decrease of 19.05% compared to USD 1,408.079 billion in 2019. The Arab States' value of foreign trade increased to USD 1,990.386 billion in 2013 after 2 years of continuous growth from 2011, marking a 10-year peak. Since then, the decline in petroleum prices and regional unrest led to a four-year decline in their foreign trade value from 2014 to 2017 (see Table 2.4). In 2018, petroleum prices recovered after several years of decreases, but then dropped due to the complex, volatile regional situations and COVID-19 outbreaks.

In 2020, the Arab States' total value of exports reached USD 571.296 billion, a decrease of 22.12% compared to USD 733.528 billion in 2019. In 2020, the Arab States' total value of imports reached USD 568.551 billion, a decrease of 15.71% compared to USD 674.521 billion in 2019. The Arab States' import value over the past six years, except for 2018, all showed negative growth (see Figure 2.4). In 2020, their trade surplus was USD 2.745 billion, down 95.35% compared to 2019. The Arab States had a foreign trade surplus from 2011 and 2014 as well as from 2017 to 2020, and demonstrated a trade deficit in both 2015 and 2016. The Arab States' foreign trade in general shows was unstable and fluctuated between

028

Chapter 2　Report on China–Arab States Trade Cooperation

2011 and 2020 (see Table 2.4 and Figure 2.4).

Table 2.4　Volume and growth rate of the Arab States' foreign trade, 2011-2020

Indicator / Year	Imports and exports		Export value		Import value		Balance of trade	
	Total amount (USD 100 million)	YoY (%)	Amount (USD 100 million)	YoY (%)	Amount (USD 100 million)	YoY (%)	Amount (USD 100 million)	YoY (%)
2011	17392.17	29.41	10906.28	37.01	6485.90	18.37	4420.38	78.17
2012	19446.23	11.81	12289.56	12.68	7156.67	10.34	5132.89	16.12
2013	19903.86	2.35	12088.30	-1.64	7815.56	9.21	4272.74	-16.76
2014	19208.59	-3.49	11205.41	-7.30	8003.18	2.40	3202.23	-25.05
2015	14392.32	-25.07	7091.00	-36.72	7301.32	-8.77	-210.33	-106.57
2016	13007.05	-9.63	6264.12	-11.66	6742.93	-7.65	-478.80	-127.64
2017	12838.43	-1.30	6744.69	7.67	6093.74	-9.63	650.95	235.95
2018	18598.23	44.86	9974.09	47.88	8624.14	41.52	1349.95	107.38
2019	14080.79	-24.29	7335.58	-26.45	6745.21	-21.79	590.37	-143.73
2020	11398.47	-19.05	5712.96	-22.12	5685.51	-15.71	27.45	-95.35

Source: Organized and calculated per statistics from the UN Comtrade Database.

Note: The Arab States are the reporting countries for the above statistics.

Classification: HS3.

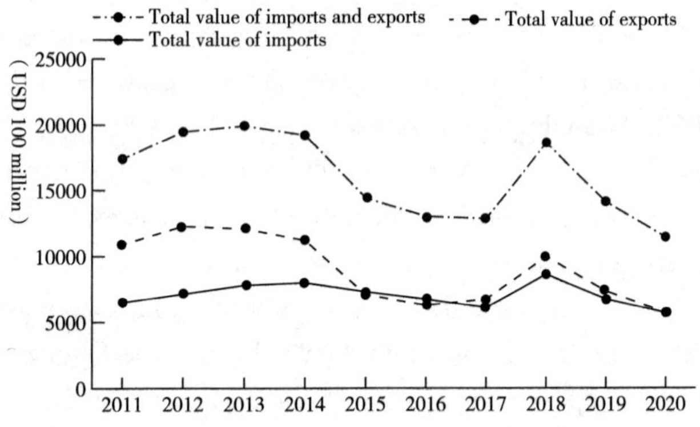

Table 2.4　Trade trends of the Arab States, 2011-2020

Source: Organized and calculated per statistics from the UN Comtrade Database.

Note: The Arab States are the reporting countries for the above statistics.

Classification: HS3.

:::: The Development Process of China-Arab States Economic and Trade Relations
:::: Annual Report 2021

In 2020, the Arab States' top four trading partners were the EU, China, the US, and India, accounting for 15.26%, 9.98%, 4.80%, and 4.28% of total imports and exports respectively, and a combined total of 34.32% of total imports and exports (see Figure 2.5). Compared with 2019, the top four trading partners of the Arab States remained the same, i.e., the EU, China, the US, and India.

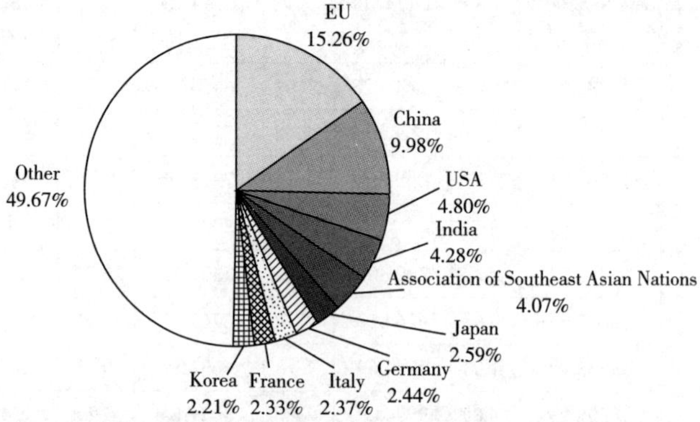

Figure 2.5   Percentage of total import and export value of the Arab States' top ten trading partners in 2020

Source: Organized and calculated per statistics from the UN Comtrade Database.

Note: The Arab States are the reporting economies for the above statistics.

Classification: HS3.

2.2.2   Basic Situation of the Arab States' Trade in Services

In 2020, the Arab States' total value of imported and exported services reached USD 401.871 billion, a decrease of 23.65% compared to USD 526.335 billion in 2019. Their imported services arrived at USD 242.371 billion, a decrease of 21.53% from USD 308.854 billion in 2019. Over the past six years, the total value of their imported and exported services as well as the total value of imported services all dropped, except for 2019. In 2020, the value of the Arab States' exported services amounted to USD 159.5 billion, a decrease of 26.66% compared with USD 217.480 billion in 2019. This was the first decrease in their export value over the past nine years (see Table 2.5 and Figure 2.6).

In 2020, the Arab States' exported services accounted for 4.05% of the global exported services, up 0.28 percentage points from 3.73% in 2019, setting a record high since 2011. Overall, the growth of their exported services remained stable (see Figure 2.7).

030

Chapter 2　Report on China–Arab States Trade Cooperation

The Arab States' trade in services has been in deficit since 2011. In 2014, their deficit peaked at USD 168.4 billion. Since then, the deficit continuously decreased year by year, arriving at USD 82.871 billion in 2020, down 9.31% from USD 91.374 billion in 2019.

Table 2.5　Value of Arab States' imported and exported services, 2011-2020

Indicator / Year	Arab States' imports and exports		Arab States' exports		Arab States' imports		Balance of trade (USD 100 million)
	Amount (USD 100 million)	YoY (%)	Amount (USD 100 million)	YoY (%)	Amount (USD 100 million)	YoY (%)	
2011	3788.23	7.7	1222.52	-0.3	2565.72	12.0	-1343.20
2012	4077.73	7.6	1305.54	6.8	2772.19	8.0	-1466.65
2013	4220.32	3.5	1324.40	1.4	2895.92	4.5	-1571.52
2014	5268.17	24.8	1792.08	35.3	3476.09	20.0	-1684.00
2015	5029.84	-4.5	1812.73	1.2	3217.12	-7.5	-1404.39
2016	4859.74	-3.4	1825.64	0.7	3034.10	-5.7	-1208.46
2017	4846.27	-0.3	1910.41	4.6	2935.87	-3.2	-1025.46
2018	4810.82	-0.7	2027.81	6.1	2783.01	-5.2	-755.20
2019	5263.35	9.41	2174.80	7.25	3088.54	10.98	-913.74
2020	4018.71	-23.65	1595.00	-26.66	2423.71	-21.53	-828.71

Source: Organized and calculated per statistics from the WTO website.

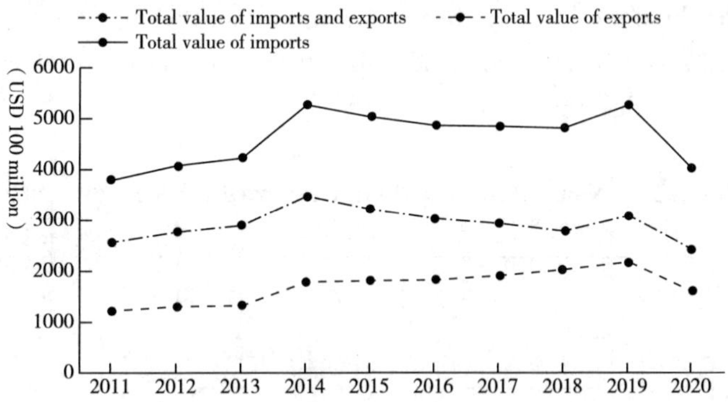

Table 2.6　Trends of the Arab States' trade in services, 2011-2020

Source: Organized and calculated per statistics from the WTO databases.

031

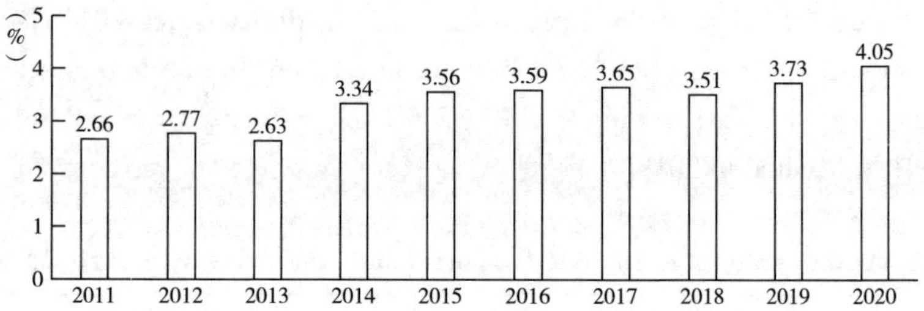

The Development Process of China-Arab States Economic and Trade Relations
Annual Report 2021

Table 2.7 Percentage of Arab States' value of exported services to the value of global exported services, 2011-2020

Source: Organized and calculated per statistics from the WTO databases.

In terms of the value of the Arab States' exported services, the five top-ranking countries in 2020 were the UAE, Qatar, Egypt, Morocco, and Bahrain. The UAE was the largest service exporter in the region, with its exported services reaching USD 62.138 billion, a decrease of 15.42% compared to 2019. Qatar was the second on the list, moving up three places compared to 2019. Its exported services amounted to USD 19.429 billion, up 1.83% compared to 2019. Egypt was in third place, with exported services amounting to USD 15.053 billion, down 28.09% compared to 2019. Morocco ranked fourth, with exported services reaching USD 13.855 billion, which was 28.47% lower than in 2019. The rankings of Egypt and Morocco in 2020 were the same as in 2019. Bahrain ranked fifth, with exported services arriving at USD 11.468 billion, which was 0.95% lower than in 2019. In 2020, the Arab country with the lowest value of exported services, i.e., USD 68 million, was the Comoros. The GCC countries, led by the UAE, have been growing fast and taking up a large share of the exported services. They accounted for 70.45% of the Arab States' exported services in 2020. (See Table 2.6).

Table 2.6 Value of the Arab States' exported services, 2013-2020

(Unit: USD 100 million)

Year / Country	2013	2014	2015	2016	2017	2018	2019	2020
Algeria	37.73	35.44	34.55	34.33	32.61	30.4	—	32
Bahrain	85.01	85.71	91.13	109.98	111.3	119.15	115.78	114.68
Comoros	0.8	0.85	0.84	—	—	—	—	0.68

032

Chapter 2 Report on China–Arab States Trade Cooperation

Continued

Year Country	2013	2014	2015	2016	2017	2018	2019	2020
Djibouti	3.66	3.82	4.55	4.06	—	2.09	11.04	—
Egypt	182.62	218.98	185.39	136.06	200.33	229.06	209.32	150.53
Iraq	32.98	41.31	62.6	48.35	—	53.06	66.37	38.03
Jordan	63.15	71.4	62.69	60.35	67.2	70.21	79.65	24.59
Kuwait	61.8	62.68	60.56	55.29	51.63	76.17	82.39	72.55
Lebanon	157.2	147.51	159.1	151.93	160.8	152.95	150.68	50.06
Libya	1.8	0.79	4.83	0.86	—	—	1	—
Mauritania	1.86	2.79	2.46	2.7	—	—	—	1.83
Morocco	143.53	162.36	146.74	153.79	172.61	178.94	193.7	138.55
Oman	29.55	31.3	33.79	36.04	—	—	—	18.3
Qatar	111.75	135.26	149.97	151.76	177.06	177.8	190.8	194.29
Saudi Arabia	118.45	125.16	144.74	172.53	180.21	173.86	241.82	102.48
Somalia	1.99	3.37	3.55	3.73	3.93	4.05	—	—
Sudan	12.58	15.68	17.27	15.45	15.17	14.86	13.68	12.3
Syria	—	—	—	—	—	—	—	—
Tunisia	48.31	47.34	32.94	32.49	32.6	36.43	42.73	22.75
UAE	212.39	583.25	607.76	655.96	704.97	708.78	734.65	621.38
Yemen	17.26	17.07	7.28	—	—	—	—	—

Source: Organized and calculated per statistics from the WTO website.

Note: "—" represents missing data.

In terms of the value of imported services, the UAE ranked first, followed by Saudi Arabia. Qatar, overtaking Kuwait, ranked third, and Kuwait and Egypt ranked fourth and fifth. The values of their imported services were respectively USD 59.523 billion, USD 53.883 billion, USD 34.698 billion, USD 18.992 billion, and USD 18.199 billion in 2020. The GCC remained the economy with the highest share of total imported services in the Arab States, i.e., 75.05%. The country with the lowest value of imported services, i.e., USD 97 million, in 2020 was the Comoros (see Table 2.7).

033

The Development Process of China-Arab States Economic and Trade Relations
Annual Report 2021

Table 2.7   Value of the Arab States' imported services, 2013-2020

(Unit: USD 100 million)

Year / Country	2013	2014	2015	2016	2017	2018	2019	2020
Algeria	107.95	118.03	110.77	108.81	115.99	104.52	—	80.03
Bahrain	70.51	67.64	65.92	75.3	76.42	79.39	80.83	92.63
Comoros	1.09	0.99	0.83	—	—	—	—	0.97
Djibouti	1.68	1.94	2.3	1.99	—	2.02	6.2	—
Egypt	164.08	175.5	175.19	170.32	173.99	178.34	209.32	181.99
Iraq	146.58	147.9	126.2	100.37	—	177.85	244.93	137.96
Jordan	46.12	46.34	45.28	45.65	46.7	46.62	47.85	30.1
Kuwait	210.04	237.87	237.96	263.48	285.66	335.67	300.67	189.92
Lebanon	130.02	132.16	136.93	132.8	138.53	143.38	144.49	57.46
Libya	84.72	74.56	46.58	28.83	—	—	62.67	—
Mauritania	9.99	9	6.41	6.05	—	—	—	8.45
Morocco	75.71	88.72	79.13	86.04	97.94	92.97	101.84	70.88
Oman	97.98	100.14	102.14	99.46	—	—	—	55.39
Qatar	274.79	328.59	307.75	315.41	314.27	307.35	354.16	346.98
Saudi Arabia	766.52	1005.45	880.36	702.67	768.18	554.77	749.73	538.83
Somalia	10.17	12.24	13.28	13.35	14.52	14.78	—	—
Sudan	20.3	20.75	17.79	15.07	19.06	6.07	14.23	13.22
Syria	—	—	—	—	—	—	—	—
Tunisia	33.04	34	30.76	30.11	29.62	29.41	30.98	23.67
UAE	621.92	846.83	818.79	838.39	855	709.87	740.64	595.23
Yemen	22.72	27.43	12.75	—	—	—	—	—

Source: Organized and calculated per statistics from the WTO website.

Note: "—" represents missing data.

2.2.3   Situation of the Arab States' Exports to China

The trends of trade between the Arab States and China fluctuated over the last decade as a result of the influence of China-Arab States relations and global dynamics. In 2020, the total value of the bilateral trade between the Arab States

Chapter 2   Report on China–Arab States Trade Cooperation

and China decreased for the first time after three years of substantial increases, arriving at USD 239.343 billion, down 10.09% from USD 266.201 billion in 2019. In 2021, however, the total value of their bilateral trade grew significantly, reaching up to USD 330.0 billion for the first time, up 37.96% compared to 2020.

In 2020, the Arab States' total value of exports to China arrived at USD 116.544 billion, a decrease of 20% compared to USD 145.682 billion in 2019. This was the first time that the export value dropped since 2016. In 2020, the Arab States' total value of imports from China reached USD 122.799 billion, up 1.89% from USD 120.521 billion in 2019. To conclude, the Arab States' imports from China steadily increased over the last decade amid fluctuations, while their exports were less stable. In 2020, the Arab States' trade deficit with China was USD 6.255billion, a significant improvement. This signals that their trade structure has been steadily optimized. (See Figure 2.8).

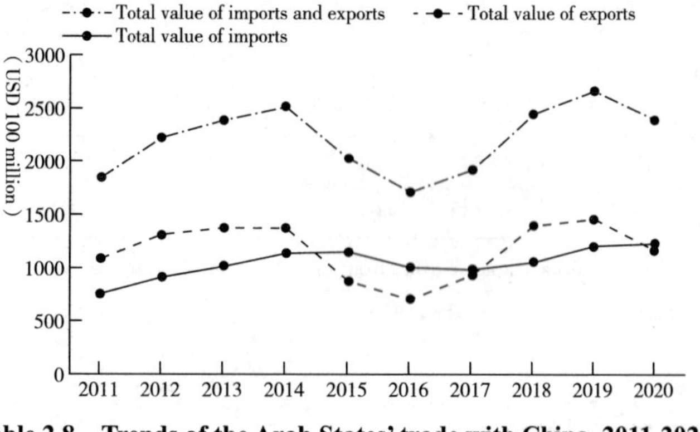

Table 2.8   Trends of the Arab States' trade with China, 2011-2020

Classification: HS3.

Source: Organized and calculated per statistics from the UN Comtrade Database.

The GCC countries are China's important partners in West Asia and North Africa. In 2020, the total value of the GCC countries' imports from and exports to China was USD 161.406 billion, accounting for 67.44% of the total import and export value between the Arab States and China. Specifically, the GCC countries exported USD 70.828 billion worth of goods and services to China, accounting for 57.68% of the Arab States' exports to China; and the GCC countries imported USD 90.578 billion worth of goods and services from China,

The Development Process of China-Arab States Economic and Trade Relations
Annual Report 2021

accounting for 77.72% of the Arab States' imports from China. The statistics testify to the fact that the GCC countries are particularly important in trade between China and the Arab States (see Table 2.8, Figure 2.9, and Figure 2.10).

Table 2.8   Overall situation of the GCC countries' trade with China, 2011-2020

Indicator \ Year	Import and export value		Import value		Export value	
	Total amount (USD 100 million)	Percentage (%)	Amount (USD 100 million)	Percentage (%)	Amount (USD 100 million)	Percentage (%)
2011	1337.14	72.53	468.68	61.78	868.46	80.05
2012	1551.12	69.74	543.3	59.52	1007.82	76.85
2013	1653.47	69.21	596.77	58.88	1056.70	76.83
2014	1751.83	69.78	685.90	60.30	1065.93	77.67
2015	1366.15	67.45	678.10	58.98	688.05	78.63
2016	1122.8	65.65	561.73	55.83	561.08	79.75
2017	1280.29	66.77	551.13	55.89	729.16	78.33
2018	1628.91	66.60	572.88	54.40	1056.03	75.83
2019	1792.59	67.34	681.5	38.02	1111.06	61.98
2020	1614.06	67.44	905.78	77.72	708.28	57.68

Source: Organized and calculated per statistics from the UN Comtrade Database.

Classification: HS3.

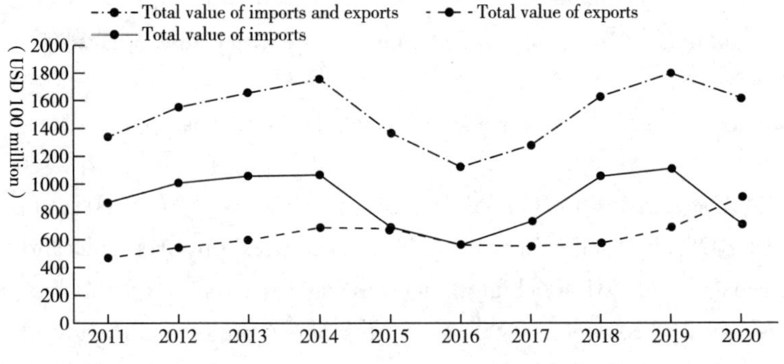

Figure 2.9   Trends of the GCC countries' trade with China, 2011-2020

Source: Organized and calculated per statistics from the UN Comtrade Database.

Classification: HS3.

036

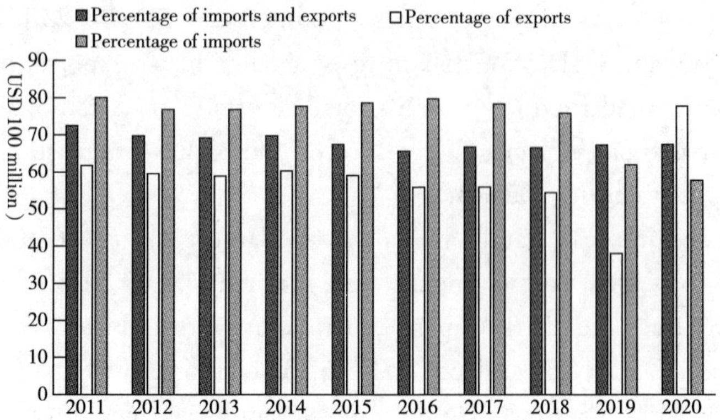

Chapter 2　Report on China–Arab States Trade Cooperation

■ Percentage of imports and exports　□ Percentage of exports
■ Percentage of imports

Figure 2.10　Percentage of the GCC countries' trade with China to the Arab States' trade with China, 2011-2020

Source: Organized and calculated per statistics from the UN Comtrade Database.

Classification: HS3.

2.3　China's Trade Relations with the Arab States

In 2020, China-Arab States trade cooperation steadily moved forward, The Arab States, the seventh largest trading partner, accounted for 5.29% of China's total foreign trade value in 2020.

2.3.1　Basic Situation of China's Major Trading Partners among the Arab States

In 2020, China's top trading partner among the Arab States was Saudi Arabia, with a total trade value of USD 67.132 billion; the second was the UAE, with a total trade value of USD 49.176 billion. Iraq, Oman, Egypt, Kuwait, Qatar, Algeria, Morocco, and Jordan ranked third to tenth on the list respectively, with Iraq, Oman, Egypt, Kuwait, and Qatar all having a total trade value of more than USD 10 billion with China. The five countries' trade values were respectively USD 30.177 billion, USD 18.643 billion, USD 14.529 billion, USD 14.285, billion, and USD 10.904 billion. Among the top ten trading partners, Kuwait had the largest increase in the value of trade with China, up 8.11%.

In terms of exports, China's largest export destination was the UAE, with exports arriving at USD 32.307 billion, followed by Saudi Arabia with exports reaching USD 28.098 billion. Egypt, Iraq, and Algeria were the next on the list.

037

China's exports to the three countries amounted to USD 13.623 billion, USD 10.924 billion, and USD 5.597 billion respectively. China's exports to these five countries accounted for 73.74% of its total exports to the Arab States. Among the top ten trading partners, Egypt showed the highest increase in terms of China's export value, up 252.84%.

In terms of imports, Saudi Arabia was the largest source of imports from the region for China, and its import value reached USD 39.033 billion. It was followed by Iraq, the UAE, Oman, and Kuwait, with imports reaching USD 19.253 billion, USD 16.869 billion, USD 15.552 billion, and USD 10.707 billion, respectively. China's imports from these five countries accounted for 87.02% of its total imports from the Arab States. Among the top ten trading partners, Kuwait showed the highest increase in terms of the value of imports from China, up 973.92%. Egypt showed the largest decrease in terms of import value, down 93.25%. (See Table 2.9).

Overall, there was no major change in China's top ten trading partners among the Arab States in 2020 compared to 2019, except that Jordan overtook Libya as China's top tenth trading partner in the region. Due to the impacts of COVID-19, import and export growth rates notably changed. Among these ten partners, only the UAE and Kuwait showed an increase in their total imports and exports, while the remaining partners all saw a decrease.

The GCC remained China's largest regional trade partner in the Arab States. In 2020, China's bilateral trade value with the GCC countries hit USD 161.406 billion, accounting for 67.44% of total China-Arab States trade value, down 9.96% from USD 179.259 billion in 2019 (see Figure 2.12).

Table 2.9 Overall situation of China's top ten trading partners among the Arab States in 2020

No.	Country	Amount (USD 100 million)			YoY growth (%)		
		Exports and imports	Exports	Imports	Exports and imports	Exports	Imports
1	Saudi Arabia	671.32	280.98	390.33	-14.13	17.45	-28.06
2	UAE	491.76	323.07	168.69	1.31	-3.42	11.81
3	Iraq	301.77	109.24	192.53	-9.32	15.30	-19.12
4	Oman	186.43	30.91	155.52	-17.07	2.36	-20.08
5	Egypt	145.29	136.23	9.06	-15.90	252.84	-93.25
6	Kuwait	142.85	35.78	107.07	8.11	-70.71	973.92
7	Qatar	109.04	26.33	82.71	-1.75	9.28	-4.81

Chapter 2　Report on China–Arab States Trade Cooperation

Continued

No.	Country	Amount (USD 100 million)			YoY growth (%)		
		Exports and imports	Exports	Imports	Exports and imports	Exports	Imports
8	Algeria	65.94	55.97	9.97	-18.46	-19.42	-12.73
9	Morocco	47.64	41.73	5.91	-34.02	70.03	-87.60
10	Jordan	36.07	31.82	4.26	-22.69	-21.05	-33.06

Source: Organized and calculated per statistics from the UN Comtrade Database.
Note: China is the reporting economy for the above statistics.
Classification: HS3.

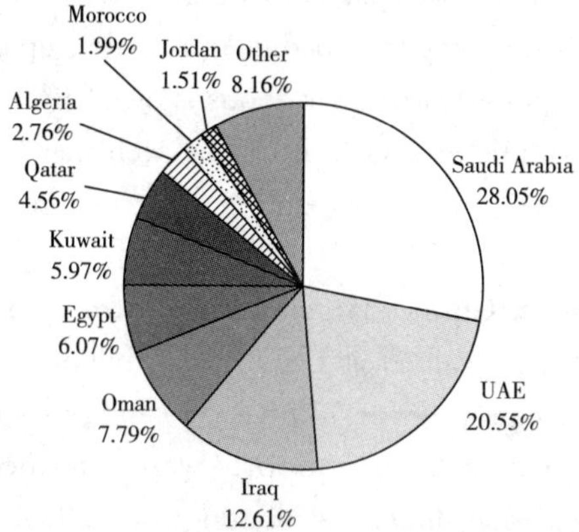

Figure 2.11　Percentage of total import and export value of China' top ten trading partners to China-Arab States total import and export value in 2020

Source: Organized and calculated per statistics from the UN Comtrade Database.
Classification: HS3.

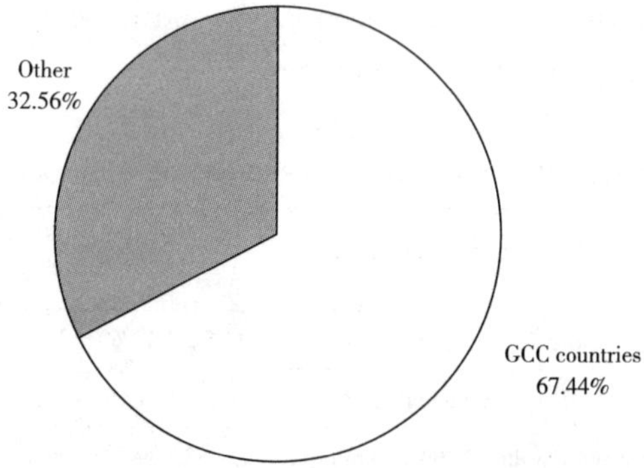

Figure 2.12　Percentage of total import and export value of the GCC countries to China-Arab States total import and export value in 2020

Source: Organized and calculated per statistics from the UN Comtrade Database.
Classification: HS3.

039

2.3.2 Structure of China-Arab States Bilateral Trade

Based on the classification method of the United Nations Conference on Trade and Development (UNCTAD) for trade commodities, below are the research results and analysis of the structure of the bilateral trade between China and the Arab States in 2020.

In 2020, China's exports to the Arab States were mainly consumer goods and capital goods, which were valued at USD 56.963 billion and USD 40.129 billion respectively. The sum of the two categories was USD 97.092 billion, accounting for 80.3% of China's total exports to the Arab States, up 3.37% compared to 2019. The value of exported consumer goods showed a relatively large increase, up 3.6% compared to 2019. As such, it can be seen that China mostly exports consumer goods to the Arab States, and the percentage of its raw materials exported was low.

In terms of imports, China's largest imports from the Arab States were raw materials, which were valued at USD 85.822 billion in 2020, down 21.3% compared to 2019, accounting for 73.85% of China's total imports from the Arab States. These second largest imports were intermediate goods, which were valued at USD 18.584 billion, accounting for 15.99%. China's imports of consumer goods and capital goods respectively accounted for 9.76% and 0.40% of its total imports from the Arab States, which indicated that China mainly imported raw materials from the Arab States. The basic structure of the bilateral trade between China and the Arab States from 2016-2019 is as described above. It shows that the bilateral trade between China and the Arab States is relatively stable (see Table 2.10, Figure 2.13, and Figure 2.14).

Table 2.10　Structure of commodities traded between China and the Arab States

UNCTAD classification of goods	Trade value and percentage	2016	2017	2019	2019	2020
Raw materials	Export value (USD 100 million)	11.52	11.69	10.56	13.15	13.22
	Percentage (%)	1.14	1.19	1	1.11	1.09
	Import value (USD 100 million)	494.82	644.81	994.81	1090.45	858.22
	Percentage (%)	70.33	69.27	71.44	74.94	73.85

040

Chapter 2　Report on China–Arab States Trade Cooperation

Continued

UNCTAD classification of goods	Trade value and percentage	2016	2017	2019	2019	2020
Intermediate goods	Export value (USD 100 million)	194.6	191.86	221.13	236.02	224.92
	Percentage (%)	19.33	19.44	21	19.86	18.6
	Import value (USD 100 million)	127.95	170.3	226.78	207.85	185.84
	Percentage (%)	18.19	18.3	16.28	14.28	15.99
Consumer goods	Export value (USD 100 million)	492.37	464.2	452.49	549.84	569.63
	Percentage (%)	48.91	47.04	42.97	46.27	47.11
	Import value (USD 100 million)	77.38	111.87	166.52	152.44	113.38
	Percentage (%)	11	12.02	11.96	10.48	9.76
Capital goods	Export value (USD 100 million)*	299.58	310.08	354.47	389.39	401.29
	Percentage (%)	29.76	31.42	33.66	32.77	33.19
	Import value (USD 100 million)	3.24	3.69	4.28	4.35	4.68
	Percentage (%)	0.46	0.4	0.31	0.3	0.4

Source: Organized and calculated per statistics from the UN Comtrade Database.

Classification of commodities: Organized and calculated per nomenclatures defined by UNCTAD

Note: China is the reporting economy for the above statistics.

Classification: HS3.

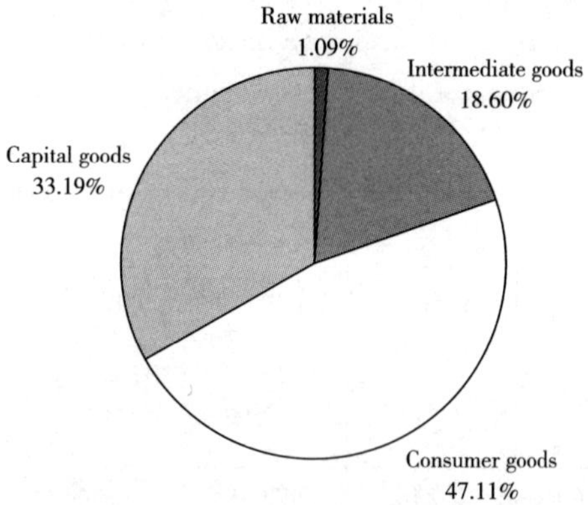

Figure 2.13　Percentage of China's exports to the Arab States under four major commodity categories in 2020

Source: Organized and calculated per statistics from the UN Comtrade Database.

Classification: HS3.

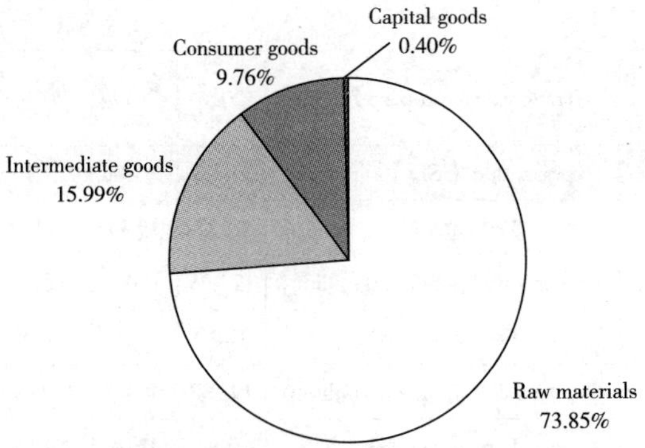

The Development Process of China-Arab States Economic and Trade Relations
Annual Report 2021

Capital goods
0.40%
Consumer goods
9.76%
Intermediate goods
15.99%
Raw materials
73.85%

Figure 2.14   Percentage of China's imports from the Arab States under four major commodity categories in 2020

Source: Organized and calculated per statistics from the UN Comtrade Database.

Classification: HS3.

From a more specific point of view, China's main exports to the Arab States in 2020 were machinery and electrical products, textiles and clothing, and miscellaneous manufactured articles, which accounted for 31.58%, 14.7%, and 13.16% respectively (59.44% in sum) of China's total exports to the Arab States. In addition, China exported metal products, plastic and rubber products, transport equipment, ores and glass, and chemical products to the Arab States. Compared to 2019, the export structure changed significantly in 2020. Only exports of machinery and electrical products, miscellaneous manufactured articles, plastic and rubber products, chemical products, vegetables, and mineral products increased in value, while the rest declined (see Table 2.11).

Table 2.11   Structure of commodities exported from China to the Arab States in 2020

(unit: USD 100 million)

Code	Commodity label	Export value in 2016	Export value in 2017	Export value in 2018	Export value in 2019	Export value in 2020
84-85	Machinery and electrical products	312.02	319.16	344.74	368.35	387.76
50-63	Textiles and clothing	192.18	179.74	164.6	192.32	180.57
90-99	Miscellaneous manufactured articles	92.22	95.74	96.02	127.02	161.57
72-83	Metal products	122.61	117.85	132.02	146.26	144.64

042

Chapter 2　Report on China–Arab States Trade Cooperation

Continued

Code	Commodity label	Export value in 2016	Export value in 2017	Export value in 2018	Export value in 2019	Export value in 2020
39-40	Plastic and rubber products	57.59	59.15	65.34	76.63	79.47
86-89	Transport equipment	42.79	36.52	56.71	72.59	68.04
68-71	Ores and glass	48.22	42.06	44.12	57.65	54.52
28-38	Chemical products	31.64	33.16	40.13	41.89	46.02
64-67	Footwear	34.05	32.71	30.22	37.68	32.92
44-49	Wood and wood products	27.74	25	26.22	29.25	27.85
06-15	Vegetables	11.6	11.56	11.82	14.34	14.84
41-43	Leather and fur products	15.63	15.17	15.26	18.67	12.31
16-24	Food	7.88	8.5	8.61	9.34	8.50
27-27	Fossil fuels and mineral oils	7.28	6.9	14.55	9.93	6.28
25-26	Mineral products	1.4	1.36	1.08	1.13	1.65
01-05	Animal products	1.89	2.14	1.67	2.14	1.04

Source: Organized and calculated per statistics from the UN Comtrade Database.

Note: China is the reporting economy for the above statistics.

Classification: HS3.

The commodity structure of China's imports from the Arab States in 2020 did not differ much from that of 2019, and the overall trend was relatively stable. Fossil fuels and mineral oils were still on the top of the import list, valued at USD 94.158 billion, accounting for 80.79% of China's total imports from the Arab States. Despite that the import value dropped compared to 2019, it did demonstrate a notable increase compared to 2016, showing fluctuating growth trends in imports from 2016. Plastic and rubber products were the next on the list, valued at USD 8.398 billion, down from USD 9.124 billion in 2019. Chemical products ranked third, valued at USD 7.836 billion. In summary, the top three imported commodities decreased in terms of total import value compared to 2019. There was still room for growth for other imported products,

043

The Development Process of China-Arab States Economic and Trade Relations
Annual Report 2021

which only took up a small share of total imports. Such trade structure reflects the Arab States' shared constraints, such as reliance on a single industry, low level of industrialization, lagging modernization, and weak manufacturing industries.

Table 2.12 Structure of commodities imported from the Arab States to China in 2019

(Unit: USD 100 million)

Code	Commodity label	Import value in 2016	Import value in 2017	Import value in 2018	Import value in 2019	Import value in 2020
27-27	Fossil fuels and mineral oils	553.04	732.1	1128.52	1205.03	941.58
39-40	Plastic and rubber products	57.09	75.4	98.08	91.24	83.98
28-38	Chemical products	58.94	81.27	115.66	100.44	78.36
25-26	Mineral products	18.18	22.11	26.09	26.73	20.75
72-83	Metal products	4.19	4.82	6.2	9.69	14.50
06-15	Vegetables	1.99	3.53	4.69	6.85	10.90
84-85	Machinery and electrical products	3.33	3.92	4.43	4.37	4.76
50-63	Textiles and clothing	2.92	3.48	4.19	4.17	3.82
16-24	Food	0.49	1.47	1.62	2.19	3.66
44-49	Wood and wood products	0.06	0.32	0.82	0.51	0.94
01-05	Animal products	0.28	0.23	0.35	2.16	0.65
68-71	Ores and glass	2.24	1.24	0.84	2.46	0.62
90-99	Miscellaneous manufactured articles	0.3	0.31	0.39	0.33	0.43
41-43	Leather and fur products	0.3	0.44	0.42	0.39	0.28
86-89	Transport equipment	0.1	0.16	0.21	0.21	0.17
64-67	Footwear	0.11	0.04	0.05	0.05	0.04

Source: Organized and calculated per statistics from the UN Comtrade Database.

Note: China is the reporting economy for the above statistics.

Classification: HS3.

2.3.3 China-Arab States Cooperation in Trade in Services

Faced with challenges posed by unprecedented changes and COVID-19 waves, China-Arab States economic and trade cooperation has demonstrated remarkable resilience and vigor. China and the Arab States have been working together to build the Belt and Road Initiative, consolidate political mutual trust, strengthen strategic coordination, and deepen pragmatic cooperation for the benefit of both the Chinese and Arab peoples.

During the COVID-19 outbreaks, China actively offered the Arab States scarce medical supplies such as vaccines and masks, and shared its anti-COVID-19 experience with them through video conferences with their health experts. Meanwhile, the Arab States also extended a helping hand in return to assist China in overcoming COVID-19. The peoples of the two sides have stood together through thick and thin, supported each other, and worked closely together. They have been using practical actions to fulfill their promise of building a China-Arab States community with a shared future, and have been invigorating the China-Arab States strategic partnership in the new era.

In terms of financial services, the ninth Ministerial Conference of the China-Arab States Cooperation Forum was held on July 6, 2020 via video conferencing, where the Execution Plan for 2020-2022 of the CASCF was adopted to help develop a comprehensive and future-oriented China-Arab States strategic partnership. This Execution Plan proposes that the two sides should strengthen mutually beneficial cooperation in the financial sector and between applicable regulatory authorities within the legal and regulatory framework, support the establishment of branches of eligible financial institutions within each other's territory, and further strengthen cooperation under the framework of the Asian Infrastructure Investment Bank.

There have been many highlights in investment between China and the Arab States. By the end of 2020, China's FDI stock in Arab countries amounted to USD 20.1 billion, and the accumulated investments from Arab countries to China arrived at USD 3.8 billion. The two sides' investments covered sectors such as crude oil, gas, construction, manufacturing, logistics, and electricity. In addition, a number of major investment projects, such as the Suez Economic and Trade Cooperation Zone and Khalifa Port Container Terminal project (Phase II) in the UAE have become landmark projects for the transformation

and upgrading of the China-Arab States economic and trade cooperation in the new era. In terms of educational services, the Confucius Institute of the University of Nouakchott Al Aasriya conducted the first Hanyu Shuiping Kaoshi (or the Chinese Proficiency Test) in December 2020, the first test of its kind in Mauritania. This enabled local Chinese learners to take the HSK and have their results certified without having to go to another country. In terms of digital services, UNESCO has been promoting distance learning and recommends a list of educational products for distance learning during COVID-19 waves, and the Chinese company NetDragon's distance learning platform is on the list. In Egypt, NetDragon's product has been designated as the national distance learning platform, offering services to around 23 million students and 2 million vocational education users in Egypt. In terms of tourism and cultural exchange, on January 11, 2020, the UAE-Guangdong Boutique Products Exhibition of Expo 2020 Dubai was held in Guangzhou via cloud services and global live streaming. The event organizer, CCPIT Guangdong, mobilized more than 300 companies to participate in the exhibition, in order to make full use of the Expo 2020 Dubai platform, help Guangdong companies expand domestic and international markets, and accelerate their integration into the new "dual circulation" development pattern. In March 2020, the China Cultural Center in Rabat based in Morocco, while prioritizing COVID-19 prevention and control measures, actively explored new cultural exchange modes. It used its Facebook, YouTube, and other online social media accounts to carry out cultural and tourism interactions, and launched the "Cloud-touring China - World Heritage in China Photo Exhibition", "Practical Chinese Lessons", and "China's Fight against COVID-19" programs to promote people-to-people interactions through cultural exchanges.

The value of China's services imported from the UAE has been rising as China-Arab States exchanges and cooperation in trade in services have been improving. The UAE, for example, is a crucial place for re-exportation, and many Chinese companies use the UAE as a base for entering the Middle East and Africa. Since the establishment of diplomatic relations between China and the UAE in 1984, their bilateral relations have been advancing steadily and economic and trade exchanges have become more frequent. In 2020, the value of bilateral trade between China and the UAE was USD 49.17 billion. China has been the UAE's top trading partner for many years, and the UAE has been China's top

Chapter 2　Report on China–Arab States Trade Cooperation

export market in the Arab States for many years.

The rapid development of China, the diversification of consumption patterns in China, and the expanding economic complementarity between China and the Arab States are the essential drivers for the quality and upgrading of their bilateral relations and cooperation achievements. The friendly China-Arab States relations and their mutual cooperation enjoy a long history and a deep foundation. For a long time, peaceful cooperation, openness and tolerance, mutual learning, and cooperation for mutual benefit have always been the underlying values of China-Arab States relations and cooperation. The China-Arab States cooperation in the new era spurs and connects the rejuvenation of both the Chinese and Arab nations, sets a model for promoting South-South cooperation, and has made substantial contributions to the promotion of regional and global governance.

Chapter 3   Report on China-Arab States Investment Cooperation

The Arab States are natural partners of China's Belt and Road initiative, and they are also important destinations for China's outward investments, which involve increasingly diversified sources of investment, investment destinations, and investment scope. According to statistics from the Ministry of Commerce of China, by the end of 2020, China's FDI stock in Arab countries amounted to USD 20.1 billion, and the accumulated investments from Arab countries to China arrived at USD 3.8 billion.[1] The two sides' investments covered sectors such as crude oil, gas, construction, manufacturing, logistics, and electricity. As their economic and trade cooperation deepens and their implementation of the Belt and Initiative advances, China and the Arab States will unleash more potential for bilateral investments.

3.1   Scale and Characteristics of China's and the Arab States' Direct Investments

In 2020, faced with sudden COVID-19 outbreaks, China and the Arab States stood by each other, overcame challenges together, and started a new chapter for the China-Arab States community with a shared future. In his congratulatory letter to the ninth Ministerial Conference of the China-Arab States Cooperation Forum, President Xi Jinping pointed out: "China and Arab States have offered

---

[1]   People's Daily Online, "Ministry of Commerce: China and the Arab States to expand new areas of economic and trade cooperation", http://world.people.com.cn/n1/2021/0618/c1002-32134414.html, June 18, 2021.

Chapter 3   Report on China–Arab States Investment Cooperation

mutual assistance and staunch support to each other, and engaged in close cooperation since the COVID-19 outbreak. This is a vivid illustration of China and Arab states sharing weal and woe." The Conference adopted the China-Arab States Joint Statement on Solidarity against COVID-19, the Amman Declaration of the 9th Ministerial Meeting of CASCF, and the Execution Plan 2020-2022 of CASCF. With regard to the implementation of the Execution Plan for the next two years, China and the Arab States have mapped out a path forward for pragmatic cooperation and mutual development. They have agreed on a total of 107 cooperation initiatives in 20 major areas, including politics, economy, energy, production capacity, science and technology, and health.

3.1.1   Scale of Foreign Direct Investments Attracted to the Arab States

Addressing investment challenges facing the Arab world is essential for raising living standards, creating jobs for young people, and addressing rapid population growth. As shown in Figure 3.1, the foreign direct investment (FDI) trend in the Arab region has witnessed several significant declines between 2008 and 2019. Global FDI fell by 35% to USD 1 trillion in 2020 due to the COVID-19 pandemic, well below the post-GFC lows over a decade ago.[1] Greenfield investments in industrial and infrastructure projects in developing countries were hit the hardest. The Arab States attracted FDI inflows of USD 38.17 billion, down 2.1% YoY from USD 38.98 billion in the previous year.[2] Their decline was much lower than the decline of FDI flows worldwide and in some other developing countries and emerging economies.

As shown in Figure 3.2, the Arab States that attracted the largest FDIs in 2020 were the UAE, Saudi Arabia, and Egypt. Driven by acquisitions in the energy sector, the FDI attracted by the UAE amounted to USD 20 billion, an increase of 11%. Saudi Arabia continued its strong momentum in attracting foreign investments, which increased to USD 5.486 billion, up 20%. FDI inflows to Lebanon and Oman rose to USD 3.067 billion and USD 4.093 billion respectively. On the other hand, Egypt's FDI inflows declined to USD 5.9 billion, down 35%. However, Egypt remained the largest recipient of FDI

---

[1]   UNCTAD, World Investment Report 2021 (Overview), June 2021, p. 5.

[2]   World Bank, Foreign direct investment, net inflows,https://data.worldbank.org/indicator/ BX.KLT.DINV.CD.WD?locations=1A, March 12, 2022.

The Development Process of China-Arab States Economic and Trade Relations
Annual Report 2021

in Africa.[①] Despite Egypt's efforts to promote diversified FDIs, its natural resources remained the major area that attracted FDIs. Meanwhile, we should note the significant decreases in greenfield investment projects in the Arab States due to the impacts of COVID-19 and the low prices of energy and primary commodities.

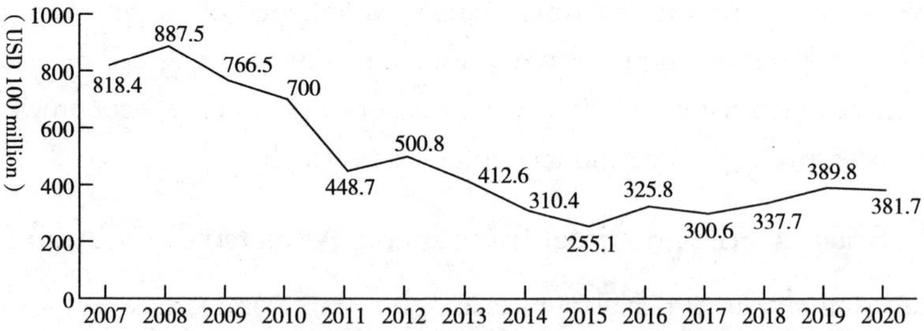

Figure 3.1   Net FDI inflows to the Arab States (2007-2020)

Source: World Bank, Foreign direct investment, net inflows.

https://data.worldbank.org/indicator/BX.KLT.DINV.CD.WD?locations=1A，March 12, 2022.

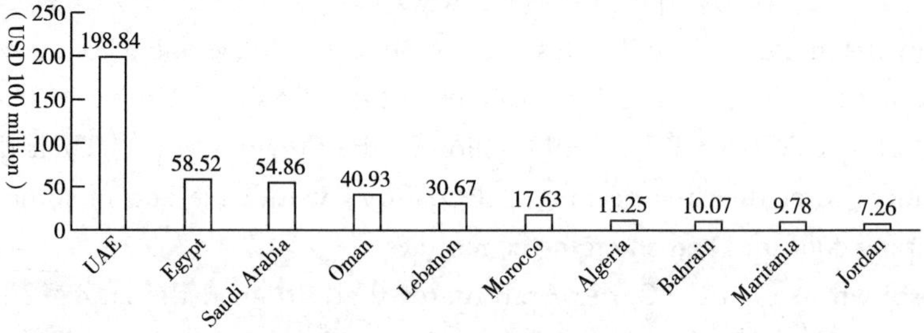

Figure 3.2   Top 10 Arab States by Received FDI Inflows in 2020

Source: UNCTAD, World Investment Report 2021, June 2021, p.248, p.250.

3.1.2   Scale of Chinese Direct Investments in the Arab States

In 2020, despite a 3.3% decline in the global economy and a nearly 40% reduction in global direct investment flows, China was the only major economy that achieved positive economic growth. It successfully coordinated the

———————————

① UNCTAD, World Investment Report 2021, June 2021, p.248, p.250.

Chapter 3　Report on China–Arab States Investment Cooperation

development of overseas employee COVID-19 prevention and control and outbound investments. China's outbound direct investment flows increased to USD 153.71 billion, up 12.3% YoY, ranking first in the world for the first time. As China-Arab States cooperation in the implementation of the Belt and Road Initiative deepens, China's direct investment flows to the Arab States grew to USD 2.833 billion in 2020, and its direct investment stocks reached USD 21.295 billion.[①] In addition, a number of major investment projects, such as the Suez Economic and Trade Cooperation Zone (SETC) and Khalifa Port Container Terminal project (Phase II) in the UAE have become landmark projects for the transformation and upgrading of the China-Arab States economic and trade cooperation in the new era. China-Arab States infrastructure cooperation is in the window period of fast development, and the level of technologies and equipment between the two sides has been continuously improving. Projects such as the Central Business District of the New Administrative Capital in Egypt and the Lusail Stadium in Qatar continued to advance amid COVID-19 outbreaks, which were highly acclaimed by the Arab States.

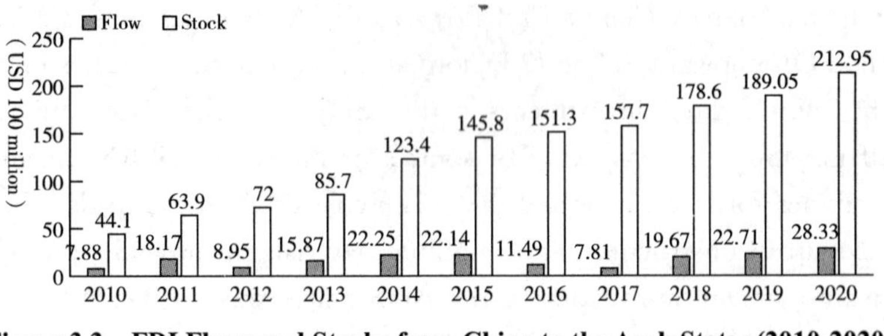

Figure 3.3　FDI Flows and Stocks from China to the Arab States (2010-2020)

Source: National Bureau of Statistics of China, 2020 Statistical Bulletin of Outbound Direct Investment, China Commerce and Trade Press, September 2021, p. 3, pp. 50-70.

3.1.3　Characteristics of Chinese Direct Investments in the Arab States

In 2020, China and the Arab States suffered terribly during the COVID-19

---

①　National Bureau of Statistics of China, 2020 Statistical Bulletin of Outbound Direct Investment, China Commerce and Trade Press, September 2021, p. 3, pp. 50-70.

051

pandemic. Thankfully, China-Arab States economic and trade cooperation withstood the impacts of COVID-19, and the all-around cooperation between them has been deepening, which is a model of South-South cooperation. China's direct investments in the Arab States in 2020 demonstrate the following characteristics: First, China-Arab States investments grew against the declining trend, with China's direct investment flows to the Arab States in 2020 rising 24.75% YoY and its investment stocks increasing by 12.6% YoY. Second, from the perspective of investment destinations, China concentrated its investments in the Arab States. As shown in Figure 3.4, the UAE, Iraq, and Saudi Arabia ranked among the top three investment destinations, but the UAE alone accounted for more than half of the total investments and ranked 11th among the top 20 countries in China's outward FDI flows in 2020. Third, the percentage of Chinese direct investments in the Arab States was still fairly low. As shown in Table 3.1, the proportion of China's FDI flows to the Arab States to the total amount of its outward FDI flows (USD 153.71 billion) in 2020 was only 1.8%, and the proportion of its investment stocks to the Arab States was as low as 0.8%. FDI inflows to the Arab States mainly came from Europe, the US, and intra-regional sources. China's FDI flows to the Arab States took up 7.4% of the total FDI inflows (USD 38.17 billion) attracted by Arab countries in 2020.[1] Fourth, Chinese direct investments in the Arab States have been increasingly diversifying. From the perspective of sources of investment, SOEs remained the major entities for investment and they mainly focused on the fields of energy, infrastructure, construction, and building materials. Meanwhile, the number of private companies investing in the Arab States was on the rise, spanning information, manufacturing, construction, trade services, and personal services. Huawei, ZTE, and Alibaba have started offering communication equipment, information technology, and other services in the Arab States. Fifth, the areas of China-Arab States cooperation continued to broaden, and China's "1+2+3" cooperation pattern for China-Arab States cooperation continued to improve and upgrade. During the COVID-19 pandemic, cross-border online communication activities between China and the Arab States were frequent, and the digital economy played a vital role in the two sides' interactions and cooperation. Sixth,

---

[1] National Bureau of Statistics of China, 2020 Statistical Bulletin of Outbound Direct Investment, China Commerce and Trade Press, September 2021, p. 3, pp. 50-70.

Chapter 3   Report on China–Arab States Investment Cooperation

China and the Arab States have been jointly developing a Health Silk Road and strengthening cooperation in medical and health fields. During the most challenging times when the Chinese people were fighting against COVID-19, the Arab States spared no effort to support China. In return, when the Arab States were faced with COVID-19 outbreaks, the Chinese government also repeatedly offered a helping hand. Such mutual assistance vividly reflects the profound friendship between China and the Arab States.

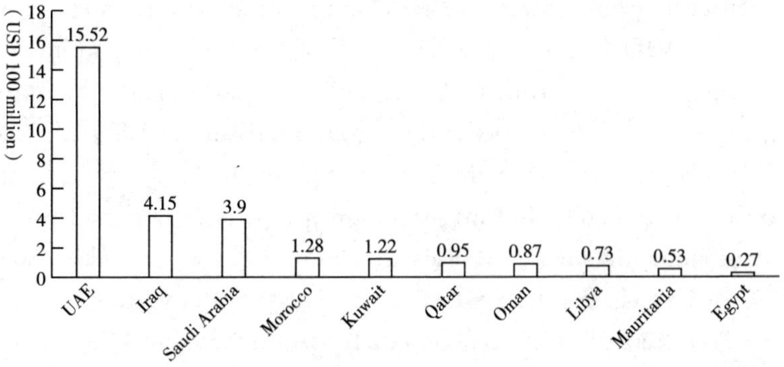

Figure 3.4   Top 10 Arab States by FDI flows received from China in 2020

Source: National Bureau of Statistics of China, 2020 Statistical Bulletin of Outbound Direct Investment, China Commerce and Trade Press, September 2021, pp. 50-70.

Table 3.1   China's FDIs in Major Economies in the World in 2020

(unit: USD 100 million)

Economy	Flow			Stock	
	Amount	YoY (%)	Percentage (%)	Amount	Percentage (%)
Hong Kong, China	891.46	-1.6	58.0	14385.31	55.7
ASEAN	160.63	23.3	10.4	1276.13	4.9
EU	100.99	5.2	6.6	830.16	3.2
USA	60.19	58.1	3.9	800.48	3.1
Australia	11.99	-42.5	0.8	344.39	1.3
Russia	5.70	-	0.4	120.71	0.5
Arab States	28.33	24.8	1.8	212.95	0.8
Total	1259.29	3.2	81.9	17970.13	69.5

Source: National Bureau of Statistics of China, 2020 Statistical Bulletin of Outbound Direct Investment, China Commerce and Trade Press, September 2021, p. 33.

053

3.1.4 Overview of the Arab States' Investments in China

The GCC countries among the Arab States are the main sources of investment for China. The Arab States' outbound investment flows declined in 2020 as a result of COVID-19, low crude oil prices, and the global recession. In 2020, the UAE's outbound investments declined to USD 19 billion from USD 20.1 billion in 2019. Saudi Arabia's outbound investments plummeted to USD 4.9 billion from USD 13.5 billion in 2019, because the Saudi Public Investment Fund (PIF) started refocusing on domestic investments to offset the negative economic impacts of COVID-19 and a slowdown in FDI. Qatar's outbound investments fell to USD 2.7 billion from USD 4.5 billion in 2019. Kuwait's outbound investments remained its momentum to grow, increasing to USD 2.4 billion in 2020. This is largely because of the Kuwait Investment Authority's new strategic focus on overseas equity and infrastructure projects rather than portfolios. Oman's outbound investments also rose to USD 1.3 billion from USD 0.6 billion in 2019.[1] As a result, the Arab States' direct investment flows to China declined by 12% YoY from USD 44.48 million in 2019 to USD 39.15 million in 2020. As shown in Figure 3.5, the UAE ranked first among the Arab States in terms of direct investments in China in 2020. Its investment flows increased from USD 21.41 million in 2019 to USD 28.02 million, accounting for about 71.6% of the total Arab investments in China in 2020. Meanwhile, Saudi Arabia and Kuwait saw a sharp decline in investments in China. Saudi Arabia's investments in China nosedived to just USD 970,000 from USD 11.7 million in 2019, while Kuwait's investments in China plunged to zero in 2020 from USD 7.42 million in 2019.[2]

To conclude, in 2020, China and the Arab States worked together to expand their areas of cooperation, providing a concrete basis for the high-quality implementation of the Belt and Road Initiative. They explored effective institutional and conceptual support in practice, and took a solid step towards building a China-Arab States community with a shared future in the new era.

---

[1] UNCTAD, World Investment Report 2021, June 2021, p.248, p.250.

[2] National Bureau of Statistics Website, "National Data", https://data.stats.gov.cn/easyquery.htm?cn=C01, April 6, 2022.

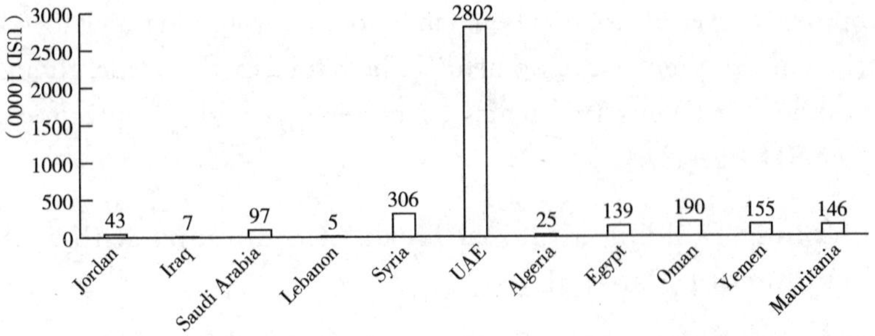

(USD 10000)

3000 ⌐
2500 ⊢
2000 ⊢
1500 ⊢
1000 ⊢
500 ⊢
0 ⌐

2802

43   7   97   5   306   25   139   190   155   146

Jordan   Iraq   Saudi Arabia   Lebanon   Syria   UAE   Algeria   Egypt   Oman   Yemen   Mauritania

Figure 3.5   FDI Flows China attracted from the Arab States in 2020

Source: National Bureau of Statistics Website, "National Data", https://data.stats.gov.cn/easyquery. htm?cn=C01, April 6, 2022.

3.2   New Trends of China-Arab States Investments

In 2021, China and the Arab States united against COVID-19, and demonstrated their resilience and vitality in their cooperation in the fields of trade, investment, and finance. In fact, with regard to infrastructure development, expansion of industrial areas, energy transformation, cross-border e-commerce, commodity trade exchanges, and alignment of financial industries, China-Arab States cooperation has successfully sped up and their investments demonstrate new characteristics and trends, thanks to the policy dividends from the implementation of the Belt and Road Initiative.

In August 2021, the 5th China-Arab States Expo yielded fruitful outcomes in terms of economic and trade cooperation. At the Expo, a total of 277 outcome documents were signed and the value of planned investments and trade totaled RMB 156.67 billion. Specifically, the documents covered 199 investment projects with an investment value of RMB 153.92 billion, 24 trade projects with a trade value of RMB 2.75 billion, and 54 policy reports and Memorandum of Agreements.[1] In April 2021, the 9th China-Arab Business Conference & 7th Investment Seminar of the China-Arab States Cooperation Forum was hosted in Beijing both online and offline. Under the theme of "Promoting China-Arab States Economic and Trade Cooperation for the Future", the participants held in-depth discussions on topics such as "strengthening economic integration

---

[1]   Ningxia News Website, "The 5th China-Arab States Expo achieved fruitful results," http://www. nxnews.net/zt/2021/dwjzablh/dwjxwzx/202108/t20210823_7244891.html, August 23, 2021.

The Development Process of China-Arab States Economic and Trade Relations
Annual Report 2021

and improving level of cooperation" and "jointly promoting digital economy and achieving common development". Their focus was on identifying new opportunities for China-Arab States economic and trade cooperation in the "post-COVID-19 era".

3.2.1 Jointly Building a Global Health Community with a Shared Future for Mankind

China has already donated and exported many batches of Chinese vaccines to the Arab States, and collaborated with the UAE and Egypt for vaccine-filling production, offering enormous support to the Arab States to address COVID-19. In the post-COVID-19 era, cooperation in public health will be an important area for China and the Arab States to jointly implement the Belt and Road Initiative. The two sides will further deepen investment cooperation in the procurement of medical supplies, vaccine production, and other health fields to support the Arab States in overcoming COVID-19 and achieving economic recoveries. The goal is to work together to build a global health community with a shared future for mankind.

In March 2021, China and the UAE collaboratively launched a local vaccine production line. Chinese State Councilor and Foreign Minister Wang Yi held talks with UAE Foreign Minister Sheikh Abdullah Bin Zayed al Nahyan in Abu Dhabi on March 28, 2021 local time, and both sides attended the cloud launch ceremony of the China-Arab States cooperation in production lines for filling Chinese vaccines. Julphar, a Gulf pharmaceutical manufacturer in the UAE, started mass producing Chinese COVID-19 vaccines. This was the first time that Chinese vaccines were manufactured through overseas production lines. The UAE became the first country in the Gulf region to have a production base for COVID-19 vaccines, and the supply shortage of vaccines in the Middle East would be notably relieved. Additionally, China provided nearly 10 million doses of COVID-19 vaccines to the UAE in batches, helping the UAE to be among the countries with the highest vaccination rates in the world. CNBG announced a joint venture with Abu Dhabi-based G42 to produce 200 million doses of coronavirus vaccine annually to support the UAE's Vaccine Hub Program. Thanks to the vaccine partnership and sufficient production capacity, preparations for Expo 2020 Dubai and the Beijing 2022 Winter Olympics went smoothly. The UAE and China have been working together in a mutually

Chapter 3   Report on China–Arab States Investment Cooperation

supportive manner to improve international health and well-being for the peace and prosperity of all peoples and the world.

3.2.2   Ushering in the New Era of China-Arab States Energy Cooperation for the Future

China-Arab States cooperation in renewable energy complies with their ideology of green, low-carbon, and sustainable development in the Belt and Road Initiative. In recent years, China and the Arab States have been stepping up energy transformation and increasing cooperation in exploring the use of clean energy. As can be seen from China-Egypt National Joint Laboratory on Renewable Energy, Qatar's green intelligent water-saving irrigation technologies, the UAE clean coal project, the and Saudi Red Sea Integrated Smart Energy Project, clean energy development has become an important area and highlight of China-Arab States cooperation in the Belt and Road Initiative. They have been actively coordinating cooperation in both oil and gas and low-carbon energy. Their focus is on driving cooperation in clean energy application technologies, low-carbon economy, and energy transformation, in order to create a new era of China-Arab States energy cooperation.

On December 26, 2021, China Weichai Group and Egypt Geyushi Motors held a signing ceremony in Cairo for cooperation projects such as green transportation and the manufacturing of gas cylinders. Egypt has been focusing on developing clean and renewable energy, promoting the upgrading and transformation of traditional industries, and striving to achieve sustainable development goals. Egypt welcomes more investments from Chinese companies, especially companies that participate in its green cooperation and local production projects, promote technology transfers, and help its green transformation. The goal is to further expand and deepen China-Egyptian cooperation in various fields, particularly clean energy and local production projects, so as to achieve remarkable progress in enhancing the China-Egyptian comprehensive strategic partnership. In August 2021, Iraq signed an agreement with Power Construction Corporation of China to build 2,000 MW solar plants. PowerChina planned to first build 750 MW of installed solar PV capacity. Meanwhile, SEPCOIII Electric Power Construction Co., Ltd. started constructing the DISI 24 MW solar PV project in Jordan, the first solar PV plant constructed by a Chinese company in the country. The completed power plant

057

will better meet the surrounding areas' demand for electricity, and relieve the pressure of electricity consumption on water factories, which could improve the factories' capacity for water supply and help reduce the local price of water.

China and the Arab States have also been jointly accelerating to transform and upgrade traditional energy. As an important supplier to the Chinese energy market, the Saudi company Aramco has been working with Chinese universities and companies to develop clean fuel systems and technologies to reduce greenhouse gas emissions. They will further cooperate to develop more new technologies. In August 2021, the joint venture contract for the China-Saudi Gulei ethylene project was officially signed via cloud services. According to the contract, Saudi Basic Industries Corporation and Fujian Petrochemical Industrial Group would establish a joint venture with a planned investment of around RMB 40 billion. The purpose is to build and operate a world-class large-scale petrochemical complex at the Gulei Petrochemical Base in Fujian Province, China. They will build a facility with a production capacity of 1.5 million tons of ethylene per year, which will be supplemented with a series of downstream production devices. Thanks to a number of global advanced technologies, the project is expected to be large-scale, economically efficient, high-end, and energy-saving that has fewer emissions and can drive downstream businesses. Fujian is the starting point of the ancient Maritime Silk Road, and Saudi Arabia is one of the first countries to participate in the Belt and Road Initiative. The China-Saudi Gulei ethylene project is vital for aligning China's Belt and Road Initiative with Saudi Arabia's Vision 2030 blueprint. Moreover, it is crucial to deepen and consolidate the long-term cooperation and friendship between China and Saudi Arabia. Abu Dhabi and Chinese state-owned oil companies have established strategic partnerships and will jointly explore opportunities for cooperation in oil and gas exploration and development, refining industry and LNG. Oil and gas trade between the UAE and China is expected to further grow in the next decade. On June 28, 2021, BGP Inc., a subsidiary of China National Petroleum Corporation, and Kuwait Oil Company (KOC) signed the West Kuwait and Mutriba 3D exploratory survey project via cross-border video conferencing. This move further consolidated BGP's leading position in the high-end market of the physical exploration industry in Kuwait and even in the Middle East, marking a gratifying achievement in the Belt and Road oil and gas cooperation between Kuwait and China.

3.2.3 Digital Transformation to Become the Focus of China-Arab States Cooperation

China-Arab States cooperation in the digital economy and cross-border e-commerce has laid the foundation for building an open, fair, and non-discriminatory digital business environment. Cooperation between China and the Arab States in high-tech-based areas not only improves cooperation between the two sides, but also facilitates the high-quality development of the Belt and Road Initiative. Many countries in the Middle East have been introducing digital strategies and supplementary policies, utilizing the development of the digital economy as an important tool to accelerate economic diversification and industrial transformation and upgrading. China boasts of leading digital technologies and has been carrying out digital cooperation with the Middle East countries. Given such advantages, future cooperation between the two sides is promising. 5G, big data, artificial intelligence, and other high-tech fields are expected to become new growth poles for cooperation between China and the Middle East. China and the Arab States should seize the opportunities brought by the digital economy, accelerate digital industrialization and industrial digitization, promote economic transformation and diversification, and work together to build a China-Arab States community with a shared future in the new era.

On July 1, 2021, the ground-breaking ceremony of the second phase of the plastic materials and electronic optics industry manufacturing base by Shengong New Materials was held in Jubail, Saudi Arabia. This project took the China-Saudi cooperation in production capacity to a new level. At the ceremony, five key cooperation deals were signed between Chinese and Saudi companies including Shengong New Materials and Saudi Basic Industries Company. The total investment value reached USD 1 billion, involving new materials, medical equipment, industrial Internet, circular economy, and green energy. In August, the 5th China-Arab States Expo, with the theme of "Deepening economic and trade cooperation, jointly building the Belt and Road", was held online for the first time. The Expo focused on sharing new opportunities for development strategies, sharing new achievements in the digital economy, and building a new future for the cloud Silk Road to achieve digital empowerment and online and offline integration. With the help of digital conferencing and exhibition methods,

059

The Development Process of China-Arab States Economic and Trade Relations
Annual Report 2021

by building cloud exhibition halls and cloud shopping malls and carrying out cloud negotiation and cloud signing via 5G, artificial intelligence, big data, cloud computing, and other information technologies, the online Expo actively guided domestic and international companies to participate in the Expo and attracted many visitors to tour cloud exhibitions and conduct cloud procurement.

In recent years, China and the Arab States have been boosting cooperation in BeiDou Navigation Satellite System (BDS). An increasing number of Arab States are collaborating with China in applications for BDS. BDS has been applied in railroad construction in the UAE as well as precision agriculture and land mapping in Saudi Arabia with fruitful results. These projects have formed accumulative experience in BDS development and application. The future prospects of applying BDS in civil aviation, petrochemical energy, and power management in the Arab States are also promising. On December 8, 2021, the 3rd China-Arab States BDS Cooperation Forum was successfully held, mapping a new blueprint for China-Arab States cooperation in BDS.

In conclusion, the Belt and Road Initiative has led to closer and deeper cooperation between China and the Arab States in various fields. Apart from traditional energy and infrastructure sectors, China and Arab States have also been innovating in clean energy, digital economy and park construction, boosting their cooperation.

3.3 New Opportunities and Challenges for China-Arab States Investment Cooperation

Despite the far-reaching impacts of COVID-19 on the global economy, which led to a sharp decline in global investment, international investment monitoring agencies still increased their focus on Arab States because of their huge investment potential, including the UAE, Saudi Arabia, Qatar, Egypt, and Oman. As natural partners in implementing the Belt and Road Initiative, the Arab States have remarkable investment dynamics and potential. In the midst of unprecedented changes, the investment cooperation between China and the Arab States faces both opportunities and challenges.

3.3.1 New Opportunities for China-Arab States Investment Cooperation

The Belt and Road Initiative has been driving the pragmatic development of China-Arab States cooperation, and China's "1+2+3" cooperation pattern for

060

Chapter 3   Report on China–Arab States Investment Cooperation

China-Arab States cooperation has been gradually improving and upgrading. Despite the impacts of the global pandemic, China-Arab States cooperation and the development of the Belt and Road Initiative did not stagnate but showed extraordinary resilience and vigor. This created new opportunities for investment and cooperation.

3.3.1.1 High-level Leadership Driving the High-quality Development of the Belt and Road Initiative

In recent years, high-level exchanges between China and the Arab States have been uninterrupted, and President Xi Jinping has exchanged phone calls with leaders of several Arab States on several occasions. In July 2020, the ninth Ministerial Conference of the China-Arab States Cooperation Forum was successfully held, opening up substantial potential for China-Arab States strategic partnership under the new situation. On April 6, 2021, the 9th China-Arab Business Conference & 7th Investment Seminar of the China-Arab States Cooperation Forum was hosted under the theme of "Promoting China-Arab States Economic and Trade Cooperation for the Future" in Beijing. On June 22, 2021, the 17th Senior Officials' Meeting and the 6th Senior Official Level Strategic Political Dialogue of the China-Arab States Cooperation Forum were held via video conferencing. At the event, participants summarized the progress of implementing the ninth Ministerial Conference of the CASCF, discussed the preparations for the China-Arab Summit and work plans for the next phase, and exchanged views on international and regional issues of mutual concern. In July 2021, State Councilor and Foreign Minister Wang Yi visited Egypt and met with the Secretary-General of the Arab League.

In recent years, the Arab League Council at the ministerial level has adopted successive resolutions on relations with China, calling on the Arab League member states to actively enhance relations with China in various fields. On March 3, 2021, the 155th session of the Arab League Council at the ministerial level adopted a resolution emphasizing that the Arab League member states should strengthen relations with China in various fields under the Belt and Road Initiative framework, reaffirming that the Arab States should uphold the one-China policy, and reiterating its support for Saudi Arabia to host the China-Arab Summit in due course so as to broaden the prospects of the strategic partnership between China and the Arab States. They also expressed their appreciation for the results of China-Arab States cooperation in the fight against COVID-19.

3.3.1.2 China and the Arab States Being Natural Partners in Implementing the Belt and Road Initiative

First, China and the Arab States enjoy a long history of friendly relations. Both sides share similar positions on major international issues, and respect and support each other in the international arena. In recent years, China and the Arab States have been closely coordinating and collaborating to address issues such as UN reform, climate change, and the Doha Round negotiations. Second, China and the Arab States have a lot in common in their future national development strategies. China has been vigorously establishing a "dual circulation" development pattern in which domestic economic cycle plays a leading role while international economic cycle remains its extension and supplement. Many Arab States are eager to fulfill their strategies for economic diversification and reduce their dependence on a single economy model. Third, in recent years, seeking peace and development has become the consensus of the majority of Arab States, and international economic cooperation is urgently needed. China has been sincerely collaborating with the Arab States to make its contributions to their peaceful development. The Arab States have gradually started to favor a "look east" policy. The two sides are expanding their areas of bilateral cooperation. Fourth, China and the Arab States are highly complementary. The two sides are highly compatible with each other in terms of transformation and development as well as industrial upgrading. In addition, they are strongly motivated to cooperate with each other. Fifth, both China and the Arab States shoulder challenging tasks for reform, development, and stability. They face similar challenges and problems in expanding youth employment, narrowing their income gap, preventing and resolving major risks, promoting national governance system and energy modernization, and enhancing environmental protection.[1]

3.3.1.3 Increasing Demand for Investments in China and the Arab States

The Arab States, regardless of their status being oil importers or exporters, have been promoting economic reforms and diversification, and have been experiencing difficulties in financing and technology shortages. In recent

---

[1] Cong Peiying, "Implementing and sharing the Belt and Road Initiative to start a new chapter for China-Arab States cooperation", http://fec.mofcom.gov.cn/article/fwydyl/zgzx/202109/20210903194173.shtml, September 2, 2021.

Chapter 3　Report on China–Arab States Investment Cooperation

years, many of them have taken sets of measures to improve their investment environment in an effort to attract foreign investment, and some have introduced new investment legislation offering preferential treatment for foreign investors, including investments and technologies from China. China is the second largest destination and source of direct investments in the world. It acts as an important hub and manufacturing center in global value chains. China has made huge strides in bringing in investments and going out as an investor, playing its roles of both investment source and destination and utilizing related resources. It has become a major power for two-way investment flows. There are enormous potential and promising prospects for China-Arab States investment cooperation.

3.3.1.4　New Growth Poles in Areas of China-Arab States Investment Cooperation

Apart from traditional energy, infrastructure, and construction contracting, cooperation between China and the Arab States has been deepening in 5G, big data, artificial intelligence, and aerospace. They have been working hand in hand to address climate change and energy transformation. The brand effects of Chinese products, Chinese technologies, and Chinese standards in the Arab world are increasing.[1] In the future, China and the Arab States will accelerate their cooperation in exploring digital transformation. On the basis of traditional energy cooperation, cooperation in clean energy and technologies will become new growth poles, and renewable energy, energy poverty reduction, and governance will become highlights of cooperation. Furthermore, they will expand their cooperation in digital economy, artificial intelligence, renewable energy, modern agriculture, and other emerging industries.

3.3.2　New Challenges for China-Arab States Investment Cooperation

The overall environment for China-Arab States investment cooperation is favorable. The two sides are complementary and have strong bilateral demand.

---

[1]　Ministry of Commerce of the People's Republic of China Website, "Jointly building a China-Arab States community with a shared future for the new era", http://www.mofcom.gov.cn/article/zwgk/bnjg/202109/20210903195308.shtml. September 6, 2021.

The Development Process of China-Arab States Economic and Trade Relations
Annual Report 2021

However, in the context of unprecedented changes, China-Arab States investment cooperation still faces enumerable risks and challenges.

3.3.2.1　Uncertainties Facing the Global Economy

In recent years, populism and anti-globalization have been on the rise, and the negative impacts of protectionism and unilateralism on the global economy have gradually emerged. What's worse, hegemonies and power politics continue to be the main source of threat to world peace and development. Against this background, the world has entered a period of turbulent changes. The impacts of the coronavirus on the global economy have been continuing, and international institutions such as the International Monetary Fund and the World Bank have lowered their expectations for global economic growth in 2022.[1] Global FDI flows skyrocketed to USD 1.65 trillion in 2021, up 77%, exceeding pre-epidemic investment levels. Direct investment flows to West Asian countries (including Turkey) rose sharply by 49% to USD 90 billion, with FDI flows to Saudi Arabia increasing threefold to USD 23 billion, partly due to an increase in cross-border mergers and acquisitions. Direct investment flows to the Arab States in North Africa, however, declined by 13% to USD 9 billion.[2] New investments in manufacturing and global value chains remain at low levels as the COVID-19 outbreaks continue and geopolitical tensions escalate in some regions. Vaccination rates, infrastructure investments, supply chain bottlenecks, energy prices, and inflation will be the main factors that determine future global investments.

3.3.2.2　High Geopolitical Risks in the Middle East

War conflicts and frequent violent terrorist attacks have been threatening the safety of personnel and property of Chinese-invested companies in Arab States. Some Western powers interfere in the internal and diplomatic affairs of the Arab States out of their own interests. They even intervene by force, making the Arab States choose sides between the US and China. They pose a potential threat to China-Arab States cooperation.

---

[1]　The IMF's World Economic Outlook report for April 2022, forecasted that the global economy will grow by 3.6% in 2022, a 0.8 percentage point decrease compared to its previous forecast in January. The lower growth forecast reflects the economic impacts of COVID-19 rebounds and the impacts of the Russia-Ukraine conflict on the global economy.

[2]　UNCTAD, Investment Trends Monitor, January 2022, p.3.

3.3.2.3 Unfavorable Investment Environment in the Arab States in General

Despite the Middle East's plentiful natural resources, the Arab States face serious challenges in attracting FDI inflows, resulting in their low global share of attracted FDI. Therefore, there is still room for development for the Arab States to benefit from FDI flows. The Arab Monetary Fund (AMF) report identifies economic freedom, governance and the quality of business environment in Arab States as key factors affecting FDI inflows to Arab States.[1] Their unfavorable business environment has been restraining private sector development and affecting foreign investment inflows. Under the impacts of COVID-19, some Arab States have been financially strained and heavily indebted, and may introduce investment policies and regulations to protect their companies, which will affect investments between China and the Arab States.

3.3.2.4 China's Economy Entering a New Stage of Development

The new development stage requires implementing the new development philosophy, creating new development dynamics, and promoting high-quality development. The pressure of the Chinese economic downturn affects the country's financial system, which will negatively restrain banks' assets of credit demand, thus further increasing financing costs of overseas investment projects. In addition, Chinese companies are likely to slow down their outbound investments owing to the expected decline in returns on investment, tight cash flows, and economic contraction in host countries.

In conclusion, as China enters the 14th Five-Year Plan period, China will continue to work with the Arab States to encourage cooperation, strengthen strategic communication, conduct bilateral dialogues, promote development through cooperation, and connect the high-quality implementation of the Belt and Road Initiative with regional national plans. The Arab States will open up to China, while China will expand its cooperation in return. Both sides will complement each other's advantages and achieve mutual benefits.[2] As President Xi Jinping said in his congratulatory letter to the 5th China-Arab States Expo: China stands ready to work with the Arab states to promote peace, cooperation

---

[1] AMF, The Role of Economic Freedom, Governance, and Business Environment in Attracting Foreign Direct Investment in the Arab Region, March 2022, p.5.

[2] Xie Fei, "Building a China-Arab States community with a shared future for the new era", Qiushi Online, http://www.qstheory.cn/qshyjx/2021-08/21/c_1127782395.htm, August 21, 2021.

The Development Process of China-Arab States Economic and Trade Relations Annual Report 2021

and development for mutual benefits and win-win results. He called on Arab states to work with China to jointly build the China-Arab states community with a shared future for a new era. His words pointed out the direction which China should work towards for its relations with the Arab States.

Chapter 4　Report on China-Arab States Agricultural Cooperation

Currently, the global food system is challenged by multiple factors such as climate extremes, the spread of COVID-19, local conflicts, wars, and sluggish markets. The global food security has been deteriorating in a spiral at four levels: supply, access, effective utilization, and stability, and the food crisis is becoming more severe. The State of Food Security and Nutrition in the World 2021, jointly prepared by FAO, WFP, IFAD, and other UN entities, shows that in 2020, a total of 720 million to 811 million people worldwide suffered from hunger. If we take its median value, i.e., 768 million, the number of hungry people grew by about 118 million in 2020 compared to 2019,[①] which increased the burden of global food security governance.

In the context of a disrupted global food system, strengthening agricultural cooperation with other countries, ensuring food security, and building a more resilient and sustainable food system have become issues of common concern for countries worldwide. As a major agricultural country, China has been promoting the development of the Belt and Road Initiative, and strengthening agricultural cooperation with countries along the route has become an important tool for promoting the high-quality development of the Belt and Road Initiative. The Arab region is an essential region for the Belt and Road Initiative, and agriculture is a major area for Arab States to protect people's livelihood and promote development. Moreover, agricultural cooperation has been becoming a core issue in the development of bilateral and multilateral relations for the

---

① FAO et al. eds., *The State of Food Security and Nutrition in the World: Transforming Food Systems for Food Security, Improved Nutrition and Affordable Healthy Diets for All*, Rome: FAO, 2021, xii.

067

Arab States. China and the Arab States highly value agriculture and food security, thus making agricultural cooperation the major path to enhancing their strategic partnership.

4.1 Current Situation of Agricultural Development in the Arab States

Agriculture for the Arab States is more than an economic issue; it is a political issue related to the stability of state power. In fact, the great turmoil in West Asia and North Africa that swept through the Arab world at the end of 2010 was connected to the global food crisis in 2008-2009;[1] the second wave of Arab Spring that erupted in Sudan, Syria, Lebanon and other countries in 2020-2021 was closely related to the "bread crisis" faced by these countries.[2] The Arab States that have undergone significant changes in the Middle East are paying unprecedented attention to agricultural development and food security. This is evidenced by the vision plans and development strategies they have prepared. For example, Saudi Arabia's Vision 2030 emphasizes the establishment of safe and sufficient strategic food reserves to ensure food supply in times of emergency, the promotion of aquaculture, and the establishment of strategic partnerships with countries blessed with natural resources such as fertile soil and water reserves. It will prioritize the use of water in agriculture for those areas with natural and renewable water sources, and will also continue to collaborate with consumers, food manufacturers and distributors to reduce any resource wastage.[3] Egypt's Vision 2030 sets out a series of agricultural development plans to increase the land under cultivation for crops, support agricultural modernization, establish distribution and storage facilities for strategic crops, develop aquaculture,

---

[1] Shuai Zhang, "Food security in Egypt: dilemmas and attributions", *West Asia and Africa,* No. 3, 2018.

[2] "Syrian Capital Sees Worsening Bread Crisis", Asharq al-Awsat, https://english.aawsat.com/ home/ article/2623156/Syrian-capital-sees-worsening-bread-crisis; "Lebanon Hikes Price of Bread by 50%", Asharq al-Awsat, https://english.aawsat.com/home/article/2736336/ lebanon-hikes-price-bread-50; "Bread and Fuel Protests Continue throughout Sudan", Dabanga, https:// www.dabangasudan.org/en/all-news/article/bread-and- fuel-protests-continue-throughout-sudan.

[3] "Kingdom of Saudi Arabia: Vision 2030", https://www.vision2030.gov.sa/media/rc0b5oy1/ saudi_vision 203.pdf.

Chapter 4   Report on China–Arab States Agricultural Cooperation

establish agricultural modernization centers, and develop national poultry breeding programs.[1] Within the framework of Jordan 2025: A National Vision and Strategy, Jordan has developed the 2020-2025 National Agricultural Development Strategy, which sets out strategic priorities to promote agricultural restructuring, agricultural informatization, application of modern technologies; increase production and productivity; develop strategic crops, logistics, and business chains; improve agricultural processing chains; develop export chains; and expand forestry and pastoral areas.[2] In addition, COVID-19 outbreaks reflected the deficient food storage in Arab States, which impelled them to make food storage a key concern in food and agriculture governance. For example, the president of the UAE issued legislation regulating the administration of strategic food reserves. Egypt further increased its strategic reserves of staple foods. Sudan announced the establishment of an emergency food reserve mechanism.[3]

Despite that agriculture has become an important area of change for self-improving development and transformation in the Arab States, the sustainable development of regional agriculture still faces multiple challenges such as shortage of arable land, limited irrigation water, declining soil fertility, continuous population growth, high poverty rate, and frequent conflicts. As a result, the overall agricultural development in the Arab region lags behind and the regional food security situation has not been effectively improved. According to the 2021 Regional Overview of Food Security and Nutrition in the Near East and North Africa: Statistics and Trends, prepared by the UN Food and Agriculture Organization, the number of undernourished people in the Near East and North Africa region reached 69 million in 2020, increasing by 4.8 million from 2019. In addition, nearly 141 million Arab people did not have access to adequate food in 2020, an increase of more than 10 million compared to 2019,[4] with Syria, Sudan, Lebanon, Yemen, and Somalia having the most severe food security

---

[1] "Guide for Outbound Investment Cooperation by Country (Region): Egypt", MOFCOM website, http://www.mofcom.gov.cn/dl/gbdqzn/ upload/aiji.pdf.

[2] "Guide for Outbound Investment Cooperation by Country (Region): Jordan", MOFCOM website, http://www.mofcom.gov.cn/dl/gbdqzn/ upload/yuedan.pdf.

[3] Overseas Agriculture-related Information Express (No. 64, 66, 67), Ministry of Agriculture and Rural Affairs website, http://www.gjs.moa.gov.cn/.

[4] FAO ed., *Near East and North Africa Regional Overview of Food Security and Nutrition: Statistics and Trends*, Cairo: FAO, 2021, v.

The Development Process of China-Arab States Economic and Trade Relations
Annual Report 2021

problems.[1]

The food security problems in the Arab States are highlighted by the imbalances between supply and demand, and they are closely related to the structure of agricultural cultivation in the region. As shown in Table 4.1, cereals such as wheat, maize, and rice account for just a small proportion of the top five crops planted in the Arab States. This is mainly because the cereals' economic returns are generally lower than those of other crops. From the perspective of national food security, such an agricultural structure does not contribute to solving food security problems in the Arab region. In addition, as shown in Table 4.1, the land under cereal production is generally larger in the Arab States of North Africa than in the Arab States of West Asia, mainly due to two reasons. First, natural and agricultural resources are generally better in the Arab States of North Africa than in the Arab States of West Asia. Second, the Arab States of North Africa have a higher demand for cereals such as wheat. In addition, Table 4.1 reflects that the shortage of arable land is the main factor that restricts the Arab States from ensuring food security.

Table 4.1　Major crops and their cultivation areas in the Arab States in 2020

(Unit: hectare)

Country	Major crops and their cultivation areas				
Egypt	Maize 1458881	Wheat 1370235	Rice 554205	Beet 263543	Potato 178608
Libya	Olive 238759	Wheat 168497	Barley 137084	Shelled almond 60396	Date palm 32868
Morocco	Wheat 2845290	Shelled almond 209233	Barley 1495190	Broad bean 107408	Olive 1068895
Algeria	Wheat 1848083	Barley 978114	Olive 438828	Date palm 170500	Potato 149465
Tunisia	Wheat 606000	Barley 542000	Olive 3642569	Shelled almond 171385	Date palm 72205
Mauritania	Sorghum 205425	Rice 69256	Dried beans 36523	Dried pea 27972	Dried cowpea 22450

[1]　FAO and WFP, "Hunger Hotpots FAO-WFP Early Warnings on Acute Food Insecurity: February to May 2022 Outlook", FAO, https://www.fao.org/3/cb8376en/cb8376en.pdf#:~:text=The%20Food%20and%20Agricultu re%20Organization%20of%20the%20United,the%20outlook%20period%20from%20February%20to%20May% 202022.

Chapter 4   Report on China–Arab States Agricultural Cooperation

Continued

Country	Major crops and their cultivation areas				
Sudan	Sorghum 5793609	Sesame seed 5173521	Shelled peanut 3197181	Foxtail millet 2424630	Dried cowpea 853088
Comoros	Coconut 27957	Rice 23570	Dried beans 17033	Cassava 11569	Clove 8130
Djibouti	Dried green beans 7082	Fresh vegetables 5010	Dried pepper 317	Maize 9	-
Saudi Arabia	Date palm 152705	Wheat 86983	Barley 81520	Sorghum 55687	Fresh fruits 41095
Kuwait	Date palm 3669	Maize 1259	Fresh vegetables 1086	Potato 895	Tomato 803
Bahrain	Date palm 2470	Fresh fruits 694	Nuts 169	Lemon 94	Banana 88
Qatar	Date palm 2216	Fresh vegetables 473	Tomato 465	Cucumber 272	Eggplant 231
Oman	Date palm 25630	Fresh vegetables 12405	Sorghum 3674	Tomato 3504	Maize 3112
UAE	Date palm 38422	Welsh onion 1022	Fresh vegetables 731	Tomato 684	Cucumber 683
Jordan	Olive 59761	Barley 43877	Wheat 10926	Tomato 9140	Potato 5161
Iraq	Wheat 2143421	Barley 1132122	Date palm 245033	Orange 104221	Rice 101716
Lebanon	Olive 62868	Wheat 41000	Potato 22649	Apple 14787	Barley 14000
Syria	Barley 1502926	Wheat 1350538	Olive 696363	Lentil 112657	Chickpea 71864
Yemen	Sorghum 322408	Foxtail millet 90000	Wheat 57218	Coffee bean 37314	Maize 37000
Somalia	Maize 100000	Sorghum 250000	Dried green beans 86202	Sesame seed 73769	Raw cotton 17901
Palestine	Olive 54336	Wheat 15147	Barley 7185	Bush vetch 3403	Grape 3200

Note: The statistics in the table mainly cover the top five crops cultivated in each Arab State; only four crops in Djibouti are listed here.

Source: Organized from the statistics released by the United Nations FAO on December 21, 2021, https://www.fao.org/fao stat/zh/#data/QCL.

The Development Process of China-Arab States Economic and Trade Relations
Annual Report 2021

The Arab States mostly resort to food imports to address their shortages of food supply. In the case of wheat, for example, it is clear from Table 4.2 that the Arab region is a major global wheat importer. In 2020, 3 Arab States ranked among the top 10 wheat imports worldwide. Only 8 of the 22 Arab States were outside the scope of the top 100 global wheat importers, while the remaining 14 States ranked among the top 100 global wheat importers. In addition, as shown in Table 4.2, most of the Arab States ranking among the top 100 global wheat importers still demonstrate a growing trend in wheat imports. Even if the wheat imports of a few countries declined compared to the previous year, their overall rankings were still high on the list. Therefore, the high volume of imports has become the major characteristic of Arab States' food trade.

Table 4.2　Wheat imports in selected Arab States in 2020

Global ranking	Country	Total import value (USD 100 million)	Change in imports (%)
1	Egypt	26.93	-10.9
7	Algeria	16.40	+11
10	Morocco	14.23	+48.2
21	Yemen	6.73	-1.8
25	Sudan	5.27	+10.5
30	Tunisia	4.66	+15
38	UAE	2.97	-12.5
44	Libya	2.44	-7.1
48	Jordan	2.15	+6.1
51	Saudi Arabia	1.94	+57.2
55	Mauritania	1.82	+23.7
61	Lebanon	1.48	+20.5
62	Oman	1.41	-10.5
68	Kuwait	1.26	-16.4

Source: "Wheat Imports by Country", https://www.worldstopexports.com/wheat-imports-by-country/.

On the whole, slow agricultural development and food insecurity issues have converged in the Arab region, and none of the major powers in the region

Chapter 4　Report on China–Arab States Agricultural Cooperation

has the capacity to build regional cooperation mechanisms to address shared development and security issues.[1] Therefore, foreign agricultural cooperation has become an effective approach for the Arab States to collectively address agriculture and food security issues. China is an indispensable partner of Arab States in agricultural cooperation, and China and the Arab States share historical ties and a foundation in agricultural exchanges. Such a relationship has created a favorable environment and beneficial conditions for China and the Arab States to jointly promote all-around and multi-dimensional agricultural cooperation.

4.2　Situation of China-Arab States Agricultural Cooperation

In 2017, the Vision and Action on Jointly Promoting Agricultural Cooperation on the Belt and Road, which was jointly released by the Ministry of Agriculture and Rural Affairs, the National Development and Reform Commission, the Ministry of Commerce, and the Ministry of Foreign Affairs, clearly states that "Agriculture remains the foundation of the national economy in B&R countries, and agricultural cooperation is their common pursuit... Therefore, under the Initiative, agricultural cooperation can be a good foothold for B&R countries to build a community of common interests and destiny."[2] Arab States are important partners of China in building the Belt and Road, and agricultural cooperation is a shared concern between them in promoting the development of the Belt and Road Initiative. This is reflected not only in the first China's Arab Policy Paper issued by the Chinese government in 2016, but also in the consensus on cooperation reached between China and the Arab States under the mechanism of the China-Arab States Cooperation Forum since its establishment in 2004.

4.2.1　China-Arab States Trade in Agricultural Products

Taken together, total China-Arab States agricultural trade in 2021 was valued at USD 4.197 billion (see Table 4.3), decreasing by USD 12 million from 2020.

---

[1]　Zhang Shuai, "Agricultural cooperation under the CASCF framework: Characteristics, motives, and challenges", *West Asia and Africa*, No. 6, 2020.

[2]　Vision and Action on Jointly Promoting Agricultural Cooperation on the Belt and Road, Ministry of Agriculture and Rural Affairs website, November 23, 2017, http://www.gjs.moa.gov.cn/ydylhzhhnyzcq/201904/t20190418_ 6184207.htm.

073

The Development Process of China-Arab States Economic and Trade Relations
Annual Report 2021

Specifically, China's total agricultural exports to the Arab States reached USD 2.41 billion (see Table 4.4), an increase of USD 39 million from 2020; and China's total agricultural imports from the Arab States are $1.787 billion (see Table 4.4), decreasing by USD 51 million from USD 1.838 billion in 2020. In 2021, China's agricultural trade with Arab States remained in surplus, and the balance of trade amounted to USD 623 million.

Specifically, as shown in Table 4.3, in 2021, the top ten agricultural products in China-Arab States agricultural trade agricultural products were medicinal plants, straw, fodder, animal and vegetable oils, coffee, tea, spices, vegetables, fruits, nuts, aquatic animals, grains, and sugars. Compared to 2020, the ranking of "Oil seeds and oleaginous fruits; miscellaneous grains, seeds and fruit; industrial or medicinal plants; straw and fodder" in terms of total trade value remained unchanged and still topped the list. The ranking of "Preparations of meat, of fish or of crustaceans, mollusks or other aquatic invertebrates" dropped to the 11th place, while the rankings of other top 10 agricultural products remained within the top 10 of the list despite fluctuations.

Table 4.3 Agricultural products traded between the Arab States and China in 2021

(unit: USD 10,000)

Ranking	Product description (HS code)	Trade value
1	Oil seeds and oleaginous fruits; miscellaneous grains, seeds and fruit; industrial or medicinal plants; straw and fodder (12)	98628.44
2	Coffee, tea, mate and spices (09)	57978.82
3	Animal or vegetable fats and oils and their cleavage products; prepared edible fats; animal or vegetable waxes (15)	43148.49
4	Residues and waste from the food industries; prepared animal fodder (23)	40533.98
5	Edible fruit and nuts; peel of citrus fruit or melons (08)	31504.63
6	Preparations of vegetables, fruit, nuts or other parts of plants (20)	30945.81
7	Edible vegetables and certain roots and tubers (07)	23146.65
8	Sugars and sugar confectionery (17)	18237.99
9	Cereals (10)	13801.51
10	Fish and crustaceans, mollusks and other aquatic invertebrates (03)	11836.33
11	Preparations of meat, of fish or of crustaceans, mollusks or other aquatic invertebrates (16)	11159.95

074

Chapter 4　Report on China–Arab States Agricultural Cooperation

Continued

Ranking	Product description (HS code)	Trade value
12	Miscellaneous edible preparations (21)	10407.98
13	Tobacco and manufactured tobacco substitutes (24)	9659.12
14	Beverages, spirits and vinegar (22)	4027.35
15	Lac; gums, resins and other vegetable saps and extracts (13)	3183.75
16	Preparations of cereals, flour, starch or milk; pastry cooks' products (19)	2947.04
17	Cocoa and cocoa preparations (18)	2268.22
18	Products of animal origin, not elsewhere specified or included (05)	1822.14
19	Dairy produce; birds' eggs; natural honey; edible products of animal origin, not elsewhere specified or included (04)	1461.75
20	Live trees and other plants; bulbs, roots and the like; cut flowers and ornamental foliage (06)	1172.10
21	Meat and edible meat offal (02)	1094.00
22	Products of the milling industry; malt; starches; inulin; wheat gluten (11)	505.05
23	Vegetable plaiting materials; vegetable products not elsewhere specified or included (14)	221.44
24	Live animals (01)	5.97

Note: For more information on the names and codes of agricultural products in this table, refer to the Import and Export Commodity Names and Codes compiled by the GACC Customs Declarer Vocational Qualification Exam Materials Preparation Committee and published by China Customs Press in 2013.

Source: Calculated per statistics from the UN Comtrade Database UN Comtrade Database, https://comtrade.un.org/data.

In terms of exports in 2021, as seen in Table 4.4, China's agricultural exports to the Arab States maintained their trade value of more than USD 100 million in eight categories of agricultural products, at the same level in 2020. "Coffee, tea, mate and spices", "Oil seeds and oleaginous fruits; miscellaneous grains, seeds and fruit; industrial or medicinal plants; straw and fodder", "Live trees and other plants; bulbs, roots and the like; cut flowers and ornamental foliage", and "Edible vegetables and certain roots and tubers" remained the top four in terms of total export value. Their rankings were the same as in 2020. Of the top four categories, the respective export value of "Coffee, tea, mate and spices" and "Oil seeds and oleaginous fruits; miscellaneous grains, seeds and fruit; industrial

The Development Process of China-Arab States Economic and Trade Relations
Annual Report 2021

or medicinal plants; straw and fodder" increased compared to 2020, while the respective export value of the remaining two categories decreased.

Table 4.4 Agricultural products exported from China to the Arab States in 2021

(Unit: USD 10,000)

Ranking	Product description (HS code)	Export value
1	Coffee, tea, mate and spices (09)	57677.23
2	Oil seeds and oleaginous fruits; miscellaneous grains, seeds and fruit; industrial or medicinal plants; straw and fodder (12)	31357.72
3	Live trees and other plants; bulbs, roots and the like; cut flowers and ornamental foliage (20)	30895.56
4	Edible vegetables and certain roots and tubers (07)	23144.14
5	Edible fruit and nuts; peel of citrus fruit or melons (08)	19098.85
6	Cereals (10)	13801.51
7	Preparations of meat, of fish or of crustaceans, mollusks or other aquatic invertebrates (16)	11116.82
8	Miscellaneous edible preparations (21)	10160.81
9	Tobacco and manufactured tobacco substitutes (24)	8676.39
10	Fish and crustaceans, mollusks and other aquatic invertebrates (03)	7746.03
11	Sugars and sugar confectionery (17)	7377.61
12	Beverages, spirits and vinegar (22)	3953.27
13	Preparations of cereals, flour, starch or milk; pastry cooks' products (19)	2898.02
14	Residues and waste from the food industries; prepared animal fodder (23)	2268.17
15	Lac; gums, resins and other vegetable saps and extracts (13)	2066.01
16	Cocoa and cocoa preparations (18)	1924.46
17	Products of animal origin, not elsewhere specified or included (05)	1691.61
18	Dairy produce; birds' eggs; natural honey; edible products of animal origin, not elsewhere specified or included (04)	1447.05
19	Live trees and other plants; bulbs, roots and the like; cut flowers and ornamental foliage (06)	1160.76
20	Meat and edible meat offal (02)	1094.00
21	Animal or vegetable fats and oils and their cleavage products; prepared edible fats; animal or vegetable waxes (15)	762.87

076

Chapter 4   Report on China–Arab States Agricultural Cooperation

Continued

Ranking	Product description (HS code)	Export value
22	Products of the milling industry; malt; starches; inulin; wheat gluten (11)	505.05
23	Vegetable plaiting materials; vegetable products not elsewhere specified or included (14)	190.04
24	Live animals (01)	5.97

Source: Calculated per statistics from the UN Comtrade Database UN Comtrade Database, https://comtrade.un.org/data.

In terms of imports, as seen in Table 4.5, China's imports of agricultural products from the Arab States exceeded USD 200 million in 2021 in three categories, at the same level in 2020. Of the three categories, the import value of "Oil seeds and oleaginous fruits; miscellaneous grains, seeds and fruit; industrial or medicinal plants; straw and fodder" and "Residues and waste from the food industries; prepared animal fodder" increased, while import value of "Animal or vegetable fats and oils and their cleavage products; prepared edible fats; animal or vegetable waxes" dropped. In terms of the import value of various agricultural products in 2021 compared to 2020, "Residues and waste from the food industries; prepared animal fodder" saw the largest increase of USD 97 million, while "Animal or vegetable fats and oils and their cleavage products; prepared edible fats; animal or vegetable waxes" saw the largest decrease of USD 263 million. Overall, China's agricultural imports to the Arab States decreased in 2021 compared to 2020. Meanwhile, as shown in Table 4.5, the import value of respective agricultural products differed substantially from each other. The import value of half of the agricultural products was less than USD 1 million. The scale of their imports was limited.

Table 4.5   Agricultural products imported from the Arab States to China in 2021

(Unit: USD 10,000)

Ranking	Product description (HS Code)	Import value
1	Oil seeds and oleaginous fruits; miscellaneous grains, seeds and fruit; industrial or medicinal plants; straw and fodder (12)	67270.72
2	Animal or vegetable fats and oils and their cleavage products; prepared edible fats; animal or vegetable waxes (15)	42385.62

077

The Development Process of China-Arab States Economic and Trade Relations Annual Report 2021

Continued

Ranking	Product description (HS Code)	Import value
3	Residues and waste from the food industries; prepared animal fodder (23)	38265.81
4	Edible fruit and nuts; peel of citrus fruit or melons (08)	12405.78
5	Sugars and sugar confectionery (17)	10860.38
6	Fish and crustaceans, mollusks and other aquatic invertebrates (03)	4090.30
7	Lac; gums, resins and other vegetable saps and extracts (13)	1117.74
8	Tobacco and manufactured tobacco substitutes (24)	982.73
9	Cocoa and cocoa preparations (18)	343.76
10	Coffee, tea, mate and spices (09)	301.59
11	Miscellaneous edible preparations (21)	247.17
12	Products of animal origin, not elsewhere specified or included (05)	130.53
13	Beverages, spirits and vinegar (22)	74.08
14	Live trees and other plants; bulbs, roots and the like; cut flowers and ornamental foliage (20)	50.25
15	Preparations of cereals, flour, starch or milk; pastry cooks' products (19)	49.02
16	Preparations of meat, of fish or of crustaceans, mollusks or other aquatic invertebrates (16)	43.13
17	Vegetable plaiting materials; vegetable products not elsewhere specified or included (14)	31.40
18	Dairy produce; birds' eggs; natural honey; edible products of animal origin, not elsewhere specified or included (04)	14.70
19	Live trees and other plants; bulbs, roots and the like; cut flowers and ornamental foliage (06)	11.34
20	Edible vegetables and certain roots and tubers (07)	2.51
21	Cereals (10)	0
22	Meat and edible meat offal (02)	0
23	Products of the milling industry; malt; starches; inulin; wheat gluten (11)	0
24	Live animals (01)	0

Source: Calculated per statistics from the UN Comtrade Database UN Comtrade Database, https://comtrade.un.org/data.

Specifically, as shown in Table 4.6, in 2021, the top ten Arab States in terms of

Chapter 4   Report on China—Arab States Agricultural Cooperation

total agricultural trade were equally distributed in West Asia and Africa. However, China's total value of agricultural trade with African Arab States such as Sudan, Egypt, Morocco, Mauritania, and Algeria (USD 1.962 billion) was higher than that with the Arab States in West Asia such as the UAE, Saudi Arabia, Iraq, Jordan, and Oman (USD 1.854 billion). Table 4.6 also shows that China had a trade surplus with 18 Arab States in terms of agricultural imports and exports, and was in a trade deficit with four Arab States, i.e., the UAE, Sudan, Mauritania and Somalia. Compared to 2020, the UAE and Somalia were no longer on the list of China's trade surplus countries. China's trade deficits in agricultural products with the UAE, Sudan, Mauritania, and Somalia, were respectively USD 36 million, USD 697 million, USD 58 million, and USD 1 million, respectively. This is mainly because China's imports of "Animal or vegetable fats and oils and their cleavage products; prepared edible fats; animal or vegetable waxes", "Residues and waste from the food industries; prepared animal fodder", and "Sugars and sugar confectionery" from the UAE exceeded its exports; its imports of "Oil seeds and oleaginous fruits; miscellaneous grains, seeds and fruit; industrial or medicinal plants; straw and fodder", "Animal or vegetable fats and oils and their cleavage products; prepared edible fats; animal or vegetable waxes", "Residues and waste from the food industries; prepared animal fodder", "Beverages, spirits and vinegar", and "Lac; gums, resins and other vegetable saps and extracts" from Jordan exceeded its exports; its imports of "Animal or vegetable fats and oils and their cleavage products; prepared edible fats; animal or vegetable waxes", "Residues and waste from the food industries; prepared animal fodder", "Fish and crustaceans, mollusks and other aquatic invertebrates", "Preparations of meat, of fish or of crustaceans, mollusks or other aquatic invertebrates", and "Products of animal origin, not elsewhere specified or included" from Mauritania exceeded its exports; and its imports of "Oil seeds and oleaginous fruits; miscellaneous grains, seeds and fruit; industrial or medicinal plants; straw and fodder", "Fish and crustaceans, mollusks and other aquatic invertebrates", and "Lac; gums, resins and other vegetable saps and extracts" exceeded its exports. In addition, Tables 4.6 also reveals that in 2021, China imported very few agricultural products from Saudi Arabia, Algeria, Oman, Kuwait, Qatar, and Bahrain, with its import values all being less than USD 100,000; and that China did not import agricultural products from Yemen, Libya, Djibouti, Comoros, and Palestine.

The Development Process of China-Arab States Economic and Trade Relations
Annual Report 2021

Table 4.6   Value of agricultural products traded between the Arab States and China in 2021

(Unit: USD 10,000)

Country name	Export value	Ranking	Import value	Ranking	Total trade value	Ranking
UAE	60622.73	1	64175.89	2	124798.62	1
Sudan	3929.54	13	73596.32	1	77525.86	2
Egypt	26918.76	3	21963.36	3	48882.12	3
Saudi Arabia	26853.25	4	4.38	13	26857.63	5
Morocco	30633.67	2	3203.83	5	33837.50	4
Mauritania	8476.48	8	14283.89	4	22760.37	6
Iraq	16179.07	5	122.71	9	16301.78	8
Algeria	13231.46	6	8.39	12	13239.85	7
Jordan	9473.73	7	19.67	11	9493.40	9
Yemen	7964.67	10	0	21	7964.67	11
Lebanon	4976.60	12	276.69	7	5253.29	12
Oman	7980.04	9	0.96	15	7981.00	10
Kuwait	3626.01	14	0.16	17	3626.17	14
Qatar	3492.15	15	0.16	16	3492.31	15
Libya	5226.96	11	0	20	5226.96	13
Tunisia	2476.45	18	146.55	8	2623.00	18
Bahrain	3022.02	17	3.80	14	3025.82	17
Syria	3335.45	16	42.57	10	3378.02	16
Somalia	773.75	20	829.22	6	1602.97	20
Djibouti	1605.72	19	0	19	1605.72	19
Palestine	434.28	21	0	22	434.28	21
Comoros	215.51	22	0	18	215.51	22

Source: Calculated per statistics from the UN Comtrade Database UN Comtrade Database, https://comtrade.un.org/data.

4.2.2   Progress of China-Arab States Agricultural Cooperation

Apart from agricultural trade, China-Arab States agricultural cooperation has achieved significant progress in terms of project promotion, agreement signing,

080

Chapter 4   Report on China–Arab States Agricultural Cooperation

and technical training. As an important segment of the 5th China-Arab States Expo, the China-Arab States Modern Agricultural Cooperation Conference was held in Ningxia on August 20, 2021. At the Conference, a total of 36 cooperation deals valued at USD 2 billion were selected and signed. Of the 36 projects, 4 were agricultural export projects under the framework of the Belt and Road Initiative; 4 were agricultural import projects about new agricultural technologies, equipment, and trade promotion; and 28 were agricultural investment and trade cooperation agreements on agricultural industries with special advantages.[1] Jordanian Ambassador to China Hussam Hosseini said at the conference that China had achieved agricultural development and modernization by using modern and renewable technologies. He welcomed China to set up an agricultural technology research and transfer center in Jordan, and looked forward to more cooperation with China in the agricultural field.[2] In addition, during the 5th China-Arab States Expo, the Arab States expressed its genuine willingness to organize activities such as technical training and supply and demand dialogues with China. In response, Ningxia Foreign Science and Technology Exchange Center organized the "2021 Online Training Course on Modern Agricultural Water Conservation Technology for the B&R Countries" on December 15, 2021, so as to facilitate the intended agricultural cooperation projects at the China-Arab States Expo and enhance international Science and technology cooperation in Ningxia.[3]

4.3   Future Prospects of China-Arab States Agricultural Cooperation

In September 2021, President Xi Jinping proposed a Global Development Initiative at the general debate of the 76th session of the United Nations

---

[1] "36 agricultural cooperation projects concluded at the 5th China-Arab States Expo Modern Agricultural Cooperation Conference," Xinhua Net, August 20, 2021, http://www.nx.xinhuanet.com/newscenter/2021-08/20/c_1127780209.htm.

[2] Lin Ziyou et al. "Science and technology cooperation injects new momentum into China-Arab States exchanges", Guangming Daily, August 21, 2021, p. 8.

[3] "2021 Online Training Course on Modern Agricultural Water Conservation Technology for the B&R Countries successfully held", China-Arab States Technology Transfer Center website, December 16, 2021, https://www.casttc.org/article/00001476.html.

081

General Assembly, which included food security as one of the eight priority areas for global teamwork.[1] Deepening China-Arab States agricultural cooperation in multiple sectors under the Belt and Road Initiative framework is an important measure for implementing the Global Development Initiative. So far, China and the Arab States have built cooperation mechanisms such as the China-Arab States Cooperation Forum, the China-Arab States Expo, and China-Arab States Technology Transfer Center, of which the CASCF is the "parent" and the China-Arab States Expo and CASTTC are the "children". All of these mechanisms provide guarantees for agricultural cooperation between the two sides. Under the CASCF framework, agriculture has become the major driver for China and the Arab States to further strengthen their future-oriented strategic partnership for comprehensive cooperation and joint development. Agriculture serves the building of the China-Arab States community with a shared future. Meanwhile, China-Arab States agricultural cooperation highlights the advantages of the CASCF mechanism, indicating that the development needs of both sides have been met during the institutionalization period of China-Arab States cooperation. As a result, "caring for the interests of both the home country and the target economy" has become an internally accepted and externally recognized method of partnership.[2] Under the China-Arab States Expo framework, agriculture has become one of the important segments of economic and trade cooperation. It enables China and the Arab States to both expand subjects of agricultural cooperation and develop agricultural partners. Under the CASTTC framework, agriculture is the main direction of technical cooperation between the two sides. China has established agricultural technology transfer centers in Mauritania, Jordan, Morocco, and other Arab States to promote the Chinese agricultural "going out" strategy and enhance the level and scale of China-Arab States cooperation in agricultural science and technology. In the future, in order to promote China-Arab States agricultural cooperation for multi-level, broad-field, and multi-dimensional development, China may consider comprehensive measures in four aspects, i.e., risk prevention, areas of cooperation, cooperation mechanisms, and cooperating entities.

---

[1] "Xi Jinping attends the General Debate of the 76th session of the UN General Assembly and delivers an important speech", *People's Daily*, September 22, 2021, p. 1.

[2] Zhang Shuai, Sun Degang, "On agricultural diplomacy with Chinese characteristics in the new era", *Ningxia Social Sciences*, No. 1, 2019.

Chapter 4　Report on China–Arab States Agricultural Cooperation

First, in terms of risk prevention, the government and the private sector should take a two-pronged approach to prevent and control overseas risks. Chinese embassies and consulates abroad serve as the "bridgeheads" for protecting overseas agricultural interests. They may consider holding regular seminars to keep abreast of the number and operation status of Chinese agricultural companies in the Arab States and help them solve their difficulties, so as to effectively play the role of diplomacy for the people. In addition, the Ministry of Agriculture and Rural Affairs may consider dispatching agricultural diplomats to major agricultural cooperation countries such as Egypt, Sudan, UAE, Morocco, Algeria, and Mauritania to coordinate China-Arab States agricultural cooperation matters and help agricultural companies mitigate economic losses. Moreover, before going abroad, agricultural companies should refer to the country-specific investment guides for the Arab States prepared by the Ministry of Commerce to understand the basic conditions of the partner countries. They may then consult with Chinese universities and appropriate think tanks on professional issues in a targeted manner before sending expert research teams to the Arab States and formulating agricultural cooperation plans. In addition, it is also advisable for agricultural companies to strengthen communication and coordination with local governments and agricultural companies in the Arab States, and for them to participate in China-Arab States agricultural cooperation, so as to reduce their investment risk and resistance in local communities.

Second, in the field of agricultural cooperation, China and the Arab States should strengthen cooperation in food crisis prevention and digital agriculture. On the one hand, the COVID-19 outbreaks reflect that there are still shortcomings in the cooperation between China and the Arab States in terms of food crisis prevention. It is advisable for the agricultural agencies of China and the Arab States to build a food public opinion sharing platform with the help of the Internet and update available information on food and agriculture related to their own countries as well as other countries. As such, when a major crisis occurs, the agricultural agencies of China and the Arab States will be able to maintain policy alignment and information symmetry, thus conducting coordination and cooperation to mitigate the impacts of sudden disturbances on the food system such as health crises. Meanwhile, China can take advantage of its infrastructure capabilities to increase cooperation with the Arab States in grain silo construction, and help them improve their grain storage capacity. On

083

the other hand, as digital technology makes huge strides, China and the Arab States should enhance the digitalization and intelligence level of their agricultural cooperation, and empower agricultural cooperation with technological innovations. For example, China may give full play to its advantages in drone technology by enhancing its application in the civilian sector in Arab States. Specifically, China may introduce drones to the Arab States for agricultural land use, so as to help them improve agricultural farming efficiency and enhance agricultural modernization by using drones for agricultural tasks such as sowing, pest removal, and spreading pesticides.

Third, in terms of agricultural cooperation mechanisms, China and the Arab States may consider establishing a comprehensive agricultural cooperation mechanism. So far, China has established an inter-departmental joint conference mechanism for international agricultural cooperation with the Minister of Agriculture and Rural Affairs as the convener and agricultural cooperation-related departments as participants. This mechanism's main purpose is to improve the comprehensive performance of international agricultural cooperation. The mechanism may be applied to China-Arab States agricultural cooperation. This is mainly because agricultural development is not just about agricultural issues; it is also related to climate, water, transportation, health, biology, and other areas. Instability in any of these areas will affect international cooperation in agriculture. This is evident from the impacts of the health crisis caused by COVID-19 and of climate extremes on the agricultural system. In this regard, China and the Arab States may consider building a comprehensive agricultural cooperation mechanism centered on the agricultural departments, incorporating departments of foreign affairs, commerce, health, ecology and environment, transportation, and other sectors related to international agricultural cooperation. They may then hold regular joint meetings with an aim of coordinating and promoting sustainable China-Arab States agricultural development. Furthermore, this mechanism will help enhance the resilience of the China-Arab States agricultural system, thus establishing a "dual circulation" development pattern for food in China.

Fourth, in terms of agricultural cooperating entities, local governments and agricultural companies in China should take the initiative to make use of existing mechanisms, and actively facilitate the implementation of the national agricultural cooperation strategy for the Arab States, so as to comprehensively

Chapter 4   Report on China–Arab States Agricultural Cooperation

improve the level of China-Arab States agricultural cooperation. Moreover, taking the China-Arab States Cooperation Forum and the implementation of Belt and Road Initiative in the Arab States as an opportunity, local governments should rely on their agricultural advantages to expand areas of cooperation, align with the needs of agricultural development in Arab States, and improve their own capacity participate in regional food security governance and agricultural development based on their understanding of the current situation of agricultural production in the Arab States. The ultimate goal is to enhance the local governments' international influence. Meanwhile, within the framework of the China-Arab States Expo, Ningxia, other Chinese thematic provinces, the host country, and guest countries may jointly explore new areas and identify new subjects, with a view to finding issues of common interests to conduct trilateral cooperation and bring out the maximum value of their respective advantageous resources. It is advisable for agricultural companies to dispatch representatives to participate in the agricultural section of the China-Arab States Expo, in order to promote their business philosophy, business direction, and technical advantages. They may also invite representatives from the Arab States for field visits.

To sum up, agricultural cooperation acts as an important tool for enhancing China-Arab States strategic partnership and is a major direction for implementing global development initiatives. It benefits from the development of China-Arab States strategic partnership, prompts positive interactions in agriculture and diplomacy between China and the Arab States, and helps guide the changing China and the Arab States through the strategic period that is full of opportunities for facilitating each other's development. As China-Arab States agricultural cooperation steadily progresses, more agricultural companies and agricultural research institutions will start exploring new markets and new areas in the Arab States. With the help of multiple stakeholders, China-Arab States agricultural cooperation will give birth to more outcomes and explore experiences from other countries, with an aim of making agricultural cooperation a new highlight of China-Arab States relations.

Chapter 5   Report on China-Arab States Energy Cooperation

With their abundant energy reserves, Arab states are of great importance in the Belt and Road Initiative. Today, as the world's largest energy consumer, China has highlighted energy factors in its diplomatic strategies. Enhancing China-Arab states' energy cooperation and building an "energy silk road" is one of the significant goals of the Belt and Road Initiative.

5.1   Overview of Energy Resources in the Arab States

5.1.1   Oil and Natural Gas Reserves and Production in Arab States

The Arab world has abundant crude oil reserves. The Arab states hold over 50% of the world's proven crude oil reserves and about 1/3 of the total production and export (bp Statistical Review of World Energy 2021). Compared with its oil reserves, the region's share of the world's natural gas reserves and production is slightly smaller. Among all the Arab states, Saudi Arabia ranks first in crude oil reserves and production, and Qatar in natural gas.

Table 5.1   Proven crude oil reserves in some Arab states

	At end-2016 (billion barrel)	At end-2018 (billion barrel)	At end-2020 (billion barrel)	Share of world total at end-2020(%)
Saudi Arabia	266.21	267.03	261.60	19.58
Iraq	148.40	148.40	148.40	11.11
UAE	97.80	97.80	107.00	8.01
Kuwait	101.50	101.50	101.50	7.60

086

Chapter 5   Report on China—Arab States Energy Cooperation

Continued

	At end-2016 (billion barrel)	At end-2018 (billion barrel)	At end-2020 (billion barrel)	Share of world total at end-2020(%)
Libya	48.36	48.36	48.36	3.62
Qatar	25.24	25.24	25.24	1.89
Algeria	12.20	12.20	12.20	0.91
Oman	4.74	4.74	4.79	0.36
Egypt	3.39	3.19	3.11	0.23
Yemen	2.67	2.67	2.67	0.20
Syria	2.50	2.50	2.50	0.19
Sudan	1.50	1.50	1.50	0.11
Tunisia	0.43	0.43	0.43	0.03
Bahrain	0.12	0.09	0.09	<0.01
Mauritania	0.02	0.02	0.02	<0.01
Total	715.08	715.67	719.41	53.85
World total	1242.6	1276.0	1336.0	100.00

Note: Share of world total at end-2020 for Tunisia, Syria, Qatar, and Libya are estimated value.

Source: Annual Statistical Report (2021), OAPEC.

Table 5.2   Proven natural gas reserves in some Arab states

	At end-2016 (billion m^3)	At end-2018 (billion m^3)	At end-2020 (billion m^3)	Share of world total at end-2020(%)
Qatar	24073	23846	23831	11.59
Saudi Arabia	8618	9074	8438	4.10
UAE	6091	6091	7730	3.76
Algeria	4504	4505	4504	2.19
Iraq	3820	3820	3820	1.86
Egypt	2221	2221	2209	1.07
Kuwait	1784	1784	1784	0.87
Libya	1505	1505	1505	0.73
Oman	705	677	674	0.33
Syria	285	285	285	0.14

The Development Process of China-Arab States Economic and Trade Relations
Annual Report 2021

Continued

	At end-2016 (billion m³)	At end-2018 (billion m³)	At end-2020 (billion m³)	Share of world total at end-2020(%)
Yemen	266	265	266	0.13
Bahrain	224	193	68	0.03
Tunisia	65	64	64	0.03
Mauritania	28	28	28	0.01
Sudan	25	25	25	0.01
Jordan	6	6	6	<0.01
Somalia	6	6	6	<0.01
Morocco	1	1	1	<0.01
Total	54227	54396	55244	26.87
World total	195388	201651	205580	100.00

Note: Share of world total at end-2020 for Tunisia, Syria, Qatar, and Libya are estimated value.

Source: Annual Statistical Report (2021), OAPEC.

Although the Arab states possess a considerable amount of oil and natural gas resources, they are unevenly distributed across the region. Saudi Arabia, Iraq, the UAE, and Kuwait hold 45% of the world's total crude oil reserves, while Oman and Bahrain, though they border the Persian Gulf, have relatively limited oil and gas resources (see table 5.1 and 5.2). For some countries such as Bahrain, the oil and natural gas resources are almost depleted. As the COVID-19 pandemic affected global resource demand and production capability, the production of oil and natural gas in Arab states decreased.

Table 5.3   Crude oil production in some Arab states

	2016 (1,000 barrels/day)	2018 (1,000 barrels/day)	2020 (1,000 barrels/day)	2020 share of world total(%)
Saudi Arabia	10488.8	10315.4	9213.2	11.33
Iraq	4164.0	4410.0	3998.0	4.92
UAE	3088.2	3007.2	2780.4	3.42
Kuwait	2954.3	2736.2	2439.0	3.00

088

Chapter 5　Report on China–Arab States Energy Cooperation

Continued

	2016 (1,000 barrels/day)	2018 (1,000 barrels/day)	2020 (1,000 barrels/day)	2020 share of world total(%)
Algeria	1020.3	970.0	838.5	1.03
Oman	908.6	870.0	765.0	0.94
Qatar	653.7	600.6	603.1	0.74
Egypt	567.0	544.1	507.3	0.62
Libya	389.0	951.0	389.3	0.48
Bahrain	202.0	194.0	194.0	0.24
Yemen	24.2	94.0	95.0	0.12
Sudan	103.6	100.3	85.6	0.11
Syria	25.0	24.1	43.0	0.05
Tunisia	59.7	51.7	35.5	0.04
Mauritania	4.8	5.0	5.0	<0.01
Morocco	0.16	0.10	0.05	<0.01
Jordan	0.01	0.02	0.02	<0.01
Total	24653.4	24873.7	21992.0	27.05
World total	79955.8	87250.0	81292.0	100.00

Note: Share of the world total in 2020 for Tunisia, Syria, Qatar, and Libya are estimated value.

Source: Annual Statistical Report (2021), OAPEC.

Table 5.4　Natural gas production in some Arab states

	2016 (billion m^3)	2018 (billion m^3)	2020 (billion m^3)	2020 share of world total(%)
Qatar	174.5	169.1	171.3	4.45
Saudi Arabia	105.3	112.1	112.1	2.91
Algeria	91.4	93.8	81.5	2.11
Egypt	40.3	58.6	58.5	1.52
UAE	59.5	58.0	55.4	1.44
Oman	31.5	36.3	36.9	0.96
Bahrain	14.4	14.6	16.4	0.43
Kuwait	16.4	16.9	15.0	0.39
Libya	14.8	13.2	13.3	0.35

The Development Process of China-Arab States Economic and Trade Relations
Annual Report 2021

Continued

	2016 (billion m3)	2018 (billion m3)	2020 (billion m3)	2020 share of world total(%)
Iraq	9.9	10.6	10.5	0.27
Syria	3.5	3.5	3.0	0.08
Yemen	0.5	0.1	0.1	<0.01
Total	562.0	586.8	574.0	14.89
World total	3552.1	3852.9	3853.7	100.00

Source: bp Statistical Review of World Energy 2021.

5.1.2 Other Energy Resources in Arab States

Arab states have small coal reserves. According to "bp Statistical Review of World Energy 2021", the total world proved reserves of coal were 1,074.108 billion tons and were heavily concentrated in a few countries such as the US (23.18%), Russia (15.10%), Australia (13.99%), and China (13.33%). As of the end of 2020, the proved coal reserves in the Middle East and Africa were only 16.04 billion tons, around 1.49% of the world total.

Because of the scarce water resource and widespread desert landforms, the Arab states are unable to develop hydropower by nature. Only a few Arab cities have hydropower plants, such as Mosul in Iraq and Aswan in Egypt. However, the Arab states have abundant solar and wind resources. Most of them have good sunlight and are not affected by humid maritime air mass. As a result, these countries rank at the top in terms of solar radiation. As the energy transition accelerates, Arab states will demonstrate their new energy potential (see Tables 5.5 and 5.6).

Table 5.5　Hydroelectricity generation in some Arab states (TWh)

	2016	2017	2018	2019	2020
Iraq	3.37	2.18	1.82	2.48	2.46
Algeria	0.07	0.06	0.12	0.15	0.05
Egypt	13.20	12.79	12.81	13.21	13.14
Morocco	1.26	1.18	1.69	1.26	1.15
World total	4018.7	4066.7	4176.7	4227.9	4296.8

Source: bp Statistical Review of World Energy 2021.

090

Chapter 5　Report on China–Arab States Energy Cooperation

Table 5.6　New energy (hydroelectricity excluded) generation in some Arab states (TWh)

	Wind	Solar	Other	Total
Iraq	—	0.377	—	0.377
Kuwait	0.018	0.153	—	0.171
Oman	—	0.206	—	0.206
Qatar	—	0.008	0.115	0.123
Saudi Arabia	—	1.038	—	1.038
UAE	—	5.553	0.006	5.559
Algeria	0.008	0.600	—	0.608
Egypt	6.776	2.909	—	9.685
Morocco	5.390	1.581	—	6.971
World total	1591.2	855.7	700.1	3147.0

Note: The mark "—" means no data. "Other" includes electricity generated from geothermal energy, biomass, and other renewable energy.

Source: bp Statistical Review of World Energy 2021.

5.2　China-Arab States Cooperation in Traditional Energy

5.2.1　Oil and Natural Gas Trade between China and Arab States

China and Arab states cooperate in the energy field through oil and gas trade. The Arab states are one of China's most important oil and natural gas suppliers. According to the General Administration of Customs, China imported 512.98 million tons of crude oil in 2021, and the top ten suppliers were: Saudi Arabia, Russia, Iraq, Oman, Angola, UAE, Brazil, Kuwait, Malaysia, and Norway. Five out of ten top crude oil suppliers are Arab states (Saudi Arabia, Iraq, Oman, UAE, and Kuwait), which contributed to 48.46% of China's total imports (see table 5.7 and figure 5.1).

Table 5.7　China's crude oil imports from Arab states

(unit: 10,000 tons)

	2017	2018	2019	2020	2021
Saudi Arabia	5217.95	5673.43	8332.96	8492.86	8756.71
Iraq	3681.53	4505.07	5179.80	6011.41	5407.49

Continued

	2017	2018	2019	2020	2021
Oman	3100.69	3290.18	3386.64	3787.77	4481.88
UAE	1015.77	1219.63	1527.96	3115.53	3194.15
Kuwait	1824.35	2321.22	2268.87	2749.75	3016.36
Qatar	101.41	134.77	85.83	619.91	785.01
Libya	322.05	856.84	940.10	169.68	613.79
Yemen	156.69	124.55	175.52	182.51	94.34
Egypt	208.42	208.69	79.52	132.33	49.00
Algeria	26.87	65.84	53.92	40.44	3.98
Sudan	72.09	44.42	63.12	16.00	—

Note: The mark "—" means no data.

Source: Customs statistics (commodity code 2709) from General Administration of Customs, P.R. China.

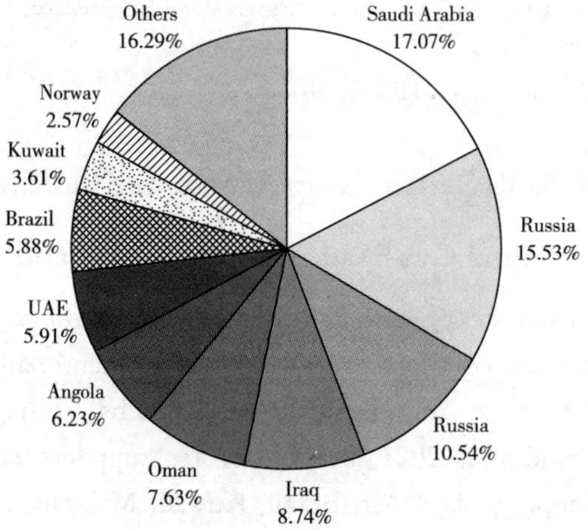

Figure 5.1 China's top 10 crude oil providers

Source: Customs statistics (commodity code 2709) from General Administration of Customs, P.R. China.

In 2021, China imported 27.12 million tons of petroleum products, of which 6.4588 million tons (around 23.82%) are from Arab states (UAE, Algeria, Qatar, Egypt, Kuwait, Iraq, Bahrain, and Oman). China's natural gas imports reached 121.36 million tons in 2021 and Qatar was the 5th largest supplier. 12.8701 tons of natural gas were from 5 Arab states (Qatar, Oman, Egypt, UAE, and Algeria), accounting for about 10.6% of the total imports. Besides natural gas, China also

Chapter 5   Report on China–Arab States Energy Cooperation

imports petroleum gases and other gaseous hydrocarbons such as liquid propane, liquid butane, liquid ethylene, propylene, butene, and butadiene from the Arab states (see table 5.8, 5.9, 5.10).

Table 5.8   China's petroleum product imports from Arab states

(unit: 10,000 tons)

	2017	2018	2019	2020	2021
UAE	110.24	243.20	184.79	146.59	282.77
Algeria	35.10	91.44	108.69	155.49	124.86
Qatar	24.07	32.91	90.00	88.71	121.50
Egypt	2.66	15.62	10.96	48.01	45.23
Kuwait	22.33	12.13	2.92	5.50	29.80
Iraq	—	12.18	14.78	5.57	21.75
Saudi Arabia	52.88	31.64	18.38	60.13	12.64
Bahrain	10.00	0.66	5.65	18.79	7.32
Oman	—	0.35	—	7.04	0.01

Note: The mark "—" means no data.

Source: Customs statistics (commodity code 2710) from General Administration of Customs, P.R. China.

Table 5.9   China's petroleum gases and other gaseous hydrocarbons imports from Arab states

(unit: 10,000 tons)

	2017	2018	2019	2020	2021
Qatar	1035.50	1235.33	1179.38	1117.51	1189.59
UAE	657.51	618.93	451.13	355.99	478.47
Oman	24.95	50.30	311.89	342.68	472.04
Kuwait	121.42	223.74	226.03	132.56	137.77
Egypt	5.61	18.24	18.55	6.43	131.20
Saudi Arabia	123.12	212.14	199.36	97.57	75.91
Algeria	29.77	26.05	46.88	39.58	40.39
Bahrain	1.26	—	4.31	—	—

Note: The mark "—" means no data.

Source: Customs statistics (commodity code 2711) from General Administration of Customs, P.R. China.

093

The Development Process of China-Arab States Economic and Trade Relations Annual Report 2021

Table 5.10 China's natural gas imports from Arab states

(unit: 10,000 tons)

	2017	2018	2019	2020	2021
Qatar	748.23	923.97	831.96	814.45	898.01
Oman	24.95	50.30	108.31	106.54	162.27
Egypt	5.61	18.24	18.55	6.43	131.20
UAE	-	-	11.99	29.60	71.15
Algeria	5.66	6.79	6.16	12.24	24.38

Note: The mark "-" means no data.

Source: Customs statistics (commodity code 271111 and 271121) from General Administration of Customs, P.R. China Code 2711 covers commodities under 271111 and 271121.

On March 22, 2021, Sinopec and QatarEnergy signed a long-term purchase and sale agreement on 2 million tons of liquefied natural gas (LNG) per annum. In 2022, QatarEnergy will start supplying 2 million tons of LNG to Sinopec every year for a term of 10 years. This is the first long-term LNG agreement between Sinopec and QatarEnergy. The cooperation between these two will further enhance Qatar's supplier capability to China, and therefore satisfy the growing demand of the Chinese market.[1]

5.2.2 Cooperation Projects on Oil and Natural Gas Production

China and Arab states have been cooperating through oil and natural gas production projects for a long time. In 2021, China and Arab states further developed their cooperation. Many Chinese companies signed new oil and gas project contracts in Arab states; others made progress in their ongoing projects. On March 8, 2021, China National Chemical Engineering Third Construction, an affiliate of China National Chemical Engineering Group Corporation, won the bid for the general construction contract of the western part of the AAP crude oil processing unit of Saudi Aramco's Berry Increasing Project. The project is located on the island of Abu Ali, Saudi Arabia, and the value of the signed contract is RMB 1.557 billion. The project is aimed at transforming and

---

[1] Sinopec and QatarEnergy Signed a Long-term Purchase and Sale Agreement on 2 million tons of Liquefied Natural Gas (LNG) Per Annum, China-Arab States Cooperation Forum, March 22, 2021, http://www.chinaarabcf.org/chn/zagx/gjydyl/202103/t20210322_9155424.htm.

Chapter 5   Report on China–Arab States Energy Cooperation

expanding the Abu Ali refinery. By the end of the project, the refinery's Arab light daily processing capacity will be increased to 500,000 barrels.[1]

In April 2021, Jereh Oil & Gas Engineering and its partners officially signed the contract for Jebel Ali Pilot Phase Project in the United Arab Emirates. This project is Abu Dhabi National Oil Company (ADNOC)'s key production project in 2021. ADNOC plans to evaluate the reserve potential in the Jebel Ali gas field located in the Northeast of Abu Dhabi, and prepare for large-scale extraction in the future. The project will build a set of production pilot facilities (PPF) to transmit processed natural gas to nearby pipelines.[2] On April 20, the international business department of Daqing Oil Field Engineering & Construction received a notice from China Petroleum Engineering & Construction Corporation (CEPCC) Iraq branch that CEPCC has won the bid of RMB 410 million for the natural gas processing project at Halfaya oilfield in Iraq.[3]

On May 20, 2021, Sinopec Fifth Construction Co., Ltd. and SAIPEM of Italy held an online signing ceremony for the Saudi Berry oil and gas processing project. The owner of the project is Saudi Aramco, and the Italian company Saipan is the general EPC contractor. The project aims to carry out equipment renovation and expansion projects to process 11 million tons of Arab light crude oil and 40,000 barrels of sulphuric hydrocarbons per day. The contract value of the two projects is around USD 200 million.[4]

In June, Jereh Oil & Gas Engineering Corporation was awarded a contract for a natural gas debottlenecking project in Algeria. The project is located in BRN-ROD fields in the eastern Algerian desert, about 300 km southeast of Hassi Messaoud. The project will upgrade and transform the original processing plant

---

[1] Third Construction Won the Bid for the General Construction Contract of Saudi Aramco's Berry Increasing Project for the Western Part of the AAP Crude Oil Processing Unit, China National Chemical Engineering Group Corporation, March 12, 2021,https://cncec.cn/articledetail/124491.

[2] New Breakthrough in the Middle East Market! Jereh Oil & Gas Engineering Wins United Arab Emirates ADNOC's Pilot Production Facility Project, Jereh Group, April 25, 2021,https://www.jereh.com/cn/news/press-release/news-detail-9626.htm.

[3] Weekly Snapshot on Chinese Company's Oversea Project (April 19, 2021 to April 25, 2021), Belt and Road Portal, April 26, 2021, https://www.yidaiyilu.gov.cn/qyfc/xmzb/175332.htm.

[4] Weekly Snapshot on Chinese Company's Oversea Project (May 17, 2021 to May 23, 2021), Belt and Road Portal, May 24, 2021, https://www.yidaiyilu.gov.cn/qyfc/xmzb/175325.htm.

that was unable to fulfill the production needs.[1] On June 30, China Petroleum Engineering & Construction Middle East branch signed a USD 690 million contract with Italian oil company Eni in Iraq for the expansion project of Zubair oilfield.[2] The project will be officially launched on August 11. The project will increase the production capacity of the Zubair oilfield from 470,000 barrels/day to 700,000 barrels/day (approximately 35 million tons/year).[3]

On September 3, 2021, CITIC Construction signed the EPC general contract for the Kirkuk oil refinery in Iraq. Located in Kirkuk Province, Iraq, the Kirkuk refinery can process 75,000 barrels of crude oil per day (with an annual capacity of about 3.5 million tons of crude oil). The products include gasoline, diesel, aviation kerosene, fuel oil, LPG, and road asphalt that are compliant with the Euro 5 emissions standard. The EPC contract value is USD 905 million and the construction lasts 46 months. As the EPC general contractor of the project, CITIC Construction will be responsible for the design, procurement, construction, and commissioning, and will also offer support on financing.[4]

On November 9, 2021, Jereh Oil & Gas Engineering won the award letter for the Phase 5 project of the National Jurassic Production Facility in the northern part of Kuwait Petroleum Company. The contract value exceeded RMB 2.7 billion. The project is located in the Jurassic gas field in northern Kuwait. It is a key strategic production project of Kuwait Petroleum Corporation from 2022 to 2023. The project applies skid installation to accelerate the construction of oil, gas, and water production plants to meet the increasing needs for natural gas power generation.[5]

---

[1] Jereh Oil & Gas Engineering Corporation Was Awarded a Contract for a Natural Gas Debottlenecking Project in Algeria, Jereh Group, June 2, 2021,https://www.jereh.com/cn/news/press-release/news-detail-9653.htm.

[2] Weekly Snapshot on Chinese Company's Oversea Project (June 28, 2021 to July 04, 2021), Belt and Road Portal, July 5th, 2021, https://www.yidaiyilu.gov.cn/qyfc/xmzb/179534.htm.

[3] Weekly Snapshot on Chinese Company's Oversea Project (August 9, 2021 to August 15, 2021), Belt and Road Portal, August 17th, 2021, https://www.yidaiyilu.gov.cn/qyfc/xmzb/183652.htm.

[4] CITIC Construction signed the General Contract for the Kirkuk Oil Refinery in Iraq, CITIC Construction, September 6, 2021,https://www.cici.citic.com/content/details_39_2567.html.

[5] Jereh Oil & Gas Engineering Wins a RMB 2.7 Billion Project of Kuwait Petroleum Company, Jereh Group, November 10, 2021,https://www.jereh.com/cn/news/press-release/news-detail-9704.htm.

5.2.3 Cooperation Projects on Other Energy Infrastructure

China and Arab states have a large number of cooperation projects on energy infrastructures such as power plants, transformer substations, and power transmission grids. On February 22, the Benban 500kV GIS transformer substation in Aswan, Egypt was put into service. China XD Group is the general contractor of the project. All high voltage power transmission and transformation equipment, including 14 500kV GIS, 10 500/220kV 167MVA single phase transformers, 500kV capacitor voltage transformer, and lightning arrester, were manufactured by China XD Group.[1]

On May 3, unit 2 of the Dubai Hassyan 4×600MW Clean Coal-fired Power Plant Project was successfully connected to the grid. Harbin Electric International is the general contractor of the project and Tianjin Electric Construction under China Energy Engineering Corporation is the constructor.[2] On September 4, unit 2 was officially put into commercial use. Hassyan power plant is equipped with 4 600MW ultra-supercritical units, ensuring 2400MW installed capacity. All 4 units will be put into commercial use in 2023. On July 20, 2020, unit 1 realized full-load power generation driven by two kinds of energy. As an important project of the Belt and Road Initiative, Hassyan will be the first clean coal-fired power plant in the Middle East.[3]

On September 29, the second unit of the Jordan Attarat oil shale power plant was successfully connected to the grid. The project was constructed by China Energy Engineering Corporation Guangdong Power Engineering. The project is one of the Belt and Road key cooperation projects between China and Jordan. It consists of two 235 MW oil shale power plants and is estimated to be the largest power plant in Jordan. The no.1 generator unit was connected to the main grid in the first half of 2021 and realized full-load power generation in July, which

---

[1] Benban 500kV GIS Transformer Substation in Aswan, Egypt Was Put into Service, China XD Group, March 2, 2021, https://mp.weixin.qq.com/s/NtK8zjMCaDJwq8kQpRBRqw.

[2] Weekly Snapshot on Chinese Company's Oversea Project (April 26, 2021 to May 9, 2021), Belt and Road Portal, May 10, 2021, https://www.yidaiyilu.gov.cn/qyfc/xmzb/175331.htm.

[3] Hassyan Project Unit 2 Designed and Constructed by China Energy Engineering Corporation is Now in Commercial Use, China Energy Engineering Corporation, September 7, 2021, http://www.ceec.net.cn/art/2021/9/7/art_11019_2512083.html.

The Development Process of China-Arab States Economic and Trade Relations
Annual Report 2021

means it can now steadily transmit electricity.[1]

On October 5, the Egyptian Ministry of Electricity and Renewable Energy and the Ministry of Energy of Saudi Arabia signed a series of memorandum of agreement on an electricity interconnection project in Cairo. The Egyptian Electricity Transmission Company and Saudi Electricity Company signed the project contract on linking the two countries' power grids. China Energy Engineering Corporation, China XD Group, and Egypt Giza Electrical Grid Company jointly signed the Egypt-Saudi ±500 kV EHVDC power transmission line EPC project.[2]

On December 13, the 650-megawatt Cairo West Supercritical Thermal Power Project constructed by China Energy Engineering Corporation Jiangsu No. 1 Electric Power Construction received TOAC issued by the owner. The project is located in the suburb region of Northwestern Cairo, Egypt. It aimed to construct a 650-MW supercritical thermal power generator unit with an oil and gas boiler. The unit is expected to generate 2 billion KWh of power annually.[3] On the morning of November 20, the PMCC 05, 10, and 15 of the Jazan project of SEPCO Electric Power Construction Corporation were officially signed. By far, the PMCC of unit 4 was all signed and transferred to Saudi Aramco.[4]

5.3 China-Arab States Cooperation in New Energy

5.3.1 Energy Transition in China and the Arab States

In the 21st century, the world is welcoming a new round of energy transition. Energy transition means that the structure of energy production and

---

[1] Jordan Attarat Oil Shale Power Plant Constructed by Chinese Company Was Successfully Connect to the Grid, Xinhua Net, September 29, 2021, http://www.news.cn/silkroad/20211015/C99004C 8CA30000175C2B38F16201A02/c.html.

[2] Weekly Snapshot on Chinese Company's Oversea Project (September 27, 2021 to October 10, 2021), Belt and Road Portal, October 15, 2021, https://www.yidaiyilu.gov.cn/qyfc/xmzb/191063. htm.

[3] Weekly Snapshot on Chinese Company's Oversea Project (November 13, 2021 to November 19, 2021), Belt and Road Portal, December 23, 2021, https://www.yidaiyilu.gov.cn/qyfc/ xmzb/208627.htm.

[4] Weekly Snapshot on Chinese Company's Oversea Project (November 20, 2021 to November 26, 2021), Belt and Road Portal, December 28, 2021, https://www.yidaiyilu.gov.cn/qyfc/ xmzb/210216.htm.

Chapter 5   Report on China—Arab States Energy Cooperation

consumption is changing.[1] Consuming new and clean energy such as nuclear energy and renewable energy instead of fossil fuels lies at the very core of this energy transition. As countries around the world put forward their energy transition strategy, new energy will play an increasingly important role in human life.

China actively participates in global energy governance and strives to find a new path toward sustainable energy development. On the general debate of the 75th session of the United Nations General Assembly, president Xi Jinping said that China will scale up its Intended Nationally Determined Contributions by adopting more vigorous policies and measures. China aims to have CO_2 emissions peak before 2030 and achieve carbon neutrality before 2060[2]. "Outline of the People's Republic of China 14th Five-Year Plan for National Economic and Social Development and Long-Range Objectives for 2035" pointed out that China will establish a modernized economic system in 2035 with reduced energy consumption and carbon dioxide emissions per unit of GDP.[3] In terms of energy cooperation, "Strategy for Energy Production and Consumption Reform (2016-2030)" stated that China should adopt a forward-looking, comprehensive, diverse, reciprocal principle, develop wide-ranging, multi-layered, full supply chain energy cooperation, and establish an energy cooperation network which connects China and the world, to build a community of shared interest and future for energy cooperation.[4]

The Arab states are also making energy transition plans and developing a new energy industry. Various forums and conferences were held in Arab states, and the "Pan-Arab Strategy for the Development of Renewable Energy Applications:2010-2030" was passed.[5] According to the energy development

---

[1]   WU, Lei. YANG, Zeyu. International Energy Transitions and the Middle East Oil. West Asia and Africa. 2018(5): 142.

[2]   Energy in China's New Era White Paper, People's Republic of China State Council Information Office, November 21, 2020,http://www.scio.gov.cn/zfbps/32832/Document/1695117/1695117. htm.

[3]   HOU, Meifang. PAN, Songqi. & LIU, Hanlin. World Energy Trend and China's Oil and Gas Sustainable Development Strategies. Natural Gas Industry. 2021(12):10.

[4]   Notice on Issuing Strategy for Energy Production and Consumption Reform (2016-2030), The State Council of People's Republic of China, April 25, 2017,http://www.gov.cn/ xinwen/2017-04/25/content_5230568.htm.

[5]   The International Renewable Energy Agency, League of Arab States, Pan Arab Renewable Energy 2030, 2014, p.38.

099

strategy of the UAE, over 10% of the total power generation will be renewable energy by 2030.[1] In 2016, Saudi Arabia published "Saudi Vision 2030" and "2020 National Transition Plan". According to these documents, Saudi Arabia has abundant solar and wind energy that is yet to be utilized, and the country has formulated its renewable energy development goals.[2] Morocco plans to increase the proportion of renewable energy to 52% by 2024. To achieve this goal, Morocco is encouraging hydroelectricity, photovoltaic, and wind energy across the country.[3]

Since October 2021, Arab states have been publishing their green gas emission reduction plans: Saudi Arabia announced that it will invest around USD 180 billion to achieve net zero by 2060; the UAE plans to go net zero by 2050; Bahrain plans to be net zero by 2060; Qatar will reduce its carbon emission by 25% by 2030.[4] These exemplify the strong will of Arab states to develop clean energy and accelerate the energy transition.

5.3.2 Overview of China-Arab States Cooperation in New Energy

Belt and Road Initiative, proposed by China in 2013, created a strategic opportunity for China-Arab states cooperation, and provide a platform for the further development of energy cooperation under the CASCF framework. China-Arab states energy cooperation is breaking through traditional oil and gas trade and is seeking cooperation on energy production and non-fossil fuels.

The "road" in Belt and Road Initiative is not only a road of "peace, prosperity, openness, and civilization", but also a road of green development. The initiative encourages China and Arab states to jointly combat climate change, protect the ecological environment, and promote sustainable development. On April 25, 2019, the Belt and Road Energy Partnership (BREP) was announced in Beijing. Under the guidance of "Cooperation Principles and Concrete Actions", all

---

① Chinese Companies Should Pay Attention to the Opportunity for New Energy Strategic Cooperation in UAE, Sunny & Forecasting, https://mp.weixin.qq.com/s/UIZoqgDbdpgpWkF6IAvBEQ.

② LIU, Chen. MA, Luanyu. Research on the New Energy Policy in Saudi Arabia. Journal of Changchun Normal University. 2021(3): 63-68.

③ GUO, Yan. Low Carbon Energy Became the New Highlight of China-Arab States Cooperation. China's Foreign Trade. 2021(9): 14-15.

④ Gulf Countries Push Forward Clean Energy Development, people.cn,http://env.people.com.cn/n1/2021/1216/c1010-32309595.html.

Chapter 5　Report on China–Arab States Energy Cooperation

participating countries collectively develop green, clean, and efficient bilateral energy cooperation. Arab states such as Iraq, Kuwait, Algeria, and Sudan are among the first group of countries to join BREP.[1]

Today, China and Arab states follow the guidance of the "1+2+3"[2] cooperation framework to enhance strategic exchange, so as to reduce the dependency on oil and natural gas resources and use energy transition as momentum for economic transition. China and the Arab states are leveraging the geographical advantage of Arab states, using their energy networks as the cooperation platform for clean energy development. As a result, the two parties are building a production center and trade hub of clean energy for Asian, European, and African countries, and establishing an energy system with clean production, wide deployment, and modern consumption, so as to meet the energy needs of all parties, increase political mutual trust, and ensure development.[3]

The CASCF execution plan for 2020-2022 was released at the ninth Ministerial Conference held in 2020. According to the plan, both parties will cooperate not only in oil, gas, and electricity but also in renewable energy. The two parties plan to make use of the PV cell and photo thermal applications in Arab states, enhance technology cooperation, and encourage the joint project. The two parties should establish a training center for clean energy, and set up a sub-center in one or many Arab states. They will also cooperate in recovering energy from non-recyclable waste, and establish policy and legislation for this new energy resource. It is encouraged to hold clean energy training courses in China under the framework of the clean energy training center in 2021 or other settled times. The parties also plan to develop a green hydrogen energy supply. It is welcome to learn and adapt China's experience in this field through research and seminars. The plan also mentions that China and Arab states will cooperate on energy

---

[1]　YU, Xiaozhong. LUO, Xia. Energy Cooperation Partnership of the "Belt and Road": Connotation and Promotion. Asia-Pacific Economic Review. 2020(4):5-17.

[2]　"1" refers to energy cooperation; "2" represents infrastructure construction and convenient trade and investment; "3" stands for three cutting-edge technology, i.e. nuclear energy, space satellite, and new energy.

[3]　Secretariat of China-Arab States Expo, Development Process of China-Arab States Economic and Trade Relations Annual Report 2019, Social Sciences Literature Press,2020, p.23.

101

efficiency and peaceful nuclear energy.[1]

Under the theme "Forward-Looking: A New Era of China-Arab States Energy Cooperation", the China-Arab States Energy Cooperation Summit was held on August 19 and 20, 2021, in Yinchuan, China. The summit participants include the energy department representatives and diplomatic envoys of Arab states, international organizations such as the International Renewable Energy Agency, and over 400 representatives from energy and financial companies. The participants believed that the energy cooperation between China and Arab states has a bright future. They were willing to cooperate in both traditional energy and new energy. Through online and on-site meetings, the summit discussed the opportunities for China-Arab states' energy cooperation during the process of achieving carbon peak and carbon neutral and encouraged each side to jointly enhance the energy development in China and Arab states.[2]

There are many fruitful cooperation projects on new energy. On August 1, 2021, the construction of the Dubai phase 5 900 MW photovoltaic project began. The project was constructed by China Energy Engineering Corporation Zhejiang Thermal Power and its commissioning was carried out by East China Electric Power Test Research Institute. The project is the largest PV power plant in Dubai and is a representative Middle East project that applies advanced solar photovoltaic power generation technology. With a total area of 10.17 m^2, the project is located in Mohammed Bin Rashid Al Maktoum Solar Park in Dubai, UAE. The construction is divided into three phases. Phase one includes a power generation unit of 300 MW and a 132 kV step-up substation.[3] On June 4, the plan was connected to the grid and operated power generation for the first time.[4]

In April 2021, China Energy Engineering Corporation Zhejiang Thermal

---

[1] China-Arab States Cooperation Forum Execution Plan for 2020-2022, China-Arab States Cooperation Forum official website, August 10, 2020,http://www.chinaarabcf.org/chn/lthyjwx/bzjhywj/djjbzjhy/202008/t20200810_6836922.htm.

[2] "China-Arab States Energy Cooperation Summit Was Held in Yinchuan", *Ningxia Daily*, August 20, 2021, front page.

[3] Weekly Snapshot on Chinese Company's Oversea Project (January 11 to January 17, 2021), Belt and Road Portal, January 18, 2021,https://mp.weixin.qq.com/s/zrledNrLjuIpNNDH4ubTOw.

[4] Dubai Phase 5 900 MW PV Project Constructed by China Energy Engineering Corporation Zhejiang Thermal Power Started Operation, China Energy Engineering Corporation, June 9, 2021,http://www.ceec.net.cn/art/2021/6/9/art_11019_2470332.html.

Power signed the RMB 1.2 billion contract for the Rabigh 300MV PV power plant EPC project in Saudi Arabia via an online meeting. The project generated 894 million kWh of electricity in the first year, and total KW will be 21.4 billion kWh of electricity per year. The project will create 900 local job positions and provide a clean power supply for 45,300 families.[①]

In May 2021, Sungrow Power signed the project contract for the Temple of Kom Ombo 200 MW PV Power Plan in Egypt. The project is located in the Temple of Kom Ombo desert area in Aswan, Egypt, where the highest temperature in summer can reach 60 ℃. High temperature and sandy environments require a highly reliable PV inverter. Therefore, Sungrow Power provides a comprehensive inverter solution to improve the power generation capacity.[②] In the same month, China National Chemical Engineering Group Corporation Middle East and Atlas Industries held the signing ceremony of the 250,000 ton/year biomass refinery project in Abu Dhabi, UAE. The project plans to invest USD 1 billion to build a biomass oil refinery plant with an annual production capacity of 1 million tons. The project is divided into several phases, and the first phase is expected to produce 250,000 tons/year. The plant will produce green oil with sustainable vegetable oil and biomass residue. Its main products include green diesel and aviation fuel.[③]

In August, a 24 MV PV power plant in Jordan started construction. Power Construction Corporation of China SEPCO3 is its general contractor. The project is located in Southern Jordan, where there are abundant solar power resources. The construction would take 270 days according to the plan. After the construction, the Chinese contractor will carry out operation and maintenance for another two years.[④] On August 19, China Energy Engineering Corporation Gezhouba Group and Egypt Peacock Energy signed the framework contract of

---

① China Energy Engineering Corporation Zhejiang Thermal Power Signed the Contract of Rabigh 300MV PV Power Plant EPC Project in Saudi Arabia, China Energy Engineering Corporation, April 14, 2021,http://www.ceec.net.cn/art/2021/4/14/art_11016_2433125.html.

② Largest in North Africa! Sungrow Power Signed a 200 MW Project in Egypt, Sungrow Power, May 7, 2021,https://cn.sungrowpower.com/news/430.html.

③ CNCECME Signed 250,000 Ton/Year Biomass Refinery Project in Abu Dhabi, China National Chemical Engineering Group Corporation Middle East, May 30, 2021,https://mp.weixin.qq.com/s/PVUJVC6jYkq1hqEOvcvwHQ.

④ Jordan PV Project with Chinese Company as the Contractor is Under Construction, Xinhuanet, http://www.xinhuanet.com/fortune/2021-08/05/c_1127734842.htm.

USD 144 million for the Gulf of Suez 120 MW wind power construction project through an online meeting.[1]

5.4   The Future of China-Arab States Energy Cooperation

5.4.1   Energy Transition: Challenge and Opportunity

The energy transition is a contemporary issue that is faced by both China and Arab states. Traditional cooperation between China and Arab states was based on these two parties' codependency on each other in terms of oil and gas. The Arab states are China's most important oil and gas supplier, and at the same time, China is a crucial oil and gas export market for the Arab states. In the context of energy transition, the fields and scope of China Arab energy cooperation have been expanded. From the perspective of fields, energy cooperation has expanded from traditional energy to wind energy, solar energy, hydropower, nuclear energy and other fields. From the perspective of scope, energy cooperation has expanded from energy exploration, mining, and trade to cooperation in the whole industry chain, thus forming a "double wheel" rotation of oil and gas and low-carbon energy, and a new situation of "oil and gas+" energy cooperation. China Arab energy cooperation should aim at building a sustainable energy partnership between China and Arab states, explore and discover new cooperation potentials and paths, and build a community of shared future for China Arab energy security.[2]

Both China and Arab states need energy transition, which creates plenty of cooperation opportunities. Many Arab states have put forward new energy development plans. To materialize the plans, they need great new energy production capacity and investment which China can offer. As the US reduces its dependency on energy from the Middle East, China is now becoming the Arab states' reliable partner in new energy development.[3] China has the world's

---

[1]   Weekly Snapshot on Chinese Company's Oversea Project (August 16, 2021 to August 22, 2021), Belt and Road Portal, Monday, August 23, 2021, https://www.yidaiyilu.gov.cn/qyfc/xmzb/184585. htm.

[2]   SUN, Xia. Energy Cooperation Between China and the Middle East and North Africa Countries Aimed at Sustainable Energy Relations. International Petroleum Economics. 2021(10): 55.

[3]   NIU, Xinchun, CHEN, Jinwen. The Impact of Global Energy Transition on Middle East Politics. Contemporary International Relations. 2021(12):7.

Chapter 5　Report on China–Arab States Energy Cooperation

highest new energy production capacity and is an ideal partner for Arab states. In the clean energy industry, China has world-leading installed capacity and power generation of hydroelectricity, wind power, and solar power. Moreover, due to the advanced technology development, the cost of clean energy in China is decreasing.[1] Meanwhile, it takes a certain amount of time for fossil fuels to be completely replaced by new energy, and energy transition can't be achieved in a short period. In addition, Arab states need more investment to increase oil and gas production capacity and develop new energy. China and Arab states should take advantage of the time gap to strengthen energy cooperation. It is foreseeable that traditional energy cooperation will still be of great importance, while energy transition creates numerous opportunities to deepen the energy cooperation between China and Arab states.

5.4.2　Remaining Economical and Political Risks Brought by the Conflict within and Outside Arab States

For a long time, the Middle East has been troubled by conflicts, either between Middle Eastern countries and other countries or between eastern countries. By 2020, some countries adjusted their policy, which alleviated the regional conflicts. On September 15, 2020, the UAE, Bahrain, and Israel signed the Abraham Accords led by the US. As a result, the relationship between the UAE and Israel was improved. In January 2021, Amiri Diwan of the State of Qatar visited Saudi Arabia and participated in the Gulf Cooperation Council Summit, which indicated that the restoration of the diplomatic relation between Qatar and Saudi Arabia since it was severed in 2017. On August 28, France and Iraq initiated the Baghdad Summit, during which Iran conducted diplomatic contact with the UAE and Saudi Arabia for the first time since 2016.[2]

However, the alleviation might be on the surface and unstable, because some crucial issues haven't been addressed yet and new disagreements are arising. On January 1, 2019, Qatar withdrew from OPEC. It was the first Middle East country that officially left OPEC since its founding 58 years ago. Qatar announced that it will significantly increase its oil production without the OPEC

---

[1]　*China Energy International Cooperation Report 2017/2018*, China Renmin University Press, 2019, p.46.

[2]　NIU, Xinchun, CHEN, Jinwen, "The Impact of Global Energy Transition on Middle East Politics", *Contemporary International Relations*, 2021(12): 4-5.

105

limit.[1] For a long time, some Arab states, especially gulf countries, have shared a similar economic development pattern, which means that their economies are not complementary and vicious competition is possible in the future. Although the issue of the nuclear program in Iran are not as severe as before, there was no substantial progress on the Palestine issue, and the future of the Iran nuclear deal is far from certain. That is to say that the fundamental reasons for these problems have not yet been addressed. Within the Arab world, the aftermaths of the political upheavals in Algeria and Sudan since 2019 remain. The internal disagreements in other countries, accumulated during their development, could morph into conflicts in the post COVID-19 era. Regional security will long be a risk factor for the cooperation between China and Arab states. The current alleviation period creates a benevolent external environment for China-Arab states energy cooperation. However, considering the long-term trend, optimism should not overshadow cautiousness. There had been plenty of cases where a Chinese company's oversea investment cooperation project suffered from great loss because of the political and economic changes in the target country. In the future, China and Arab states should push forward energy cooperation with a rational and practical mindset, evaluate all the factors in cooperation projects, and avoid conflict as much as possible, so as to maximize mutual interests.

5.4.3 The Long-term Advantage of China-Arab States Energy Cooperation: Beneficial Political Foundation

There's no pending historical issue between China and Arab states. China has long been keeping a friendly relationship with Arab states and other Middle East countries. Both parties are willing to continue the practical cooperation in every field. In 2018, at the opening ceremony of the eighth Ministerial Conference of CASCF, president Xi Jinping's speech offered guidance for the future energy cooperation between China and Arab states. President Xi pointed out that China and Arab states should actively push forward cooperation in both oil-gas energy and low-carbon energy. China and Arab states should follow the "oil and gas plus" cooperation model and enhance cooperation along the whole oil and gas production chain, including exploration, extraction, refining, storage, and

---

[1] NIU, Xinchun, CHEN, Jinwen, "The Impact of Global Energy Transition on Middle East Politics", *Contemporary International Relations*, 2021(12):5.

Chapter 5   Report on China–Arab States Energy Cooperation

transportation. They should also keep up with the global energy revolution and the development of green low-carbon industry, cooperate in peaceful nuclear energy, solar power, wind power, and hydroelectricity, and build a cooperation framework that is led by oil and gas, followed by nuclear energy, and propelled by clean energy, so as to create a reciprocal and friendly long-term strategic cooperation.[1]

According to Amman Declaration, a document released at the ninth Ministerial Conference of CASCF, China and Arab states will further strengthen the "future-oriented strategic partnership of comprehensive cooperation and common development", jointly build a community with a shared future for China and Arab states, and contribute to the community with a shared future for mankind.[2] Today, with Belt and Road Initiative as the overall guidance, China and Arab states are improving cooperation mechanisms such as the CASCF, the China-Arab states energy cooperation conference, and the China-Arab states energy cooperation league, in order to strengthen the foundation for strategic cooperation on oil, gas, and new energy.[3] At the China-Arab States Energy Cooperation Summit held in August 2021, Jianhua Zhang, Director of National Energy Administration, said in his speech that China is willing to enhance cooperation in issues such as oil, natural gas, energy transition, and the establishment of efficient cooperation platform. Zhang also stated that China stood ready to achieve energy transition with Arab states, and upgrade China-Arab states energy cooperation.[4] China and Arab states leaders' political guidance builds a solid foundation for China-Arab states relations and provides a long-term advantage for continuous energy cooperation, which to some extent could counteract the negative effect of regional geopolitical issues and economic status on cooperation.

---

[1] The Strategic Partnership between China and Arab States in the New Era: the Speech on the Opening Ceremony of the Eighth Ministerial Conference of CASCF, people.cn, July 10, 2018,http://jhsjk.people.cn/article/30138530.

[2] Amman Declaration on the Ninth Ministerial Conference of CASCF, August 10, 2020, http://www.chinaarabcf.org/chn/lthyjwx/bzjhywj/djjbzjhy/202008/t20200810_6836914.htm.

[3] Build Belt and Road: Deepen Chin-Arab States Energy Cooperation, Belt and Road Energy Cooperation, July 6, 2018,http://obor.nea.gov.cn/detail2/3098.html.

[4] China-Arab States Energy Cooperation Summit was Held, National Energy Administration, August 20, 2021,http://www.nea.gov.cn/2021-08/20/c_1310138987.htm.

Chapter 6　Report on China-Arab States Digital Economy Cooperation

Arab states are by nature China's partner in the Belt and Road Initiative. When the COVID-19 pandemic impacted the traditional economy, the accelerating digital economy development provides new momentum for the global economy and society and brings new opportunities for China-Arab states digital economy cooperation in the new era. China and the Arab states should jointly strive to make the digital economy a practical approach to ensure the quality development of the Belt and Road Initiative.

6.1　The Digital Economy Development in the Arab States

As a new form of economy that integrates with socio-economic activities, the digital economy, with information communication as its core technology, has been playing an unprecedented role in every aspect of socio-economy[1]. The "boundary-less, globalized, ubiquitous" digital economy has connected the development of all countries. In recent years, some developed countries limited their high technology export, and the oversea investment of some Chinese digital economy companies was faced with limitations and obstacles, which deteriorated the international environment for the development of the digital economy in China. Fortunately, Arab states, represented by Saudi Arabia and the UAE, have adopted a practical mindset when it comes to high-technology application, and value the broad application potential of new infrastructure represented by 5G

---

[1]　PEI, Changhong, NI, Jiangfei, LI, Yue, "Approach Digital Economy from the Perspective of Political Economics", *Finance & Trade Economics*, 2018(9):5.

Chapter 6   Report on China–Arab States Digital Economy Cooperation

technology. In addition, Arab states are against the technology monopolization of western countries, and welcome Chinese companies to participate in their 5G infrastructure construction despite of political pressure. As a result, the Arab states are becoming a crucial partner in terms of digital economy cooperation.

The current development status of the digital economy in Arab states is a key factor in determining the level and quality of China-Arab states digital economy cooperation. This paper follows the five dimensions defined by EU Member States' Digital Economy and Society Index report to evaluate the development of digital economy status in Arab states in the following five aspects: connectivity, Internet application, e-commerce, e-government, and human capital.

6.1.1   Connectivity

Digital infrastructures provide momentum for digital economy development, and connectivity is the foremost index for digital economy development evaluation. According to the Digital trends in the Arab States Region 2021[1] published by International Telecommunication Union, the Internet market penetration and household Internet access in Arab states are at around the same level as in China. As telecommunication develops rapidly, the proportion of mobile phone users in the Arab region is rising, especially in countries that are suffering from war and unstableness such as Tunisia and Syria, whose market penetration of mobile phones is close to or even surpass that of China. However, the connectivity index in about half of the Arab states is below the average number of developing countries. Generally, Internet connectivity in Arab states is improving but remains at a low level. There's an obvious regional "digital gap".

Table 6.1   Internet connectivity in Arab states

(unit: %)

Dimension	Top 5 Arab states	Last 5 Arab states	Arab states	China
Internet penetration rate	Bahrain (99.7), Qatar (99.65), Kuwait (99.6), UAE (98.5), Saudi Arabia (93.31)	Somalia (2), Comoros (8.48), Mauritania (20.8), Libya (21.76), Yemen (26.72)	54.6	54.3

---

[1] International Telecommunication Union (ITU): Digital trends in the Arab States region 2021, https://www.itu.int/en/myitu/Publications/2021/04/07/12/19/Digital-Trends-in-the-Arab-States-region-2021.

| | | | | Continued |
Dimension	Top 5 Arab states	Last 5 Arab states	Arab states	China
Mobile phone penetration rate	UAE (200), Kuwait (174), Qatar (138), Oman (138), Morocco (128)	Djibouti (42), Somalia (51), Yemen (54), Lebanon (62), Comoros (67)	99	115.53
Mobile broadband penetration rate	UAE (239.9), Kuwait (131.8), Bahrain 122.6, Qatar (120), Saudi Arabia (116.9)	Somalia (2.5), Comoros (6), Mauritania (9.5), Syria (11.5), Palestine (19.3)	62	96.7
Fixed broadband penetration rate	UAE (31.17), Saudi Arabia (19.85), Iraq (11.6), Oman (10.24), Saudi Arabia (10.2)	Sudan (0.08), Comoros (0.14), Mauritania (0.24), Somalia (0.67), Yemen (1.36)	7.7	31.34
The proportion of households with Internet access	Saudi Arabia (99.2), Oman (94.5), Lebanon (84.4), Morocco (80.8), Palestine (79.6)	Comoros (5.56), Yemen (6.3), Mauritania (14.3), Libya (23.7), Sudan (33.6)	58.9	59.6

Source: International Telecommunication Union "Digital Trends in the Arab States Region" and "Digital Trends in Asia & the Pacific 2021", International Telecommunication Union, "Digital Trends in Asia & the Pacific 2021", https://www.itu.int/en/myitu/Publications/2021/03/08/09/13/Digital-Trends-in-Asia-Pacific-2021, 2021-03-08.

6.1.2 Internet Application

6.1.2.1 Time spent

According to the data in "Digital 2020: Global Overview Report"[1], about 70% of users in the Arab region spend more than 2 hours per day using the Internet on their phones, and around 17% use the Internet over 10 hours a day. Around 47% of users spend 2 hours a day using the Internet on computers. The majority of Internet users in Arab states choose to use smartphones to access the Internet, and the time spent per person on the Internet is increasing.

6.1.2.2 Internet users

In terms of age group, ITU's "Measuring digital development: Facts and figures 2020"[2] shows that 67.2% of youths (aged between 15-24) in Arab states are Internet users, which is higher than developing countries' average of 65.6% but slightly lower than world average 69.4%.

---

[1] Data Reportal: Digital 2020: Global Overview Report, https://datareportal.com/reports/digital-2020-global-digital-overview.

[2] ITU, "Measuring digital development: Facts and figures 2020", https://www.itu.int/en/ITU-D/Statistics/Documents/facts/FactsFigures2020.pdf, 2020-11-30.

Chapter 6   Report on China–Arab States Digital Economy Cooperation

In terms of gender distribution, 61.3% of men in Arab states are Internet users, which is higher than the world average of 55.2% and developing country average of 48.9%. 47.3% of women in Arab states are Internet users, which is slightly lower than the world average of 48.3% while higher than the developing country average of 40.4%. Generally speaking, the gender gap still exists in Internet access in the Arab region: compared with men, women have fewer opportunities to acquire knowledge through the Internet. However, in Gulf Cooperation Council countries where the economic status is better, the proportion of female Internet users is close to that of male Internet users. One reason behind this is that countries with a better economy have higher literacy rates and better education, especially higher education, which can help reduce the gender gap in Internet usage. The other reason is that the proportion of female mobile users in these economically developed Arab states is considerably high. As the most common Internet access device, the mobile phone can effectively close the gender gap in Internet usage.

As for ICT skills, the share of users with different levels of skills varies in all countries, while a small group of countries, including Oman, UAE, Bahrain, Kuwait, Egypt, Saudi Arabia, and Morocco, rank the highest in every skill level. Moreover, the proportions of users with different ICT skills vary greatly even within each country. For example, the penetration rate of users with basic skills in Oman is over 75%, while the number for standard skills and advanced skills are less than 40% and 10% respectively. Comparatively, the proportion of different skill levels in Tunisia is evenly distributed, which is between 16% and 20% for each skill level (see Table 6.2).

Table 6.2   the gender of Internet users and their ICT skills in Arab states

(unit: %)

Country	Men	Women	Basic skills	Standard skills	Advanced skills
UAE	99	99.5	72.3	60.4	17.9
Kuwait	99.5	99.6	57.7	43.7	13.4
Qatar	100	99.3	44.8	30.1	5.1
Oman	94.4	96.2	75.4	36.7	8
Morocco	78.6	70.2	36.6	27.8	9.3
Tunisia	72.5	61.1	20	17.1	16.1

The Development Process of China-Arab States Economic and Trade Relations
Annual Report 2021

Continued

Country	Men	Women	Basic skills	Standard skills	Advanced skills
Saudi Arabia	96.5	94.6	56.7	49.6	13.8
Bahrain	99.9	99.3	60.8	42	18.1
Algeria	55.1	42.9	17	12.1	6.9
Egypt	61.5	53	57.5	36.2	7.9
Iraq	98.3	51.2	23.1	11.3	4.7
Palestine	72.3	68.9	—	—	—
Sudan	16.9	11	3	2.2	1.6
Djibouti	59.9	51.6	15.8	12.6	4.5

Source: International Telecommunication Union "Digital Trends in the Arab States Region".

Note: The "—" mark means the data is unavailable.

6.1.3 E-commerce

E-commerce is one of the most active and typical forms of the digital economy and is an important foothold of digital economy development. In general, Arab states do not score high in terms of e-commerce. Three Arab states, namely the UAE, Saudi Arabia, and Qatar, have higher scores than China's 70.1 and are among the top 50 out of 152 countries in e-commerce ranking (see Table 6.3). The UAE has the best e-commerce in the Arab world. In 2017, over half of its Internet users shop online. Compared with the online shopping rate of China in the same year (69%), however, the gap is still obvious. Besides, although 42% of Internet users in Sudan shop online, its national online shopping rate is less than 2% because of the low Internet penetration and connectivity. Generally speaking, e-commerce in Arab states is still in its beginning stage, which means there's huge space and potential for future development.

Table 6.3 E-commerce index and online shopping in Arab states

Regional ranking	Country	Score	World ranking	Share of online shopping users	
				In Internet users	In total population
1	UAE	78.2	37	54	49.6
2	Saudi Arabia	72.3	49	30	24.9

112

Chapter 6   Report on China–Arab States Digital Economy Cooperation

Continued

Regional ranking	Country	Score	World ranking	Share of online shopping users	
				In Internet users	In total population
3	Qatar	72.1	50	-	-
4	Kuwait	68.7	58	21	20.2
5	Lebanon	60.4	64	16	13.8
6	Bahrain	59.7	66	27	25
7	Jordan	54.7	76	9	7.1
8	Tunisia	54.6	77	11	4.7
9	Algeria	52.2	80	5	2.8
10	Libya	49.7	85	20	14.6
11	Morocco	44.8	95	22	14.2
12	Egypt	36.6	109	7	2.4
13	Djibouti	27.7	125	-	-
14	Iraq	25.4	129	16	8.6
15	Sudan	21.7	132	42	1.7
16	Syria	21.1	133	-	-
17	Yemen	18.5	138	-	-
18	Mauritania	15	145	5	1.5
19	Comoros	12	149	-	-

Source: UNCTAD B2C E-commerce Index 2020, UNCTAD, "UNCTAD B2C E-commerce Index 2020", https://unctad.org/system/files/official-document/tn_unctad_ict4d17_en.pdf, 2021-02-17.

In 2020, the outbreak of the COVID-19 pandemic stimulated online shopping activities in Arab states. According to PricewaterhouseCoopers (PwC) "Global Consumer Insights Survey 2020"[1], about 58% of respondents in the Middle East stated that they already started shopping online, and 49% suggested that their online shopping activities would greatly increase after the pandemic ends. These numbers rank the top among all regions in the PwC survey. At the same time, a global online payment solution provider surveyed 5000 consumers in Gulf Cooperation Council countries and Middle East countries including Egypt,

---

[1]   PwC, "Global Consumer Insights Survey 2020: The consumer transformed", https://www.pwc.com/gx/en/consumer-markets/consumer-insights-survey/2020/pwc-consumer-insights-survey-2020.pdf，2020-07-07.

Jordan, and Pakistan. The survey found that around 47% of consumers will increase their online shopping activities in the upcoming year.[1] At the end of 2020, the industry value of e-commerce in the Middle East increased by 52% to USD 22 billion. Egypt, Saudi Arabia, and the UAE consist of 80% of the total value.[2] Currently, e-commerce transactions are mainly processed through foreign platforms,[3] but as the habit of smartphone users changes and online shopping activity increases, local companies such as Souq and Noon are starting to develop their mobile services, hoping to become the next Amazon or Taobao. This will no doubt leave a positive influence on the promotion of digital payment and digital inclusion in the Arab states.

6.1.4　E-government

The digital economy is an effective approach to efficient governance, and e-government serves as the best way to empower the digital economy. The digital economy has created the trend where traditional government transforms into "e-government", and countries start to put more emphasis on improving the foundation of e-government. United Nations Department of Economic and Social Affairs defined the "e-government development index" (EGDI) based on the e-government development in 193 member states to evaluate the performance of e-government in each country. Since 2001, the United Nations has published 9 biennial EGDI reports. The EGDI value of each country is scored from 0 to 1, and the countries are divided into four groups according to their scores. Scores over 0.75 are defined as a very high EGDI value, 0.50 to 0.75 as a high EDGI value, 0.25 to 0.50 as a middle EDGI value, and less than 0.25 as a low EDGI value.

As the global e-government develops, the world average EDGI is increasing from 0.55 in 2018 to 0.6 in 2020. According to the data about Arab states in

---

[1]　Checkout.com，"Seizing opportunity in MENA and Pakistan (2020)"，https://www.checkout.com/newsroom/news/connected-payments-seizing-opportunity-in-mena-and-pakistan-report-launch，2020-11-10.

[2]　Egypt Pushed Forward the Development of E-commerce in Northeast Africa in 2020, Ministry of Commerce, http://www.mofcom.gov.cn/article/i/jyjl/k/202103/20210303047853.shtml，2021-08-10.

[3]　KPMG International,"The Truth about Online Consumers: 2017 Global Online Consumer Report", https://assets.kpmg/content/dam/kpmg/xx/pdf/2017/01/the-truth-about-online-consumers.pdf,2017-01-30.

Chapter 6　Report on China–Arab States Digital Economy Cooperation

E-Government Survey 2020, 11 countries (52.38%) in the Arab world have high EDGI values, and 8 Arab states (38.1%) have higher EDGI values than the world average of 0.6 (see Table 6.4). It is worth mentioning that the UAE, Bahrain, and Saudi Arabia have higher EDGI values than China (0.795), and the EDGI value of 10 countries including Saudi Arabia, Kuwait, Oman, Egypt, and Algeria has increased therefore ranked higher. The only country in the Arab region and Asia that has decreased EDGI value is Lebanon.

Table 6.4　E-government development index in Arab states

Group	Country (world ranking)
Very high	UAE (21), Saudi Arabia (38), Saudi Arabia (43), Kuwait (46), Oman (50)
High	Qatar (66), Tunisia (91), Morocco (106), Egypt (111), Jordan (117), Algeria (120)
Middle	Lebanon (127), Syria (131), Iraq (143), Libya (162), Sudan (170), Yemen (173), Mauritania (176), Comoros (177), Djibouti (179)
Low	Somalia (191)

Source: E-Government Survey 2020, United Nations, "E-Government Survey 2020: Digital Government in the Decade of Action for Sustainable Development", https://publicadministration.un.org/egovkb/en-us/#.WgMZJq-GO71, 2020-12-07.

6.1.5　Human Capital

Human capital is a key momentum for sustainable and inclusive economic growth.[1] It plays a key role in technology innovation in an era of the digital economy and is a factor behind the technology gap among countries. The World Bank designed the human capital index (HCI) to measure the human capital that children born today can expect to attain by their 18th birthday. The value is scored from 0 to 1.[2] In 2020, the HCI values of 11 countries in the Arab region were higher than 0.5 (see Table 6.5), and 4 countries' HCI values were above 0.6. The UAE is the only one with an HCI value higher than that of China (0.653). In general, the HCI value in Arab states is comparatively low, mainly because the

---

① World Bank: Human capital investment determines the future; digital economy requires new tax system, yicai, October 12, 2018, https://www.yicai.com/news/100038465.html

② For example, the HCI value of the UAE in 2020 is 0.673, which means in 2038, around 2/3 of the 18-year-olds can attain human capital.

values vary greatly within the region. The HCI value in West Asia countries is higher than that of countries in North Africa, and the less developed countries such as Sudan, Mauritania, and Yemen have HCI values that are less than 0.4. These factors have severely affected the overall HCI value of the Arab region.

Table 6.5   Human capital index in Arab states

Regional ranking	Country	Value	Regional ranking	Country	Value
1	UAE	0.673	10	Tunisia	0.517
2	Bahrain	0.652	11	Lebanon	0.515
3	Qatar	0.638	12	Morocco	0.504
4	Oman	0.608	13	Egypt	0.494
5	Palestine	0.580	14	Iraq	0.408
6	Saudi Arabia	0.576	15	Comoros	0.405
7	Kuwait	0.563	16	Mauritania	0.382
8	Jordan	0.553	17	Sudan	0.377
9	Algeria	0.535	18	Yemen	0.373

Source: World Bank, "Human Capital Index", World Bank, "Human Capital Index", https://data.worldbank.org/indicator/HD.HCI.OVRL, 2021-02-14.

The human capital status of a country is highly related to its economic status and is determined by its education quality and condition. As resource-based economies and rentier states, the Arab states have a low level of industrialization and unequal economic distribution. Most countries are faced with challenges when it comes to education access and quality. The lack of human capital investment, inadequate education quality reform, and inactive employment market, all these factors have led to the increasing unemployment of local youths. The gender gap in education is also serious in Arab states. The average years of education received by women are 0.6 years less than that of men, while the world average gap is only 0.1 years.[1] In 2020, 18% of youths (around 10% of the total male population and 27% of the female population) in Arab states are "NEET",

---

[1]   UNDP, "Arab Human Development Report Research Paper: Leaving No One Behind: Towards Inclusive Citizenship in Arab Countries", https://arab-hdr.org/wp-content/uploads/2020/12/UNDP_Citizenship_and_SDGs_report_web.pdf, 2019-08-22, p.16.

Chapter 6　Report on China–Arab States Digital Economy Cooperation

which stands for "Not in Education, Employment or Training".[1] In addition, the human capital factor can affect the ICT skill level of Internet users, and a country's e-government development is highly relevant to education and people's other general skills. Underdeveloped human capital and lower public education expense can seriously deteriorate the development of e-government. In other words, the overall educational status of Arab states, especially the inadequate public education, can to some extent impede the transition to a new industry and thus result in negative impacts on local digital economy development.[2]

6.2　China-Arab States Cooperation in Digital Economy

6.2.1　The Foundation of China-Arab Digital Economy States Cooperation

Firstly, Arab states highly emphasize their digital economy development strategies. As a new round of technology revolution and digital industry transformation accelerates, the Arab states emphasize their digital economy development plan. In the UAE, in particular, there's an outstanding digital transformation strategy that consists of a series of targeted plans based on the national vision. The strategy includes many cutting-edge technology development plans, such as "UAE Centennial 2071" released in 2017 to realize prosperity and development over five decades through communication technology and digital economy, and the "UAE Strategy for Artificial Intelligence 2031" proposed in 2019, and the "Blockchain strategy" in 2020. It is worth mentioning that the UAE attaches great importance to the development of smart cities, and established the "UAE smart government plan", "Smart Dubai 2021 Strategy", and "smart Abu Dhabi". Today, smart cities account for around 50% of the total cities in the UAE, which is the highest in Arab states.[3]

Other countries also attach great importance to digital development in their

---

[1]　ESCWA," التقرير العربي للتنمية المستدامة ",https://asdr.unescwa.org/sdgs/pdf/ar/ASDR2020-Final-Online.pdf,2019-02-14,p.60.

[2]　ESCWA,"2030 الابتكار والتكنولوجيا من أجل التنمية المستدامة آفاق واعدة في المنطقة العربية لعام ", https://archive.unescwa.org/sites/www.unescwa.org/files/publications/files/arab-horizon-2030-innovation-perspectives-sdgs-arab-region-arabic_0.pdf,2019-02-12.

[3]　AMF: Smart Cities in the UAE is Leading the Way, Ministry of Commerce, http://www.mofcom.gov.cn/article/i/jyjl/k/201908/20190802893678.shtml, 2019-08-28.

117

national development plans and visions, although the digital economy plans are not as targeted and precise as those in the UAE. For example, "Saudi Vision 2030" includes plans to increase investment in technology innovation, cloud service, and digital transformation. In Bahrain's 2030 vision, there are plans for technology development, cloud service, data center, etc. "Oman Vision 2040" and "Digital Oman 2030" cover cutting-edge technology such as artificial intelligence, blockchain, big data, smart city, Internet of Things, and virtual reality. According to the "New Kuwait Vision 2035", the country plans to innovate its technology and accelerate the establishment of a modern infrastructure system. There are other plans and visions that serve as the digital foundation of regional economic development, such as "Jordan 2025 vision", "2030 digital transformation strategy" in Syria, Egypt's "Vision 2030" and "ICT 2030 strategy", Mauritania's national broadband strategy (2019-2022), and Sudan's national strategy (2007-2031).[1]

Secondly, China can offer development experience to Arab states. China has long joined the global innovation network and has become an important participant and propeller in the new round of technology revolution and industrial transformation.[2] China's prosperous digital economy indicates that its development capacity and potential are no less than traditional developed countries, which makes Arab states realize the importance of digital transformation in industrial transformation and economic development, and improves the confidence of Arab states in developing digital economy. Different from the Western countries, China respects the specific conditions and autonomy of their countries, and adheres to the principles of "creating more space and opportunities for developing countries" and "teach a man to fish and you feed him for a lifetime". China will cooperate with the Arab states and "seize opportunities created by digital, networked and smart development, and build

---

[1] ESCWA, "Arab Digital Development Report 2019: Towards Empowering People and Ensuring Inclusiveness", https://www.unescwa.org/sites/www.unescwa.org/files/publications/files/arab-digital-development-report-2019-english_0.pdf, 2019-06-30. Huawei, GCI 2016, ttps://www.huawei.com/minisite/gci/assets/files/gci_2016_whitepaper_cn.pdf?v=20201217v2, 2016-04-11. Huawei, GCI 2019, https://www.huawei.com/minisite/gci/assets/files/gci_2019_whitepaper_cn.pdf?v=20201217v2, 2019-11-17.

[2] Find the Direction and Breakpoint of Technology Innovation, people.cn, http://theory.people.com.cn/n1/2019/0725/c40531-31254734.html, 2019-07-25.

Chapter 6   Report on China–Arab States Digital Economy Cooperation

the digital Silk Road and the Silk Road of innovation."[1] The goal of the China-Arab states economy cooperation is to reduce the gap in economic development, facilitate high-level cooperation and mutual benefit. Today, China is leading the way in the development of the Internet and telecommunication. However, most Arab states need improvement, and the penetration of information technology and transmission speed is unable to support the further development of their digital economy. China can share its results from digital transformation to improve the Arab states' digital development ability, make use of its advantage on the Internet and digital economy to make the smart product serve the digital economy development needs of Arab states; promote the concepts such as "shared economy" and "Internet + Finance" to encourage the open and innovative development of digital economy in the Arab states; provide matured platform building and logistics service management technology and experience in terms of e-commerce, in order to guide Arab states towards the digital economy.

Thirdly, the Arab states need support from China to construct their digital infrastructure. The large number of Internet users in the Arab states creates an enormous 5G market, which is an important momentum for China to accelerate the cooperation in digital infrastructure. According to the telecommunication giant Ericsson, 5G technology is expected to make breakthroughs in the Middle East and North Africa. In 2025, 5G users in this region are estimated to reach 80 million, accounting for 10% of the global total[2]. Therefore, a fundamental task of China-Arab states digital economy cooperation and a key to promoting the application of 5G technology in the Arab states is to change the status quo where the Arab states lack robust digital infrastructure, and the regional development gap persists.

Chinese companies such as Huawei and ZTE broadly expand their oversea business. Huawei, in particular, has a long cooperation history with the Middle East by initiating cooperation in wireless Internet, smart end devices, etc. through its 5G communication technology. Initially, 5G users concentrated in the Gulf countries, with the UAE being one of the first countries to apply 5G

---

[1]   Keynote speech given by President Xi Jinping at the opening ceremony of the Belt and Road Forum, xinhuanet, http://www.xinhuanet.com/world/2019-04/26/c_1210119584.htm, 2019-04-26.

[2]   5G: Users in Middle, East, and North Africa Will Reach 80 million in 2025, Ministry of Commerce, http://www.mofcom.gov.cn/article/i/jyjl/k/202006/20200602976533.shtml, 2020-06-22.

119

technology in the commercial sector, and Saudi Arabia is one of the Middle East countries that deployed 5G infrastructures.[1] At MWC Barcelona 2019, Saudi Telecommunication signed the "Aspiration" project contract with Huawei. The project will facilitate the modernization of the wireless network and the construction of a 5G network in Saudi Arabia and will help the country implement its Vision 2030 and National Transformation Program 2020.[2] By the end of September 2019, 11 telecommunication companies from Middle East countries such as the UAE, Saudi Arabia, Kuwait, Oman, and Bahrain have signed a 5G technology contract with Huawei.[3] Since the pandemic containment measures were implemented, China and the Gulf Arab states have accelerated their new technology cooperation. In June 2020, Huawei signed an agreement with SC2, a Saudi Arabian smart city solution provider, to start a cooperation project in Saudi Arabia[4]. In October, Saudi Data and AI Authority established a partnership with Huawei and signed a memorandum of understanding on the national AI development plan, so as to jointly push forward the AI development plan in Saudi Arabia.[5] Besides, Egypt is the first Arab state with Huawei 5G base station. During the COVID-19 pandemic, "AI Smart Classroom", the AI technology training program established by Huawei and the Egypt Ministry of Communications and Information Technology in Aswan University, provided technical training for Aswan and other provinces with inadequate educational resources.[6]

6.2.2 The Progress of China-Arab States Digital Economy Cooperation

First, China has been innovating the China-Arab states digital economy

---

[1] Ren Zhengfei Was Interviewed by Middle East Media Agency, guancha.cn, https://www.guancha. cn/economy/2019_11_04_523846.shtml, 2019-11-04.

[2] Huawei and STC Signed 5G Aspiration Project Contract, Huawei, https://www.huawei.com/cn/ news/2019/2/stc-huawei-5g-aspiration-project, 2019-02-26.

[3] Ren Zhengfei Was Interviewed by Middle East Media Agency, guancha.cn, https://baijiahao.baidu. com/s?id=1649237516262391504&wfr=spider&for=pc, 2019-11-04.

[4] Huawei Cooperate with SC2 to Build Saudi Arabia into a Smart City, https://baijiahao.baidu.com/ s?id=1670917657561774548&wfr=spider&for=pc, 2020-06-30.

[5] Saudi Data and AI Authority and Huawei Established Partnership, https://baijiahao.baidu.com/ s?id=1681265438967428264&wfr=spider&for=pc, 2020-10-22.

[6] Jing Yue, Huang Peizhao, "China and Arab States Strengthen Digital Cooperation", *People's Daily*, July 9, 2020.

Chapter 6   Report on China–Arab States Digital Economy Cooperation

cooperation mechanism in recent years, China is committed to jointly building through consultation to meet the interests of all and improving the China-Arab states digital economy cooperation mechanism. In December 2016, China approved the "China-Arab states online silk road economic cooperation pilot zone and Ningxia hub project". The project has become an online platform for China and Arab states leaders to communicate, initiate economic and trade cooperation, and carry out the cultural exchange. The most important cooperation fields include cutting-edge industries such as broadband infrastructure, satellite application service, big data, cloud computing, cross-border e-commerce, and smart city.[1] In 2017, at the fourth World Internet Conference, China launched the "Belt and Road" Digital Economy International Cooperation Initiative[2] with countries including the UAE and Saudi Arabia, and signed the "Memorandum of Understanding on Building Cyber Silk Road and Promoting Information Interconnectivity" with Egypt.[3] In July 2018, President Xi Jinping said in his speech at the opening ceremony of the eighth Ministerial Conference of CASCF that China and Arab states should ensure "financial cooperation go in tandem with collaboration on new and high technology", and implement "China-Arab states technology partnership", and "accelerate the work on a cyber-Silk Road, and strive for more cooperation consensus and outcomes in Internet infrastructure, big data, cloud computing, and e-commerce". China will "invite 300 science professionals" from Arab states, and "provide 10,000 training opportunities".[4] In July 2020, the ninth Ministerial Conference of CASCF published the execution plan for 2020-2022. The plan pointed out that China and the Arab states should cooperate and learn from each other in terms of Internet and digital economy through bilateral economic cooperation, increase exchanges on technological humanity in technology cooperation, and

---

[1]   Build Cyber Silk Road to Facilitate Belt and Road, State Council Information Office, http://www. scio.gov.cn/31773/35507/35519/Document/1537340/1537340.htm, 2016-12-29.

[2]   Multiple Countries Jointly Launched "Belt and Road" Digital Economy International Cooperation Initiative, xinhuanet, http://www.xinhuanet.com/zgjx/2017-12/04/c_136798586.htm, 2017-12-04.

[3]   National Development and Reform Commission and Egypt Ministry of Communications and Information Technology Signed the Memorandum of Understanding on Building Cyber Silk Road and Promoting Information Interconnectivity, http://www.gov.cn/xinwen/2017-01/22/content_5162147.htm, 2017-01-22.

[4]   Xi Jinping, "Jointly Develop China-Arab States Strategic Partnership in the New Era", *People's Daily*, July 11, 2018.

121

invite technology management professionals and technicians to participate in the annual "advanced technology and technology management training course" held by the Ministry of Science and Technology, and research on how to conduct cooperation between science and technology parks.[1] China and the Arab states have built a multi-layered cooperation platform for stable communication, which will further facilitate and strengthen bilateral digital economy cooperation

Secondly, China and the Arab states have made many achievements in the digital economy. In the new era, China and the Arab states are expanding their relations and demonstrating new development trends. In the past couple of years, in particular, the spreading COVID-19 pandemic has helped the China-Arab states digital economy cooperation to reach a new level. In the medical field, G42, an artificial intelligence company from the UAE launched a cooperation project in March 2020 with BGI Group from Shenzhen, China. This project aimed to build a test laboratory for COVID-19 diagnosis and testing. For the first three months, the lab conducted over 3 million tests for around 10 million people in the UAE, and as a result, the UAE became one of the countries with the highest test rate.[2] In the education and culture field, Edmodo, the online education and digital learning platform developed by the Chinese company NetDragon Websoft was recommended by Tarek Shawky, Minister of Education and Technical Education in Egypt. The platform provided remote learning support to 2.2 million students and over 1 million teachers in Egypt during the pandemic.[3] In November 2020, the first China-Arab States Digital Culture Exhibition launched by the Chinese Ministry of Culture and Tourism and the UAE Ministry of Culture and Youth used "CBox", a 3D virtual architecture space, as its online exhibition platform to allow audiences from both countries to experience the charm of digital culture in an immersion space without time

---

[1] China-Arab States Cooperation Forum Execution Plan for 2020-2022, China-Arab Research Center on Reform and Development, http://infadm.shisu.edu.cn/_s114/07/09/c7779a132873/page.psp, 2018-08-19.

[2] The Partnership Between China and Gulf Countries Can Survive Global Crisis, Silk Road Promotion Center for International Production Capacity Cooperation, http://weixin.bricc.org.cn/Module_Think/ThinkPortal/ArticleDetail.aspx?aid=2756, 2020-07-22.

[3] China and Arab States Promote Digital Cooperation, people.cn, http://arabic.people.com.cn/n3/2020/0709/c31660-9708802.html, 2020-07-09.

Chapter 6   Report on China–Arab States Digital Economy Cooperation

and space barriers.[1] As for economy and trade, in July 2020, the first China-UAE Economic and Trade Digital Expo, co-hosted by the China Council for the Promotion of International Trade and the UAE Ministry of Economy, applied a cloud exhibition platform which attracted 2100 companies from China and the UAE and about 12,000 purchasers from 11 countries including China, the UAE, Egypt, and Morocco. On May 24, 2021, China held the 4th CIIE online promotional event targeting Middle Eastern countries. Around 150 representatives from the Middle Eastern government and companies, such as the Dubai Customs, Abu Dhabi National Oil Company, and Qatar Free Zone, participated in the online event.[2] From August 19 to 22, 2021, the 5th China-Arab States Expo was held online and attracted over 10 million visits. It was the first time that the exposition had been held online. During the China-Arab States Expo, China and the Arab states signed 277 documents with a total planned investment and trade value of RMB 156.67 billion and published and signed 54 policy reports and memorandums.[3]

6.3 The Future of China-Arab States Cooperation in the Digital Economy

The digital economy is the future of global development.[4] China and the Arab states could follow the Belt and Road principle of "jointly building through consultation to meet the interests of all" to facilitate digital economy cooperation. According to the analysis of the current status of the digital economy in the Arab states, the cooperation between China and the Arab states still needs further development.

Firstly, we should strengthen cooperation in digital infrastructure construction

---

[1] School of Animation and Digital Art Participated the Design of China-Arab States Digital Culture Exhibition, Communication University of China, http://www.cuc.edu.cn/news/2020/1127/c1902a176264/page.htm, 2020-11-27.

[2] The 4th CIIE Applied "Cloud Expo" in the Middle East, http://www.ce.cn/xwzx/gnsz/gdxw/202105/28/t20210528_36596486.shtml, 2021-05-28.

[3] Jointly Build the China-Arab States Community with a Shared Future: The 5th China-Arab States Expo Was Held Successfully, Ministry of Commerce, http://xyf.mofcom.gov.cn/article/cr/202109/20210903195308.shtml, 2021-09-06.

[4] Xi Jinping: Digital economy is the future of global development and innovation is the wing of Asian-pacific economy, http://www.gov.cn/xinwen/2020-11/20/content_5563088.htm, 2020-11-20.

with the Arab states. Network infrastructure is the prerequisite for digital economy development. The Arab states have significant demand for digital infrastructure, which makes it possible for China and the Arab states to match their needs and supplies for the construction of digital infrastructures such as the 5G network, big data, and cloud platform. On one hand, as mobile communication in some Arab states is gradually freed from governmental control and starts welcoming market competition, the local digital companies in those countries now enjoy a beneficial environment for development. Digital companies in China should leverage the open and competitive mobile communication market in the Arab states.[1] On the other hand, China has the world's most sophisticated industrial chain and can use advanced technology to help Arab states build and upgrade their digital infrastructure, encourage the middle class in Arab states to accept and develop the habit of online shopping, and therefore facilitate the integrated development of payment and data. Besides, China could integrate pandemic containment and infrastructure construction to apply the new technology and application of healthcare infrastructure to the post-pandemic restoration in the Arab states.

Secondly, implement plans for China-Arab states digital talents exchange and training. The digital industry development in different Arab states varies greatly. China and Arab states could build a shared community that benefit both science and education development, while they can also create targeted talent exchange and training project according to the different development status of each Arab state. China and the Arab states could hold digital ability-building workshops and have in-depth exchanges[2]. Universities and educational institutes in China and the Arab states can cooperate to design digital economy programs, curricula, and training centers, in order to provide quality education services such as course design and personnel training to the Arab states. Chinese research institutes and companies such as Huawei, ZTE, and Tencent could establish joint R&D centers and innovation platforms, so as to provide targeted digital education solutions for the training of professional technical talents. In addition, to facilitate communication, China and the Arab states should train interdisciplinary talents

---

[1] Lin Ying, Chen Bingfu, Li Yidong, Ke Guanyan, Feng Songhe, "Activating Information Infrastructure Development in Countries along the Belt and Road with Basic Information Application", *Strategic Study of CAE*, 2019(4):37.

[2] "Jointly Build a Prosperous and Beautiful Future", *People's Daily*, July 18, 2021.

Chapter 6　Report on China−Arab States Digital Economy Cooperation

that master not only technology but also foreign languages such as Arabic, French, and English.

Thirdly, cross border e-commerce market should be the focus. Although the Arab states still need to improve their digital economy, they are complementary to the Chinese economy and are the seventh greatest trade partner of China while China has become the Arab states' largest trade partner. According to the statistical data, over 80% of Internet users in the six Gulf countries use Chinese e-commerce platforms.[1] As the daily time spent online, youth Internet user ratio, and online shopping rate in the Arab states keep increasing, and the COVID-19 pandemic forced countries that used to rely on traditional international trade such as Saudi Arabia and the UAE to adopt e-commerce, the cross border e-commerce between China and the Arab states is welcoming broad opportunities. However, we should realize that because of the increasingly heated competition in the Arabic cross-border e-commerce market and the global commodity mobility impeded by the China-US trade dispute and the COVID-19 pandemic, a large number of e-commerce companies have inadequate supply chains and founding will struggle to survive. Therefore, the Silk Road e-commerce companies in China should transform into a targeted and precise industry[2], because cross-border e-commerce that focuses on digital products and services, and digital knowledge and information will gain larger market space in the Arab states.

Fourthly, the smart city will become the highlight of China-Arab states digital economy cooperation. Smart cities and new infrastructure construction are connected by nature. The smart city is the main application scenario of new infrastructure, and new infrastructure construction plays an irreplaceable role in upgrading smart city infrastructure and empowering smart city governance.[3] As the bilateral cooperation in digital infrastructure develops, the exchange between smart cities in China and the Arab states will become an important part of the China-Arab states digital economy cooperation in the future. At the same time,

---

[1]　China-Arab States Cooperation Initiative on Data Security Opened a New Chapter of Global Digital Government, http://www.gov.cn/xinwen/2021-03/30/content_5596690.htm, 2021-03-30.

[2]　Qiao Cai, Cross Border E-commerce is Developing Rapidly, people.cn, http://finance.people.com.cn/n1/2021/0222/c1004-32033286.html, 2021-02-22.

[3]　Du Qinghao, "The Main Direction of Digital Economy Development in the New Era", *China Opening Journal*, 2020(6):79.

125

China should be aware of the fact that the digital economy status in different Arab states varies greatly. As a result, the development of the smart city is uneven. China should initiate targeted smart city cooperation according to the existing policy and technology in different Arab states. According to the "Smart City Index 2020"[1] by IMD Business School World Competitiveness Center, the ranking of Arab cities such as Abu Dhabi and Dubai keeps increasing in recent years and surpass some major cities in China. Therefore, the Arab states' policies on smart city development can serve as an important reference for China. A smart city requires the integration of the latest technology including cloud computing, big data, and blockchain into public transportation, healthcare, information security, environmental protection, etc., which is a great challenge to the scientific innovation ability and technology talent pool in the Arab states and creates many opportunities for China-Arab states smart city cooperation.

---

[1] IMD, "Smart City Index 2020", https://www.imd.org/smart-city-observatory/smart-city-index/, 2021-04-14.

Chapter 7 Report on China-Arab States Cooperation in Science, Technology, and Eco-environmental Governance

Science, technology, and eco-environmental governance is an important area of China-Arab states economy and trade cooperation and is of great importance to improve the level of comfort, convenience, and happiness of people in China and the Arab states.

7.1 The China-Arab States Science and Technology Cooperation Framework and Traditional Cooperation Field

Science and technology constitute a primary productive force. Since the reform and opening up in the 1970s, China has formulated a medium- and long-term science and technology revitalization strategy, from learning rules and benchmarking norms to guiding regulation, to strengthen international science and technology cooperation. In the past two decades, the Chinese government has actively issued relevant science and technology policy documents to continuously deepen the top-level design of China-Arab states science and technology exchanges in the new era, providing systematic planning and indicating the directions of development for China-Arab states science and technology exchanges and cooperation.

7.1.1 Cooperation Framework

The framework of China-Arab states cooperation in science and technology has been steadily promoted with the China-Arab States Cooperation Forum as the main long-term mechanism. The cooperation has been developing, showing

127

a multilateral and multi-faceted cooperation model with the CASCF as the framework, the China-Arab States Expo and the China-Arab States Technology Transfer and Innovation Cooperation Conference as the platform, and the China-Arab States Technology Transfer Center and Joint Research Center as the cooperation base.

The China-Arab States Cooperation Forum has played a key leading role in facilitating China-Arab States bilateral science and technology exchanges and has continuously promoted China-Arab States cooperation toward formalization and institutionalization. Relying on the China-Arab States Expo, the China-Arab States Technology Transfer Center closely focuses on the practical needs of China-Arab states science and technology cooperation, welcomes the construction of the China-Arab technology transfer collaboration network, establishes a comprehensive information service platform, carries out a series of technology matching and transfer activities, and continuously builds a professional and institutional China-Arab States Technology Transfer Center. Since September 2015, China and Arab states have jointly established 8 bilateral technology transfer centers, including LAS, Egypt, and Oman, held more than 20 training courses for transnational technical talents, and trained more than 300 international technology transfer cooperation talents.[1] China and Arab states have jointly established a network of technology transfer collaborative institutions with 4264 network members including domestic and foreign enterprises, scientific research institutions, higher education institutions, and intermediary service institutions. With the increasingly expanded and improved collaborative network, the China-Arab States Technology Transfer Center hosts or participates in various collaborative network proposal seminars, academic seminars on science and technology transformation and science and technology strategy, etc. Relying on the China-Arab States Science and Technology Park, more than 20 science and technology projects have been launched, and a series of China-Arab states science and technology innovation platforms have been established in the fields including date palm, agricultural Internet of Things, green intelligent water-saving equipment, satellite data services, potato food development.

---

[1] WANG, Lili, "Jointly Build the Belt and Road to Energize China-Arab States Cooperation", *China's Foreign Trade*, September, 2021.

Chapter 7   Report on China-Arab States Cooperation in Science, Technology, and
Eco-environmental Governance

7.1.2   The Traditional Field and Model of the China-Arab States Science and Technology Cooperation

Since China and the Arab states established diplomatic relations, the cooperation between the two sides has been expanding and deepening based on agriculture, energy, and infrastructure development in the 20th century. In the 21st century, China has made rapid progress in the field of science and technology. With the continuous depletion of the resources which used to be abundant, the Arab states now pay more attention to scientific and technological research and development, and their intention to cooperate with China has been strengthened, laying a solid foundation for China-Arab states cooperation in science and technology. In recent years, studies conducted by domestic and foreign academics have shown that China-Arab states cooperation in science and technology has begun to focus on environmental protection, water resources, information networks, high-speed rail, new energy, etc., while gradually strengthening technology transfer and the application of research results.

In May 2017, President Xi Jinping proposed at the Belt and Road Forum to launch the Belt and Road Science, Technology and Innovation Cooperation Action Plan to carry out four actions, namely technological humanity exchanges, joint laboratories, science and technology park cooperation, and technology transfer.

From 2020 to 2021, the COVID-19 pandemic affected the exchange, visits, and cooperation between China and the Arab states, but the CASCF and the China-Arab States Technology Transfer and Innovation Cooperation Conference mechanism stayed functional, and the 9th Ministerial Conference, the 3rd China-Arab States BDS Cooperation Forum, the 4th China-Arab States Technology Transfer and Innovation Cooperation Conference, and a series of product and technology promotion activities and cooperation promotion and exchange meetings were held successfully. The China-Arab States Technology Transfer Center has maintained close contact with institutions and enterprises in Arab states and carried out science and technology cooperation at all levels in an orderly manner. According to statistics, within two years, China-Arab States Technology Transfer Center held two training courses for Arab states (agricultural water conservation technology and COVID-19 prevention), facilitated an investment agreement of USD 1.264 billion (Ningxia University and Qatar Free

129

Zone), and promoted three major engineering projects (Hassyan clean coal-fired power plant project in Dubai, UAE, etc.), which practically promoted China-Arab states cooperation in science and technology and technology transfer.

The four science and technology cooperation has been steadily pushed forward, and large science and technology projects, either jointly constructed by China and Arab states companies or constructed by Chinese general contractors, have been established in Arab states, mostly in the fields of new energy and aerospace. Technology transfer refers to the international transfer of certain mature technologies from China to Arab countries, such as desalination technology, aerospace technology, etc., and the most representative one is the technology transfer of healthcare in 2020-2021. During the pandemic, the export of Chinese vaccine technology provided life support for countless people in the Arab states. Humanity exchanges are represented by the training of technology talents in the Arab states. In the past two years, China-Arab state exchanges in the field of artificial intelligence have been very common. Huawei, for example, has extensively carried out the "Seeds for the Future" program in the Arab states and has trained a large number of local high-tech talents with an international vision in the fields of communication technology, 5G and cloud computing, laying a solid foundation for China-Arab states cooperation and exchanges.

7.2   Key Fields of China-Arab States Science and Technology Cooperation

In addition to traditional energy, China and Arab states have explored fields such as clean energy, artificial intelligence, digital economy, healthcare, and aerospace under the guidance of the Belt and Road Initiative, providing new momentum for the cooperation between the two sides.

In the new era, China-Arab states cooperation in science and technology has shifted from traditional energy to low-carbon energy, and gradually expanded to renewable energy, especially the photovoltaic power generation projects, large-scale energy storage projects, and clean energy projects in 2020 and 2021. In addition, breakthroughs have been made in healthcare, communication technology, and aerospace. China and the Arab states have actively cooperated to jointly promote the production and supply of COVID-19 vaccines in Arab countries. In terms of key high-tech projects including 5G, artificial intelligence,

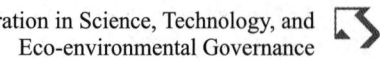

Chapter 7   Report on China-Arab States Cooperation in Science, Technology, and Eco-environmental Governance

cloud computing, electronic industrial technology, and electronic optical industry, China has cooperated with the Arab states through talent exchange and training, and technology transfer to promote the development of the digital economy and cross-border e-commerce. For space satellite research and production, China has actively provided technical support and technology transfer and promotion through forums, dialog, and cooperation.

7.2.1   Cooperation in New Energy

China and the Arab states are both facing the issue of energy security and energy transformation, and the low-carbon energy sector has become the focus of attention for both sides. Vigorously developing renewable energy and building a clean, low-carbon, safe and efficient energy system has become a global trend, which offers a good opportunity to deepen China-Arab states energy cooperation. From 2020 to 2021, China and the Arab states broadened their energy cooperation fields and shifted from traditional energy cooperation to diversified energy cooperation, and as a result, the quality of cooperation has improved. At the current stage, China-Arab states energy cooperation is mainly expanding from oil and gas to solar energy and electricity.

7.2.1.1   Cooperation projects on renewable energy such as solar energy

In the field of new energy, solar photovoltaic power generation features the most extensive and in-depth cooperation projects that have achieved fruitful results and good international influence. Cooperation in solar energy is mainly located in the Gulf countries. For example, China's PV project in Qatar will become the world's third largest single-site PV power plant and the largest PV project that uses tracking systems and bifacial modules. The project will be the power supply of the 2022 Qatar World Cup venues. The Red Sea integrated intelligent energy project with Saudi Arabia not only develops solar energy and renewable energy but also provides integrated infrastructure for seawater desalination and wastewater management. In August 2021, China signed an agreement with Iraq to build a 2,000 MW photovoltaic power plant. Dubai Maktoum Solar Park Phase V 900 MW photovoltaic project Phase A, a key project of the Belt and Road Initiative, was officially connected to the grid at full capacity, becoming the largest PV power plant project in Dubai so far. At the same time, the first photovoltaic power plant project built by a Chinese company in Jordan — the 24MW photovoltaic project — will start construction in

131

August 2021.

The implementation of these projects will not only solve the plight of power shortage in Arab states, bring healthy, safe, and clean life to local residents, but also create a large number of job opportunities. At the same time, they can help Arab states reduce their dependence on traditional energy and develop a diverse economy.

7.2.1.2 Cooperation projects on clean energy such as natural gas

In recent years, China has accelerated the process of the green energy transition. Coal is gradually replaced by gas, natural gas consumption is increasing rapidly, and the proportion of clean energy in total energy consumption continues to rise. Arab states are also actively seeking energy transition to reduce their dependency on fossil fuels.

In terms of natural gas storage and transportation technology, China Shipbuilding Group Corporation, and Qatar Petroleum Corporation jointly signed an agreement on the "China Shipbuilding-Qatar Petroleum LNG Vessel Construction Project" in April 2020 and completed the first order in October 2021 for four 174, 000 cubic meters LNG carriers. China and Qatar plan to make this project a cornerstone of cooperation between China Shipbuilding Group and Qatar Petroleum and Qatar Gas, and a bridge and example for the China-Qatar cooperation during the development of the Belt and Road Initiative. In October 2020, China Petroleum Pipeline Engineering Cooperation Abu Dhabi Branch officially confirmed the winning bid for the UAE National Gas Pipeline Network Upgrade FEED (Front End Engineering Design) project. The project will play a vital role in the UAE's energy security and is a strategic national energy project for the livelihood of the people.

As for clean coal-fired power in June 2016, Harbin Electric International Co., Ltd. and General Electric Co. formed a consortium and won the contract for the Hassyan 4×600MW clean coal-fired power plant project in Dubai, UAE. In May 2020, Unit 1 of the Hassyan Project was successfully connected to the grid. As a major project of the Belt and Road international cooperation and the first clean coal-fired power plant in the Middle East, Hassyan's successful grid connection marks a major breakthrough in the construction of the world's first dual-fuel full-load power plant. At the same time, the Hassyan project is also an important step toward energy diversification in Dubai.

132

Chapter 7　Report on China-Arab States Cooperation in Science, Technology, and Eco-environmental Governance

7.2.1.3　Cooperation in electrical energy

In terms of electric energy transportation, on October 5, 2021, a consortium consisting of China Energy Engineering, China XD Group, and Giza Cables Industries of Egypt, successfully signed the Egypt-Saudi Arabia ±500 kV ultra-high voltage DC transmission line EPC project. The project is the DC transmission project with the highest voltage level and longest transmission distance in the Middle East and North Africa region. The total length of the project line is 335 km, which is of great significance to optimizing the structure of Egypt's power system, improving local employment, and boosting local economic and social development. Yao Gang, General Manager of China Energy Engineering Egypt Representative Office, said that it has taken ten years to negotiate and select the location for the project. During this period, the Chinese enterprises have always stood firm and implemented the project amid the pandemic.

7.2.2　Cooperation in Artificial Intelligence

In the past two years, the main form of China-Arab states cooperation in artificial intelligence is the training of talents in the Arab states. The most representative project is "Seeds for the Future", a flagship CSR program initiated by Huawei. Launched in 2008, the program aims to train local ICT talents, enhance knowledge transfer, and promote international exchanges in the ICT industry. Currently, 130 countries and regions have joined the program, of which 14 are Arab countries.

On October 20, 2020, the launching ceremony of the fifth Seeds for the Future program and the award ceremony of the second Huawei ICT Competition was held in Algeria, attracting over 3,000 Algerian students to participate. On March 16, 2021, Huawei held "Tunisia Talent Day" in Tunisia. Since Huawei established the ICT Training Academy in Tunisia, it has signed agreements with dozens of universities, provided online courses for more than 4,000 Tunisian students, and selected more than 80 Tunisian students to join the "Seeds for the Future" program. On August 23, 2021, the "Seeds for the Future" program in Bahrain was recognized by international AI organizations. Dr. Jassim Haji, president of the International Group of Artificial Intelligence, called the program "a key pillar to support the ICT ecosystem in Bahrain". In September of the same year, Huawei held the graduation ceremony of the 2021 "Seeds for

the Future" program in Qatar.

In addition to the "Seeds for the Future" program, China has launched multi-faceted talent training and technical support initiatives in the Arab states. In June 2020, Huawei and the Egypt Ministry of Communications and Information Technology launched the "Artificial Intelligence Classroom" program at Aswan University to provide training in 5G, artificial intelligence, cloud computing, and other technologies for Aswan and other provinces where educational resources are relatively scarce. Huawei has also agreed to train 200 national-level instructors for the National Institute of Communications of Egypt.

In addition, China-Arab states cooperation in artificial intelligence also includes digital cooperation centered on technology transfer. An e-commerce platform operated by Zhejiang Zhiyu Information Technology Co., Ltd. now covers more than 80% of Internet users in the UAE, Oman, Bahrain, Qatar, Kuwait, and Saudi Arabia. The company works with government departments to actively share advanced technologies and experiences in developing digital platforms. At the Global AI Summit on October 22, 2020, Huawei and the Saudi Data and Artificial Intelligence Authority signed a memorandum of understanding online for the National Artificial Intelligence Capability Development Program to support Saudi Arabia's digital transformation. Huawei stands ready to create new value for artificial intelligence and other technologies through cooperation with Saudi Arabia.

7.2.3　Cooperation in Aerospace Technology

As a representative of today's cutting-edge technology, aerospace is an important field of cooperation between China and the Arab states. Under the framework of the Belt and Road initiative, China and the Arab states are jointly building the "Space Silk Road". China will make use of its advanced technology in aerospace and integrate various aerospace resources to carry out international cooperation in space science, launch services, satellite applications, deep space exploration, human spaceflight, and space infrastructure construction, to support economic development, social progress, and improvement of people's livelihood in Belt and Road initiative participating countries.

In the past two years, China-Arab states aerospace cooperation was represented by a series of space cooperation projects, including the Chinese-Egyptian satellite project MisrSat II and the China-Arab states BeiDou Navigation Satellite System

Chapter 7   Report on China-Arab States Cooperation in Science, Technology, and
Eco-environmental Governance

cooperation project. The former is the first overseas satellite project undertaken by the China Academy of Space Technology, a subsidiary of China Aerospace Science and Technology Corporation, and financially supported by the Ministry of Commerce and the China International Development Cooperation Agency. On July 15, 2020, the MisrSat II project announced that all of its technical documents have passed the evaluation, which means the satellite has fully entered the development and production phase.

MisrSat II is a satellite developed in the joint mode under the framework of the Belt and Road Initiative. Part of the development work will be completed in the satellite assembly and integration test center constructed by Chinese company. The project will deliver a 2m/8m resolution optical remote sensing satellite in orbit, construct a supporting ground measurement and control station and ground application system, and conduct training for Egyptian space experts and talents. Upon the completion of the project, Egypt will become the first African country with complete satellite assembly and integration test capability, and the parallel development capability of two 600 kg class satellites. The project enhances Egypt's aerospace capability, shows China's competence in the space field, and promotes friendly cooperation between China and Egypt.

More attention is drawn to the China-Arab states BeiDou cooperation project, which is a priority cooperation project specified in the memorandum of understanding on China-Arab satellite navigation cooperation signed by the China Satellite Navigation Office and the Arab Information and Communication Technologies Organization on the initiative of President Xi Jinping. At present, the BeiDou system has established CORS systems in Tunisia and Algeria, providing users with real-time, continuous, stable, and accurate GNSS positioning data and time information; in countries such as Saudi Arabia, Algeria, Lebanon, Oman, Morocco, BeiDou system has been used in many fields such as territorial mapping, transportation, precision agriculture, environmental monitoring, and non-traditional security; in the UAE, Beidou is integrated with technologies such as the Internet of Things and has applied to various railroads construction regulation scenarios such as construction machinery, materials, personnel, and entry/exit gates.

On December 8, 2021, the 3rd China-Arab States BDS Cooperation Forum was successfully held in Beijing, which was also the first forum held after the BeiDou-3 Navigation Satellite System was in operation. At the forum, China and

135

The Development Process of China-Arab States Economic and Trade Relations
Annual Report 2021

the Arab states summarized the experience and achievements of China-Arab cooperation in Beidou over the past five years, and jointly signed the "Action Plan for Cooperation between China and Arab States in Navigation Satellite (2022-2023)". The plan states that China and Arab states will implement no less than five demonstration application projects in key areas of using BeiDou/GNSS technology; establish 1-2 additional Beidou/GNSS centers in Arab states that are interested in the technology; hold 1-2 short-term training courses on satellite navigation technology each year; provide 3-5 scholarships every year for master's degree students in navigation and communication in Arab states; send 1-2 groups of short-term visiting scholars to each other annually; continue to carry out BeiDou/GNSS joint testing and evaluation and publish test results; conduct performance tests for the return link of Beidou international search and rescue service; use the China-Arab satellite navigation cooperation website to publish the cooperation results, attract more participants, promote cooperation, and strengthen the development. The plan wishes to enable BeiDou to better serve the Arab states in a win-win situation.

7.2.4 Cooperation in Healthcare

The year 2021 is a critical period when the healthcare systems in all countries were challenged since the outbreak of the COVID-19 pandemic. Facing the pandemic, China and the Arab states focused on the urgent needs of both sides in the healthcare sector, closely cooperating on key projects such as vaccine R&D and production, the training of medical personnel, and technology transfer to jointly tackle COVID-19.

China has been promoting Chinese vaccines as a global public product and actively helping Arab states to build vaccine production lines to ensure adequate supply. In March 2021, the Chinese vaccine production line project was launched in the UAE. The vaccine plant has 3 filling lines and 5 automatic packaging lines, with an annual production capacity of 200 million doses. As such, the UAE will become the Gulf country to have a production base for COVID-19 vaccine, and its vaccine supply will serve the whole Middle East region. On May 21, 2021, Egypt procured a new batch of Sinopharm BBIBP vaccines and its first batch of undiluted CoronaVac vaccines from China, thus becoming the first African country to cooperate with China to produce COVID-19 vaccine. It is China's solemn commitment to "strive to make vaccines a public product that

136

Chapter 7   Report on China-Arab States Cooperation in Science, Technology, and
Eco-environmental Governance

is accessible and affordable to all peoples". The China-Arab states cooperation in vaccine technology facilitates pandemic containment in the Middle East. It is also China and Arab states' effort to the global COVID-19 containment.

In addition, China initiated online meetings and invited experts who had fought on the front line of epidemic prevention to introduce their recommended personal protective measures and China's experience in the prevention and control of COVID-19. On March 25, 2021, the first online training on understanding and preventing COVID-19 for Belt and Road participating countries was held by Ningxia International Technology Exchange Center (China-Arab States Technology Transfer Center). The training course was fully supported by the Social Development Office of Ningxia Science and Technology Department and the Scientific Research Department of Ningxia Medical University General Hospital and invited medical experts to offer lectures on relevant topics. More than 20 participants from countries including Egypt, UAE, Sudan, Iraq, Nigeria, and Thailand attended the training.

7.3   The Current Status and Future Development of China-Arab States Cooperation in Eco-environmental Governance

"Ecological Civilization: Building a Shared Future for All Life on Earth" framed the 15th meeting of the Conference of the Parties to the United Nations Convention on Biological Diversity held in Kunming, China in October 2020. This is the first time that the Conference has adopted "ecological civilization" as its theme. Living in harmony with nature is a decisive task in the 21st century. President Xi Jinping emphasized green low-carbon development and eco-environmental governance at the third symposium on the development of the BRI, pointing out the need to support low-carbon energy development in developing countries, promote information sharing and capacity building for low-carbon development, and deepen cooperation in eco-environmental and climate governance. China and the Arab states are both facing air pollution, water pollution, and other emerging environmental problems during economic development, industrialization, and urbanization. The two sides share board common ground in terms of environmental protection and are welcoming new opportunities for cooperation in this field.

137

7.3.1 The Current Status of China-Arab States Cooperation in Ecology and Environment

The Arab countries are mainly located in dry regions. The arid zone in western China belongs to the dry zone in the hinterland of inland Eurasia, in which the ecological environment is extremely fragile. China and Arab states share the same ecological and environmental problems. Most Arab states have low agricultural productivity and further degradation of natural resources due to insufficient investment in science and technology and agricultural development. Therefore, developing and implementing long-term strategic sustainable development plans that encompass the environment is a top priority for Arab states. In recent years, some Arab states in the Gulf region and North Africa have begun to put more emphasis on regional cooperation to encourage domestic and foreign investment in green infrastructure projects. Countries including Qatar, Saudi Arabia, UAE, Jordan, and Kuwait have included environmental protection as one of the core issues in their national development visions[1], which undoubtedly opens up a new platform and provides new opportunities for China-Arab states cooperation in ecology and environment.

In 2006, the China-Arab Conference on Environmental Cooperation was held in Dubai, UAE, which heralds the future research and practices of China-Arab states environmental cooperation. Today, China-Arab states cooperation has a solid foundation and a good operating mechanism. Based on the framework of the China-Arab Cooperation Forum established in 2004, with the Ministerial Meeting of China-Arab Cooperation Forum and the China-Arab States Environmental Protection Cooperation Forum under the China-Arab States Expo as long-term mechanisms, the whole cooperation system regulates and enables the China-Arab cooperation in the long term. The fourth China-Arab States Technology Transfer and Innovation Cooperation Conference announced the signing of the China-Qatar Technology Transfer Center and planned to increase the number of China-Arab bilateral technology transfer centers to nine by the fifth conference. China's achievements in ecology and environment are being introduced to Arab states through an increasing number of efficient and practical technology transfer information service platforms.

---

[1] ZOU, Zhiqiang, "Development Transformation of Arab Countries from the Perspective of the 2030 Agenda for Sustainable Development", *Arab World Studies*, 2020(3) .

Chapter 7   Report on China-Arab States Cooperation in Science, Technology, and Eco-environmental Governance

On one hand, with a similar ecological environment to Arab states, western China has accumulated rich experience in ecological environment restoration represented by desertification prevention and control since the 1960s. In recent years, under the guidance of President Xi Jinping's environment protection concept, the ecological environment construction has developed rapidly, represented by natural forest protection, farmland to forest and grass project, grazing regulation, ecological restoration and construction, and the "ten environment protection articles" for atmosphere, water, and soil. On the other hand, China-Arab states cooperation in the traditional energy development and desertification control has formed a comprehensive cooperation system.

The Execution Plan for 2020-2022 of the CASCF, formulated at the 9th Ministerial Conference in 2020, covers China-Arab states cooperation in natural resources, environment, agriculture, and human resource development. From 2020 to 2021, relying on China-Arab States Cooperation Forum and the China-Arab Technology Transfer Center, China actively promoted cooperation with the Arab states in environmental protection, agriculture, and desertification control, and carry out various cooperation activities through projects, technology development, and personnel training.

In terms of agriculture and water resources, China has initiated long-term cooperation projects with Gulf countries that lack water resources and have an urgent need for desalination. The cooperation in this field from 2020 to 2021 includes several projects on water-saving irrigation and desalination. In August 2020, China and Qatar NAAAS Group signed the USD 1.264 billion contract for the "Beautiful Doha" project through an online meeting. The project aimed to promote the application of Ningxia University's green and intelligent water-saving irrigation technology and equipment in Qatar. The project is related to many technologies, such as food production, water-saving greening, water-saving agriculture, and ecological protection. In June 2021, the Desalination Technology Institute of Saline Water Conversion Corporation in Saudi Arabia and the Chinese Ministry of Natural Resources cooperated to develop new desalination technologies. The cooperation project focused on osmosis technology, evaporation technology, and developing a multi-stage effect approach to standardize desalination technologies. In August 2021, the 150MIDG desalination project in Umm Al Quwain, the UAE, one of the world's top five desalination projects constructed by the China Railway 18th Bureau,

139

officially entered the finishing stage. As one of the important projects of the "UAE Water Security Strategy 2036", it is a key livelihood project integrating seawater desalination, water storage, and water supply. In November 2021, the world's largest desalination project under construction by CEC EPC — Taweelah Desalination Plant in the UAE — started to produce qualified drinking water.

Combating desertification and land degradation has always been an area of concern for Arab states. As mentioned in the white paper "China's International Development Cooperation in the New Era" released by the Information Office of the State Council in January 2021, China actively shares its effective desertification control technology and experience with other countries and has organized and implemented several training programs on desert control technology, integrated soil erosion control, etc. Gansu province has built an international platform for technical assistance and exchange on desertification and land desertification control and has held 36 "international training courses on desert control technology and desertification control in China". In 2006, the first "Training Course on Desertification Control Technology for Arab Countries" was held in Ningxia, and 12 courses have been held so far. China has also promoted bamboo and Juncao (plants used as a medium for fungi) cultivation and processing technologies. These technologies have effectively controlled soil erosion and land degradation and played a positive role in protecting the ecological environment while promoting economic development. During the 5th China-Arab States Expo, the Chinese Academy of Sciences, Ningxia University, and other research institutes introduced microalgae carbon fixation sand, desert seed rain ecological engineering technology using drones, etc.

In terms of environmental protection, China attaches great importance to ecological civilization, and its power infrastructure cooperation with Arab states has been transformed and upgraded from traditional thermal power, hydropower, and power transmission projects to innovative projects such as clean coal-fired and large-scale combined cycle power plants, cultivating new momentum for development, minimizing air pollution emissions, and taking the protection of the local ecosystem environment as an important policy in the process of joint development. The HEC-Dubai Hassyan clean coal-fired power plant project in Dubai, UAE, which was successfully connected to the grid in May 2020, has been highly recognized by the Dubai government for its efforts in environmental

140

Chapter 7 Report on China-Arab States Cooperation in Science, Technology, and Eco-environmental Governance

protection.[1]

The science and technology section of the 5th China-Arab States Expo launched a series of promotion sessions related to clean energy and green low-carbon transition technologies. Chinese enterprises and research institutions are forging ahead in the development and innovation work of various green technologies, showing a blueprint for Arab countries, and the activities cover areas such as ultra-low concentration gas technology, efficient management and ecological restoration of urban rivers, full biodegradable film soil environmental protection and restoration technology for arid zones in Central Asia, oil refining and purification technology, water security assessment and efficient use of water resources, and integrated water environment management and optimization technology across the drainage basin.[2]

China has long been an important driver of China-Arab states cooperation in science and technology, mainly because China attaches great importance to the development of human resources in science and technology fields in Arab countries and regularly organizes training courses to share experiences and good practices. In addition to the "training course on sand control technology for Arab states", "training course on integrated soil erosion management" and "2021 online training course on modern agricultural water conservation technology for Belt and Road participating countries", the 5th China-Arab States Expo held a technology transfer and innovation cooperation conference and 6 technology promotion and matchmaking sessions. Ten advanced technologies were introduced to the "Belt and Road" participating countries, and academicians and experts were invited to provide advice on solving technical problems. During the conference, the Arab Academy of Science, Technology and Maritime Transport, the Cultural, Educational and Scientific Department of the Egyptian Embassy in China, and other Arab institutions expressed their strong willingness to jointly hold technology training and match the demand with supply in these two markets. They believe that the training courses are closely related to the technical needs of the Belt and Road participating countries, and will strongly promote the cooperation plan formulated during the China-Arab States Expo

---

[1] The First Clean Coal-fired Power Plant in the Middle East Was Successfully connected to the Grid in Dubai, http://www.sasac.gov.cn/n2588025/n2588124/c14632536/content.html.

[2] China-Arab States Technology Transfer Center, https://www.casttc.org.

141

and continuously improve the quality of China-Arab states technical cooperation and exchange.

7.3.2 The Future Development of China-Arab States Cooperation in Ecology and Environment

In "The Vision and Actions on Jointly Building the Silk Road Economic Belt and the 21st Century Maritime Silk Road", China calls for giving prominence to the ecological civilization in the process of cooperation and trade, strengthening cooperation in the ecological environment, biodiversity protection and addressing climate change, building the Green Silk Road, enhancing green and low-carbon construction and operation management of infrastructure, and considering the impact development on climate change.

In the process of developing the Belt and Road, China and the Arab states are embracing "multi-faceted and deep" cooperation in ecology and the environment. In particular, the Ningxia autonomous region, which has high similarity with Arab countries in terms of natural conditions, economic culture, and ecological environment, has the most representative cooperation cases. Ningxia is not only the main hub for economic, trade, and cultural exchanges between China and Arab states but also an important support point for the Belt and Road Initiative. With complementary economies, the central and western regions of China, led by Ningxia, and the Arab states have good foundations, prerequisites, and a strong desire for cooperation in many areas.

China-Arab states cooperation in ecology and environment should make good use of the China-Arab States Cooperation Forum, China-Arab States Expo, China-Arab States Technology Transfer and Innovation Cooperation Conference, and other improving cooperation mechanisms to actively set up new projects, design programs and put forward initiatives about science and technology innovation. China and the Arab states have initiated technology transfer, cooperation projects, and humanistic exchanges for their cooperation in environmental protection in the energy field, irrigation technology, desalination and desertification control for agricultural production, etc. Cooperation in major projects can facilitate the flow and sharing of scientific and technological resources within and between regions and forms the basis for the technological and economic spillover effects, which can bring "engineering dividends" to the economies, promote economic growth, and ensure the economy and

142

Chapter 7   Report on China-Arab States Cooperation in Science, Technology, and
Eco-environmental Governance

infrastructure for science and technology development. For example, the Dubai Maktoum Solar Power Plant Project, the "2021 Online Training Course on Modern Agricultural Water Conservation Technology for Belt and Road Participating Countries" and the "Training Course on Sand Control Technology for the Arab States" have effectively promoted the introduction of Chinese advanced technology, equipment, and talents into Arab states, and ensured the mutual benefit and win-win situation in science and technology development and technology transfer.

China should leverage its development strategy, understand the characteristics and needs of Arab states, identify the key field of cooperation, and create an ecological and environmental cooperation model with Arab characteristics that suits the needs of Arab states. Arab states are an important market for China and have considerable import demand for China's food security and ecological environment industries. For Arab countries with a shortage of natural resources, backward agricultural production methods, and shortage of food supply, China should strengthen the export of agricultural technology, encourage the exchange and training of scientific researchers, and build production bases and demonstration parks. For example, China can establish production bases or test areas in Arab states for the breeding, improvement, and research of the mature grass and livestock industries and desert cash crops from the Ningxia region.[①] For Arab countries with more developed economies and higher scientific research and innovation capacity, such as Saudi Arabia and the UAE, more efforts should be made to build joint R&D centers and laboratories to help China and these Arab states to cooperate in cutting-edge technologies and make breakthroughs. For example, in the "Beautiful Doha" project, China wishes to build China-Qatar Technology Transfer Center with Qatar Free Zone to promote the implementation of China-Qatar science and technology cooperation projects, striving to implement 2-3 technology transfer projects every year. China and Arab states work together to plan the specific direction and path for future cooperation with a clear focus, ensuring that the results of cooperation can effectively serve both sides.

---

① WANG, Linling, "A Study of the Cooperation in Ecological Environment between China and Arab Countries — Based on the Discussion of Desertification Cooperation and Technological Output", *Journal of Ningxia Communist Party Institute*, 2013, 15(06).

China-Arab states cooperation in the ecological environment is represented by environmental cooperation in desertification control and energy development, and the cooperation mechanism has been improving with a solid foundation and adequate demand for cooperation. Continuing to promote China-Arab states cooperation in ecological and environmental innovation is beneficial at the macro level to both sides in addressing global environmental issues and improving the global environmental governance system. At the micro level, it has a positive influence on facilitating sustainable development of both sides. "Both China and the Arab states are developing countries that seek cooperation adhering to the principle of equality. Arab states are willing to introduce and learn from China's technology to improve their industries. Both sides have great potential for cooperation in areas such as desertification control, clean energy, green international production capacity cooperation, and infrastructure construction, green trade, and green finance. All these contribute to the promising prospects of China-Arab states cooperation."

7.4 The Future of China-Arab States Science and Technology Cooperation

Arab states are by nature strategic partners of the Belt and Road Initiative. Science and technology cooperation should continue to be an important approach to friendly China-Arab states relation.

On the one hand, although China-Arab states cooperation involves a large number of countries with different political systems, science, and technology, as a basic contractual transaction, is usually less hindered by political factors. On the other hand, most Arab states are emerging economies and developing countries with greater demand for science and technology in economic development, which makes science and technology cooperation a key and breaking point for the effective promotion of the China-Arab states cooperation mechanism. In addition, nuclear energy, aerospace, and new energy in the "1+2+3" pattern of China-Arab states cooperation is ultimately dependent on science and technology innovation. China-Arab states cooperation in science and technology is in line with the core concept of China-Arab strategic partnership in the new era and is conducive to the mutual development and long-term interests of both sides.

With the new promising opportunity, China-Arab states science and

Chapter 7   Report on China-Arab States Cooperation in Science, Technology, and
Eco-environmental Governance

technology cooperation should quickly adapt to the changes and needs, demonstrate the characteristics of the two sides, and strive to achieve sustainable long-term cooperation and development goals, so that China-Arab states science and technology cooperation can play a full role in China's science and technology development strategy, "go global" strategy and diplomatic strategy. We can start from the following aspects.

Firstly, develop a science and technology cooperation model with Arab characteristics that meets the needs of Arab countries. The current science and technology innovation in most Arab states is still at a relatively low level. According to the Global Innovation Index (GII) 2020 report, the UAE (34), Tunisia (65), and Saudi Arabia (66) are the only Arab states in the top 50% of the ranking, while most of the other Arab states are at the lower end of the list, with a relatively weak science and technology innovation capacity in general. In contrast, China's S&T innovation capacity ranks 14th and is the strongest among upper-middle-income countries. Therefore, the current China-Arab S&T cooperation is not at a high level. To boost the development of China-Arab states cooperation in science and technology, China must adopt a country-specific approach, identify key areas of cooperation, understand the science and technology capabilities and strengths of the target countries, and recognize their urgent needs, so as to accelerate technology transfer in countries with insufficient technology and enhance R&D cooperation with technologically developed countries, thereby improving the quality and effectiveness of cooperation.

In particular, starting with science and technology humanities exchange can help avoid political barriers and encourage people-to-people contact. At the same time, science and technology humanities exchanges can reduce information costs, promote trust and understanding between countries, and deepen scientific and technological professionals' understanding of the technologies, and thus enhance R&D and innovation capabilities. Building joint R&D centers and technology transfer platforms is the key to meeting the specific needs of Arab states and promoting the long-term and stable development of China-Arab states science and technology cooperation. Technology transfer is the most direct and effective way for Arab states with less science and technology innovation capacity to improve their productivity levels. It also provides a safeguard for the sustainable development of the countries. Although the transfer of proprietary or patented technologies cannot directly enhance the capacity of independent innovation, it

145

can help break through technological bottlenecks and serves as a foundation for future S&T innovation. Joint R&D centers, on the other hand, can help China cooperate with Arab states that have economic and technological advantages to achieve breakthroughs in high-tech fields. Therefore, building joint laboratories and technology transfer platforms can best reflect the characteristics of science and technology development in Arab states, and is of strategic importance in China-Arab science and technology cooperation.

Secondly, efforts should be made to create a multi-level cooperation space. In addition to leveraging the China-Arab States Cooperation Forum and other platforms to carry out project cooperation and technology transfer, we should conduct field surveys and studies on the development of science and technology in Arab states, build mechanisms for civil interaction, parallel official cooperation, and civil cooperation, and expand the scope of cooperation subjects. The overall level of science and technology innovation in Arab states is still not ideal, and the internal and external causes of the situation are worthy of in-depth study and analysis. Only through a comprehensive and in-depth understanding of the impediments to science and technology innovation in Arab countries and their key concerns and needs for science and technology development can we better promote comprehensive and regular China-Arab states science and technology cooperation. The possible causes include, for example, inadequate science and technology development in private companies in Arab states, limited capital for research and development, weak attraction for high-tech talents, and poor information communication. Moreover, the complex international environment and different cultures could result in the inactive China-Arab states cooperation in science and technology, which is mainly promoted by the government[1]. Take the China-Arab states cooperation in science and technology in 2020 as an example. China and Arab states promoted renewable energy projects such as solar energy and expanded the cooperation in ecology and environment through clean energy projects etc., all of which are led by the government with state-owned enterprises, instead of private enterprises, as the main participants. In such a case, China could build a civil interaction mechanism for science and technology cooperation and introduce more entities for science and technology

---

[1] WANG, Hui, *Annual Report on Development of Sino-Arab Cultural Communication* (2018), Social Sciences Academic Press, 2019, p.59.

146

Chapter 7   Report on China-Arab States Cooperation in Science, Technology, and Eco-environmental Governance

cooperation. S&T enterprises should also actively participate in the China-Arab states science and technology cooperation, take the initiative to leverage the existing cooperation platforms and mechanisms, introduce the advanced technologies through China-Arab States Expo, meet the needs of science and technology development in Arab states, and enhance the service capacity and international visibility.

Thirdly, develop sustainable China-Arab states cooperation in science and technology. China adheres to the Scientific Outlook on Development and insists on sustainable development, attaches great importance to science and technology innovation, and believes that innovation is the first driving force for development. China actively follows the trend of international science and technology cooperation, joins the global innovation network, and implements a more open and inclusive, mutually beneficial, and shared international science and technology cooperation strategy. China-Arab states cooperation in science and technology will also move towards sustainable development and keep its vitality through innovation.

The Fifth China-Arab States Expo held on August 19, 2021, expanded the cooperation between China and Arab states in the digital economy, artificial intelligence, new energy, and other emerging fields, which means that the China-Arab "1+2+3" cooperation pattern has been upgraded again in the new era. The cooperation between China and the Arab states in science and technology not only improves the level of cooperation between the two sides but also provides new momentum for the high-quality development of the Belt and Road Initiative. China-Arab states cooperation in new energy and clean energy materialized the concept of green, low-carbon, and sustainable development of the Belt and Road Initiative.[1]

In terms of cooperation fields, China-Arab states cooperation in science and technology still has great potential in technology transfer, basic research, and application of artificial intelligence, information technology, Internet of Things and smart cities, clean and renewable energy, the peaceful use of nuclear energy, environmental protection, desertification control, and sustainable development, rapid construction technology, etc. In addition, the two sides will strive to strengthen cooperation in biodiversity conservation and jointly promote

---

[1]   http://www.china.com.cn/opinion2020/2021-08/24/content_77710484.shtml.

147

The Development Process of China-Arab States Economic and Trade Relations
Annual Report 2021

the integration of biodiversity in energy, mineral, industry, healthcare, and infrastructure.

In terms of platforms, China is building the Belt and Road Ecology and Environment Protection Big Data Service Platform and the Belt and Road International Alliance for Green Development, both of which encourage the participation of the Arab states to jointly promote the building of the Green Silk Road. Meanwhile, China and the Arab states are cooperating in achieving the 2030 Sustainable Development Goals, exchanging experiences and organizing seminars and activities to discuss and introduce the best practices from both sides. China also supports and participates in the Arab Sustainable Development Week.[1]

In conclusion, from a macro perspective, promoting China-Arab states cooperation in science and technology innovation will have positive effects on achieving sustainable development, addressing global challenges, improving global science and technology governance, and promoting the development of developing countries. At the meso and micro levels, the sustainable cooperation in science and technology between China and the Arab states is an important practice for the development of the Belt and Road Initiative and is a solid step toward a China-Arab States community with a shared future.

---

[1] China-Arab States Cooperation Forum Execution Plan for 2020-2022, http://www.chinaarabcf. org/chn/lthyjwx/bzjhywj/djjbzjhy/202008/t20200810_6836922.htm.

148

Chapter 8   Report on China-Arab States Healthcare and Pandemic Containment Cooperation

Faced with the sudden and non-traditional security threat — the COVID-19 pandemic — China and the Arab states have stood by each other through thick and thin, supported each other, faced threats and challenges, and strengthened cooperation through supplying medical material, dispatching medical teams, exchanging medical experience, procuring medical material, and supporting vaccine supply and production. China and Arab states resolutely opposed the attempts to politicize and stigmatize the virus, hoping to achieve a full-coverage pandemic containment.

8.1   The Overall Status of China-Arab States Pandemic Containment Cooperation

Since 2020, the COVID-19 pandemic has affected the world and the international reality is changing rapidly. In the face of various difficulties and challenges, China and Arab states have been deepening their cooperation in terms of epidemic containment concepts, material supply, experience exchange, medical team support, vaccine donation, and production, making great contributions to building a healthcare community for all.

8.1.1   Deepening China-Arab States Pandemic Containment Cooperation

8.1.1.1   Epidemic Containment Cooperation Concept
Since the outbreak of COVID-19, China and the Arab states community have

149

issued many joint declarations and statements and proposed the Belt and Road Vaccine Partnership Initiative, which has provided guidance for both sides to strengthen cooperation in COVID-19 containment.

A joint declaration titled Working Together to Defeat the COVID-19 Outbreak and Build a Community with a Shared Future for China and Arab States in the New Era was adopted at the China-Arab States Political Parties Dialog Extraordinary Meeting on June 24, 2020. The declaration states that "the COVID-19 outbreak has once again laid bare that interests of countries are closely interwoven, and we humans share a common future. In deep appreciation of the vision of President Xi Jinping for a community with a shared future for mankind, political parties of Arab states share the view that cooperation in solidarity is the most powerful weapon against the virus. We oppose any attempt to politicize the epidemic and label the virus. We call on all countries to enhance anti-epidemic cooperation and policy coordination, support the leading role of the WHO, strengthen the collective response at the international level, and work together to build a global community of health for all. The CPC will take steps to promote the implementation of what General Secretary Xi Jinping announced at the 73rd World Health Assembly, i.e., COVID-19 vaccine development and deployment in China, when available, will be made a global public good, which will be China's contribution to ensuring vaccine accessibility and affordability in developing countries."[1]

On 6 July 2020, at the ninth Ministerial Conference of the China-Arab States Cooperation Forum, China and Arab states held an in-depth discussion on COVID-19 containment and signed the "China-Arab States Joint Statement on Solidarity Against COVID-19". The statement goes as follows: "First, solidarity and cooperation are the most powerful weapons for the international community to overcome the epidemic. We call for enhancing the awareness of the community of a shared future and building a China-Arab States community with a shared future and a China-Arab community of healthcare through the cooperation in COVID-19 containment. Second, we emphasize the importance of multilateralism and further strengthen and improve the global governance system with the United Nations at its core. We support the World Health

---

[1] China-Arab States Political Parties Dialog Extraordinary Meeting Adopted a Joint Meeting, xinhuanet, June 24, 2020, http://www.xinhuanet.com/world/2020-06/24/c_1126156410.htm.

Chapter 8   Report on China-Arab States Healthcare and Pandemic Containment
Cooperation

Organization to play a leading role in global public health governance. We call on all parties in the international community to enhance coordination, form synergies and effectively carry out international joint prevention and control to reduce the negative impact of the pandemic. Third, strengthen information communication, policy coordination, and operational cooperation, and carry out exchanges and cooperation on epidemic prevention and control. China is willing to continue providing support and assistance within its capabilities to Arab states in urgent need of support by providing medical supplies, holding video conferences with experts, and dispatching medical expert groups to build a 'Healthcare Silk Road'. Fourth, in the face of the global health crisis, responsible public information communication is crucial. Professional exchanges on prevention and treatment should be conducted in a scientific manner, and statements and practices that discriminate against any country, region, nationality, or individual should be opposed in accordance with the resolution on the COVID-19 pandemic adopted by the 73rd World Health Assembly. Fifth, use the health cooperation mechanism under the framework of the China-Arab States Cooperation Forum to carry out COVID-19 containment cooperation and convene China-Arab States Health Cooperation Forum meetings when necessary. We should Implement the China-Arab Countries Health Cooperation 2019 Beijing Initiative, promote the development of the 'China-Arab States Medical and Health Cooperation Alliance', and boost cooperation in public health, traditional medicine, health policy research, and the health industry. Sixth, encourage the continuation of Belt and Road cooperation while preventing and controlling COVID-19, strengthen macroeconomic policy coordination, and promote economic and social development in an integrated manner. China and Arab states should keep trade and investment markets open, and jointly maintain the stability of global financial markets, industrial chains, and supply chains. We should also actively share and utilize digital trade and innovative technologies to promote scientific combat against the pandemic. We will work together to ensure post-pandemic recovery and economic development and maintain the well-being and sustainable growth of people on both sides."[1]

---

[1] China-Arab States Joint Statement on Solidarity against COVID-19, August 10, 2020, China-Arab States Cooperation Forum, http://www.chinaarabcf.org/chn/lthyjwx/bzjhywj/djjbzjhy/202008/t20200810_6836919.htm.

151

On June 23, 2021, China and 29 other countries, including Saudi Arabia and the United Arab Emirates, launched the Initiative for Belt and Road Partnership on COVID-19 Vaccines Cooperation during the Asia and Pacific High-level Conference on Belt and Road Cooperation to promote rational global vaccine distribution. The initiative goes as follows: "We recognize that solidarity and cooperation are key to fight against the COVID-19 pandemic, a challenge confronting all countries in the world. We believe that in combating the pandemic, people and their lives must be put first, and no one can be safe until everyone is safe. We stress that vaccines, as an important part of our toolkit for pandemic response, should be equitably distributed as a global public good, inter alia, in a way that their availability, accessibility, and affordability in developing countries are ensured. Recalling the relevant resolutions of the United Nations General Assembly and the World Health Assembly as well as the "Political Declaration on Equitable Global Access to COVID-19 Vaccines", we call for open, fair, and non-discriminatory international cooperation on vaccines. We commend the efforts made by the United Nations system, in particular the World Health Organization (WHO), as well as by relevant countries in carrying out cooperation on vaccines. We call upon Belt and Road cooperation partners to focus on the following: a. Strengthen communication on vaccine regulatory policies to jointly ensure the safety and efficacy of vaccines. b. Encourage vaccine-producing countries, which are in a position to do so, to support vaccine companies in providing more vaccines to the COVID-19 Vaccine Global Access (COVAX) facility of the WHO. c. Support the provision of vaccines by governments and companies to developing countries either through donation or export at affordable prices. d. Facilitate joint vaccine research, development, and technological exchanges, and encourage transferring relevant technologies to developing countries. e. Promote partnerships between vaccine producers and developing countries for joint vaccine production towards the scaling up of global production. f. Encourage regional and multilateral development banks to provide more concessional financing to developing countries for their vaccine procurement and production, while respecting each country's right to select its preferred vaccines. g. Strengthen Belt and Road cooperation on connectivity to ensure cross-border flows of vaccines. We look forward to the participation of

Chapter 8   Report on China-Arab States Healthcare and Pandemic Containment
Cooperation

more partners in this initiative.[1]

8.1.1.2　Medical Supplies

After the outbreak of COVID-19 in China, member countries of the Arab League donated more than 10 million masks, nearly 3.2 million pairs of medical gloves, 100,000 sets of protective suits, and 65,000 goggles to China.[2] Algeria was the first country to take the initiative to donate anti-epidemic supplies to China; Saudi Arabia donated medical supplies worth RMB 50 million to China; Egypt's Minister of Population and Health visited China with 10 tons of medical supplies as a special presidential envoy; the UAE, Kuwait, Qatar, and other countries have donated medical supplies to China multiple times. After the pandemic spread to the Arab states, China provided medical supplies to Arab states, such as nucleic acid testing reagents, masks, protective suits, thermometers, and ventilators, and helped these countries to build virus testing laboratories. As of December 2020, the Chinese government has provided more than 1 million testing kits and 18 million masks to Arab states.[3]

In 2021, China's COVID-19 containment supplies for Arab states mainly targeted Palestine and the United Nations Relief and Works Agency for Palestine Refugees in the Near East (UNRWA), as well as countries suffering from unrest such as Iraq, Yemen, Lebanon, Syria and other extremely underdeveloped countries such as Comoros. The supplies include medical equipment such as testing reagents, respirators, oxygen machines, N95 masks, oximeters, ambulances, electric medical beds, electrocardiogram machines, and office supplies such as computers. China's aid to the United Nations Relief and Works Agency for Palestine Refugees in the Near East has been distributed to local refugees through health centers in Palestine, Jordan, Lebanon, Syria, etc.

In addition, enterprises, universities, civil organizations, and individuals from both sides have also donated countless supplies to each other through different channels.

---

[1]　Initiative for Belt and Road Partnership on COVID-19 Vaccines Cooperation, xinhuanet, June 23, 2021, http://www.xinhuanet.com/2021-06/24/c_1127592302.htm.

[2]　Wang Guangda, "Pandemic Control Has Deepened China-Arab States Cooperation", *Guangming Daily*, June 22, 2020.

[3]　Chinese Foreign Ministry Donates Second Batch of COVIS-19 Containment Supplies to the Arab League, Beijing Daily, December 11, 2020, https://news.sina.com.cn/c/2020-12-11/doc-iiznezxs6365863.shtml.

153

The Development Process of China-Arab States Economic and Trade Relations
Annual Report 2021

8.1.1.3　Medical Experience Exchange

In addition to medical supplies, China and the Arab states actively informed the status of the epidemic in China and exchanged experiences in fighting against the pandemic through multiple bodies and channels, which provided many useful experiences for both sides to conquer COVID-19 together. Immediately after the outbreak of the pandemic, Chinese embassies in Arab states shared information on the pandemic with other countries through different channels. As of April 2021, China and the Arab states have held more than 50 video conferences with health experts, both multilaterally and bilaterally. The video conferences were held by the Ministry of Foreign Affairs, embassies abroad, the Health and Welfare Commission, local governments, and other government departments, as well as through cooperation mechanisms such as friendly hospitals. For example, the two China-Arab states health expert video conferences organized by the Chinese Ministry of Foreign Affairs with the National Health and Wellness Commission and the Ministry of Science and Technology on April 9 and September 29, 2020, respectively, were multilateral meetings with the participation of 10 or more Arab states, and some of the meetings had more than 100 participants. In these meetings, China and the Arab states conducted in-depth exchanges and discussions on the epidemiological characteristics of the epidemic, development trends, prevention and control strategies, clinical treatment, scientific research and research, epidemic risk assessment and graded prevention and control, vaccine development, and the evolution of the virus, making important contributions to the prevention and control of the pandemic.

In addition, the National Health and Wellness Commission and several domestic universities also shared their experience in COVID-19 containment with Arab states through the compilation of documents and children's books. For example, the e-book version of the children's picture book "Get Out, COVID-19" translated by Shanghai International Studies University has been published in Arab states, sharing the experience of COVID-19 prevention and control with the Arab people through vivid illustrations.

8.1.1.4　Medical Expert Support

To further enhance the ability of Arab states to deal with the COVID-19 pandemic, Chinese epidemic control experts went to eight Arab countries to share their experience in treating COVID-19 patients experiences and introduce their prevention and control programs, which were warmly welcomed by

Chapter 8   Report on China-Arab States Healthcare and Pandemic Containment
Cooperation

all countries. China's successful experience in combating the pandemic and the dedication and ability of the expert teams were highly recognized and appreciated by the Arab states. The Prime Minister of Djibouti, Mr. Kamil, awarded the "June 27 Independence Day" national medal to 12 members of the Chinese medical expert team in recognition of their contribution to the combat against COVID-19 in Djibouti.[1] The Chinese medical team to Comoros was awarded the "Knight of the Order of the Green Crescent of Comoros" by President Azali, [2] and was also awarded by the National Health Commission of China as a "group with outstanding performance in 2021 oversea healthcare aid".[3] Other countries have also held activities such as appreciation ceremonies to express their gratitude.

Table 8.1   COVID-19 containment medical expert team sent by China to the Arab states

No.	Date range	Target country	Number of experts	Dispatching organization
1	March 7, 2020 - April 20, 2020	Iraq	7	Red Cross Society of China
2	April 15, 2020 - April 27, 2020	Saudi Arabia	8	Health Commission of Ningxia Hui Autonomous Region
3	April 27, 2020 - May 2, 2020	Kuwait	8	
4	April 30, 2020 - May 12, 2020	Djibouti	12	Health Commission of Sichuan Province
5	May 13, 2020 - May 29, 2020	Algeria	20	Chongqing Municipal People's Government (15 experts); Government of Macao Special Administrative Region (5 experts)
6	May 29, 2020 - June 10, 2020	Sudan	20	
7	June 10, 2020 - June 18, 2020	Palestine	10	Health Commission of Chongqing
8	March 17, 2021 - June 15, 2021	Comoros	12	People's Government of Guangxi Autonomous Region

Source: news reports.

---

[1]   The Ministry of Foreign Affairs Introduced the Work of Chinese Medical Experts to Ethiopia and Djibouti, xinhuanet, May 13, 2020, http://www.xinhuanet.com/world/2020-05/13/c_1125981547.htm.

[2]   Comoros President Azali Elevated Chinese Medical Aid Team, Embassy of the People's Republic of China in the Union of Comoros, June 16, 2021, http://km.china-embassy.org/zxdt/202106/t20210616_9117355.htm.

[3]   On the Award of Group with Outstanding Performance in 2021 Oversea Healthcare Aid by National Health Commission, National Health Commission of People's Republic of China, January 24, 2022, http://www.nhc.gov.cn/gjhzs/s7958/202201/20478922ea8e40bba008f8eaf74b3fa1.shtml.

155

The Development Process of China-Arab States Economic and Trade Relations
Annual Report 2021

In addition, China's resident medical aid teams in Arab states have also played an important role in assisting Arab states to fight against the pandemic. As of 2021, China has sent permanent medical aid teams to nine LAS member countries, namely Algeria, Djibouti, Kuwait, Mauritania, Morocco, Tunisia, Sudan, Yemen, and Comoros. From 2020 to 2021, the 20th resident medical team to Djibouti, the 13th-14th to Kuwait, the 33rd-34th to Mauritania, the 180th-193rd to Morocco, the 24th-25th to Tunisia, the 26th to Algeria, the 35th-36th to Sudan, and the 13th-14th to Comoros were all awarded as "group with outstanding performance in oversea healthcare aid" for their outstanding contributions to COVID-19 containment in Arab states.[1][2] Take the 35th batch of a medical team dispatched to Sudan as an example, the medical team members devoted themselves to COVID-19 control during their year in Sudan. They held seven training sessions for Sudanese medical personnel on epidemic prevention and control and gave lectures to local people through the national TV of Sudan and other media to popularize epidemic prevention and control knowledge and share China's experience in COVID-19 containment, which helped local people and made contributions to the people-to-people relations between China and Sudan.[3]

8.1.2　World-leading Vaccine Cooperation

The vaccine has always been the focus and highlight of China-Arab states cooperation in COVID-19 containment. Vaccine cooperation has always been the focus and highlight of China-Arab states cooperation in COVID-19 containment. China and Arab states have been actively carrying out vaccine

---

[1] On the Award of Group with Outstanding Performance in 2020 Oversea Healthcare Aid by National Health Commission, National Health Commission of People's Republic of China, Monday, February 8, 2021, http://www.nhc.gov.cn/gjhzs/s7958/202102/d6ec37af0ad94babbba96 4ac7628f0de.shtml.

[2] On the Award of Group with Outstanding Performance in 2021 Oversea Healthcare Aid by National Health Commission, National Health Commission of People's Republic of China, January 24, 2022, http://www.nhc.gov.cn/gjhzs/s7958/202201/20478922ea8e40bba008f8eaf74b3fa1. shtml.

[3] The Speech of Ambassador to Sudan at the Video Meeting of the 35th Batch of Medical Aid Team to Sudan, Embassy of the People's Republic of China in Sudan, November 2, 2020, http:// sd.china-embassy.org/dsxx/dsjhhsmwz/202011/t20201103_7285862.htm.

Chapter 8   Report on China-Arab States Healthcare and Pandemic Containment
Cooperation

cooperation and working together to build a "healthcare silk road" and a "healthcare community for all". China upholds the principle of treating vaccines as global public goods, donated vaccines to Arab states, facilitated vaccine procurement, and supported local processing, production, and use of vaccine products, helping to improve regional and global production capacity. At present, China has initiated vaccine cooperation with several Arab states.

8.1.2.1   Arab States' Support for Chinese Vaccine

On the one hand, Arab states supported the clinical trials of China's COVID-19 vaccine, and dignitaries from various Arab states participated in the trials. In 2020, China's vaccine was tested in Phase III clinical trials in the UAE, Bahrain, Egypt, and Morocco, among which the UAE cooperated with China to conduct the world's first Phase III international clinical trial of inactivated COVID-19 vaccine.[1] Once the Chinese vaccine was approved for marketing, several Arab dignitaries took the initiative to publicly inoculate themselves, showing their confidence in the safety and efficacy of the Chinese vaccine.

On the other hand, after the Chinese vaccine was put into mass production for vaccination, Arab states quickly granted official registration and bulk purchase, which once again demonstrated their trust in China and Chinese medicine standards. On September 14 and November 3, 2020, the UAE and Bahrain announced the emergency use of the Sinopharm vaccine respectively, making the UAE the first country outside of China to approve the Sinopharm vaccine for emergency use.[2] At the beginning of 2021, more Arab states started to authorize the use of the Sinopharm BBIBP vaccine. In just one month, five countries, including Egypt, Jordan, Algeria, Iraq, and Morocco, have officially approved the use of the Chinese COVID-19 inactivated vaccine. On May 7[3] and June 1[4] respectively, WHO added the Chinese Sinopharm vaccine and CoronaVac vaccine to the list of vaccines for emergency use, and most Arab states have

---

① Ni Jian, China-Arab States Relation is at a New Historic Starting Point, China Daily, February 16, 2022, https://cn.chinadaily.com.cn/a/202202/16/WS620ca52da3107be497a06876.html.

② International Insight: The Safety of Chinese COVID-19 Vaccine was recognized by the International Community, people.cn, December 16, 2020, http://world.people.com.cn/n1/2020/1216/c1002-31968601.html.

③ WHO approves Sinopharm BBIBP vaccine for emergency use, UN news, May 7, 2021, https://news.un.org/zh/story/2021/05/1083742.

④ WHO validates Sinovac COVID-19 vaccine for emergency use and issues interim policy recommendations, UN news, June 1, 2021, https://news.un.org/zh/story/2021/06/1085102.

officially approved the emergency use of Chinese vaccines. On December 27, 2021, the UAE approved the emergency use of the Sinopharm second-generation recombinant protein COVID-19 vaccine, which is the first second-generation recombinant protein COVID-19 vaccine approved for emergency use in the world, setting another "world first" record for China-Arab states pandemic containment cooperation.[1] The Arab states' approach fully demonstrated their trust in China and confirmed the sincere friendship between the two sides.

8.1.2.2　China's Vaccine Aid to the Arab States

In addition to medical supplies, China has also provided vaccines to Arab states. According to data released by Bridge Beijing, a consulting company, as of December 31, 2021, China has sold 1.64 billion doses of the COVID-19 vaccine to countries around the world and donated 133 million doses. Of the total 1.773 billion doses of vaccine, 1.34 billion doses have been delivered. China has shipped 84,350,400 doses of vaccines sold and donated to Arab states. China has shipped 84,350,400 doses of vaccines sold and donated to Arab states. Among them, Morocco ranks sixth in terms of Chinese vaccine delivery, Egypt ranks sixth in the number of vaccines sold, and second in the number of donations among all target countries.[2]

Table 8.2　The number of Chinese vaccines delivered to Arab states (as of December 31, 2021)

Target country	Vaccines delivered (10,000 doses)
Egypt	1612.44
Libya	506
Tunisia	110
Algeria	520
Morocco	4550
Sudan	65
Mauritania	33
Djibouti	140
Comoros	40

[1]　Sinopharm's Second Generation COVID-19 Vaccine Was Approved for Emergency Use in the UAE, people.cn, December 29, 2021, http://world.people.com.cn/n1/2021/1229/c1002-32319663.html.

[2]　China COVID-19 Vaccines Tracker, Bridge Beijing, December 31, 2021, https://bridgebeijing.com/our-publications/our-publications-1/china-covid-19-vaccines-tracker/.

Chapter 8　Report on China-Arab States Healthcare and Pandemic Containment Cooperation

Continued

Target country	Vaccines delivered (10,000 doses)
Somalia	70
Lebanon	74
Palestine	30
Jordan	69.6
Syria	80
Iraq	225
UAE	300
Oman	10
Total	8435.04

The above data are from Bridge Beijing, excluding vaccines produced through COVAX or co-production programs.

At the same time, China has actively participated in the UN's COVID-19 Vaccines Global Access (COVAX) initiative, facilitating the vaccine supplies in Arab states. Since China announced providing the first 10 million doses of vaccine to COVAX in June 2021, China supplied more than 200 million doses of vaccine to the program by the end of 2021. In August 2021, China announced a $100 million donation to COVAX for the distribution of vaccines to developing countries.[1] According to reports, Algeria, Libya, Yemen, and other Arab states have received Chinese vaccines from COVAX.

Overall, China has donated and exported nearly 100 million doses of COVID-19 vaccine to Arab states, based on statistics as of August 2021.[2] By the end of December 2021, China had assisted and exported 440 million doses of vaccine to Middle Eastern countries, including Arab states.[3]

8.1.2.3　China-Arab States Cooperation in Vaccine Production

Arab countries have given full trust and recognition to Chinese vaccines and

---

[1]　China signed the COVAX Donation Agreement with the Global Alliance for Vaccines and Immunization, xinhuanet, February 15, 2022, http://www.news.cn/world/2022-02/15/c_1128376818.htm.

[2]　China: China and Arab States will Continue Strengthen Cooperation in Medical Supply Procurement and Vaccine Production in the Post-pandemic Era, chinanews.com, August 23, 2021,https://www.chinanews.com.cn/gn/2021/08-23/9549638.shtml.

[3]　2021: Remember these Moments, China-Arab States Cooperation Forum, December 27, 2021, http://www.chinaarabcf.org/zagx/sssb/202112/t20211227_10475895.htm.

159

were one of the first regions to cooperate with China in vaccine production. The UAE, Egypt, Algeria, and Morocco have already cooperated with China in vaccine production, providing a boost to the region to fight against COVID-19.

The UAE was the first Arab state to cooperate with China in vaccine production. On January 5, 2021, the UAE Ministry of Health and Prevention announced that the UAE authorities' cooperative scientific research institute has reached an agreement with Sinopharm to produce Sinopharm vaccines locally under the authorization of China.[1] On March 28, the project of the Chinese vaccine filling line in cooperation with the UAE was launched online.[2] The main manufacturers of Chinese vaccines are the Ras Al Khaimah factory and the new Hayat-Vax factory, which is under steady construction. According to an interview of The National in June 2021 with Ni Jian, Chinese Ambassador to the UAE, the Ras Al Khaimah factory will be able to produce 3 million doses of COVID-19 vaccine per month and the Hayat-Vax factory will have an annual production capacity of 200 million doses when it is in operation.[3] Thanks to the joint efforts of both countries, the UAE has become one of the most vaccinated countries in the world[4] and the center of vaccine production and transit in the Middle East.

Egypt is the first African country to cooperate with China in the production of the COVID-19 vaccine. On April 21, 2021, the Egyptian company VACSERA and Sinovac signed an agreement for vaccine production in Egypt. On May 21, the first batch of undiluted CoronaVac vaccines from China arrived in Cairo for filling and production. On July 5, Egypt completed the production of the first 1 million doses of the CoronaVac vaccine. By then, the daily production capacity could reach 300,000 doses and the annual production capacity could reach 200 million doses, providing 2 million doses of locally filled and produced CoronaVac

---

[1] The UAE Announced Local Production of Sinopharm Vaccine, people.com, January 6, 2021, http://world.people.com.cn/n1/2021/0106/c1002-31991467.html.

[2] China-Arab Vaccine Production Project Shows China's Commitment, china.com, March 28, 2021, http://www.china.com.cn/opinion2020/2021-04/02/content_77370854.shtml.

[3] Chinese Ambassador to the UAE Interviewed by The National, Embassy of the People's Republic of China in United Arab Emirates, June 16, 2021, http://ae.china-embassy.org/xwdt/202106/t20210616_8910634.htm.

[4] Ni Jian, China-Arab States Relation is at a New Historic Starting Point, China Daily, February 16, 2022, https://cn.chinadaily.com.cn/a/202202/16/WS620ca52da3107be497a06876.html.

Chapter 8   Report on China-Arab States Healthcare and Pandemic Containment
Cooperation

vaccines to vaccination centers in Egypt every week.[1] The cooperation between China and Egypt in vaccine production has not only advanced the vaccination program in Egypt itself but also push forward the process of pandemic control in the Middle East and Africa. In July 2021, China and Egypt jointly donated 500,000 doses of vaccines produced in the vaccine filling plant to Palestine in the Gaza Strip.[2] With the efforts of the two countries, Egypt is gradually becoming a regional vaccine production and export center in Africa.

Algeria is the second country in Africa to produce Chinese vaccines. On September 29, 2021, the first doses of the CoronaVac vaccine were produced in Constantine in partnership with Algeria's pharmaceutical group Saidal. Saidal planned to have a monthly production of 5 million doses and an annual production of 96 million doses by January 2022, according to the report.[3] The Algerian Prime Minister hailed the Chinese vaccine production project as "the first seed of the new Algeria.[4]

In addition, on July 5, 2021, in the presence of King Mohammed VI of Morocco, China National Biotec, Sinopharm International, and the Moroccan Ministry of Health signed a memorandum of cooperation on the COVID-19 inactivated vaccine. Under the supervision and guidance of the Moroccan Ministry of Health, the Moroccan company Sothema will cooperate with Sinopharm to produce the COVID-19 vaccine using the existing sterile filling line, with an estimated monthly production capacity of up to 5 million doses.[5] The cooperation project, when implemented, will have a significant impact on the global combat against the pandemic.

The China-Arab states cooperation in combating the pandemic has demonstrated the ability of both sides to deal with public health emergencies in

---

[1]   From Face Masks to Vaccine: The Upgrading China-Egypt Pandemic Containment Cooperation, people.cn, October 23, 2021,http://world.people.com.cn/n1/2021/1023/c1002-32262038.html.

[2]   China and Egypt Will Donate Vaccine to Palestine People in Gaza Strip, xinhuanet, July 19, 2021, http://www.xinhuanet.com/2021-07/19/c_1127668131.htm.

[3]   Algeria Started Producing Chinese COVID-19 Vaccine, China-Arab States Cooperation Forum, October 2, 2021, http://www.chinaarabcf.org/zatjky/202110/t20211002_9592955.htm.

[4]   2021: Remember these Moments, China-Arab States Cooperation Forum, December 27, 2021, http://www.chinaarabcf.org/chn/zagx/sssb/202112/t20211227_10475895.htm.

[5]   China National Biotec, Sinopharm International and the Moroccan Ministry of Health Signed a Memorandum of Cooperation on COVID-19 Inactivated Vaccine, guancha.com, July 6, 2021, https://www.guancha.cn/politics/2021_07_06_597192.shtml.

a collaborative manner, which is an example of global health governance and a model of building a healthcare community for all.

8.2 The Characteristics and Meaning of China-Arab States Pandemic Containment Cooperation

8.2.1 The Characteristics of China-Arab States Pandemic Containment Cooperation

From medical supplies to vaccine production cooperation, all of them reflect the inclusiveness and comprehensiveness of China-Arab states cooperation in combating COVID-19.

8.2.1.1 Multiple Participants

The participants of China-Arab states cooperation against the pandemic not only include the central government and the Red Cross but also local governments, enterprises, chambers of commerce, public welfare organizations, think tanks, and even individuals, showing remarkable breadth and diversity. The participants are different in size and function but are complementary to each other. While governments of China and Arab states continue to donate supplies and vaccines, some enterprises and chambers of commerce also raised supplies and donate them to Arab states. Universities and think tanks organized and translated materials on epidemic prevention and control experience, providing advice to government agencies on cooperation during the epidemic. Cultural organizations wrote poems and recorded videos to express their support. Landmarks in Arab states, such as the Burj Khalifa, the tallest building in the world, and the Pyramids in Egypt, put up light shows with the text "Go Wuhan". The Chinese People's Association for Friendship with Foreign Countries, the China Arab Friendship Association, and the Arab China Friendship Association have also contributed to the China-Arab states cooperation in the battle against the pandemic. There are many participants in China-Arab states cooperation in combating the pandemic. All of them are empowering each other with their ideas and suggestions for the prevention and control of the pandemic in Arab states and the China-Arab cooperation in the pandemic era.

8.2.1.2 Comprehensive Cooperation

China-Arab states cooperation in COVID-19 containment is holistic and comprehensive. It covers all the 22 Arab states, and covers the whole process

Chapter 8 Report on China-Arab States Healthcare and Pandemic Containment
Cooperation

of COVID-19 control and prevention. China's relief supplies to Arab states cover not only the general population, but also the Palestinian people, Palestinian refugees, and people in areas suffering from conflict such as Syria. According to reports, the Syrian embassy is filled with relief supplies donated by various Chinese provinces, private enterprises, and individuals.[1] At the end of 2021, China donated 80,000 doses of COVID-19 vaccine to Palestinian refugees in Jordan.[2] China Arab states cooperation in the fight against the pandemic has been carried out in different forms, including verbal support, supply donation, experience exchange, medical teams dispatch, vaccine procurement, and production.

8.2.1.3 Expanding Pandemic Containment Cooperation to Other Fields

In the face of the pandemic, China and the Arab states have not only deepened cooperation in the field of healthcare but also strengthened cooperation in material production, scientific research, academic consultation, public welfare donations, logistics and transportation, economic development, and humanistic exchanges. For healthcare, the two sides have cooperated deeply in COVID-19 rapid testing, clinical diagnosis and treatment, and vaccine filling and production; for material production, China has not only facilitated the import of medical supplies for Arab states, but also cooperated with Egypt to build a mask factory to provide masks for Arab and African countries; for logistics, Qatar Airways has opened a green channel to help Chinese enterprises and overseas Chinese people to transport relief supplies to China, becoming the first Middle East airline to undertake the task.

8.2.1.4 Taking the Lead in Vaccine Production Cooperation

In the face of the pandemic, China and the Arab states have taken the lead in all aspects of cooperation. After the outbreak, Saudi King Salman was the first foreign head of state to call President Xi Jinping to support China's fight against the pandemic. In terms of vaccine cooperation, Arab states are the first to join China's vaccine cooperation. The UAE was the first country to conduct Phase III trials of the Chinese vaccine outside China and is also one of the fastest

---

[1] We Are on the Same Boat: A Report on China's Oversea Support, August 28, 2020, https://ishare.ifeng.com/c/s/7zJ7pYiRJwU.

[2] COVID-19 Vaccine Donated by China for Palestine Refugees Arrived in Jordan, Office of the People's Republic of China to the State of Palestine, December 24, 2021, http://www.pschinaoffice.org/zxxx/202112/t20211224_10475538.htm.

163

countries to introduce the Chinese vaccine.[1] Some Arab heads of state and senior government officials have taken the lead to vaccinate with the Chinese vaccine, showing their confidence in the Chinese vaccine and making outstanding contributions to the development and promotion of the Chinese vaccine.

8.2.1.5 Like-minded Participants

The most fundamental philosophy of China-Arab states cooperation in pandemic containment is that we share the same destiny. In the face of the pandemic, the destiny of mankind is connected, and China and Arab states share the same fate. We support international cooperation against the pandemic and issued a joint statement on solidarity against the pandemic, unanimously emphasizing that international cooperation should be strengthened, and the World Health Organization should play a leading role. We carried out international joint prevention and control to build a global firewall against the pandemic. We jointly oppose the politicization of the pandemic and the labeling of the virus and make contributions to promote the formation of global consensus and the convergence of forces against the pandemic. At the same time, China has taken practical actions to promote the fair and reasonable distribution of vaccines worldwide and is actively engaged in international cooperation in vaccine research and development, production, and use.

8.2.2 The Meaning of China-Arab States Pandemic Containment Cooperation

The China-Arab states cooperation in combating the pandemic has made a contribution to the victory of both sides over the pandemic, consolidated the deep friendship established since the ancient Silk Road, and set a model for the international community to respond to major public health emergencies in a united and cooperative manner, and put the idea of China-Arab States community with a shared future into practice.

The cooperation in COVID-19 containment enhanced and developed the traditional friendship between China and Arab states. The cooperation proved that both China and Arab states have always been good partners for mutual benefit and good brothers who share the hardships and sufferings and that

---

[1] China-Arab Vaccine Production Project Shows China's Commitment, china.com, Friday, April 2, 2021, http://www.china.com.cn/opinion2020/2021-04/02/content_77370854.shtml.

Chapter 8   Report on China-Arab States Healthcare and Pandemic Containment
Cooperation

China-Arab relations have stood the test of the storm. The pandemic will only strengthen the friendship and facilitate the in-depth development of the strategic partnership between China and Arab states.

The cooperation proved the ability of China-Arab States Cooperation in dealing with non-traditional security threats. Viruses know no borders and pandemics know no race. In the face of the sudden emergence of COVID-19, it is more important than ever for China and the Arab states to strengthen cooperation, overcome the difficulties, and move forward together, so as to create a strong synergy to overcome the crisis through joint response and enhanced cooperation. The practice of China and the Arab states in combating the pandemic fully demonstrates that China and the Arab states have a strong capacity to deal with non-traditional security threats.

The cooperation has boosted the confidence of the international community in the fight against the pandemic. The China-Arab cooperation has set a successful example of working together to contain COVID-19 and has set an example for the international community to gain confidence in overcoming the pandemic, enhance mutual trust among countries, and maintain international solidarity in combating the pandemic. Solidarity and cooperation will eventually become the mainstream choice of the international community.

The cooperation exemplified the idea of building a community with a shared future for mankind. Since the outbreak of the epidemic, many individuals, enterprises, and social organizations have transcended national borders to show their empathy for the people in the outbreak areas, fully demonstrating the appeal and relevance of the community with a shared future. China is not only the advocate of the concept but also the practitioner. In the face of the pandemic, China and the Arab states have been helping each other and supporting each other, and putting the idea of the China-Arab States community with a shared future into practice.

8.3   The Outlook of China-Arab States Healthcare Cooperation

In the post-pandemic era, China-Arab states healthcare cooperation has both challenges and opportunities. Although it faces challenges such as recurring epidemics, anti-globalization thinking, changes in relations between major powers, and a lack of international discourse, it has a promising future

165

in improving health cooperation mechanisms, mobilizing global resources to combat the pandemic, improving early warning and monitoring capabilities for major infectious diseases, improving healthcare aid systems, deepening cooperation in the production of vaccines and medicine, and promoting the development of digital healthcare.

8.3.1   The Challenge of China-Arab States Healthcare Cooperation

COVID-19 is very stubborn and difficult to eradicate, and the global fight against the pandemic has not yet achieved full victory. At present, there are four major challenges facing China-Arab states cooperation in pandemic containment.

Repeated outbreaks bring pressure to epidemic control. The recurring outbreaks have increased the pressure on governments and health systems, making the China-Arab states cooperation against the pandemic more challenging.

The "anti-globalization" affects the global combat against the pandemic. Some trade and investment protectionists, under the banner of maintaining public health security, have recklessly adop ted border control measures to restrict the movement of people and goods, resulting in a poor global supply chain and the untimely delivery of various supplies. Some countries even hoard vaccines, which leads to waste and affects global combat, and also brings inconveniences to China-Arab states cooperation in combating COVID-19.

The "great power competition" affects the effectiveness of cooperation in combating the pandemic. The US defines China-US relations as a "great power competition" and strategically extrudes Russia, which makes the international situation more volatile and brings more uncertainty to the China-Arab states cooperation in containing COVID-19.

The "political virus" concept constitutes an obstacle to cooperation against COVID-19. Some Western countries have called COVID-19 the "Chinese virus" without any actual evidence, which politicized the virus and made groundless speculations about its origin, and repeatedly stigmatized China.[1] The "political virus" is the biggest obstacle to the global combat against the pandemic and its origin tracing, posing a major challenge to the China-Arab states cooperation in containing COVID-19.

---

[1]   SONG, Xiaoxiao, Exploring the International Cooperative Governance Model from the Sino-Arab Anti-epidemic Cooperation, China-Arab States Science and Technology Forum, 2020(12): 22-23.

Chapter 8   Report on China-Arab States Healthcare and Pandemic Containment
Cooperation

8.3.2   The Future of China-Arab States Healthcare Cooperation

China-Arab states healthcare cooperation has a long history and is one of the important areas of cooperation between the two sides. Under the current situation, the importance of strengthening healthcare cooperation has become more prominent. In the post-pandemic era, public health cooperation will be an important area for China-Arab states cooperation in developing Belt and Road Initiative, and both sides will continue to deepen investment cooperation in medical supplies procurement, vaccine production, and other areas to jointly build a Healthcare Silk Road. Looking ahead, the two sides can continue to improve cooperation in the following areas.

Give full play to the existing mechanisms and promote systematic cooperation. Give full play to the existing mechanisms and promote systematic cooperation. At present, China-Arab states healthcare cooperation has been incorporated into the framework of cooperation mechanisms such as the China-Africa Cooperation Forum, China-Arab States Cooperation Forum, Belt and Road initiative, China-Arab States Expo, and China International Import Expo. In the future, the two sides should further leverage the above-mentioned cooperation mechanisms in fields such as medical supplies, medical personnel, and cooperation in diagnosis and treatment technology, give full play to the role of the China-Arab States Health Cooperation Forum, and form a fixed exchange mechanism, explore new cooperation models based on existing cooperation, and develop systematic cooperation.

Make full use of the international organizations and mobilize global resources to jointly contain COVID-19. As the specialized agency of the United Nations in the field of health, the World Health Organization should play a more timely and effective role in responding to the outbreak. China and the Arab states actively support international cooperation to contain the pandemic, and can further participate in cooperation mechanisms such as the United Nations, the World Health Organization, APEC, SCO Health Ministers' Meeting, G20 Health Ministers' Meeting, etc. By jointly participating in and supporting the above-mentioned international organizations and international activities, we can build a multilateral healthcare cooperation mechanism, mobilize global resources to join efforts to combat the pandemic, and build a stronger healthcare community for all.

167

Build a prevention and control system for major infectious diseases and improve surveillance and early warning capabilities. The outbreak of the COVID-19 pandemic has made the world realize once again that major infectious diseases are the enemy of all mankind, and a more extensive and effective prevention and control system has become a top priority. In the future, China and the Arab states need to strengthen the construction of major infectious disease prevention and control systems, exchange comprehensive prevention and control strategies, carry out technical cooperation through bilateral or multilateral health cooperation mechanisms, improve disease monitoring, laboratory monitoring, and early warning capabilities, establish mechanisms for infectious disease detection, outbreak notification, information sharing, and joint disposal, and improve the capacity of both sides to prevent and control infectious diseases.

Improve the oversea healthcare aid system and help the Arab states upgrade their health system. At present, China's oversea medical aid mainly includes hospital construction, medicine, and medical equipment, medical teams, medical personnel training, and joint exchange and cooperation with developing countries on disease prevention and treatment.[1] Overall, the public health aid mechanism for emergencies still needs to be built. China and the Arab states have been exploring this area. In the future, the two sides can further improve the aid system, form long-term and short-term medical aid mechanisms, infectious disease specialist medical assistance, etc. China is committed to helping the Arab states to enhance the health system's independent development capacity and promote the transformation and upgrading of the Arab states' health system through medical technology aid, public health cooperation, medical personnel training, and pharmaceutical industry development.

Strengthen cooperation in vaccine R&D and production to form a stable medicine supply chain. At present, China and the Arab states have achieved certain results in vaccine R&D and production cooperation. In the post-pandemic era, the two sides can use the existing vaccine cooperation basis to expand cooperation in other categories of vaccines, medicine, and medical devices. China can further build vaccine production lines, medicine, and medical

---

[1] Overview of China's Oversea Healthcare Aid, China International Development Cooperation Agency, October 16, 2018, http://www.cidca.gov.cn/2018-10/16/c_129972289.htm.

Chapter 8   Report on China-Arab States Healthcare and Pandemic Containment
Cooperation

device production plants in the UAE and Egypt, establish a production and supply system for medical supplies based in the target country, and actively expand the third-party market to form a stable medicine supply chain in Arab states.

Accelerate the transformation and upgrading of the medical and healthcare industry and promote the development of digital healthcare. Today, digital healthcare has achieved greater development and satisfies people's need to live a life where they can buy medicines without leaving home. Currently, both China and the Arab states are vigorously promoting the digital transformation of the healthcare industry and encouraging the development of new industries such as telemedicine. In the future, China-Arab states digital healthcare can continue to promote cooperation in various fields such as medical data management, cloud diagnosis/portable diagnosis, virtual reality telemedicine, wearable health monitoring devices, and precision medicine.

At present, the world is entering a new period of turbulence and change due to the overlap between the unprecedented changes of the century and the impact of the COVID-19 pandemic. Both China and the Arab states should have firm confidence and courage to move forward with the health and safety of the Chinese and Arab peoples as the top priority, develop health cooperation, build a "healthcare community for all" and create a better world in the post-pandemic era.

Chapter 9   Report on the Opening up of Ningxia

After the 3rd Plenary Session of the 11th CPC Central Committee, Northwest China has taken the initiative in promoting opening up to the outside world and achieved many significant results. Since 1984, Ningxia has been proactively exploring the Arab markets, which has encouraged the inland areas of the Northwest to emulate. After the Chinese government decided to open up to the countries to the west, the provinces and areas in West China have been developing economic and trade cooperation with Central and West Asian regions and countries, and scholars have been actively exploring development strategies and implementation methods to promote the opening up of Northwest China to the countries to the west. After China implemented the Great Western Development Strategy, Ningxia applied for the establishment of the China-Arab States Economic and Trade Forum based on its advantages in international trade and economic cooperation. The Forum serves as a new platform for economic and trade cooperation between China and the Arab States, West Asia, and the North Africa region. It is conducive to integrating the advantageous resources of the northwestern region of China and promoting the overall opening up of the western region to the Middle East. Moreover, it further complements and improves China's overall diplomatic strategic landscape.

9.1   General Situation of Economic and Trade Cooperation between Ningxia and the Arab States

In the mid-1980s, Ningxia's amicable interactions with the Arab States laid a solid good foundation for economic and trade exchanges. On February 9,

Chapter 9　Report on the Opening up of Ningxia

1985, the People's Government of Ningxia Hui Autonomous Region hosted a reception for Arab envoys and dignitaries in Beijing, to which more than 30 diplomatic officials and representatives of the Arab States were invited. At the reception, the Ningxia government actively promoted Ningxia and expressed its intention to develop economic and trade cooperation with the Arab States for mutual benefit. From April to May 1985, then-Chairman of the Ningxia Hui Autonomous Region Hei Boli and Vice Chairman Ma Tengyi led a Ningxia delegation on a 44-day visit to Pakistan, Egypt, Yemen Arab Republic, Kuwait, and Saudi Arabia. The delegation was received by Egyptian President Hosni Mubarak and called on the Egyptian Minister of Foreign Affairs, Minister of Economy, Minister of Agriculture, and members of the business community. The delegation then made a historic visit to Saudi Arabia, which had not established diplomatic relations with China back then, with the help of the Embassy of Pakistan in Saudi Arabia. The delegation visited factories, hospitals, and universities in the cities of Riyadh, Jeddah, Jubail, and Taif, and met with the presidents of local chambers of commerce and banking executives over a period of 12 days. Ningxia delegation's interactions with Saudi Arabia contributed to the formal establishment of diplomatic relations between China and Saudi Arabia later.

9.1.1　Economic and Trade Cooperation between Ningxia and the Arab States (1980-2000)

In the early 1980s, there was almost no direct economic and trade cooperation between Ningxia and the Arab States. Their knowledge of each other's markets was little to none. This lack of mutual understanding gradually changed from the mid-1980s, and the economic and trade interactions between the two sides increased considerably. In the 1990s, the general idea of Ningxia's opening up to the outside world was to strengthen international economic and technological exchanges and cooperation; promote horizontal economic cooperation within China; strive to increase exports; develop international markets on all fronts and at multiple levels; further enhance labor export and overseas construction and tourism; and increase non-trade foreign currency income. It further actively and effectively utilized foreign investments, took various measures to absorb and guide foreign investments, and effectively combined absorbing foreign investments with accelerating the technological progress of companies.

First, Ningxia actively carried out two-way economic and trade negotiations

171

and exhibitions. In terms of imports, in September 1984, Ningxia held the International Economic and Technical Cooperation Fair in Yinchuan city, which was attended by diplomats and business leaders from 12 Arab States based in China. From September 12 to 22, 1991, Ningxia hosted the Ningxia Yinchuan International Yellow River Cultural Festival. Through exhibiting export commodities, foreign trade companies in the autonomous region negotiated with nearly 100 business people from more than 10 countries and regions, and the total foreign trade turnover reached USD 5.04 million. In sum, they signed 4 formal contracts, and 10 agreements and letters of intent with 14 companies from 8 countries and regions, with a total investment of RMB 29.626 million, including a foreign investment of RMB 2.796 million. In terms of exports, from March 30 to April 15, 1988, Ningxia participated in the 12th World Fair held in Dubai, UAE, through which Ningxia commodities entered the UAE and the Gulf markets for the first time. More than 160 categories of Ningxia commodities were exhibited and the value of signed futures contracts amounted to RMB 2,416,500. After the fair ended, Ningxia and the exhibitors from Northwest China continued their journey to Egypt, Kuwait, and other countries to promote their products, which yielded excellent outcomes.

Second, Ningxia created professional international trade and economic institutions. In July 1985, Ningxia set up the International Economic and Technical Cooperation Company, whose scope of business was contracting construction, labor export, joint venture operations, cooperative production, technology introduction, export compensation trade, and information consulting. It started business operations in Egypt, Kuwait, Thailand, Hong Kong (China), and other countries and regions. In November 1985, Ningxia established the International Trust and Investment Company, which attracted the attention of Chinese and international financial circles. The company forged partnerships with more than 60 banks, consortia, and commercial companies in more than 30 countries and regions. It also actively expanded its business in North China, Northeast China, Southwest China, and coastal areas in China, serving as a platform for opening up Ningxia to the outside world and introducing foreign capital and advanced technologies. In addition, the People's Bank of China and the State Administration of Foreign Exchange authorized the company to collaborate with the Arab National Bank to establish the first investment company that China jointly funded with an international institution. In 1987, Ningxia International Trust and Investment Company introduced a USD 10 million loan at preferential interest rates for the first time in Ningxia. Within

Chapter 9   Report on the Opening up of Ningxia

the first three years of operations, the company's revenue grew to RMB 14.2 million, its capital increased over 100% compared to the beginning, and it paid more than RMB 700,000 in taxes.

Third, Ningxia explored construction labor cooperation with the Arab States. Ningxia's major main channels for exporting labor services to the Arab States were the International Economic and Technical Cooperation Company and the CSCEC Ningxia Branch. From 1980 to 1986, Ningxia dispatched laborers 1,460 times to the then North Yemen, gaining profits of RMB 3.056 million and foreign currency income of USD 1.404 million. In 1984, Ningxia subcontracted 4,475 residential homes, a total of around 350,000 square meters, from CSCEC which won the contract in Egypt. From 1981 to 1983, Ningxia provided Arabic translation services to CSCEC's operations in Iraq and Libya. Later, Ningxia signed a deal with Egypt for 1,000 residential homes in Mansour at a total price of USD 15.12 million and signed a deal for a defense housing project in Kuwait at a total price of USD 17.7 million.

Fourth, Ningxia boosted exports to generate foreign currency income. In 1991, Ningxia's foreign trade department, under the situation that exports transition from being subsidized by state policies to being fully self-funding, accelerated its adjustments to export commodity structures and changed its business philosophy. It generated 82% of the foreign currency income target in the first half of the year, which reached USD 50.72 million, an increase of 61%. Of its total foreign currency income, USD 36.78 million were generated by local self-funded exports, which accounted for 88%, of the annual target and ranked among the top in terms of its growth rate in China. By the end of September 1991, Ningxia generated a foreign currency income of nearly USD 70 million, which was 13% more than the annual export target. At the 70th Canton Fair in October, Ningxia's turnover arrived at a total of USD 20.7 million, a record high.

Overall, there was still room for improvement in Ningxia's economic and trade relations with the Arab States. The value of its trade with the Arab States only accounted for a small proportion of its total foreign trade value. This was inconsistent with both the enormous trade demand of the Arab market, and China's economic and trade transactions with the developed areas in the Arab States. On the other hand, through this period of economic and trade interactions, Ningxia's foreign trade departments and market entities broadened their international horizons, gained a preliminary understanding of

173

The Development Process of China-Arab States Economic and Trade Relations
Annual Report 2021

the characteristics, needs and cooperation methods of the Arab market in the Middle East, and accumulated valuable experience for the further development of Ningxia-Arab States economic and trade cooperation in the future.

9.1.2 Economic and Trade Cooperation between Ningxia and the Arab States (2000-2021)

In 2010, the China-Arab States Economic and Trade Forum was held in Ningxia. Three sessions of China-Arab States Economic and Trade Forum and two sessions of the China-Arab States Expo not only brought Ningxia closer to the Arab countries, but also added momentum to the opening-up of inland Ningxia. After Ningxia hosted three sessions of China-Arab States Economic and Trade Forums, the Ningxia Inland Opening-up Pilot Economic Zone and Yinchuan Comprehensive Free Trade Zone were approved by the State Council, which fully empowered Ningxia to innovate policies and encouraged it to take early and pilot measures. As a result, Ningxia's opening-up to the countries to the west became a national strategy and a new path for cooperation between China and the Arab States. It significantly promoted the development of Ningxia's inland opening-up economy, greatly enhanced the province's popularity at home and abroad, and effectively promoted bilateral trade between Ningxia and the Arab States.

In 2010, the trade value between Ningxia and the Arab States arrived at USD 23.298 million. In 2015, their bilateral trade value reached USD 129 million, increasing nearly five times within five years, with an average annual growth rate of 92.2%, higher than that of traditional trading countries.

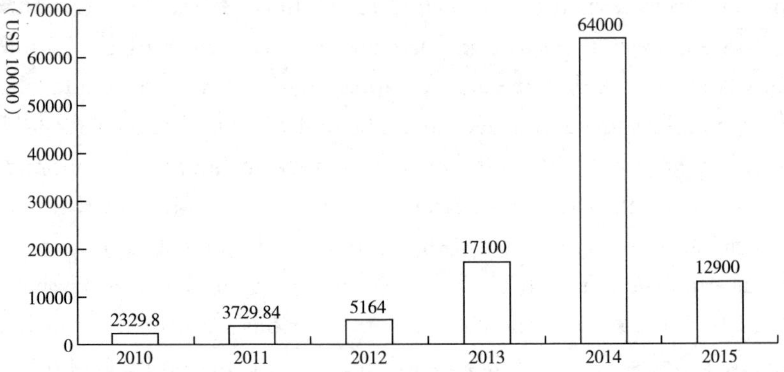

Figure 9.1   Total trade value between Ningxia and the Arab States, 2010-2015

Source: China Customs Statistics.

Chapter 9   Report on the Opening up of Ningxia

In terms of the proportion of Arab States in Ningxia's total international trade value, the proportion was increasing YoY. In 2010, the total international trade value between Ningxia and Arab accounted for 1.19% of the total imports and exports of the year; 1.16% in 2011; 2.33% in 2012; 5.30% in 2013, an increase of 2.97 percentage points over the previous year; 11.78% in 2014, an increase of 6.48 percentage points over the previous year. In 2015, Ningxia's total trade value with the Arab States accounted for 3.41% of China-Arab States trade value, 8.37 percentage points lower than the previous year. Despite such a decrease, however, the overall trend demonstrated spiraling growth.

From the perspective of commodities, Ningxia mainly exported to the Arab States rubber products, metal products, cashmere and wool products, chemical products, and activated carbon. From the perspective of the number of trade partners, Ningxia developed trade relations with 17 Arab States in 2010, and the number of its trade partners increased to 22 in 2015, covering all Arab States.

From 2013 to 2020, Ningxia steadily promoted foreign economic and trade cooperation, with total imports and exports, actual utilization of foreign capital, and foreign direct investments reaching USD 28.19 billion, USD 1.71 billion, and USD 4.47 billion. Among them, Ningxia's total imports and exports, actual utilization of foreign investments, and foreign direct investments with the B&R countries respectively arrived at USD 8.53 billion, USD 108 million, and USD 150 million, accounting for 30.3%, 6.32%, and 3.4% of the total amounts. The province's scale of international economic and trade cooperation continued to expand.[1] According to China Customs Statistics, the value of Ningxia's trade with the Arab States was USD 136 million in 2017, USD 242 million in 2018, USD 52.03 million in 2019, and USD 19.557 million in 2020. In 2021, the total value of Ningxia's imports and exports arrived at USD 3.45 billion. Its trade value with the EU grew to USD 610 million, an increase of 112.1%, making the EU Ningxia's largest trading partner. The value of Ningxia's trade with ASEAN reached USD 460 million, an increase of 88.5%.[2] The value of Ningxia's trade with the Arab States amounted to USD 68.171 million, and the UAE, Saudi Arabia, and Egypt were the top three trading partners among the Arab States.

---

[1]   "The major opportunity of jointly building the Belt and Road allows Ningxia's inland open economy to develop rapidly and smoothly", *Ningxia Daily*, November 22, 2021.

[2]   Ningxia's export growth rate to rank first in China in 2021, China News Service website, https://t.ynet.cn/baijia/32120418.html, accessed on February 20, 2022.

The Development Process of China-Arab States Economic and Trade Relations
Annual Report 2021

In summary, since the beginning of the 21st century, the economic and trade relations between Ningxia and the Arab States have further deepened and developed. In particular, after the founding of the China-Arab States Expo, its trading partners include all member states of the Arab League, the scale of its international trade has been expanding and reached an unprecedented level in 2014. The share of Ningxia-Arab States trade in the overall international trade of Ningxia is low and its potential for development is enormous.

9.2 Report on the First Five Sessions of China-Arab States Expo

The China-Arab States Expo serves as an important platform for China-Arab States cooperation in building the Belt and Road. President Xi Jinping sent congratulatory letters to five consecutive sessions of the Expo, which fully reflects the importance that the Chinese government attaches to China-Arab States cooperation. It also points out the way forward and provides a fundamental guideline for better utilizing the platform of the China-Arab States Expo and deepening China-Arab States cooperation in building the Belt and Road. The China-Arab States Expo has been playing a special and essential role in expanding the functional cooperation under the CASCF framework and in promoting the economic and trade cooperation of local governments, companies, and communities with the Arab States. It has also provided institutional experience for China to better participate in economic governance and inter-regional economic and trade cooperation in the Middle East.

9.2.1 General Situation

Since 2013, the Ministry of Commerce, CCPIT and the People's Government of Ningxia Hui Autonomous Region have organized five sessions of China-Arab States Expo. Focusing on the key areas of China-Arab States cooperation such as infrastructure construction, production capacity, advanced technologies, health, modern agriculture, and logistics, the Expo has seen an opening ceremony, a series of activities for guests of honor and theme provinces, as well as conferences, forums, exhibitions, and investment and trade promotion activities. Overall, the mechanism of "co-organization by China and the Arab States, co-organization by the State Ministry and the regional departments, and assistance from the private sector" has taken shape. So far, a total of 24 Chinese

176

Chapter 9   Report on the Opening up of Ningxia

and foreign dignitaries, 318 Chinese and foreign ministerial guests, 115 diplomats based in China, more than 6,000 Chinese and foreign companies, and nearly 45,000 exhibitors and buyers from 112 countries, regions, and international organizations participated in the Expo,[1] at which 1,524 deals of various kinds were signed. The Expo has contributed to deepening the economic and trade cooperation between China and the B&R countries and regions, including the Arab States. In terms of the mechanism for organizing the Expo, the 5th China-Arab States Expo focused on building a "dual circulation" development pattern, taking the initiative to join the Belt and Road development, responding to the needs of Morocco, the United Arab Emirates, and other countries for further strengthening economic and trade cooperation with China, and setting up a double guests of honor mechanism for the first time. The Expo was committed to further expanding the depth and width of regional cooperation, establishing a mechanism of double theme provinces (cities), i.e., Henan and Chongqing, for the first time. The Expo, held in an online and offline manner, fully integrated market resources in brand development and brand marketing, and increased the marketization level, thus enhancing its mechanism of marketization.

9.2.2   Progress of Economic and Trade Cooperation under the China-Arab States Expo Mechanism

The Arab States highly value the China-Arab States Expo, which further drives and enhances the pragmatic cooperation in multiple fields in China-Arab States trade and economy.

9.2.2.1   Cooperation in Production Capacity

Production capacity, a key area of the Belt and Road Initiative, is a major topic at the China-Arab States Expo. The industrial parks built by China in Egypt, Saudi Arabia, Oman, and other Arab States are the buttress for promoting China-Arab States cooperation in production capacity, and they help with implementing China-Arab States development strategies. The way that the China-Arab Expo promotes Sin China-Arab cooperation in production capacity is by facilitating the signing of contracts between local companies and overseas industrial parks and providing support in follow-up investments and policy coordination. Under

---

[1]   See the website of China-Arab States Expo, https://cn.cas-expo.org.cn/index.html, accessed on February 22, 2022.

the framework of the China-Arab States Expo, China has made initial progress in production capacity cooperation with Egypt, Saudi Arabia, and Oman.

First, in May 2016, Ningxia, the Ministry of Commerce, and CCPIT successfully held a series of activities of "China-Arab States Expo in Egypt" in Cairo, an important initiative for Ningxia to implement the achievements of President Xi Jinping's visit to Egypt and to participate in the celebration of the 60th anniversary of the establishment of diplomatic relations between China and Egypt. The 3rd China-Arab States Expo invited Egypt as the guest of honor to promote the China-Egypt Mankai Textile Industrial Park to be located in the industrial city of Sadat, Egypt, which was highly appreciated by the Egyptian President Abdel Fattah El Sisi. Second, China-Saudi Arabia (Jizan) Industrial Park has become a large-scale investment project to deepen China-Saudi cooperation in production capacity, and progress has been made in communication and coordination mechanisms, park infrastructure construction, and investments. The first investment project of the park, Guangzhou petrochemical and chemical fiber integrated project in Saudi Arabia, has started.[1] Third, two investment deals, the Cirata floating PV plant project in Indonesia and the Saudi Red Sea Integrated Smart Energy Project, were signed. They highlighted the supporting role of the platform "focusing on economic and trade cooperation and building the Belt and Road", and improved the mechanisms and achievements of economic and trade, technologies, and energy cooperation between China and the B&R countries.

9.2.2.2 Technical Cooperation

Cooperation in science and technology and agriculture is indispensable for China's overall cooperation with the Arab States. It is of strategic importance to the development and improvement of people's livelihood in the Arab States. The China-Arab States Technology Transfer and Innovation Cooperation Conference, the China-Arab States Technology Transfer Center and the China-Arab States Agricultural Technology Transfer Center, which were founded under the framework of the China-Arab States Expo, act as the major channels for the centralized exhibition of the achievements of China-Arab States science and technology cooperation and for the promotion of regular technology transfers.

First, the China-Arab States Technology Transfer Center promotes all-around

---

[1] Z. Yang et al, "The China-Saudi Arabia (Jizan) Industrial Park under the Belt and Road Initiative", *Asian Journal of Middle Eastern and Islamic Studies*, Vol.14, No.4, 2020, pp.528-537.

Chapter 9   Report on the Opening up of Ningxia

China-Arab States cooperation in high-tech fields, which is conducive to the scientific and technological progress and social development of both sides. It also contributes to the progress of developing countries that are technologically backward and are striving to keep up with the Fourth Industrial Revolution.[1] Under the framework of China-Arab States cooperation in science and technology, the China-Arab Technology Transfer Center facilitated the joint construction of the 4G-LTE laboratory by Huawei and King Abdulaziz City for Science and Technology; the cooperation projects between China and Saudi Arabia such as satellite navigation, the China-Arab States platform for green intelligent control and water conservation technology, and the construction project of the China-Jordan Potato Industry Science and Technology Demonstration Park all commenced smoothly.[2] The intelligent wind-solar complementary water-saving irrigation system designed by Sun Zhaojun's team at Ningxia University has been introduced to Oman and Qatar. In October 2018, Ningxia University signed a water-saving equipment technology transfer agreement and a water-saving irrigation technology transfer contract valued at RMB 110 million with the Suwadi Farm in Muscat, Oman. In August 2020, Ningxia University, Qatar NAAAS Holding Group, and Huaxin Guolian (Beijing) Enterprise Management Co., Ltd. held an online signing ceremony for the Beautiful Doha project, with an investment of about USD 1.264 billion.[3] After the outbreak of COVID-19, at the request of the Arab Academy for Science, Technology and Maritime Transport (AAST AASTMT), a sub-center of the China-Arab States Technology Transfer Center, the China-Arab States Technology Transfer Center held two online training sessions on COVID-19 prevention and control for countries along the Belt and Road, which was fully recognized by the Arab side.[4] Secondly, the China-Arab States Agricultural

---

[1]   Sun Degang, Wu Tongyu, "The Fourth Industrial Revolution and China's science and technology diplomacy with the Arab States", *West Asia and Africa*, No. 6, 2020, p. 116.

[2]   Shu Mu, "The China-Arab States Expo expands the circle of friends along the Silk Road", *People's Daily*, August 31, 2017.

[3]   "Ningxia University and the Qatar Free Zones reaching cooperation agreement valued at USD 1.264 billion," China-Arab States Technology Transfer Center website: http://www.casttc.org/article/00001108.html, 2021-01-01.

[4]   "The second online training session on COVID-19 prevention and control for countries along the Belt and Road successfully held", China-Arab States Technology Transfer Center website: http://www.casttc.org/article/00001194.html, 2021-1-26.

179

Technology Transfer Center, based in Ningxia, has played its role as a fulcrum of overseas sub-centers to assist Arab countries in their upgrading of agricultural science and technology.[1] For example, the overseas sub-center in Mauritania has carried out cow embryo transfers, as well as the introduction and trial planting of high-quality forage grass and tropical fruits; the overseas sub-center in Jordan has carried out agricultural cooperation, such as the cultivation, demonstration and promotion of vegetable seeds from Ningxia, the seeds of which have been since exported to 12 countries and regions in the Middle East and Africa; the overseas sub-center in Morocco has focused on the demonstration and experiment of fish meal processing, and the production and aquatic product processing and trade.[2]

In addition, according to the national overall arrangements for international cooperation against COVID-19, from the middle of April to early May, 2020, Ningxia selected and dispatched 8 experts in laboratory tests, the prevention and control of infectious diseases, PCCM, nursing, traditional Chinese medicine and other professional fields, to form a medical team to go to Saudi Arabia and Kuwait to help fight COVID-19. They were provided with relevant medical protective supplies, shared China's experience of fighting COVID-19, and given guidance and training on the prevention and control, diagnosis and treatment of the virus.[3] On September 29, 2020, the National Health Commission of the People's Republic of China and the Ministry of Foreign Affairs jointly hosted a video conference for experts from China and members of the Arab League on the joint fight against COVID-19. Representatives from the Health Commission of the Ningxia Hui Autonomous Region attended the conference, making positive contributions toward the co-construction of the China-Arab States health community with a shared future.[4]

---

[1] Zhang Shuai, "Agricultural cooperation under the CASCF framework: Characteristics, motives, and challenges", *West Asia and Africa*, No. 6, 2020, p. 98.

[2] Jin He, "Ningxia promotes the development of overseas sub-centers of China-Arab States Agricultural Technology Transfer Center," Xinhua Silk Road Network: https://www.imsilkroad.com/news/p/383973.html, 2021-01-27.

[3] Liang Hongxin: "Experts dispatched from Ningxia to Saudi Arabia and Kuwaiti to return to Yinchuan", People's Daily Online: http://nx.people.com.cn/n2/2020/0502/c192493-33991919.html, 2021-1-27.

[4] "China-Arab League joint expert video conference on combating coronavirus successfully held", in National Health Commission website, http://www.nhc.gov.cn/cms-search/xxgk/getManuscriptXxgk.htm?id= 17139fc8846b46b99eff15bdcfb5a747, 2021-01-27.

9.2.2.3　Economic and Trade Promotion

According to statistics, a total of 1,084 projects of all kinds were signed during the five sessions of the China-Arab States Expo, with a total contractual investment amount of RMB 268.571 billion (excluding the statistics of the fifth session). However, the contractual investment amount for each session fluctuated considerably (see Table 9.1). Taking the projects signed at the 2nd China-Arab States Expo held in 2015 as an example, "a total of 60 China-Arab States cooperation deals were concluded, with an investment amount of RMB 75.43 billion. Meanwhile, there were 15 other foreign cooperation projects with an investment amount of RMB 11.126 billion".[1]

Table 9.1　Scale and project investments of the five sessions of the China-Arab States Expo

	First session	Second session	Third session	Fourth session	Fifth session
Number of attendees (person)	7348	10856	7478	12600	140000 (online)
Number of attending companies	1200	1000	1283	2900	1094
Number of signed deals	158	163	124	362	277
Total amount of investments (RMB 100 million)	2599.01	1712	2187.34	1854.2	1566.7
Amount of contractual investments (RMB 100 million)	1058.83	269.9	815.06	541.92	-

Note: "Number of signed deals" comprises contracted projects and agreed (intentional) projects. The 4th China-Arab States Expo for the first time classified signed deals into "investment projects" and "trade projects". "Amount of contractual investments" does not include statistics outside Ningxia; and the investment amount is in RMB.

Source: Based on public reports of the signing ceremony and field research data of the five sessions of the China-Arab States Expo.

The 5th China-Arab States Expo, due to the COVID-19 outbreak, was held in an online and offline manner, and most of its activities were held online. At the national level, three policy reports were released, including the Annual Report on

---

[1] "Project signing ceremony held at the 2015 China-Arab States Expo attended by Li Jianhua and Liu Hui", Chinese Communist Party News website: http://cpc.people.com.cn/n/2015/0912/c117005-27575582.html, 2021-03-07.

the Development Process of China-Arab States Economic and Trade Relations 2020, the Report on the Development of Economic and Trade Cooperation between China and Arab States 2021, and the Achievements of the UNIDO Center for South-South Industrial Cooperation in China (UCSSIC China) Project - Phase II. At the level of Ningxia, 154 cooperation deals were signed in 9 key industries with a total investment of RMB 127.68 billion, accounting for 55.6% and 81.5% of the total number of cooperation outcomes and total investment amount. Specifically, the deals include: 33 clean energy projects with an investment of RMB 61.33 billion; 47 new materials projects with an investment of RMB 45 billion; 32 green food projects with an investment of RMB 7.36 billion; 6 beef cattle and sheep projects with an investment of RMB 4.4 billion; 4 wine projects with an investment of RMB 2.84 billion; 3 dairy industry with an investment of RMB 2.44 billion; 8 cultural tourism projects with an investment of RMB 2.19 billion; 19 electronic information projects with an investment of RMB 1.5 billion; and 2 Chinese wolfberry projects with an investment of RMB 620 million.[A] Meanwhile, People's Government of the Ningxia Hui Autonomous Region signed strategic cooperation framework agreements with China Resources Group, China Motor Corporation, Huawei Group, China Energy Engineering Group, Shanghai Electric Wind Power Group, and Guangdong Ming Yang Wind Power Group, with an aim to promoting high-end, green, intelligent, and integrated development of key industries in Ningxia, and adding momentum for building the Yellow River Basin pioneer area for ecological protection and high-quality development.

The 5th China-Arab States Expo for the first time set up the mechanism of double theme provinces. This further served provinces and cities in expanding economic and trade cooperation. For example, Beijing, Tianjin, Hebei, Zhejiang, Hubei, Henan, Guangdong, and Shaanxi, by utilizing the China-Arab States Expo platform, successfully signed 12 investment deals totaling RMB 7.43 billion with the Arab States and other B&R countries. In particular, Zhejiang Post & Telecommunication Construction, Gezhouba Group, and Tianjin Sino-Saudi TEDA Industrial Park signed 5G, AI, and aerospace cooperation projects

---

① Ma Xiaofang, Monday Qing, Jiang Lu: "The 5th China-Arab States Expo project signing and cooperation results released: 277 signed deals and total planned investment and trade value RMB 156.67 billion", *Ningxia Daily*, August 20, 2021, p. 1.

Chapter 9   Report on the Opening up of Ningxia

with Saudi Arabia, Egypt, the United Arab Emirates, and Iraq, which effectively broadened the areas and improved the quality of economic and trade cooperation between China and the Arab States. Henan theme province and Chongqing theme city precisely positioned their comparative advantages. By adopting the online and offline dual-venue approach, they promoted their advantageous industries through dedicated sessions -- "Wonderful Henan, Global Partnership" and "Chongqing: A Land of Natural Beauty, A City with Cultural Appeal". They signed 46 cooperation projects (agreements) with a total investment of RMB 24.98 billion, involving green food, clean energy, new materials, dairy industry, aviation, channel, and business. They initiated ripple effects as theme province (city) and injected new momentum for expanding China's inward opening-up and promoting high-quality development.

In summary, in the context of the unprecedented pandemic and global challenges brought about by extraordinary changes, China-Arab States cooperation and the development of the Belt and Road Initiative have been showing remarkable resilience and vigor. Serving major participating entities, Ningxia has been consistently and organically coordinating domestic and international opening-up. Hence, it has accumulated experience in establishing a "dual circulation" development pattern in which domestic economic cycle plays a leading role while international economic cycle remains its extension and supplement.

东、陕西等8个省市，利用中阿博览会平台与阿拉伯国家和其他"一带一路"共建国家签订投资类项目12个，投资总额74.3亿元。特别是浙江省邮电工程建材公司、葛洲坝集团、天津中沙泰达工业园区分别与沙特、埃及、阿联酋、伊拉克等国家签署的5G、人工智能、航空航天等合作项目，有效拓展了经贸合作领域，提升了经贸合作质量。河南主题省、重庆主题市精准定位自身比较优势，分别采取线上线下双会场的方式，专题推介了优势特色产业，展示了"与世界携手，让河南出彩""山水之城·美丽重庆"的主题省（市）风采，签署了合作项目（协议）46个，投资总额249.8亿元，涉及绿色食品、清洁能源、新型材料、奶产业、航空、通道、商务等多个领域，释放了主题省（市）的示范带动效应，为扩大对内开放、促进高质量发展注入了新动力。

综上，面对世纪疫情叠加百年变局带来的全球挑战，中阿合作和"一带一路"建设展现出强大韧性和旺盛活力，宁夏服务各有关参会主体，坚持对内开放与对外开放有机联动，为加快构建以国内大循环为主体、国内国际双循环相互促进的新发展格局积累了新经验。

表 9.1　5 届中阿博览会规模及项目投资情况

	第一届	第二届	第三届	第四届	第五届
参会人数（人）	7348	10856	7478 人	12600	140000（线上）
参会企业（家）	1200	1000	1283	2900	1094
签约项目（个）	158	163	124	362	277
总投资额（亿元）	2599.01	1712.00	2187.34	1854.20	1566.70
合同投资额（亿元）	1058.83	269.90	815.06	541.92	—

说明："签约项目"由合同项目和协议（意向性）项目组成；第四届中阿博览会首次按"投资类项目"和"贸易类项目"分类统计签约项目，合同投资额不包括宁夏以外的数据。

资料来源：根据 5 届中阿博览会项目签约仪式公开报道及实地调研数据整理。

第五届中阿博览会受新冠肺炎疫情影响，采取"线上线下相结合，以线上为主"方式举办。在国家层面，发布了《中阿经贸关系发展进程 2020 年度报告》《中国与阿拉伯国家经贸合作发展报告 2021》《联合国工发组织中国南南工业合作中心二期项目成果》等 3 个政策报告。在宁夏层面，九大重点产业签署合作项目 154 个，投资总额 1276.8 亿元，分别占合作成果项目总数和投资总额的 55.6%、81.5%，其中：清洁能源产业项目 33 个、投资额 613.3 亿元，新型材料产业项目 47 个、投资额 450 亿元，绿色食品产业项目 32 个、投资额 73.6 亿元，肉牛和滩羊产业项目 6 个、投资额 44 亿元，葡萄酒产业项目 4 个、投资额 28.4 亿元，奶产业项目 3 个、投资额 24.4 亿元，文化旅游产业项目 8 个、投资额 21.9 亿元，电子信息产业项目 19 个、投资额 15 亿元，枸杞产业项目 2 个、投资额 6.2 亿元。[①] 同时，宁夏回族自治区人民政府分别与华润集团、中车集团、华为集团、中国能建集团和上海电气风电集团、广东明阳集团签署了战略合作框架协议，将有力推动宁夏重点产业高端化、绿色化、智能化、融合化发展，为努力建设黄河流域生态保护和高质量发展先行区注入了强劲动力。

第五届中阿博览会首次设立"双主题省（市）"，服务各省市拓展经贸合作的质量进一步提升，北京、天津、河北、浙江、湖北、河南、广

---

① 马晓芳、周一青、姜璐：《第五届中阿博览会项目签约合作成果发布：签约成果 277 个计划投资和贸易总额 1566.7 亿元》，《宁夏日报》2021 年 8 月 20 日第 1 版。

力阿拉伯国家农业科技升级。① 例如,宁夏在毛里塔尼亚海外分中心开展奶牛胚胎移植、优质牧草、热带水果引进及试种实验;在约旦海外分中心开展了宁夏蔬菜种子栽培示范推广等农业合作,宁夏的蔬菜种子进入中东、非洲12个国家和地区;在摩洛哥海外分中心重点开展鱼粉加工生产、水产品加工贸易领域的试验示范。②

此外,按照国家抗疫国际合作总体安排,2020年4月中旬至5月初,宁夏选派实验室检测、传染病防控、呼吸与重症、护理、中医等专业领域的8名专家组成抗击新冠肺炎疫情医疗专家组,并携带相关医疗防护物资赴沙特、科威特分享中国抗疫经验,提供防控和诊疗指导培训。③ 2020年9月29日,国家卫生健康委和外交部共同举办中国与阿拉伯国家联盟(阿盟)成员国联合抗击新冠肺炎疫情专家视频会,宁夏回族自治区卫生健康委派代表参会,为共建"中阿卫生健康共同体"作出了积极贡献。④

9.2.2.3 经贸促进

根据公开数据,5届中阿博览会共签订各类项目1084个,累计合同投资金额2685.71亿元人民币(不含第五届数据),但历届合同投资额波动较大(见表9.1)。以2015年举办的第二届中阿博览会签约项目为例,"中阿合作项目60个,投资金额754.3亿元;其他国外合作项目15个,投资金额111.26亿元"。⑤

---

① 张帅:《中阿合作论坛框架下的农业合作:特征、动因与挑战》,《西亚非洲》2020年第6期。
② 靳赫:《宁夏推进中阿农业技术转移中心海外分中心建设》,新华丝路网站,https://www.imsilkroad.com/news/p/383973.html,2021年1月27日。
③ 梁宏鑫:《宁夏支援沙特、科威特专家返银》,人民网,http://nx.people.com.cn/n2/2020/0502/c192493-33991919.html,2021年1月27日。
④ 《中国—阿盟联合抗击新冠肺炎疫情专家视频会召开》,国家卫生健康委员会网站,http://www.nhc.gov.cn/cms-search/xxgk/getManuscriptXxgk.htm?id=17139fc8846b46b99eff15bdcfb5a747,2021年1月27日。
⑤ 《2015中阿博览会举行项目签约仪式 李建华刘慧出席》,中国共产党新闻网,http://cpc.people.com.cn/n/2015/0912/c117005-27575582.html,2021年3月7日。

9.2.2.2 技术合作

科技合作是中国对阿拉伯国家整体合作的重要组成部分,对于阿拉伯国家发展和改善民生具有战略意义。在中阿博览会框架下创办的中阿技术转移与创新合作大会、中阿技术转移中心、中阿农业技术转移中心,是集中展示中阿科技合作成果、推进常态化技术转移的主渠道。

其一,中阿技术转移中心促进了中阿在高科技领域的全方位合作,有利于双方的科技进步和社会发展,也有利于技术相对落后的发展中国家跟上第四次工业革命的时代步伐。[1] 在中阿科技合作框架下,中阿技术转移中心推动华为与沙特国王科技城共建联合创新"4G-LTE"实验室,中国与沙特开展卫星导航领域合作,中阿绿色智能控制节水技术平台建设、中阿(约旦)马铃薯科技试验示范基地建设等项目顺利开展。[2] 宁夏大学孙兆军团队的绿色智能节水灌溉技术与装备实质性进入阿曼和卡塔尔。2018年10月,宁夏大学与阿曼马斯喀特苏瓦迪(Suwadi)农场签订了节水设备技术转移合作协议和价值1.1亿元人民币的节水灌溉技术转移合同;2020年8月,宁夏大学、卡塔尔纳阿斯(NAAAS)集团、华新国联(北京)企业管理有限公司三方举行"美丽多哈"项目线上签约仪式,项目投资额约12.64亿美元。[3] 新冠肺炎疫情发生后,中阿技术转移中心应中阿(阿拉伯国家科技与海运学院)技术转移分中心请求,连续举办了2期面向"一带一路"共建国家新冠肺炎疫情防控线上培训,得到阿方充分肯定。[4]

其二,中阿农业技术转移中心立足宁夏,发挥海外分中心支点作用助

---

[1] 孙德刚、武桐雨:《第四次工业革命与中国对阿拉伯国家的科技外交》,《西亚非洲》2020年第6期。
[2] 书牧:《中阿博览会扩大丝路朋友圈》,《人民日报》2017年8月31日第20版。
[3] 《宁夏大学与卡塔尔自由区达成12.64亿美元合作协议》,中阿技术转移中心网站,http://www.casttc.org/article/00001108.html,2021年1月1日。
[4] 《第二期面向"一带一路"国家新冠肺炎疫情防控线上培训成功举办》,中阿技术转移中心网站,http://www.casttc.org/article/00001194.html,2021年1月26日。

等方面的市场资源，全面提升了市场化水平。

9.2.2 中阿博览会机制下的经贸合作进展

中阿博览会受到阿拉伯国家高度重视，也进一步带动和提升了中阿经贸方面多领域的务实合作。

9.2.2.1 产能合作

产能合作是中国与阿拉伯国家共建"一带一路"的重点合作领域，也是中阿博览会的重要议题。中国在埃及、沙特、阿曼等阿拉伯国家设立的产业园区则是推进中阿产能合作的重要支点，担负着将中阿发展战略对接落实落地的使命。中阿博览会推动中阿产能合作的主要途径是促成企业与境外产业园区签约，并在后续招商和政策协调等方面给予支持。在中阿博览会框架下，中国与埃及、沙特、阿曼产能合作取得初步进展。

其一，2016年5月，宁夏与商务部、中国贸促会在开罗成功举办了中阿博览会走进埃及系列活动，这是宁夏落实习近平主席访埃成果、参与中埃建交60周年庆祝活动的重要举措，第三届中阿博览会邀请埃及担任主宾国，推动中埃曼凯纺织产业园落地埃及萨达特市工业城，受到埃及总统塞西的高度赞赏。其二，中国—沙特（吉赞）产业园成为深化中沙产能合作的大型投资项目，在沟通协调机制、园区基础设施建设和招商方面取得进展，首个入园项目广州泛亚聚酯有限公司沙特石油化工化纤一体化项目开工建设。[1] 其三，签订了印尼奇拉塔漂浮光伏项目、沙特红海综合智慧能源投资类项目2个，凸显了"聚焦经贸合作·共建一带一路"的平台支撑作用，丰富完善了我国与"一带一路"共建国家经贸、技术、能源合作机制与成果。

---

[1] Z. Yang et al., "The China-Saudi Arabia (Jizan) Industrial Park under the Belt and Road Initiative", *Asian Journal of Middle Eastern and Islamic Studies*, Vol. 14, No. 4, 2020, pp. 528-537.

9.2 前五届中阿博览会专题报告

中阿博览会是中阿共建"一带一路"的重要平台,习近平主席连续向五届中阿博览会致贺信,充分体现了中国政府对中阿合作的高度重视,也为更好地发挥中阿博览会平台作用、深化中阿共建"一带一路"指明了前进方向,提供了根本遵循。中阿博览会为拓展中阿合作论坛框架下的功能性合作,促进地方政府、企业和民间对阿经贸合作发挥了特殊而重要的作用,也为中国更好地参与中东地区经济治理和区域间经贸合作提供了制度经验。

9.2.1 总体情况

自2013年以来,商务部、中国贸促会和宁夏回族自治区人民政府已举办了五届中阿博览会。大会聚焦基础设施建设、产能合作、高新技术、卫生健康、现代农业、物流等中阿重点合作领域,举办开幕大会,主宾国、主题省(区、市)系列活动,以及会议论坛、展览展示和投资贸易促进活动,基本建立了"中阿共办、部区联办、民间协办"的办会机制。截至目前,共有112个国家、地区和国际机构,24位中外政要,318位中外部长级嘉宾,115位驻华外交官,6000多家国内外企业,近4.5万名参展商、采购商参会,[①] 签订各类项目1524个,为深化中国与包括阿拉伯国家在内的"一带一路"共建国家和地区的经贸合作发挥了一定作用。在办会机制上,第五届中阿博览会着眼构建双循环新发展格局,更加积极主动融入"一带一路"建设,顺应摩洛哥、阿联酋等国家进一步加强与我国经贸合作的需求,首次设置了双主宾国;致力于进一步拓展区域合作的深度和广度,首次建立了河南、重庆双主题省(市)机制。强化市场化办会机制,通过线上线下相结合的方式,充分整合博览会在品牌开发、品牌营销

---

① 参见中阿博览会网站,https://cn.cas-expo.org.cn/index.html。

出口总额的1.19%；2011年占比1.16%；2012年占比2.33%；2013年占比5.30%，较上年提高了2.97个百分点；2014年占比11.78%，较上年提高了6.48个百分点；2015年，中阿贸易额在宁夏外贸总额中占比达到3.41%，较上年降低了8.37个百分点；但总体来看呈现螺旋式快速增长态势。

从商品角度来看，宁夏对阿拉伯国家主要出口商品有橡胶制品、金属制品、羊绒羊毛制品、化工制品、活性炭等。从贸易国别数量来看，2010年宁夏共与17个阿拉伯国家发展贸易关系，2015年贸易国别数量增加到22个，涵盖全部阿拉伯国家。

2013年至2020年，宁夏稳步推进对外经贸合作，累计实现进出口总额、实际利用外资、对外直接投资分别为281.9亿美元、17.1亿美元和44.7亿美元。其中，与"一带一路"共建国家实现进出口总额、实际利用外资、对外直接投资85.3亿美元、1.08亿美元和1.5亿美元，分别占全区总额的30.3%、6.32%和3.4%，对外经贸合作规模不断扩大。① 海关总署数据显示，宁夏与阿拉伯国家贸易额2017年为1.36亿美元，2018年为2.42亿美元，2019年为5200.3万美元，2020年为1955.7万美元。2021年，宁夏对外贸易进出口总值34.5亿美元，宁夏与欧盟贸易总值6.1亿美元，增长112.1%，欧盟成宁夏第一大贸易伙伴；宁夏与东盟贸易总值为4.6亿美元，增长88.5%；② 宁夏与阿拉伯国家贸易额为6817.1万美元，阿联酋、沙特、埃及为前三大贸易伙伴。

综上，进入21世纪后，宁夏与阿拉伯国家的经贸关系进一步深化发展，特别是在创办中阿博览会之后，贸易国别覆盖阿盟所有成员国，贸易规模不断扩大，并在2014年达到最高点，宁阿贸易在宁夏对外贸易总体格局中所占份额较低，发展潜力较大。

---

① 《迎共建"一带一路"重大机遇 宁夏内陆开放型经济"乘风"而行》，《宁夏日报》2021年11月22日。
② 《2021年宁夏外贸出口增速居全国第一》，中国新闻网，https://t.ynet.cn/baijia/32120418.html，2022年2月20日。

视野得以开阔,对中东阿拉伯国家市场的特点、需求、合作方式等有了初步了解,为将来进一步发展宁阿经贸合作积累了宝贵经验。

9.1.2 宁夏与阿拉伯国家的经贸合作（2000~2021年）

2010年,中阿经贸论坛在宁夏召开。三届中阿经贸论坛和两届中阿博览会的举办,不仅拉近了宁夏与阿拉伯国家之间的距离,还给宁夏内陆开放增加了助推剂。举办三届中阿经贸论坛之后,宁夏内陆开放型经济试验区和银川综合保税区获得国务院批复,充分赋予宁夏政策创新空间,鼓励宁夏先行先试。由此,宁夏向西开放上升为国家战略,也成为中国与阿拉伯国家合作的新路径,极大促进了宁夏内陆开放型经济发展,极大提升了宁夏在国内外的知名度,有效促进了宁夏与阿拉伯国家的双边贸易。

2010年,宁夏与阿拉伯国家贸易额2329.8万美元。2015年,双边贸易额达到1.29亿美元,五年间扩大近5倍,年均增长率为92.2%,高于传统贸易国家。

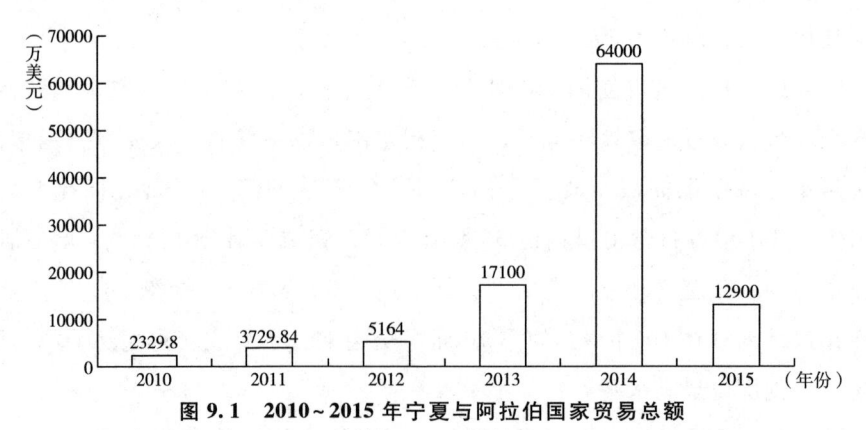

图9.1 2010~2015年宁夏与阿拉伯国家贸易总额
资料来源:中国海关总署数据。

从阿拉伯国家在宁夏外贸总额的比重来看,阿拉伯国家占宁夏外贸中的份额呈逐年上升趋势。2010年,宁夏与阿拉伯国家贸易总额占当年进

引进和开展出口补偿贸易、信息咨询等，相继在埃及、科威特、泰国等国家开拓业务。1985年11月，宁夏成立了国际信托投资公司，引起国内外金融界的关注，并与30多个国家和地区的60多家银行、财团及商贸企业建立合作关系，该公司还积极拓展华北、东北、西南及沿海地区业务，发挥了宁夏对外开放、引进外资和先进技术的窗口作用。中国人民银行和国家外汇管理局还授权该公司与阿拉伯国家银行合作，建立我国第一家中外合资的国际投资公司。1987年，宁夏国际信托投资公司在宁夏历史上首次引进了1000万美元优惠利率贷款。开业前三年，该公司营收达到1420万元，资本金比开业时增加了1倍多，上缴税款70多万元。

第三，发展对阿工程劳务合作。宁夏对阿劳务输出的渠道主要有经济技术合作公司和中国建筑总公司宁夏分公司。1980年至1986年，宁夏在当时的北也门提供劳务人员1460人次，获得利润305.6万元，外汇额度140.4万美元。1984年，宁夏还分包中建总公司在埃及中标承包的4475套住宅工程，约35万平方米。1981年至1983年，宁夏还为中建总公司在伊拉克和利比亚的业务提供了阿拉伯语翻译。此后，宁夏又与埃及签订了曼苏尔1000套住宅工程项目，总价为1512万美元，以及科威特的一处国防住房工程，总价为1770万美元。

第四，扩大出口创汇。1991年，宁夏外贸部门在出口由国家补贴转向全面自负盈亏的政策形势下，加快调整出口商品结构，改变经营理念，上半年出口创汇完成全年任务的82%，创汇达5072万美元，同比增长61%，其中地方自营出口创汇3678万美元，完成年计划的88%，增幅居全国前列；截至9月末，宁夏出口创汇近7000万美元，超额13%完成全年出口计划。在10月举办的第70届广交会上，宁夏成交总额达2070万美元，创历史最高水平。

总体来看，这一时期宁夏与阿拉伯国家的经贸关系还不够密切，对阿贸易额只占本地区对外贸易总量的很小的一部分，既与阿拉伯国家市场巨大的贸易需求不相匹配，与我国对阿贸易先进地区的经贸往来也难相比。但是，通过这一时期的经贸互动，宁夏外经贸主管部门和市场主体的国际

拜会了埃及外交部部长、经济部部长、农业部部长和工商界人士。随后，代表团在巴基斯坦驻沙特大使馆的帮助下历史性地访问了当时还未与中国建交的沙特，在12天内参观了利雅得、吉达、朱贝勒、塔伊夫等城市的工厂、医院、大学，会见了当地商会主席及银行界高管。宁夏代表团与沙特的接触和互动，为日后中沙两国正式建立外交关系增加了正向因素。

9.1.1 宁夏与阿拉伯国家的经贸合作（1980~2000年）

20世纪80年代前期，宁夏和阿拉伯国家几乎没有直接的经贸合作往来，双方对彼此市场的认知处于很低的水平。这种双向不了解的情况从20世纪80年代中期逐步发生转变，双方的经贸互动明显增强。20世纪90年代，宁夏对外开放的总体思路是：进一步扩大对外开放，加强对外经济技术交流合作，推进国内的横向经济联合；努力增加出口，全方位、多层次开拓国际市场，继续发展劳务输出，对外承包工程和旅游业、增加非贸易外汇收入；继续积极有效地利用外资，采取多种形式吸收和引导外商投资，更好地把吸收外资与加快企业技术进步有效地结合起来。

第一，积极开展双向经贸洽谈和展览活动。"请进来"方面，1984年9月，宁夏在银川举办了国际经济技术合作洽谈会，12个阿拉伯国家的驻华外交官和工商界人士参会。1991年9月12日至22日，宁夏在银川举办了宁夏国际黄河文化节，自治区外贸公司通过举办出口商品展览等，与10多个国家和地区的近百名客商洽谈交易，对外贸易成交总额达504万美元，与8个国家和地区的14家企业签订正式合同4项，协议和意向书10项，投资总额2962.66万元，其中外商投资279.66万元。"走出去"方面，1988年3月30日至4月15日，宁夏参加了在阿联酋迪拜举办的第12届国际博览会，宁夏商品首次通过博览会进入阿联酋及海湾地区市场，共展出160多种商品，签订期货合同214.65万元。博览会结束后，宁夏与西北地区参展企业赴埃及、科威特等国家推介产品，取得良好效果。

第二，组建专业外经贸机构。1985年7月，宁夏组建了国际经济技术合作公司，主营业务为承包工程、劳务输出、合资经营、合作生产、技术

第9章 宁夏对外开放专题报告

党的十一届三中全会后,西北地区在推动对外开放的进程中主动作为,取得了很多重要成果。自1984年开始,宁夏以先行先试的魄力积极开拓阿拉伯国家市场,在西北内陆地区形成良性带动作用。随着中国政府决定大力实施向西开放,西部各省区相继开展与中亚、西亚地区和国家的经贸合作,理论界也积极探讨推动西北地区向西开放的发展战略及实施路径。2000年国家实施西部大开发战略以后,宁夏从自身对外经贸合作的优势出发,申请创办了中阿经贸论坛,形成中国与阿拉伯国家及西亚北非地区经贸合作的新平台,有利于整合中国西北地区优势资源,推动西部地区整体面向中东地区和国家"向西开放",进一步补充和完善国家总体外交战略布局。

9.1 宁夏与阿拉伯国家经贸合作总体情况

20世纪80年代中期,宁夏与阿拉伯国家的友好往来为经贸互动奠定了良好基础。1985年2月9日,宁夏回族自治区人民政府在北京召开阿拉伯国家驻华使节和友好人士招待会,30多位阿拉伯国家的外交官员和代表应邀出席。自治区政府在招待会上积极宣传宁夏,表达了与阿拉伯国家互惠互利开展经贸合作的愿望。1985年4月至5月,时任自治区主席黑伯理、副主席马腾霭率领宁夏代表团对巴基斯坦、埃及、也门、科威特、沙特进行了为期44天的友好访问,代表团受到埃及总统穆巴拉克的接见,

前，中阿双方都在大力推动医疗健康产业数字化转型，鼓励发展远程医疗等新兴产业。未来，中阿数字医疗可以继续推动在医疗数据管理、云诊断/便携式诊断、虚拟现实远程医疗、可穿戴健康监测设备、精准医疗等多个领域的合作。

当前，百年未有之大变局与新冠肺炎疫情影响相叠加，世界进入新的动荡变革期，中阿双方均应坚定信心、勇毅前行，以中阿民族的健康与安全为首要任务，发展卫生健康合作，共建"人类卫生健康共同体"，共创后疫情时代美好世界。

效。中阿双方积极支持国际合作抗疫,可以进一步参与联合国、世界卫生组织、亚太经合组织、上合组织卫生部长会、二十国集团卫生部长会等合作机制,通过共同参与和支持上述国际组织、国际活动,构建多边卫生合作机制,调动全球资源合力抗疫,构建更强大的人类卫生健康共同体。

构建重大传染病防控体系,提高监测预警能力。新冠肺炎疫情的发生让世界再次意识到重大传染性疾病是全人类共同的敌人,构建覆盖面更广、更有效的防控体系成为重中之重。未来,中阿双方需加强重大传染病防控体系建设,交流综合性防治策略,通过双边或多边卫生合作机制开展技术合作,提高疾病监测、实验室监测检测和预警能力,建立传染病监测、疫情通报、信息分享和联合处置机制,提高各方传染病防控能力。

完善对外卫生援助制度,帮助阿方升级卫生体系。目前,中国对外医疗援助主要包括援建医院、提供药品和医疗设备、派遣医疗队、培训医疗人员、与发展中国家共同开展疾病防治交流合作等形式。① 整体来看,针对紧急情况的公共卫生援助机制还有待建设。疫情之下,中阿已初步探索该领域,未来可进一步完善相关援助体系,形成长短期配合医疗援助、传染病专科医疗援助等,致力于帮助阿方提升卫生体系的自主发展能力为主,通过医疗技术援助、公共卫生合作、医疗人才培养及医药产业发展等方式,促进阿方卫生体系转型升级。

加强疫苗研发与生产合作,形成稳定药品供应链。目前,中阿在疫苗研发与生产合作领域已取得一定成果,双方可利用现有疫苗合作基础,扩大其他类别疫苗、药物、医疗器械的合作,在阿联酋、埃及等国进一步建造疫苗生产线、药品及医疗器械生产厂,建立起立足本国的医疗用品生产供应体系,并积极拓展第三方市场,形成稳定的阿拉伯国家药品供应链。

加快医疗健康产业转型升级,促进数字医疗发展。疫情之下,数字医疗满足了人们足不出户便能购买药品的生活需求,实现了较大发展。目

---

① 《我国医疗卫生领域对外援助情况综述》,国家国际发展合作署网站,http://www.cidca.gov.cn/2018-10/16/c_129972289.htm,2018年10月16日。

惮采取边境管制措施,限制人员、货物流动,导致全球供应链不畅,一些国家甚至囤积疫苗导致浪费,影响全球抗疫,也对中阿抗疫合作造成不便。第三,"大国竞争"影响合作抗疫效果。美国一味以"大国竞争"定义中美关系,战略挤压俄罗斯,致使国际局势动荡加剧,给中阿抗疫合作带来更多不确定性。第四,"政治病毒"构成合作抗疫障碍。疫情之下,一些西方国家在没有任何实际证据情况下将新冠肺炎病毒称为"中国病毒",将病毒政治化且对病毒的起源进行无端猜测,反复对中国进行污名化。[①]"政治病毒"作为全球抗疫和科学溯源的最大障碍,对中阿抗疫合作带来重大挑战。疫情反复之下,各国政府和卫生体系压力剧增,为中阿抗疫合作带来较大难度和挑战。

8.3.2 中阿卫生健康合作展望

中阿卫生健康合作历史悠久,是双方重要的合作领域之一。疫情之下,加强卫生健康合作的重要性更加凸显。后疫情时代,公共卫生合作将是中阿共建"一带一路"的重要领域,双方将不断深化医疗物资采购、疫苗合作生产等领域的投资合作,共同打造健康丝绸之路。展望未来,双方可在下述领域继续完善合作。

充分发挥现有机制作用,推动实现系统性合作。目前,中阿卫生健康合作已纳入中非合作论坛、中阿合作论坛、"一带一路"倡议、中阿博览会、中国国际进口博览会等合作机制框架内。未来,双方要在医疗物资、医护人员、诊疗技术合作等方面进一步发挥上述合作机制作用,充分发挥中阿卫生合作论坛作用,形成固定交流机制,在现有合作基础上探索新合作模式、新合作空间,形成系统性合作。

充分发挥国际组织作用,调动全球资源合力抗疫。世界卫生组织作为联合国在卫生领域的专门机构,在应对疫情方面发挥作用还应更加及时有

---

① 宋萧萧:《中阿双边国家合作抗疫治理模式的构建》,《中阿科技论坛(中英文)》,2020年第12期,第20~22页。

分种族。面对突如其来的新冠肺炎疫情，中阿双方比以往任何时候都更需要加强合作、共克时艰、携手前行，通过携手应对、加强合作，凝聚起战胜疫情的强大合力。中阿携手抗疫的生动实践充分说明中阿具备成功应对非传统安全威胁的强大能力。

树立了国际社会合作抗疫的信心。中阿合作抗疫树立了携手抗疫的成功典范，为国际社会树立战胜疫情的信心、展现团结抗疫的姿态和胸怀、增进国家间互信、维护国际团结抗疫大局作出示范。团结合作、同舟共济最终将成为国际社会的主流选择。

践行了人类命运共同体理念。疫情发生以来，众多的个人、企业、社会组织超越国家边界，与疫情发生地区的人民感同身受、同舟共济，充分展现了人类命运共同体的普遍感召力和现实性。中国不仅是人类命运共同体理念的倡导者，更是理念的践行者。疫情之下，中阿守望相助、互相支持，中阿命运共同体建设也由理念走向实践。

8.3 中阿卫生健康合作展望

后疫情时代，中阿卫生健康合作既有挑战又有机遇，虽面临疫情反复、逆全球化思潮、大国关系变化、缺少国际话语权等挑战，但在完善卫生合作机制、调动全球资源抗疫、提高重大传染病预警监测能力、完善卫生援助制度、深化疫苗等药品生产合作、促进数字医疗发展等方面合作前景广阔。

8.3.1 中阿卫生健康合作面临的挑战

新冠病毒十分顽固，难以根除，全球抗疫尚未取得全面胜利。目前来看，中阿合作抗疫主要面临四大挑战。

第一，疫情反复带来抗疫压力。疫情反复之下，各国政府和卫生体系压力剧增，为中阿抗疫合作带来较大难度和挑战。第二，"逆全球化"影响全球抗疫。贸易投资保护主义者打着维护公共卫生安全的旗号，肆无忌

8.2.1.4 敢为先，合作生产疫苗

面对疫情，中阿在各方面合作中敢为人先。疫情发生后，沙特国王萨勒曼是第一个致电习近平主席支持中国抗疫的外国元首。在疫苗合作领域，阿拉伯国家是中国对外疫苗合作的第一方阵，阿联酋是最先接受中国疫苗境外三期试验的国家，也是中国以外接种国药疫苗速度最快的国家之一，① 一些阿拉伯国家的元首和政府高官带头接种中国疫苗，为中国疫苗投下信任票，为中国疫苗成功研发与推广作出突出贡献。

8.2.1.5 意相通，支持国际合作

中阿抗疫合作最根本的信念是命运与共。在重大疫情面前，人类命运相连，中阿休戚与共，支持国际抗疫合作，共同发表团结抗疫联合声明，一致强调应加强国际合作，发挥世界卫生组织领导作用；开展国际联防联控，构筑全球抗疫防火墙；共同反对把疫情政治化、病毒标签化，为促进形成全球共识、汇聚抗疫力量作出重要贡献。同时，中国以实际行动推动全球疫苗公平合理分配，在疫苗研发、生产、使用等方面均在积极开展国际合作。

8.2.2 中阿抗疫合作的意义

中阿抗疫合作为双方战胜疫情作出重要贡献，巩固了双方自古丝绸之路建立起的深厚友谊，为国际社会团结合作应对重大突发公共卫生事件树立了典范，也让中阿命运共同体理念的建设从理论走向了实践。

巩固和提升了中阿传统友谊。中阿携手抗疫证明，双方始终是互惠互利的好伙伴、同甘共苦的好兄弟，中阿关系经得起风浪考验，疫情的淬炼只会让中阿传统友谊更加牢固和坚韧，让中阿战略伙伴关系得到进一步深化。

检验了中阿合作应对非传统安全威胁的能力。病毒没有国界，疫情不

---

① 《中阿启动疫苗生产线项目，再证中国重承诺敢担当》，中国网，http：//www.china.com.cn/opinion2020/2021-04/02/content_77370854.shtml，2021 年 4 月 2 日。

人、高校、智库整理翻译疫情防控经验资料、为政府机构提出疫情时期的合作建议，文化机构则创作诗歌、录制视频互相表达支持，世界最高楼阿联酋哈利法塔、埃及金字塔等阿拉伯国家地标建筑纷纷亮起"武汉加油"等感人标语，中国人民对外友好协会、中国阿拉伯友好协会、阿拉伯中国友好协会等组织也为中阿抗疫合作贡献了民间智慧与力量。中阿抗疫合作主体众多，但都在互相给予力量，为阿拉伯国家疫情防控及疫情时期的中阿合作集思广益、建言献策。

8.2.1.2 全覆盖，实现全面合作

中国对阿拉伯国家的抗疫合作实现了"全覆盖"，不仅是对22个阿拉伯国家的全覆盖，也是对抗疫全过程的覆盖。中国对阿拉伯国家的物资援助，不仅覆盖了普通民众，也覆盖了巴勒斯坦人民及周边巴勒斯坦难民、叙利亚等冲突地区人群。据相关报道，叙利亚大使馆内堆满了来自中国各个省份、民间企业及个人捐赠的救援物资；[1] 2021年底，中国向在约旦的巴勒斯坦难民捐赠8万剂新冠疫苗。[2] 同时，从互相声援到物资援助，从视频交流经验到派遣医疗队，从疫苗采购到本地化生产，中国与阿拉伯国家的抗疫合作都未缺席。

8.2.1.3 多领域，共面疫情影响

面对疫情，中阿不仅加深了医疗卫生领域合作，更实现了物资生产、科学研究、学术咨询、公益捐助、物流运输、经济发展、人文交流等领域的进一步合作。在医疗卫生领域，双方在新冠快速检测、临床诊疗、疫苗灌装生产等领域深入合作；在物资生产领域，中国不仅为阿拉伯国家进口医疗物资提供便利，还与埃及合作建造口罩厂，为阿拉伯国家和非洲国家提供口罩；在物流运输方面，卡塔尔航空开辟绿色通道，帮助中资企业、华侨向中国运输救援物资，成为首个积极承担救援物资任务的中东航空公司。

---

[1]《寰宇同舟——中国援外纪实》，凤凰网，https://ishare.ifeng.com/c/s/7zJ7pYiRJwU，2020年8月28日。

[2]《中国援助巴勒斯坦境外难民新冠疫苗交付运抵》，中国驻巴勒斯坦办事处网站，http://www.pschinaoffice.org/zxxx/202112/t20211224_10475538.htm，2021年12月24日。

月29日，阿尔及利亚塞达尔集团与中国科兴公司合作的首批新冠疫苗克尔来福在康斯坦丁正式投入生产。据报道，塞达尔集团计划到2022年1月的月产量达到500万剂，年产量达到9600万剂。① 阿尔及利亚总理称赞中国疫苗投产项目是"新阿尔及利亚的第一粒种子"。②

此外，2021年7月5日，在摩洛哥国王穆罕默德六世的见证下，中国生物、国药国际与摩洛哥卫生部共同签署新冠灭活疫苗合作备忘录。摩洛哥Sothema公司将在摩卫生部的监督指导下，与国药集团合作，利用现有无菌灌装线生产新冠疫苗，据估计每月产量可达500万剂。③ 该项合作落实后，将对全球抗疫产生重要意义。

中阿抗疫合作，充分展现了双方协同处置突发公共卫生事件的能力，是全球卫生治理的范例，也是共建人类卫生健康共同体的典范。

8.2 中阿抗疫合作的特点与意义

8.2.1 中阿抗疫合作的特点

从医疗物资援助到疫苗生产合作，无不体现出中阿抗疫合作主体众多、全面覆盖、领域广泛、敢为人先、理念相通的特点。

8.2.1.1 多主体，联动合力抗疫

中阿合作抗疫的主体不仅是中央政府、红十字会，也包括地方政府、企业、商会、公益组织、智库乃至个人，呈现显著的广泛性和多样性。各主体虽大小有别、分工各异，但能够优势互补。在双方政府持续不断捐赠物资、疫苗的同时，一些企业、商会也积极筹集物资捐赠给阿拉伯国家友

---

① 《阿尔及利亚正式开始生产中国新冠疫苗》，中阿合作论坛网站，http://www.chinaarabcf.org/zatjky/202110/t20211002_9592955.htm，2021年10月2日。
② 《2021年，请记住我们这些精彩的瞬间》，中阿合作论坛网站，http://www.chinaarabcf.org/chn/zagx/sssb/202112/t20211227_10475895.htm，2021年12月27日。
③ 《中国生物、国药国际与摩洛哥卫生部共同签署新冠灭活疫苗合作备忘录》，观察者网站，https://www.guancha.cn/politics/2021_07_06_597192.shtml，2021年7月6日。

日,阿联酋卫生和预防部宣布,阿联酋当局合作科研机构已与中国国药集团达成协议,将在中方授权下在当地生产国药疫苗。① 3月28日,中阿两国合作灌装中国疫苗生产线项目"云启动"。② 生产中国疫苗的厂家主要为拉斯海玛工厂和正在稳步建设的Hayat-Vax新工厂,根据中国驻阿联酋大使倪坚在2021年6月接受阿联酋《国民报》的专访,拉斯海玛工厂每月可生产新冠疫苗300万剂,Hayat-Vax工厂投产后年产量将达2亿剂。③ 在两国的共同努力下,阿联酋已成为全球疫苗接种率最高的国家之一④及中东的疫苗生产与转运中心。

埃及是第一个与中国合作生产新冠疫苗的非洲国家。2021年4月21日,埃及生物制品与疫苗公司(VACSERA)和中国科兴公司签署在埃及生产科兴疫苗的协议。5月21日,埃及从中国采购的首批科兴疫苗原液运抵开罗,开始灌装生产。7月5日,埃及完成首批100万剂中国科兴疫苗的生产,当时日产量可达30万剂,年产能可达2亿剂,每周可为境内疫苗接种中心提供200万剂本土灌装生产的科兴疫苗。⑤ 两国的疫苗生产合作不仅推进了埃及本土的疫苗接种计划,也进一步推动了中东、非洲的抗疫进程。2021年7月,中埃双方依托在埃及合作建立的疫苗灌装厂,并联合向加沙地带的巴勒斯坦民众援助50万剂疫苗。⑥ 在两国的共同努力下,埃及正逐步实现成为非洲地区疫苗生产、出口中心的目标。

阿尔及利亚是非洲第二个实现中国疫苗本土化生产的国家。2021年9

---

① 《阿联酋宣布将在当地生产中国国药疫苗》,人民网,http://world.people.com.cn/n1/2021/0106/c1002-31991467.html,2021年1月6日。
② 《中阿启动疫苗生产线项目,再证中国重承诺敢担当》,中国网,http://www.china.com.cn/opinion2020/2021-04/02/content_77370854.shtml,2021年4月2日。
③ 《驻阿联酋大使倪坚接受阿联酋〈国民报〉专访》,中国驻阿联酋大使馆网站,http://ae.china-embassy.org/xwdt/202106/t20210616_8910634.htm,2021年6月16日。
④ 倪坚:《中阿关系站在新的历史起点上》,中国日报网,https://cn.chinadaily.com.cn/a/202202/16/WS620ca52da3107be497a06876.html,2022年2月16日。
⑤ 《通讯:从口罩到疫苗,中埃抗疫合作不断升级》,人民网,http://world.people.com.cn/n1/2021/1023/c1002-32262038.html,2021年10月23日。
⑥ 《中埃决定向加沙地带巴勒斯坦民众援助疫苗》,新华网,http://www.xinhuanet.com/2021-07/19/c_1127668131.htm,2021年7月19日。

续表

对象国	已运达量	对象国	已运达量
摩洛哥	4550	叙利亚	80
苏丹	65	伊拉克	225
毛里塔尼亚	33	阿联酋	300
吉布提	140	阿曼	10
科摩罗	40	合计	8435.04

资料来源：以上数据来自播锐智咨询（北京）有限公司网站，只包括直接来自中国的疫苗，不包括COVAX项目、合作生产等数据。

同时，中国积极参与联合国"新冠肺炎疫苗实施计划"（COVAX），为阿拉伯国家提供了疫苗便利。自2021年6月中国宣布向COVAX首批提供1000万剂疫苗以来，截至2021年底中国已向该计划供应超过2亿剂疫苗。2021年8月，中国宣布向COVAX捐赠1亿美元用于向发展中国家分配疫苗。[1] 根据报道，阿尔及利亚、利比亚、也门等阿拉伯国家均收到了来自COVAX的中国疫苗。

根据截至2021年8月的统计数据，中国已向阿拉伯国家援助和出口近1亿剂新冠疫苗。[2] 截至2021年12月底，中国已向包括阿拉伯国家在内的中东国家援助和出口4.4亿剂新冠疫苗。[3]

8.1.2.3 中阿合作生产疫苗

阿拉伯国家对中国疫苗给予了充分信任和肯定，是最先同中国开展疫苗生产合作的地区之一。阿联酋、埃及、阿尔及利亚和摩洛哥已先后与中国开展了疫苗生产合作，为地区国家抗疫提供助力。

阿联酋是最早与中国开展疫苗生产合作的阿拉伯国家。2021年1月5

---

[1] 《中国与全球疫苗免疫联盟签署"新冠疫苗实施计划"捐款协议》，新华网，http://www.news.cn/world/2022-02/15/c_1128376818.htm，2022年2月15日。

[2] 《中方：后疫情时代，中阿将不断深化医疗物资采购、疫苗合作生产等合作》，中国新闻网，https://www.chinanews.com.cn/gn/2021/08-23/9549638.shtml，2021年8月23日。

[3] 《2021年，请记住我们这些精彩的瞬间》，中阿合作论坛网站，http://www.chinaarabcf.org/zagx/sssb/202112/t20211227_10475895.htm，2021年12月27日。

使用中国新冠灭活疫苗。世卫组织分别于5月7日①、6月1日②将中国国药疫苗与科兴疫苗列入紧急使用名单,大多数阿拉伯国家已正式批准紧急使用中国疫苗。2021年12月27日,阿联酋批准紧急使用国药集团中国生物二代重组蛋白新冠疫苗,这是目前全球首个获批紧急使用的二代重组蛋白新冠疫苗,再为中阿抗疫合作创下"世界第一"的纪录。③阿拉伯国家的做法充分展现了对中国的信任,证实了双方诚挚的友谊。

8.1.2.2 中国向阿拉伯国家提供疫苗援助

除医疗物资援助外,中国还向阿拉伯国家提供了疫苗援助。根据播锐智咨询(北京)有限公司发布的数据,截至北京时间2021年12月31日,中国已向世界各国出售新冠疫苗16.4亿剂,直接捐赠1.33亿剂,其中13.4亿剂已送达。中国向阿拉伯国家出售、捐赠的疫苗已运达8435.04万剂(见表8.2)。其中,中国向摩洛哥交付疫苗的总数在所有对象国中排名第六,向埃及出售疫苗的数量在所有对象国中排名第六、捐赠的数量在所有对象国中排名第二。④

表8.2 中国向阿拉伯国家运送新冠疫苗数量(截至2021年12月31日)

单位:万剂

对象国	已运达量	对象国	已运达量
埃及	1612.44	索马里	70
利比亚	506	黎巴嫩	74
突尼斯	110	巴勒斯坦	30
阿尔及利亚	520	约旦	69.6

---

① 《世卫组织批准紧急使用中国国药集团新冠疫苗》,联合国新闻网站,https://news.un.org/zh/story/2021/05/1083742,2021年5月7日。

② 《中国科兴新冠疫苗获得世卫组织紧急使用许可》,联合国新闻网站,https://news.un.org/zh/story/2021/06/1085102,2021年6月1日。

③ 《国药集团二代新冠疫苗在阿联酋获批紧急使用》,人民网,http://world.people.com.cn/n1/2021/1229/c1002-32319663.html,2021年12月29日。

④ 《中国新冠病毒疫苗跟踪》,播锐智咨询(北京)有限公司网站,https://bridgebeijing.com/our-publications/our-publications-1/china-covid-19-vaccines-tracker/,2021年12月31日。

苏民心相通作出积极贡献。①

8.1.2 疫苗合作成为全球典范

疫苗合作一直是中阿抗疫合作的重点，也是亮点。中阿双方积极开展疫苗合作，为共建"健康丝路"、"人类卫生健康共同体"，共享健康共同努力。中国始终秉持将疫苗作为全球公共产品的原则，向阿拉伯国家捐赠更多疫苗、提供疫苗采购便利，并支持和协助地区国家当地加工、生产和使用疫苗产品，助力地区乃至全球产能提升。目前，中国已同多个阿拉伯国家展开疫苗合作。

8.1.2.1 阿拉伯国家支持中国疫苗

一方面，阿拉伯国家积极支持中国新冠疫苗临床试验，各国政要纷纷参与试验。2020年，中国疫苗先后在阿联酋、巴林、埃及、摩洛哥等国进行三期临床试验，其中中国与阿联酋合作开展的是全球首个新冠灭活疫苗三期国际临床试验。② 中国疫苗一经获批上市，多位阿拉伯国家政要主动公开接种，为中国疫苗的安全性和有效性投下信任票。

另一方面，中国疫苗投入批量生产接种后，各国迅速给予正式注册并批量采购，再次展现了对中国和中国医药水平的信任。2020年9月14日和11月3日，阿联酋和巴林分别宣布紧急使用中国国药集团新冠疫苗，阿联酋成为中国以外首个紧急批准使用中国国药疫苗的国家。③ 2021年初，更多阿拉伯国家开始授权使用中国国药集团新冠疫苗。短短1个月内，埃及、约旦、阿尔及利亚、伊拉克、摩洛哥等5个国家相继正式批准

---

① 《用医者仁心传承中苏友谊——驻苏丹大使马新民在第35批援苏丹医疗队表彰暨送行视频会上的讲话》，中国驻苏丹大使馆网站，http://sd.china-embassy.org/dsxx/dsjhhsmwz/202011/t20201103_7285862.htm，2020年11月2日。
② 倪坚：《中阿关系站在新的历史起点上》，中国日报网站，https://cn.chinadaily.com.cn/a/202202/16/WS620ca52da3107be497a06876.html，2022年2月16日。
③ 《国际观察：中国新冠疫苗安全性获国际社会认可》，人民网，http://world.people.com.cn/n1/2020/1216/c1002-31968601.html，2020年12月16日。

活动，对专家组的工作表示感谢。

表 8.1 中国向阿拉伯国家派遣抗疫医疗专家组信息

序号	时间	对象国	专家人数	派出单位
1	2020年3月7日~4月20日	伊拉克	7	中国红十字会总会选派
2	4月15~27日	沙特	8	宁夏卫生健康委选派
3	4月27日~5月2日	科威特	8	
4	4月30日~5月12日	吉布提	12	四川卫生健康委选派
5	5月13~29日	阿尔及利亚	20	重庆市人民政府选派15人，澳门特区政府选派5人
6	5月29日~6月10日	苏丹	20	
7	6月10~18日	巴勒斯坦	10	重庆卫生健康委选派
8	2021年3月17日~6月15日	科摩罗	12	广西壮族自治区选派

资料来源：根据新闻报道内容整理。

此外，中国常驻阿拉伯国家援助医疗队也在协助阿拉伯国家抗疫方面发挥了重要作用。截至2021年，中国向阿尔及利亚、吉布提、科威特、毛里塔尼亚、摩洛哥、突尼斯、苏丹、也门和科摩罗9个阿盟成员国派有常驻援助医疗队。2020年至2021年，第20批援吉布提、第13~14批援科威特、第33~34批援毛里塔尼亚、第180~193批援摩洛哥、第24~25批援突尼斯、第26批援阿尔及利亚、第35~36批援苏丹、第13~14批援科摩罗常驻医疗队均因在阿拉伯国家抗疫工作中贡献突出而被中国国家卫健委评为援外医疗工作表现突出集体。[①] 以第35批中国援苏丹医疗队为例，医疗队队员在援苏一年间投身当地抗疫，为苏丹医护人员举行7次防疫抗疫知识培训，并通过苏丹国家电视台等媒体为苏丹百姓进行疫情防控讲座，普及防疫知识，传播中国疫情防控经验，广泛惠及当地民众，为中

---

① 《国家卫生健康委关于通报表扬2020年援外医疗工作表现突出集体的通知》，国家卫生健康委员会网站，http：//www.nhc.gov.cn/gjhzs/s7958/202102/d6ec37af0ad94babbba964ac7628f0de.shtml，2021年2月8日；《国家卫生健康委关于通报表扬2021年卫生援外工作表现突出集体的通知》，国家卫生健康委员会网站，http：//www.nhc.gov.cn/gjhzs/s7958/202201/20478922ea8e40bba008f8eaf74b3fa1.shtml，2022年1月24日。

2021年4月，中阿双方已举办50多次卫生专家视频会，视频会既有多边形式亦有双边形式，既有由外交部、驻外使馆、卫生健康委、地方政府等政府部门组织的，也有通过友好医院等合作机制举办的。例如，中国外交部同国家卫生健康委、科技部分别于2020年4月9日、9月29日举办的两次中阿卫生专家视频会，均是10个及以上阿拉伯国家参与的多边会议，有些参会人数还超过百人。在这些会议中，中阿双方就疫情流行病学特征、发展趋势、防控策略、临床诊疗、科研攻关、疫情风险评估和分级防控、疫苗研发、新冠病毒毒性演化等议题进行了深入交流与探讨，为疫情防控作出重要贡献。

此外，国家卫生健康委、国内多个高校还通过资料汇编、抗疫童书等方式向阿拉伯国家传递抗疫经验。例如，上海外国语大学翻译的儿童绘本《新型冠状病毒走啦》，以电子书形式在阿拉伯国家广泛传播，通过生动形象的方式向阿拉伯民众传递了抗疫经验。

8.1.1.4 医疗专家援助

为进一步提升阿拉伯国家应对新冠肺炎疫情的能力，中国抗疫专家前往8个阿拉伯国家分享诊疗经验和防控方案，受到各国各界热烈欢迎（见表8.1）。中国抗疫成功经验、专家组的敬业精神和专业水平受到阿拉伯国家的高度赞扬和肯定。其中，吉布提总理卡米勒专门向中国赴吉布提抗疫专家组12名成员颁授"6·27独立日"国家勋章，表彰专家组为吉布提抗疫所作的贡献。① 中国赴科摩罗短期抗疫医疗队获得了由科摩罗总统阿扎利授予的"科摩罗绿新月骑士勋章"，② 还被中国国家卫健委评选为2021年卫生援外工作表现突出集体。③ 其他国家也纷纷举办了答谢仪式等

---

① 《外交部介绍中国赴埃塞俄比亚和吉布提抗疫医疗专家组工作情况》，新华网，http://www.xinhuanet.com/world/2020-05/13/c_1125981547.htm，2020年5月13日。
② 《科摩罗总统阿扎利向中国援科短期抗疫医疗队授勋》，中国驻科摩罗大使馆网站，http://km.china-embassy.org/zxdt/202106/t20210616_9117355.htm，2021年6月16日。
③ 《国家卫生健康委关于通报表扬2021年卫生援外工作表现突出集体的通知》，国家卫生健康委员会网站，http://www.nhc.gov.cn/gjhzs/s7958/202201/20478922ea8e40bba008f8eaf74b3fa1.shtml，2022年1月24日。

七、我们欢迎更多伙伴加入本倡议。"①

8.1.1.2 医疗物资援助

新冠肺炎疫情在中国发生后，阿盟成员国向中国捐赠口罩1000多万只，手套近320万双，防护服10万套，护目镜6.5万个。②阿尔及利亚是第一批主动向中方捐助抗疫物资的国家，沙特各界分多次向中方捐助了价值5000万元人民币的医疗物资，埃及人口与卫生部部长作为总统特使携10吨医疗物资访华，阿联酋、科威特、卡塔尔等国家均多次向中国捐赠运输医疗物资。新冠肺炎疫情在阿拉伯国家发生后，中国对阿拉伯国家的物资援助实现了全覆盖，先后向阿拉伯各国提供核酸检测试剂、口罩、防护服、温度计、呼吸机等医疗物资，协助其建设病毒检测实验室。截至2020年12月，中国政府已向阿拉伯国家提供100多万份检测试剂盒，1800多万只口罩。③

2021年，中国对阿抗疫物资援助的对象主要为巴勒斯坦及联合国近东巴勒斯坦难民救济和工程处（UNRWA），伊拉克、也门、黎巴嫩、叙利亚等动荡国家及科摩罗等极度不发达国家。援助的物资既包括检测试剂、呼吸机、制氧机、N95口罩、血氧仪、救护车、电动医疗床、心电图机等医疗物资，也包括电脑等办公用品。中国援助联合国近东巴勒斯坦难民救济和工程处的物资已通过巴勒斯坦、约旦、黎巴嫩、叙利亚等地卫生中心发放给当地难民。

此外，双方企业、高校、民间组织、个人等也通过不同途径互相捐赠了难以计数的物资。

8.1.1.3 医疗经验交流

除医疗物资援助之外，中阿双方通过多主体、多渠道积极通报中国疫情状况、交流抗疫经验，为双方共克疫情提供了诸多有益经验。疫情发生后，中国驻阿拉伯国家使馆立即通过不同渠道与各国共享疫情信息。截至

---

① 《"一带一路"疫苗合作伙伴关系倡议（全文）》，新华社网站，http://www.xinhuanet.com/2021-06/24/c_1127592302.htm，2021年6月24日。
② 王广大：《携手抗疫推动中阿合作达到新高度》，《光明日报》2020年6月22日第12版。
③ 《中国外交部向阿盟捐赠第二批抗疫援助物资》，新浪网，https://news.sina.com.cn/c/2020-12-11/doc-iiznezxs6365863.shtml，2020年12月11日。

展，推进公共卫生、传统医药、卫生政策研究、健康产业等方面的合作。
六、鼓励在防控疫情的同时，继续开展共建'一带一路'合作，加强宏观经济政策协调，统筹推进经济社会发展。保持贸易投资市场开放，共同维护全球金融市场、产业链和供应链稳定。积极分享并利用数字贸易和创新技术，推动科学抗疫。共同致力于疫后复苏和经济发展，维护双方人民福祉和可持续增长。"①

2021年6月23日，中国与沙特、阿联酋等29个国家在"一带一路"亚太区域国际合作高级别会议期间共同发起"一带一路"疫苗合作伙伴关系倡议，推动全球疫苗合理分配。倡议指出："一、我们认为新冠肺炎疫情大流行是世界各国面临的共同挑战，团结合作是战胜疫情的关键。二、我们坚信应对疫情必须坚持人民至上、生命至上，只有各国普遍安全，本国才能安全。三、我们强调疫苗是应对疫情的重要工具，应作为全球公共产品公平分配，确保在发展中国家的可获得性、可及性和可负担性。四、我们忆及联合国大会及世界卫生大会有关决议以及联合国《全球公平获得新冠疫苗政治宣言》，呼吁开展开放、公平、非歧视的国际疫苗合作。五、我们赞赏联合国系统特别是世卫组织以及有关国家之间开展疫苗合作的努力。六、我们倡导'一带一路'合作伙伴聚焦以下合作：（一）加强疫苗监管政策沟通，共同确保疫苗的安全性和有效性。（二）鼓励有条件的疫苗生产国支持企业向世卫组织'新冠肺炎疫苗实施计划'（COVAX）提供更多疫苗。（三）支持各国政府和企业向发展中国家无偿捐赠疫苗，或以可负担的价格出口疫苗。（四）促进疫苗联合研发和技术交流，鼓励向发展中国家转让相关技术。（五）推动疫苗生产方与发展中国家建立疫苗联合生产伙伴关系，扩大全球疫苗生产。（六）鼓励区域和多边开发银行为发展中国家采购和生产疫苗提供更多优惠融资，同时尊重各国自主选择疫苗的权利。（七）加强'一带一路'互联互通合作，确保疫苗跨境运输畅通。

---

① 《中国和阿拉伯国家团结抗击新冠肺炎疫情联合声明》，中阿合作论坛网站，http://www.chinaarabcf.org/chn/lthyjwx/bzjhywj/djjbzjhy/202008/t20200810_6836919.htm，2020年8月10日。

发生再次表明，各国利益紧密相连，人类命运休戚与共。阿拉伯国家政党高度赞赏习近平主席提出的人类命运共同体理念，认为团结合作是战胜疫情最有力的武器，反对将疫情政治化、病毒标签化，呼吁各国加强抗疫合作和政策协调，支持世卫组织发挥领导作用，推进国际联防联控合作，共同构建人类卫生健康共同体。中方表示将推动落实习近平总书记在第73届世界卫生大会上作出的承诺，即中国新冠疫苗研发完成并投入使用后，将作为全球公共产品，为实现疫苗在发展中国家的可及性和可担负性作出中国贡献。"[1]

2020年7月6日，在中国—阿拉伯国家合作论坛第九届部长级会议中，中阿双方就团结抗击新冠肺炎进行了深入探讨，并共同签署《中国和阿拉伯国家团结抗击新冠肺炎疫情联合声明》，达成六点共识。"一、强调团结合作是国际社会战胜疫情的最有力武器。呼吁增强人类命运共同体意识，在抗疫合作中打造中阿命运共同体和中阿卫生健康共同体。二、强调多边主义的重要性，进一步加强和完善以联合国为核心的全球治理体系。支持世界卫生组织在全球公共卫生治理中发挥领导作用。呼吁国际社会各方加强协调，形成合力，有效开展国际联防联控，减少疫情负面影响。三、加强信息沟通、政策协调、行动配合，开展疫情防控交流与合作。中方愿继续通过提供物资援助、召开专家视频会议、派遣医疗专家组等方式，向急需支持的阿拉伯国家提供力所能及的支持和帮助，共建'健康丝绸之路'。四、强调面对全球卫生危机，负责任的公共信息传播至关重要。应本着科学的态度就防治等开展专业性交流，根据第73届世界卫生大会通过的新冠肺炎疫情决议，反对歧视任何国家、地区、民族和个人的言论和做法。五、利用中阿合作论坛框架下卫生合作机制开展抗疫合作，适时召开中国—阿拉伯国家卫生合作论坛会议。落实《中国—阿拉伯国家卫生合作2019北京倡议》，促进'中国—阿拉伯国家医疗健康合作联盟'发

---

[1] 《中国—阿拉伯国家政党对话会特别会议发表共同宣言》，新华社，http://www.xinhuanet.com/world/2020-06/24/c_1126156410.htm，2020年6月24日。

第8章 中阿卫生健康（抗疫）合作专题报告

面对新冠肺炎疫情这一突如其来的非传统安全威胁，中阿双方风雨同舟、守望相助，始终相互扶持，共同面对威胁与挑战，在医疗物资援助、专项医疗队援助、医疗经验交流、医疗物资采购、疫苗援助与生产等层面加强合作，并坚决反对将病毒标签化、政治化、污名化的企图，实现抗疫合作"全覆盖"。

8.1 中阿抗疫合作的总体情况

2020年以来，新冠肺炎疫情席卷全球，国际局势日新月异，面对各种困难与挑战，中阿在抗疫理念、物资援助、经验交流、医疗队援助、疫苗捐赠与生产等方面不断深化合作，为构建人类卫生健康共同体作出巨大贡献。

8.1.1 中阿抗疫合作不断深化

8.1.1.1 抗疫合作理念

新冠肺炎疫情发生以来，中阿各界多次发表共同宣言、联合声明，提出"一带一路"疫苗伙伴关系倡议，为双方加强抗疫合作指明方向。

2020年6月24日，中阿政党对话会特别会议发表题为《携手抗疫，共建新时代中阿命运共同体》的共同宣言，其中提到："新冠肺炎疫情的

作不仅提升了双方的合作水平，也为"一带一路"高质量发展注入新动力。中阿在新能源、清洁能源等领域的合作，实现了"一带一路"绿色、低碳、可持续发展的理念。①

在合作领域上，中阿的科技合作在诸多领域仍有广泛的开发空间，如技术转移、人工智能基础研究及其应用、信息技术、物联网和智慧城市、清洁能源和可再生能源、和平利用核能、环境保护、荒漠化防治和可持续发展、快速施工技术等。此外，双方还将努力加强在生物多样性保护领域的合作，共同推动生物多样性在能源、矿产开发、工业、健康和基础设施等领域的主流化。

在平台建设上，中国积极建设"一带一路"生态环保大数据服务平台，以及"一带一路"绿色发展国际联盟，均鼓励阿方参与，以共同推动绿色丝绸之路建设。同时，中阿双方在实现2030年可持续发展目标方面积极合作，交流经验并举办专门研讨会和联合活动，讨论和介绍双方在实现2030年可持续发展目标方面的最佳成功实践，中方还支持举办和参与阿拉伯可持续发展周。②

总之，从宏观上看，推动中阿科技创新协作，对于实现可持续发展、应对全球性挑战、完善全球科技治理、促进发展中国家发展均有积极意义。在中观、微观层面，中阿推行可持续的科技合作，是实现高质量共建"一带一路"的重要实践，向打造新时代中阿命运共同体迈出了坚实一步。

---

① 中国网，http://www.china.com.cn/opinion2020/2021－08/24/content＿77710484.shtml，2021年8月24日。
② 参见中阿合作论坛《中国—阿拉伯国家合作论坛2020年至2022年行动执行计划》，http://www.chinaarabcf.org/chn/lthyjwx/bzjhywj/djjbzjhy/202008/t20200810＿6836922.htm，2020年8月10日。

体现阿拉伯国家科技发展的特点，具有重要的战略意义。

第二，努力开拓多层次的合作空间。除了继续发挥中阿合作论坛等主要平台优势，开展项目合作、技术转移等合作模式以外，应加强对阿拉伯国家科技发展情况的实地调查和研究，建设民间交往机制，官方合作和民间合作并行，扩大合作主体范围。阿拉伯国家的科技创新水平总体上仍处于偏低水平，其内因、外因都值得深入研究分析，只有全面、深入了解阿拉伯各国科技创新的阻碍、挖掘其科技发展的重点关注和需求，才能更好推动中阿科技合作全面和常态化。例如，阿拉伯国家民营企业的科技水平较低，用于研发的资本有限，对于高科技人才的吸引力较弱，信息沟通不畅；复杂的国际形势，有差异的文明，都导致了中阿民间科技合作不够活跃，中阿科技合作主要靠政府推动。[①] 以2020年的中阿科技合作为例，中国与阿拉伯国家推进太阳能等可再生能源的项目、扩大天然气等清洁能源的项目等生态环境领域的合作，都是以政府为主导，国企为主体，民营企业参与较少。在这种情况下，可以建设科技合作的民间交往机制，引入更多的科技合作主体，科技企业也宜积极响应国家对阿拉伯国家的科技合作战略的号召，主动借力已有的合作平台和机制，通过参与中阿博览会等，向阿拉伯国家展示企业的技术特点和优势领域，对接阿拉伯国家科技发展的需求，提升企业的服务能力和国际知名度。

第三，开展可持续的中阿科技合作。中国坚持可持续发展的科学发展观，高度重视科技创新，坚持把创新作为引领发展的第一动力；积极顺应国际科技合作的大趋势，主动融入全球创新网络，实施更加开放包容、互惠共享的国际科技合作战略。中阿科技合作也将向可持续方向迈进、在创新中保持发展活力。

2021年8月19日召开的第五届中阿博览会，拓展了中阿之间在数字经济、人工智能、新能源等新兴领域的合作，意味着中阿"1+2+3"的合作格局在新时代再次实现了提质升级。中阿双方在科技含量更高领域的合

---

① 王辉：《中阿文化交流发展报告（2018）》，社会科学文献出版社，2019，第59页。

为中阿合作机制建设有效推进的关键点和突破口。此外,中阿合作目前主要推行的"1+2+3"合作格局,其中诸如核能、航天、新能源等领域的发展,归根结底也离不开科技创新。中阿科技合作符合新时期中阿战略伙伴关系的核心理念,有利于双方的共同发展和长远利益。

在新的大好形势下,中阿科技合作要迅速适应变化和需求,体现中阿特色,努力实现可持续的长期合作发展目标,使中阿科技合作在中国的科技发展战略、"走出去"战略、外交战略中充分发挥作用。我们可从以下几条路径着手。

第一,制定一套适合阿拉伯国家需求、体现阿拉伯特色的科技合作模式。大部分阿拉伯国家目前的科技创新水平仍处于较低水准。根据《2020年全球创新指数(GII)报告》,阿拉伯国家中只有阿联酋(34)、突尼斯(65)、沙特(66)处于榜单的前50%,其余大部分阿拉伯国家都处于较为靠后的位置,科技创新能力普遍不高。相比之下,中国的科技创新能力排在第14位,在中偏上收入国家中科技创新能力最强。因此,当前中阿科技合作总体而言水平不高。要推动中阿科技合作快速发展,中方必须因国施策,在确定重点合作领域的前提下,也要了解合作对象国的科技能力和优势,知晓对方发展的迫切需求,在技术薄弱国家加速技术转移,同技术发达国家加强技术研发合作,从而提高合作层次和效果。

其中,以科技人文交流为切入点可有效避开政治障碍,促进民心相通。同时,开展科技人文交流可以降低信息成本,促进国家间的信任与了解,还可以加深科技人员对相关技术的了解,进而提升研发创新能力。共建联合研发中心和技术转移平台是满足阿拉伯国家个性化需求、推进中阿科技合作长期稳定发展的关键。技术转移是科技创新能力较弱的阿拉伯国家提高本国生产力水平最直接有效的方式,也为国家的可持续发展提供保障。专有或专利技术的转移虽无法直接提升自主创新能力,却能够帮助突破技术瓶颈,在此基础上开展科技创新。而联合研发中心则能够帮助中国与具有经济和技术优势的阿拉伯国家在高新技术领域展开合作,实现突破。因此,在中阿科技合作中,联合实验室、技术转移平台的建设最能够

基地或试验区进行育种、繁殖、改良或研究。① 对于经济较发达、科研创新能力较高的阿拉伯国家，如沙特、阿联酋，则应加大力度建设联合研发中心，共建实验室，帮助中国与具有经济和技术优势的阿拉伯国家在高新技术领域展开合作，实现突破。如在"美丽多哈"项目中，中方表示希望与卡塔尔自由区共同建设中国—卡塔尔技术转移中心，共同推动中卡科技合作项目的落地实施，争取每年联合实施2~3个技术转移项目。中阿双方共同规划具体合作方向与路径，明确合作重点，确保合作成果切实服务于双方。

中阿生态环境方面的合作以荒漠化防治和能源开发领域的环保合作为主，合作机制逐渐完善，有良好的合作基础与需求。继续推动中阿生态环境创新合作，在宏观上有利于双方在应对全球环境问题、完善全球环境治理体系中实现合作共赢。在微观层面，对促进双方可持续发展均有积极意义。"中阿双方同属发展中国家，谋求合作时秉承平等原则。阿拉伯国家有意愿引进并学习我国技术，完善自身相关产业。双方在荒漠化防治、清洁能源、国际产能合作与基础设施建设的绿色化、绿色贸易、绿色金融等方面合作潜力巨大。这些都使得中阿合作前景广阔。"②

7.4 中阿科技合作展望

阿拉伯国家是"一带一路"倡议的天然战略合作伙伴，科技合作理应继续成为中阿关系友好发展的重要途径。

一方面，中阿合作涉及的国家众多，政治体制各不相同，科技作为一种基础性的契约交易，受到的阻碍通常较小；另一方面，阿拉伯国家多为新兴经济体和发展中国家，经济发展对科技的需求较大，科技合作因此成

---

① 王林伶：《中国与阿拉伯国家生态环境领域合作研究——兼论防沙治沙合作与技术输出》，《宁夏党校学报》2013年第6期。
② 《中阿博览会：面向世界讲述合作共赢新故事》，光明日报，https://m.gmw.cn/baijia/2021-08/23/35099322.html，2021年8月23日。

生态环境、生物多样性保护与应对气候变化方面的合作，共建绿色丝绸之路，强化基础设施绿色低碳化建设和运营管理，在建设中充分考虑气候变化的影响。

在共建"一带一路"的过程中，中阿生态环境合作正呈现出"多方面、深层次"的趋势。其中尤以与阿拉伯国家在自然条件、经济文化、生态环境等方面有着高度相似性的宁夏最具代表性。宁夏既是中阿进行经贸往来、文化交流的最主要通道，也是"一带一路"建设的重要支撑点。以宁夏为主的中国中西部地区与阿拉伯国家在许多方面具有良好的合作基础、合作条件和强烈的合作愿望，还具有很强的互补性与借鉴性。

第一，中阿生态环境合作要利用好已有的中阿合作论坛、中阿博览会及中阿技术转移与创新合作大会等逐步完善的合作机制，围绕科技创新积极设立新项目、开启新计划、提出新倡议。在中阿重点关注的能源开发领域的环保合作，农业生产领域的灌溉技术、海水淡化和荒漠化防治等合作中，开展以技术转移、项目合作、人文交流等为主的合作。重大项目的合作能够为科技资源在区域内及区域间的流动和共享提供便利，是发挥技术、经济溢出效应的基础，可为经济体带来"工程红利"，促进经济增长，为其科技发展提供经济和基础设施的保障。比如迪拜马克图姆太阳能电站项目，"2021面向'一带一路'国家现代农业节水技术线上培训班""阿拉伯国家防沙治沙技术培训班"等已有效推动中国先进技术、设备和人才走进阿拉伯国家，实现中阿在科技发展、技术转移方面的互利共赢。

第二，结合中国的发展战略，明确阿拉伯国家的发展特点及发展需求，确定重点合作领域，打造适合阿拉伯国家需求体现阿拉伯特色的生态环境合作模式。阿拉伯国家是我国实施"走出去"的重要市场，同时阿拉伯国家对我国粮食安全、生态环境等行业有可观的进口需求。对于自然资源短缺、农业生产方式落后、粮食供应短缺的阿拉伯国家，我国应加强农业技术输出，积极推动科研人员交流与培训，建立生产基地示范园区等。例如，可将宁夏成熟的草畜产业、沙漠经济作物等在阿拉伯地区建立生产

成功的哈电集团—阿联酋迪拜哈斯彦清洁燃煤电站项目,在环境保护方面付出的努力获得了迪拜政府的高度认可。①

2021年第五届中阿博览会的科技板块活动推出一系列清洁能源与绿色低碳转型技术相关的推介会,中国企业和研究机构在各类绿色环保技术的开发创新工作中锐意进取,为阿拉伯国家展示了一幅蓝图,活动涉及领域包括超低浓度瓦斯技术、城市黑臭河道高效治理与生态化修复技术、中亚干旱区全生物降解膜土壤环境保护与修复技术、成品油提炼净化技术、水安全评估与水资源高效利用技术、流域水环境综合治理优化技术等。②

长期以来,中阿科技人文交流一直是中阿科技合作的重要推手,主要表现为中国高度重视阿拉伯国家相关领域的人力资源开发,定期举办阿方人才培训班,促进分享重点领域的成功经验及良好实践。除"阿拉伯国家防沙治沙技术培训班"、"水土流失综合治理培训班"、"2021面向'一带一路'国家现代农业节水技术线上培训班"(2021年12月)之外,第五届中阿博览会举办技术转移与创新合作大会及6场技术成果推介对接会,形成十项具有推广价值的先进技术向"一带一路"共建国家推介,邀请院士专家为解决相关产业技术难题出谋划策。会议期间,阿拉伯科技与海运学院、埃及驻华大使馆文化教育科技处等阿拉伯国家机构表达了与中方联合举办技术培训、供需对接等活动的强烈意愿,认为培训班紧扣"一带一路"共建国家技术需求,将有力推动中阿博览会合作意向落地,持续提升中阿科技合作交流水平。

7.3.2 中阿生态环境合作前景

中国在《推动共建丝绸之路经济带和21世纪海上丝绸之路的愿景与行动》中,要求在合作贸易的过程中把生态文明建设放在突出位置,加强

---

① 《"中国造"中东首个清洁燃煤电站在迪拜一次并网成功》,国务院国有资产监督管理委员会网站,http://www.sasac.gov.cn/n2588025/n2588124/c14632536/content.html,2020年5月20日。

② 中国—阿拉伯国家技术转移中心网站(https://www.casttc.org/)2020~2021年新闻数据。

淡化公司（SWCC）通过其海水淡化技术研究所与中国自然资源部合作，着手开发海水淡化新技术，合作包括开发使用反渗透技术和蒸发技术的项目，采用多级效应方法标准化海水淡化技术。① 2021年8月，由中铁十八局参建的世界五大海水淡化工程之一阿联酋乌姆盖万150MIDG海水淡化项目正式进入收尾移交阶段。作为"2036阿联酋水安全战略"的重要工程之一，该项目是集海水淡化、蓄水、供水于一体的重点民生工程。② 2021年11月，中国电建EPC总承包的全球在建最大海水淡化工程——阿联酋塔维勒海水淡化项目正式产出合格饮用水。③

农业领域中的防治荒漠化和土地退化一直是阿拉伯国家关注的领域。国务院新闻办公室2021年1月发布的《新时代的中国国际发展合作》白皮书中提到，中国积极同其他国家分享自身有效的治沙技术和经验，围绕沙漠治理技术、水土流失综合治理等专题，组织实施了多期研修项目。甘肃打造国际荒漠化和土地沙化防治技术援助交流平台，先后举办了36期"中国沙漠治理技术和荒漠化防治国际培训班"。2006年首次在宁夏举办"阿拉伯国家防沙治沙技术培训班"，迄今已举办12期。中国还推广竹子、菌草种植与加工技术，在促进有关国家发展经济的同时，有效控制了水土流失和土地退化，为保护生态环境发挥了积极作用。第五届中阿博览会期间，中科院及宁夏大学等科研院校介绍了微藻固碳沙产业、基于无人机的荒漠种子雨生态工程技术等。

在环境保护方面，中国高度重视生态文明建设，与阿拉伯国家的电力基建合作从传统的火电、水电、输变电项目向清洁燃煤、大型联合循环电站等创新项目转型升级，培育发展新动能，最大限度减少大气污染排放，把保护当地生态圈环境作为共商共建过程中的重要方针。2020年5月并网

---

① 《沙特与中国合作开发海水淡化新技术》，中阿合作论坛网站，http://www.chinaarabcf.org/zagx/gjydyl/202106/t20210614_9155449.htm，2021年6月14日。

② 《中国企业在阿联酋助力民生发展》，中阿合作论坛网站，http://www.chinaarabcf.org/zagx/gjydyl/202108/t20210825_9155469.htm，2021年8月25日。

③ 《中国电建承包全球最大海水淡化工程》，中阿合作论坛网站，http://www.chinaarabcf.org/zagx/gjydyl/202111/t20211118_10449806.htm，2021年11月18日。

的运行机制。以 2004 年成立的"中阿合作论坛"框架为主，中阿合作论坛部长级会议、中阿博览会下设的中国—阿拉伯国家环境保护合作论坛等长效机制，规范并长期带领着中阿合作有效运行。第四届中阿技术转移与创新合作大会上宣布签署共建中国卡塔尔技术转移中心，计划在第五届会议时中阿双边技术转移中心增至 9 个。中国在生态环境方面取得的瞩目成就正通过越来越多的高效务实的技术转移信息服务平台向阿拉伯国家推广。

一方面，与阿拉伯国家生态环境相似的中国西部地区，自 20 世纪 60 年代迄今在以防沙治沙为代表的生态环境恢复方面积累了丰富的经验。近年来，在习近平主席"绿水青山就是金山银山"思想指导下，生态环境建设发展迅速，开展了规模宏大的天然林保护、退耕还林还草工程、封山禁牧、生态恢复与建设工程，实施了大气、水、土壤"十条"等环保计划，取得了丰硕的成果。另一方面，中阿在传统的能源开发领域的环保合作和荒漠化防治领域的合作已经构建了全方位立体的合作体系。

2020 年中阿第九届部长级会议制定的《中国—阿拉伯国家合作论坛 2020 年至 2022 年行动执行计划》中，涉及中阿生态环境的合作分别属于自然资源和环境、农业和人力资源开发等方面。2020 年至 2021 年，中方依托中阿合作论坛及中阿技术转移中心积极推进与阿方在环境保护、农业、荒漠化防治等方面的合作，通过项目建设、技术开发、专业人员培训等多渠道开展活动。

农业与水资源方面，中国与水资源缺乏、海水淡化需求迫切的海湾国家建立了长期合作项目。2020 年至 2021 年，该领域合作主要在节水灌溉、海水淡化上达成了多个项目合作。2020 年 8 月，中国与卡塔尔 NAAAS 集团通过线上签约达成投资额约 12.64 亿美元的"美丽多哈"项目，联合推动宁夏大学绿色智能节水灌溉技术与装备在卡塔尔示范应用，项目涉及粮食生产、节水绿化、节水农业、生态保护等领域。[①] 2021 年 6 月，沙特海水

---

① 《宁夏大学与卡塔尔自由区达成 12.64 亿美元合作协议》，中国—阿拉伯国家技术转移中心网站，https://www.casttc.org/article/00001107.html，2020 年 8 月 11 日。

7.3 中阿生态环境治理合作现状和前景

2021年10月在云南昆明召开的联合国《生物多样性公约》缔约方大会第十五次会议将主题定为"生态文明：共建地球生命共同体"，这是联合国环境公约缔约方大会首次将"生态文明"作为大会主题。与自然和谐相处是21世纪的一个决定性任务。习近平主席在第三次"一带一路"建设座谈会上重点提到绿色低碳发展和生态环境治理，指出要支持发展中国家能源绿色低碳发展，推进绿色低碳发展信息共享和能力建设，深化生态环境和气候治理合作。中国和阿拉伯国家在快速的经济发展工业化、城镇化的进程中，面临着同样的大气、水以及一些新兴的环境问题，在环境保护领域开展合作有高度的契合点，双方正迎来新的环保合作机遇。

7.3.1 中阿生态环境合作现状

阿拉伯国家主要分布在干旱地区。中国西部干旱区属于欧亚大陆内陆腹地旱区，是生态环境严重脆弱地区。中阿存在相同的生态环境问题。然而，多数阿拉伯国家由于对科学技术和农业发展的投资不足，其农业生产率低下，自然资源进一步退化。因此，制定和实施包含环境的长期战略可持续发展计划是阿拉伯国家的当务之急。近年来，海湾地区和北非的部分阿拉伯国家开始重视区域合作，鼓励国内外对绿色基础设施项目的投资。卡塔尔、沙特、阿联酋、约旦、科威特等国在国家发展愿景中，都提出将环境保护作为核心议题之一，[①] 这无疑为中阿在生态环境领域的合作打开了新的格局，提供了更广阔的合作空间。

2006年，中阿环境合作会议在阿联酋迪拜召开，拉开了中阿环境合作实践与研究的帷幕。如今，中阿双方合作已经形成了坚实的基础和良好

---

① 邹志强：《2030年可持续发展议程与阿拉伯国家发展转型》，《阿拉伯世界研究》2020年第3期。

7.2.4 医疗卫生合作

2021年是全球疫情发生以来各国医疗卫生遭受严峻考验的关键时期，中国与阿拉伯国家不畏疫情，紧紧围绕双方在医疗卫生领域的急切需求，密切开展疫苗研发与生产、医护人员培训、技术转移等重点项目的深度合作，共同应对全球疫情。

其一，中方全力推动中国疫苗成为全球公共产品，积极帮助阿拉伯国家建设新冠疫苗生产线，以改善阿拉伯国家的疫苗供应情况。2021年3月，中国疫苗生产线项目在阿联酋启动，该疫苗工厂拥有3条灌装线和5条自动包装线，疫苗年生产量将达到2亿剂，使阿联酋将成为海湾地区第一个拥有新冠疫苗生产基地的国家，其疫苗供应将辐射整个中东地区。2021年5月21日，埃及从中国采购新一批国药疫苗和首批科兴疫苗原液，由此成为非洲大陆第一个同中国合作生产新冠疫苗的国家。"努力让疫苗成为各国人民用得上、用得起的公共产品"是中国的庄严承诺。中阿疫苗技术合作将为中东抗疫注入动力，也是中阿两国为全球早日取得抗疫胜利贡献力量。

其二，中方采用线上培训的创新方式，邀请曾奋战在防疫一线的专家分享个人防护措施以及我国在防控新冠肺炎疫情中的经验，为阿拉伯国家学员答疑解惑。2021年3月25日，由宁夏对外科技交流中心（中阿技术转移中心）举办的首期面向"一带一路"沿线国家正确认识和预防新型冠状病毒线上培训如期进行。本次培训班得到了宁夏科技厅社发处与宁夏医科大学总医院科研处的鼎力支持，协调专家专题授课，共有来自埃及、阿联酋、苏丹、伊拉克、尼日利亚、泰国等国家的20多名学员参加了此次培训。[1]

---

[1]《首期面向"一带一路"沿线国家正确认识和预防新型冠状病毒线上培训如期举行》，中国—阿拉伯国家技术转移中心网站，https://www.casttc.org/article/00001074.html，2021年3月26日。

建设配套地面测控站和地面应用系统，并对埃及的航天专家和人才进行联合培训。项目完成后，埃及将成为第一个具有完备的卫星总装集成测试能力的非洲国家，具备两颗 600 公斤级卫星的并行研制能力，这提升了埃及的航天能力，展现了航天领域的中国风貌，促进了中埃之间的友好合作关系。

更受瞩目的是中阿北斗合作项目，该项目是由习近平主席倡议、中国卫星导航系统管理办公室与阿拉伯信息通信技术组织签署的中阿卫星导航合作谅解备忘录中明确的优先合作项目。目前，北斗已在突尼斯、阿尔及利亚等地建立 CORS 系统，可为用户提供实时、连续、稳定的精确 GNSS 定位信息数据及时间信息；在沙特、阿尔及利亚、黎巴嫩、阿曼、摩洛哥等国家，北斗已用于国土测绘、交通运输、精细农业、环境监测、非传统安全等多个领域；在阿联酋，北斗与物联网等技术相结合，应用于铁路建设的施工机械、物料、人员、场地进出关口等各类监管对象中。

2021 年 12 月 8 日，第三届中阿北斗合作论坛在北京成功举办，这也是北斗三号全球卫星导航系统正式建成开通后举办的首届论坛。会上，总结了中阿北斗五年来的合作经验与成果，共同签署了《中国—阿拉伯国家卫星导航领域合作行动计划（2022—2023 年）》，计划将于 2022 年至 2023 年，通过运用北斗/GNSS 技术，在具有应用规模的重点领域，联合实施不少于 5 个示范应用项目；共同推动在感兴趣的阿拉伯国家，增建 1~2 个北斗/GNSS 中心；每年举办 1~2 次卫星导航技术短期培训班；中方每年为阿拉伯国家提供 3~5 名导航与通信专业硕士学位研究生奖学金名额；每年互派 1~2 批短期访问学者；继续联合开展北斗/GNSS 联合测试与评估活动并发布测试结果；联合开展北斗国际搜救返向链路性能测试；利用中阿卫星导航合作网站，宣传双方合作成果，吸纳更多参与者，促进合作深化与发展，让北斗更好地服务阿拉伯国家，实现共享共赢。①

---

① 《第三届中阿北斗合作论坛在北京成功举办》，北斗卫星导航系统网站，http：//www.beidou.gov.cn/zt/gjhz/202112/t20211214_23441.html，2021 年 12 月 8 日。

供包括5G、人工智能、云计算等技术培训,并承诺为埃及国家通信研究院培养200名国家级培训讲师。①

此外,中阿科技在人工智能领域的合作还包括开展以技术转移为中心的数字化合作。浙江执御信息技术有限公司运营的电商平台,目前已覆盖阿联酋、阿曼、巴林、卡塔尔、科威特和沙特六国80%以上的互联网用户,公司与政府部门合作,积极分享数字平台的先进技术与经验。2020年10月22日举办的全球人工智能峰会上,华为与沙特数据与人工智能局在线签署了国家人工智能能力发展计划谅解备忘录,支持沙特实现数字化转型,并通过与沙特的合作,创造人工智能等技术领域的新价值。

7.2.3 航天合作

航天作为当今尖端科技的代表,是中阿双方重要的合作领域。在"一带一路"合作倡议的框架下,中阿双方共同建设"天基丝绸之路"。中国利用在航天领域的优势技术,围绕空间科学、发射服务、卫星应用、深空探测、载人航天和航天基础设施建设等议题,整合各类航天资源开展国际合作,为"一带一路"共建国家的经济发展、社会进步和民生改善提供有力支撑。

近两年,中阿在航天领域主要以项目合作的方式进行,包含中国援埃及二号卫星项目和中阿北斗合作项目。前者是首个由中国航天科技集团所属的中国空间技术研究院负责、由商务部和国家国际发展合作署出资支持的海外卫星项目。2020年7月15日,中国援埃及二号卫星项目宣布,其技术文件近日已全部通过评审,这标志着该卫星已全面进入研制生产阶段。

中国援埃及二号卫星是在"一带一路"倡议框架下,采用联合模式研制的卫星,部分研制工作将在中国援建的埃及卫星总装集成测试中心完成。项目内容包括:为埃及在轨交付1颗2米/8米分辨率光学遥感卫星,

---

① 《中阿加强数字化合作》,中阿合作论坛网,http://www.chinaarabcf.org/zagx/gjydyl/202007/t20200710_6842182.htm,2020年7月10日。

签约埃及—沙特±500千伏超高压直流输电线路EPC项目。该项目是中东北非区域电压等级最高、输送距离最长的直流输电项目。项目线路总长335千米，对优化埃及电力系统结构、解决当地就业、促进当地经济社会发展具有重要意义。中国能建埃及代表处总经理姚刚表示，该项目从谈判到近期确定选址历经十年，中国企业始终坚守，并在疫情中实现项目落地。①

7.2.2 人工智能合作

近两年，中阿在人工智能领域的合作主要体现在中国对阿人才培养上，其中最具代表性的是华为企业社会责任旗舰项目"未来种子"。该项目于2008年启动，旨在培养当地的信息和通信技术（ICT）人才，加强知识转移，促进ICT行业的国际交流。目前，已有130个国家和地区加入该项目，其中阿拉伯国家占据14席。

2020年10月20日，第五届"未来种子"项目在阿尔及利亚举行启动仪式，暨第二届阿尔及利亚华为ICT大赛颁奖仪式，吸引超3000名阿尔及利亚学生踊跃参与。2021年3月16日，华为在突尼斯举办"突尼斯人才日"，自华为在突尼斯建立信息通信技术培训学院以来，已与数十所高校签署协议，为4000余名突尼斯学生提供线上课程，选拔超过80名突尼斯学生加入"未来种子"项目。2021年8月23日，"未来种子"项目在巴林获得了国际人工智能组织的认可，国际人工智能集团总裁贾西姆·哈吉博士称其为"支持巴林ICT生态系统的关键支柱"。同年9月，华为在卡塔尔举行了2021年"未来种子"项目的结业仪式。

除"未来种子"项目外，中国在阿拉伯国家开展了多方位的人才培养和技术支持行动。2020年6月，华为与埃及通信和信息技术部在阿斯旺大学开设了"人工智能教室"项目，为教育资源相对匮乏的阿斯旺等省份提

---

① 《中企承建埃及—沙特超高压直流输电线路项目签约》，新华网，https：//baijiahao.baidu.com/s？id=1712866235672971841&wfr=spider&for=pc，2021年10月6日。

快速增长,清洁能源在能源消费总量中的比重持续提升。阿拉伯国家也正在积极寻求能源转型,改变依赖化石能源的局面。

在天然气储能、运输技术方面,2020年4月中国船舶集团有限公司与卡塔尔石油公司联合签署《中国船舶—卡塔尔石油液化天然气船建造项目协议》,并于2021年10月完成首批订单:建造4艘17.4万立方米液化天然气(LNG)运输船。中卡双方表示,要将该项目打造成中国船舶集团与卡塔尔石油、卡塔尔天然气合作的基石,中卡两国"一带一路"建设的桥梁和典范。[①] 2020年10月中国石油天然气管道工程有限公司阿布扎比分公司正式确认中标阿联酋国家天然气管网升级FEED(前端工程设计)项目,该项目作为阿联酋民生工程,将对阿联酋能源安全起到至关重要的作用,是阿联酋国家能源战略性项目。[②]

在清洁燃煤领域合作方面,2016年6月,哈电集团哈尔滨电气国际工程有限责任公司与通用电气公司组成联合体,赢得阿联酋迪拜哈斯彦4×600兆瓦清洁燃煤电站项目合同。2020年5月,迪拜哈斯彦项目1号机组一次并网成功。作为"一带一路"国际合作重大工程项目,同时也是中东首个清洁燃煤电站,哈斯彦成功并网发电标志着世界第一个能实现双燃料满负荷供电的电站建设取得重大突破。同时,哈斯彦项目也是实现迪拜能源多元化的重要一步。[③]

7.2.1.3 电力能源合作有效推进

在电力能源运输方面,2021年10月5日,中国能源建设股份有限公司、中国西电集团有限公司和埃及吉萨电缆工业公司组成的联合体,成功

[①] 《"一带一路"新成果》,中阿合作论坛网站,http://www.chinaarabcf.org/zagx/gjydyl/202110/t20211011_10131714.htm,2021年10月11日。

[②] 《中国石油管道工程有限公司中标阿联酋国家天然气管网升级FEED项目》,中阿合作论坛网站,http://www.chinaarabcf.org/zagx/gjydyl/202010/t20201012_6842267.htm,2020年10月12日。

[③] 《"中国造"中东首个清洁燃煤电站在迪拜一次并网成功》,国务院国有资产监督管理委员会网站,http://www.sasac.gov.cn/n2588025/n2588124/c14632536/content.html,2020年5月20日。

点项目，中方通过人才交流培训与技术转移与阿方展开合作，推动数字经济、跨境电商等领域的发展；在航天卫星研制技术方面，中方积极开展相关技术援助，并通过论坛对话合作形式进行技术的转移与推广。

7.2.1 新能源合作

中阿共同面临着保障能源安全和实现能源转型的重大课题，低碳能源领域成为双方关注的焦点。大力发展可再生能源，构建清洁低碳、安全高效能源体系已成为全球趋势，这一趋势也是深化中阿能源合作的良机。2020年至2021年，中阿能源合作领域不断拓宽，由传统能源合作转向多元能源合作，且合作水平有效提升。现阶段，中阿双方的能源合作主要从油气领域向太阳能、电力等领域扩展。

7.2.1.1 太阳能等可再生能源项目合作遍地开花

在新能源领域，中阿以太阳能光伏发电技术项目合作最为广泛、深入，取得了丰硕的成果和良好的国际效应。该领域的合作对象主要以海湾国家为主，如：中国在卡塔尔建设的光伏项目将成为世界第三大单体光伏项目及最大运用跟踪系统和双面组件的光伏项目，该项目将为2022年卡塔尔世界杯的比赛场馆供电；与沙特合作的红海综合智慧能源项目，不仅开发太阳能和可再生能源，还为海水淡化、废水处理等提供综合基础设施；2021年8月，中国还与伊拉克签署了建设2000兆瓦光伏电站的协议；"一带一路"重点项目——迪拜马克图姆太阳能公园五期900兆瓦光伏项目A期正式实现全容量并网发电，成为迄今为止迪拜境内最大的光伏电站项目；中资企业在约旦承建的首个光伏电站项目——约旦第仕24兆瓦光伏项目于2021年8月正式施工。

这些项目的成功实施不仅可以解决阿拉伯国家电力短缺的困境，为当地居民带去健康、安全、清洁的生活，还创造了大量的就业机会，同时，帮助阿拉伯国家降低对传统能源的依赖，推动了经济多元化发展。

7.2.1.2 天然气等清洁能源项目合作稳步推进

近年来，我国加快推进能源绿色转型进程，煤改气等带动天然气消费

坛、第四届中阿技术转移和创新合作大会，开展了一系列产品、技术推介活动与合作推进交流会。中阿技术转移中心与阿拉伯国家机构、企业保持密切联系，有序开展各个层次的科技合作。据统计，两年内中阿技术转移中心举办面向阿拉伯国家的行业培训班2次（农业节水技术及新冠肺炎预防），促成投资协议12.64亿美元（宁夏大学与卡塔尔自由区），推进重大工程项目3次（阿联酋迪拜哈斯彦清洁燃煤电站项目等），务实推动中阿科技合作与技术转移工作向前迈进。

四项科技合作稳步推进，并以联合共建或中方承建的形式，在阿拉伯国家建立大型科技项目，多为新能源和航天领域的合作；技术转移指中国向阿拉伯国家关于某种成熟技术的国际转移，如海水淡化技术、航天技术等，其中2020~2021年以医疗卫生的技术转移为甚。疫情期间，中国疫苗技术的输出为无数阿拉伯人民提供了生命保障。人文交流则更多体现在中国对阿拉伯科技领域人才的培养上，过去两年中阿在人工智能领域的交流非常普及，以华为公司为例，在阿拉伯国家广泛开展"未来种子"计划，在当地培养出了一大批在通信技术、5G、云计算等领域具有国际化视野的高新技术人才，为中阿的合作和交流奠定了坚实的基础。

7.2 中阿科技合作的重点领域

在"一带一路"倡议推动下，中阿各领域合作愈加密切深入，除传统能源领域外，清洁能源、人工智能、数字经济、医疗卫生、航天合作等领域也不断开拓创新，为双方合作注入新动力。

新时期中阿科技合作的重点领域在延续了传统能源合作的基础上，更多转向低碳能源领域，并且逐渐扩展到可再生能源领域，2020年至2021年尤其以光伏发电项目、大规模储能项目、清洁能源项目最为蓬勃发展。在其他产业合作中，医疗卫生、通信技术与航天领域的合作都取得新的突破：中阿双方积极合作，共同推进阿拉伯国家新冠疫苗的生产与供应；围绕5G、人工智能、云计算、电子产业技术、电子光学产业等高新技术重

络，打造综合信息服务平台，开展一系列技术对接与转移活动，不断推进中阿技术转移中心工作的专业化、机制化。自2015年9月起，中国与阿拉伯国家相继共建了阿盟、埃及、阿曼等8个双边技术转移中心，举办20多期跨国技术人才培训班，培养出300多名具有"种子"效应的国际合作技术转移人才；① 中阿双方共建中阿技术转移协作机构网络，与国内外企业、科研机构、高等学校、中介服务机构等组建协作机构网络，协作网络成员已达4264家；依托日益扩大完善的协作网络，中阿技术转移中心主持或参与各类协作网络建议研讨会、科技转化与科技战略学术研讨会等探讨活动；依托中阿科技园专项，启动中阿科技项目20多个，在椰枣、农业物联网、绿色智能节水装备、卫星数据服务、马铃薯食品开发等领域建立了一系列中阿科技创新平台。

7.1.2 中阿科技合作传统领域与合作模式

中国和阿拉伯国家建交以来，双方的合作在20世纪农业、能源、基建等领域的基础上不断拓展深化。迈入21世纪之后，中国在科学技术领域快速进步，而阿拉伯国家虽大多资源较为丰富，但随着资源的不断消耗，其对科技研发的重视不断升级，与中国的合作意向日渐加强，为中阿科技合作奠定了坚实基础。近年来国内外学界开展的相关研究显示，中阿在科技领域的合作，开始聚焦于环境保护、水资源、信息网络、高铁、新能源等领域，同时逐渐加强技术转移和成果应用转化。

2017年5月，习近平主席在"一带一路"国际合作高峰论坛上提出启动"一带一路"科技创新行动计划，开展科技人文交流、共建联合实验室、科技园区合作、技术转移等四项行动。

2020年至2021年，在新冠肺炎疫情影响全球的形势下，中阿交流互访和合作开展受到较大影响，但中阿合作论坛、中阿技术转移创新合作大会机制保持积极运作，分别举办了第九届部长级会议、第三届中阿北斗论

---

① 王莉莉：《共建一带一路，中阿合作不断焕发新活力》，《中国对外贸易》2021年第9期。

第7章 中阿科技与生态环境治理合作专题报告

中阿科技与生态环境治理合作是中阿经贸合作的重要领域，对提升中阿人民的生活舒适度、便利度和幸福指数都具有十分重要的意义。

7.1 中阿科技合作框架和传统领域

科学技术是第一生产力。改革开放以来，中国制定了中长期科技振兴战略，加强国际科技合作，从学习规则、对标规范到引领规制。近二十年来，中国政府积极出台相关科技政策文件，不断深化新时代中阿科技往来的顶层设计，为中阿科技交流与合作提供了系统规划并指明发展方向。

7.1.1 合作框架

中阿科技合作框架以中阿合作论坛为主的长效机制稳步推进，合作层次不断提高，呈现以论坛为框架，以中阿博览会、中阿技术转移与创新合作大会等为平台，以中阿技术转移中心、联合研究中心为合作基地的多边、多面开展模式。

中阿合作论坛在推动中阿双边科技交往中起到了关键的引领作用，并不断推进中阿合作向正规化、机制化发展。中阿技术转移中心依托中阿博览会，紧紧围绕中阿科技合作的切实需求，开放构建中阿技术转移协作网

建设的政策措施、重点实施领域可以作为中国建设智慧城市的重要参照。智慧城市建设需要将云计算、大数据、区块链等最新技术大量运用至公共交通、医疗卫生、信息安全、环境保护等领域，这对阿拉伯国家的科技创新能力和科技人才储备提出极大挑战，也为中阿智慧城市合作提供广阔空间。

第三，精耕跨境电子商务市场。阿拉伯国家数字经济发展水平整体偏低，但与中国贸易往来优势互补，是中国第七大贸易伙伴，中国也已成为阿拉伯国家第一大贸易伙伴。据统计，中国电商平台在海湾六国互联网用户覆盖率已达80%。① 随着阿拉伯国家在日均上网时长、青年上网率和在线购买率等方面水平不断攀升，以及新冠肺炎疫情因素倒逼沙特、阿联酋等原本倚重传统国际贸易方式的阿拉伯国家逐渐转向电子商务，中阿跨境电商发展迎来拓展空间。但我们同时也应意识到，由于阿拉伯地区跨境电商市场竞争愈发激烈，以及中美贸易摩擦叠加新冠肺炎疫情对全球商品流动性产生阻碍，大量缺乏供应链、资金链优势的电商企业难以为继。因此，中国丝路电商需要从"野蛮生长"向"精耕细作"转型，② 未来以数字产品与服务、数字化知识与信息作为贸易标的的跨境电商，在阿拉伯地区将会获得更大的市场空间。

第四，智慧城市将成为中阿数字经济合作亮点。智慧城市与新基建存在天然的联系。智慧城市是新基建的主要应用场景，新基建在升级智慧城市基础设施、赋能智慧城市治理方面发挥着不可替代的作用。③ 中阿智慧城市交流互鉴也会因双边数字基础设施建设合作的不断深化，成为未来中阿数字经济合作的重要方向。同时，我国要认识到阿拉伯各国数字化水平的严重差异导致不同国家在智慧城市建设中呈现出不均衡态势的现实，可参考不同阿拉伯国家的政策体系和技术层面的完善程度，有针对性地开展智慧城市合作。根据洛桑国际管理学院世界竞争力中心的《智慧城市指数2020》④ 排名，近些年阿布扎比、迪拜等阿拉伯城市的发展趋势不断提升，超过中国的主要城市。所以，海湾阿拉伯国家智慧城市

---

① 《〈阿数据安全合作倡议〉开启全球数字治理新篇章》，中华人民共和国中央人民政府网站，http://www.gov.cn/xinwen/2021-03/30/content_5596690.htm，2021年3月30日。
② 乔彩：《跨境电商增长势头猛》，人民网，http://finance.people.com.cn/n1/2021/0222/c1004-32033286.html，2021年2月22日。
③ 杜庆昊：《新时代数字经济发展的主要方向》，《开放导报》2020年第6期。
④ IMD, "Smart City Index 2020", https://www.imd.org/smart-city-observatory/smart-city-index/, 2021-04-14.

的"共商、共建、共享"原则，共同推进数字经济合作。基于阿拉伯国家数字经济水平现状分析，中阿数字经济合作还需继续取得进展。

第一，加强与阿拉伯国家的数字基础设施建设合作。网络基础设施水平是推动一国数字经济发展的首要条件，基于阿拉伯国家对发展数字基础设施的强大需求，双方可进一步深化需求对接，例如推动5G网络、大数据存储、云平台等数字基础设施建设。一方面，随着部分阿拉伯国家的移动通信从完全的政府垄断逐渐走向竞争，当地国外数字企业获得了良好的发展与成长环境，我国数字企业应及时把握该地区具有开放性和竞争性的移动通信市场机遇；[①] 另一方面，我国具备全球最完整的产业链，能够依托成熟技术推动阿拉伯国家迅速建成和升级数字基础设施，间接促进该地区中产阶级接受并形成网络购物的消费习惯，从而带动支付与数据一体化发展。此外，中国还可将抗击疫情与新基建结合起来，助推医疗健康基础设施建设领域产生的新技术与新应用扩展到阿拉伯国家的疫后重建。

第二，实施中阿数字人才交流和培训计划。阿拉伯国家数字产业发展基础差异较大，我国既可以与阿拉伯国家联合推动构建深度融合的科教互利合作共同体，也可以根据阿拉伯各国不同的发展特点，开展差异化人才交流和培养合作项目。双方可考虑举办数字能力建设研讨会开展深入交流；[②] 通过加强中阿高校和教育机构合作，联建数字经济特色学科、专业和培教基地，搭建人才培养、科技研发平台载体，为阿拉伯国家提供课程研发、人员培训等方面的优质教育服务；鼓励中国科研机构、企业（如华为、中兴、腾讯）等同阿拉伯各国设立联合研发中心和创新平台，为当地培养专业性技术人才提供针对性的数字教育解决方案。在合作过程中也要重视培养既懂技术又懂阿拉伯语、法语、英语等外语的复合型人才，提升沟通的能力。

[①] 林颖、陈炳福、李泡东、柯冠岩、冯松鹤：《以基础型信息应用激活"一带一路"沿线国家信息基础设施建设》，《中国工程科学》2019年第4期。
[②] 和音：《共创共享繁荣美好的未来》，《人民日报》2021年7月18日第2版。

网龙网络公司开发的在线教育电子学习平台"埃德莫多"受到埃及教育和技术教育部部长塔里克·史威基的强烈推荐，为埃及受停课影响的2200万名学生和100万多名教师提供远程学习支持。① 2020年11月，中国文化和旅游部与阿联酋文化和青年部共同主办的首届"中阿数字文创展"采用3D虚拟建筑空间"CBox"作为线上展示平台，让两国观众不受时空约束，沉浸式体验中阿特色文创作品的数字文化魅力。② 在经贸合作领域，2020年7月，由中国贸促会和阿联酋经济部联合主办的首届"中国—阿联酋经济贸易数字展览会"采用云展平台方式吸引了中国和阿联酋的2100家企业参展，来自中国、阿联酋、埃及、摩洛哥等11国的1.2万余家采购商参与对接。2021年5月24日，我国成功举办了第四届进博会中东国家线上推介会，来自迪拜海关、阿布扎比国家石油公司、卡塔尔自由贸易区等近150位中东国家政府和企业代表线上参会。③ 2021年8月19～22日，第五届中国—阿拉伯国家博览会首次以线上为主方式举办，总访问量突破1000万人次。其间，中阿双方签订各类合作文件277个，涉及计划投资和贸易总额1566.7亿元人民币，并发布政策报告、签署备忘录协议54个。④

6.3 中阿数字经济合作前景

数字经济是全球未来的发展方向。⑤ 中阿可结合"一带一路"所秉承

---

① 《中国与阿拉伯国家促进数字合作》，人民网，http://arabic.people.com.cn/n3/2020/0709/c31660-9708802.html，2020年7月9日。
② 《动画与数字艺术学院参与设计"中阿数字文创展"》，中国传媒大学网站，http://www.cuc.edu.cn/news/2020/1127/c1902a176264/page.htm，2020年11月27日。
③ 《第四届进博会"云招展"走进中东》，中国经济网，http://www.ce.cn/xwzx/gnsz/gdxw/202105/28/t20210528_36596486.shtml，2021年5月28日。
④ 《携手打造面向新时代的中阿命运共同体 推动中阿共建"一带一路"达到更高水平——第五届中国-阿拉伯国家博览会成功举办》，商务部网站，http://xyf.mofcom.gov.cn/article/cr/202109/20210903195308.shtml，2021年9月6日。
⑤ 《习近平：数字经济是全球未来的发展方向，创新是亚太经济腾飞的翅膀》，中央人民政府网站，http://www.gov.cn/xinwen/2020-11/20/content_5563088.htm，2020年11月20日。

建设合作促进信息互联互通的谅解备忘录》。① 2018年7月，国家主席习近平在中阿合作论坛第八届部长级会议开幕式上的讲话指出：中阿双方"要努力实现金融合作、高新技术合作'两翼'齐飞"，"要落实好中阿科技伙伴计划"，以及"要加快网上丝绸之路建设，争取在网络基础设施、大数据、云计算、电子商务等领域达成更多合作共识和成果"，中国将再从阿拉伯国家"邀请300名科技人员来华研讨"，"再为阿拉伯国家提供1万个各类培训名额"。② 2020年7月，中国—阿拉伯国家合作论坛第九届部长级会议发表《中国—阿拉伯国家合作论坛2020年至2022年行动执行计划》并指出，在双边经济领域合作上"加强双方在互联网和数字经济发展领域的合作与互鉴"，在科技合作领域要"加强科技人文交流合作"，并"邀请阿方科技管理和技术人员参与中国科技部每年举办的'先进适用技术与科技管理培训班'"，共同"探讨开展科技园区合作"。③ 中阿已建立了稳定交流的多层机制合作平台，常态化的多层交流机制将促进双边数字经济合作走深走实。

第二，中阿在关键领域数字经济合作进展卓有成效。中阿关系在新时代正在拓展新边疆并呈现新的发展态势，尤其近一两年，新冠肺炎疫情持续肆虐全球，推进中阿数字经济合作上升至新高度。在医疗合作领域，2020年3月阿联酋人工智能公司（G42）宣布与中国深圳的"华大基因"合作，设立用于检测和诊断新冠肺炎病例的大型检测实验室。该实验室在最初3个月内为阿联酋约1000万人完成超过300万次检测，阿联酋也因此跻身全球检测率最高的国家行列。④ 在人文教育领域，疫情期间由中国

---

① 《发展改革委与埃及通信和信息技术部签署关于加强"网上丝绸之路"建设合作促进信息互联互通的谅解备忘录》，中央人民政府网站，http：//www.gov.cn/xinwen/2017-01/22/content_5162147.htm，2017年1月22日。
② 习近平：《携手推进新时代中阿战略伙伴关系》，《人民日报》2018年7月11日第2版。
③ 《中国—阿拉伯国家合作论坛2020年至2022年行动执行计划》，中阿改革发展研究中心网站，http：//infadm.shisu.edu.cn/_s114/07/09/c7779a132873/page.psp，2018年8月19日。
④ 《中国与海湾国家间的伙伴关系能够度过当前全球危机》，丝路国际产能合作促进中心网站，http：//weixin.bricc.org.cn/Module_Think/ThinkPortal/ArticleDetail.aspx？aid=2756，2020年7月22日。

技术协议。① 疫情防控以来，中国与海湾阿拉伯国家快速推进新技术领域合作。2020年6月，华为与沙特智慧城市解决方案公司（SC2）签署协议，开展沙特智慧城市项目合作；② 10月，沙特数据与人工智能局与中国华为公司建立合作伙伴关系，与华为在线签署了国家人工智能能力发展计划谅解备忘，将共同推动沙特国家人工智能发展计划。③ 此外，埃及是阿拉伯世界首个建立华为5G基站的国家，疫情防控期间其通信和信息技术部与华为在阿斯旺大学建立的人工智能培训项目"人工智能教室"，为当地和其他相对缺乏教育资源的省份提供必要的技术培训。④

6.2.2 中阿数字经济合作进展

第一，中国不断创新中阿数字经济合作机制。近年来，我国秉承"共商共建共享"原则不断创新中阿数字经济合作机制。2016年12月，"中国—阿拉伯国家网上丝绸之路经济合作试验区暨宁夏枢纽工程"获国家批复，成为中国与阿拉伯国家开展高层对话、经贸合作、文化交流的网上平台，重点在宽带信息基础设施、卫星应用服务、大数据、云计算、跨境电商、智慧城市等新兴产业领域开展对阿合作。⑤ 2017年，中国与阿联酋、沙特等国家在第四届世界互联网大会上共同发起《"一带一路"数字经济国际合作倡议》⑥、与埃及政府联合签署了《关于加强"网上丝绸之路"

---

① 《任正非接受中东媒体采访：华为没犯错，美国制裁是政治目的》，观察者网，https://baijiahao.baidu.com/s?id=1649237516262391504&wfr=spider&for=pc，2019年11月4日。
② 《华为与SC2公司达成合作 为沙特打造智慧城市》，环球网，https://baijiahao.baidu.com/s?id=1670917657561774548&wfr=spider&for=pc，2020年6月30日。
③ 《沙特数据与人工智能局与华为建立合作伙伴关系》，新华社网站，https://baijiahao.baidu.com/s?id=1681265438967428264&wfr=spider&for=pc，2020年10月22日。
④ 景玥、黄培昭：《中阿加强数字化合作（患难见真情 共同抗疫情）》，《人民日报》2020年7月9日第3版。
⑤ 《打造网上丝绸之路，助力"一带一路"建设》，国务院新闻办公室网站，http://www.scio.gov.cn/31773/35507/35519/Document/1537340/1537340.htm，2016年12月29日。
⑥ 《〈多国共同发起"一带一路"数字经济国际合作倡议〉发布》，新华网，http://www.xinhuanet.com/zgjx/2017-12/04/c_136798586.htm，2017年12月4日。

国家的信息技术渗透程度和传输速度难以支撑本国数字经济的进一步发展。中国可分享数字化转型的变革红利，提升阿拉伯国家的数字化建设能力；发挥中国互联网、数字经济产业的优势，推动中国智能化产品服务阿拉伯国家数字经济发展需求；推广我国共享经济、"互联网+金融"等先进理念，促进阿拉伯国家数字经济开放、创新发展；共享我国电子商务在平台建设、物流服务管理方面的成熟技术与经验，引领阿拉伯国家数字经济走向高速发展道路。

第三，阿拉伯国家数字基础设施建设需要中国支持。阿拉伯国家数字人口红利带来的庞大5G市场规模，是中国与之加速数字基础设施合作的重要因素。据电信巨头爱立信预测，5G技术将在中东北非地区取得较大突破，预计到2025年其5G用户数将达到8000万，占全球移动用户的10%。[1] 因此，改变阿拉伯各国数字基础设施不健全、区域内发展差距大的现状，是中阿开展数字经济合作的重要基础性任务，也是推动5G技术在阿拉伯世界应用的必要支撑。

中国的华为、中兴等企业广泛开展全球性业务，尤其华为多年深耕中东，利用其5G通信核心技术提供无线网、智能终端等业务合作。5G初始用户主要集中在海湾国家，其中阿联酋是最早将5G技术应用于商业领域的国家之一，沙特是较早在中东地区部署5G基础设施的国家。[2] 在"2019年世界移动通信大会"上，沙特电信为加强本国无线网络现代化及5G网络建设，与华为签署了"Aspiration项目"合同，助力沙特"2030愿景"及"国家转型2020"等计划的落地。[3] 截至2019年9月，阿联酋、沙特、科威特、阿曼和巴林等中东国家的11家电信公司与华为签署了5G

---

[1] 《5G：2025年中东北非地区用户数将达到8000万》，商务部网站，http://www.mofcom.gov.cn/article/i/jyjl/k/202006/20200602976533.shtml，2020年6月22日。
[2] 《任正非接受中东媒体采访：华为没犯错，美国制裁是政治目的》，观察者网，https://www.guancha.cn/economy/2019_11_04_523846.shtml，2019年11月4日。
[3] 《华为与沙特电信（STC）签署5G Aspiration项目合同》，华为官网，https://www.huawei.com/cn/news/2019/2/stc-huawei-5g-aspiration-project，2019年2月26日。

盖人工智能、区块链、大数据、智慧城市、物联网和虚拟现实等前沿内容；科威特"2035新愿景"涉及技术创新、加快建设现代化国家基础设施体系等内容。此外，约旦"2025愿景"、叙利亚"2030数字化转型战略"、巴勒斯坦"国家信息技术战略"、埃及"2030愿景"和"ICT 2030战略"、毛里塔尼亚"国家宽带战略（2019~2022）"、苏丹"国家战略（2007~2031）"等愿景与规划，也都能满足为区域经济发展提供基础信息化支撑的需求。①

第二，中国数字经济发展经验可供阿拉伯国家借鉴。中国已深度嵌入全球创新网络，成为新一轮科技革命和产业变革的重要参与者和推动者，②其数字经济蓬勃发展显示出不弱于传统发达国家的发展能力和潜力，让阿拉伯国家更强烈地意识到数字转型在产业变革和经济增长中的重要性，也帮助本国增强发展数字经济的信心。与西方国家不同，中国更加注重探寻尊重他国国情及其自主性的发展道路，秉承"为发展中国家创造更多的发展机遇和空间"的宗旨和"授人以鱼，不如授人以渔"的理念，与阿拉伯国家"共同把握数字化、网络化、智能化发展机遇，建设数字丝绸之路、创新丝绸之路"③；中阿数字经济合作目标在于逐步缩小双方数字差距，实现高层次合作及普惠共赢。当前，中国互联网和电信建设水平在全球处于领先地位，而大多数阿拉伯国家仍处于数字经济的"洼地"，不少

---

① 以上内容根据西亚经社会《阿拉伯数字发展报告2019》、华为《全球联接指数2016》和《全球联接指数2019》中的数据内容整理而得，链接分别为 ESCWA, "Arab Digital Development Report 2019: Towards Empowering People and Ensuring Inclusiveness", https://www.unescwa.org/sites/www.unescwa.org/files/publications/files/arab-digital-development-report-2019-english_0.pdf, 2019-06-30；华为《GCI 2016：量化数字经济进程》，https://www.huawei.com/minisite/gci/assets/files/gci_2016_whitepaper_cn.pdf?v=20201217v2, 2016年4月11日；华为《GCI 2019：智能联接，共塑新常态》，https://www.huawei.com/minisite/gci/assets/files/gci_2019_whitepaper_cn.pdf?v=20201217v2, 2019年11月17日。
② 《找准科技创新的主攻方向和突破口》，人民网，http://theory.people.com.cn/n1/2019/0725/c40531-31254734.html, 2019年7月25日。
③ 《习近平在第二届"一带一路"国际合作高峰论坛开幕式上的主旨演讲》，新华网，http://www.xinhuanet.com/world/2019-04/26/c_1210119584.htm, 2019年4月26日。

的教育及相关通用技能息息相关的还有本国的电子政务水平，较低的人力资本水平和教育公共支出可能会严重影响电子政务的发展，所以阿拉伯地区总体教育状况特别是公共教育水平较低，一定程度上阻碍该地区国家向创新产业过渡，对当地数字经济发展产生不利影响。①

6.2　中阿数字经济合作现状

6.2.1　中阿数字经济合作基础

第一，阿拉伯国家高度重视制定本国数字经济发展战略。随着新一轮科技革命与产业变革数字化进程加快，阿拉伯国家纷纷重视制定本国数字经济发展计划，其中以阿联酋的数字化战略最为卓越，在国家愿景基础上制定了"一揽子"具有针对性的数字计划。其中，2017年的"阿联酋百年计划2071"，旨在依靠通信技术和数字经济实现国家未来50年的繁荣与发展；2019年的"2031年人工智能战略"和2020年"阿联酋区块链战略"都是具有针对性的尖端技术规划。值得一提的是，阿联酋非常重视智慧城市建设，制定了"阿联酋智慧政府计划""智慧迪拜2021""智慧阿布扎比"等重点规划。目前，阿联酋国内智慧城市占主要城市比重约为50%，覆盖率居阿拉伯地区之首。②

其他阿拉伯国家虽然赶不上阿联酋制定计划的精准程度，但普遍将相关数字发展条款作为国家发展规划的重要成分，置于本国重要的发展愿景中。例如，沙特"2030愿景"涵盖加大投入科技创新、云技术以及推动数字化等内容；巴林"2030年愿景"包括科技创新、云服务和打造数据中心等内容；阿曼"2040愿景"和"数字阿曼战略2030"覆

---

① ESCWA, "2030 الابتكار والتكنولوجيا من أجل التنمية المستدامة آفاق واعدة في المنطقة العربية لعام", https://archive.unescwa.org/sites/www.unescwa.org/files/publications/files/arab-horizon-2030-innovation-perspectives-sdgs-arab-region-arabic_0.pdf, 2019-02-12.
② 《AMF：阿联酋智慧城市处于地区领先位置》，商务部网站，http://www.mofcom.gov.cn/article/i/jyjl/k/201908/20190802893678.shtml，2019年8月28日。

表 6.5 阿拉伯国家人力资本指数

阿拉伯地区排名	国别	指数	阿拉伯地区排名	国别	指数
1	阿联酋	0.673	10	突尼斯	0.517
2	巴林	0.652	11	黎巴嫩	0.515
3	卡塔尔	0.638	12	摩洛哥	0.504
4	阿曼	0.608	13	埃及	0.494
5	巴勒斯坦	0.580	14	伊拉克	0.408
6	沙特	0.576	15	科摩罗	0.405
7	科威特	0.563	16	毛里塔尼亚	0.382
8	约旦	0.553	17	苏丹	0.377
9	阿尔及利亚	0.535	18	也门	0.373

资料来源：根据《世界银行人力资本指数 2020》（World Bank，"Human Capital Index"，https：//data.worldbank.org/indicator/HD.HCI.OVRL，2021-02-14）整理。

一国的人力资本水平与该国的经济状况息息相关，由该国的教育条件与水平决定。受单一资源依赖型和地租型经济发展模式的长期影响，阿拉伯国家工业化程度不高，社会贫富差距大，大多数国家的教育获取途径和质量一直面临严峻挑战，在人力资本投入不足、教育质量改革乏力、就业市场疲软等方面都不同程度地存在些问题，导致本地区青年失业问题日益严峻。阿拉伯国家受教育人口性别差异化程度也同样严重，女性平均受教育年限比男性少 0.6 年，远超世界平均水平 0.1 年。[1] 2020 年阿拉伯地区有 18%的"NEET"（Not in Education, Employment or Training，不升学、不就业、不进修）青年，其中男、女性别名比分别为 10%、27%。[2] 另外，同样受一国人力资本因素影响的还有互联网用户技能水平，而与一国人口

---

[1] UNDP, "Arab Human Development Report Research Paper: Leaving No One Behind: Towards Inclusive Citizenship in Arab Countries", https://arab-hdr.org/wp-content/uploads/2020/12/UNDP_Citizenship_and_SDGs_report_web.pdf, 2019-08-22, p.16.

[2] ESCWA, "التقرير العربي للتنمية المستدامة", https://asdr.unescwa.org/sdgs/pdf/ar/ASDR2020-Final-Online.pdf, 2019-02-14, p.60.

伯地区和亚洲地区唯一倒退的国家。

表 6.4 阿拉伯国家电子政务发展指数

组别	国别（世界排名）
极高分组	阿联酋（21）、巴林（38）、沙特（43）、科威特（46）、阿曼（50）
高分组	卡塔尔（66）、突尼斯（91）、摩洛哥（106）、埃及（111）、约旦（117）、阿尔及利亚（120）
中等组	黎巴嫩（127）、叙利亚（131）、伊拉克（143）、利比亚（162）、苏丹（170）、也门（173）、毛里塔尼亚（176）、科摩罗（177）、吉布提（179）
低分组	索马里（191）

资料来源：根据《联合国电子政务调查报告 2020》（United Nations, "E-Government Survey 2020: Digital Government in the Decade of Action for Sustainable Development", https://publicadministration.un.org/egovkb/en-us/#.WgMZJq-GO71, 2020-12-07）整理。

6.1.5 人力资本

人力资本是可持续、包容性经济增长的一个关键驱动力,[①] 既是数字经济时代国家实现技术创新的主体，也是导致国家间技术水平差异的要素。世界银行采用人力资本指数估计某国出生的新生儿预计在 18 周岁时人均人力资本情况将达到"理想前沿"状态下的百分比，取值范围 0~1。[②] 2020 年阿拉伯地区人力资本指数高于 0.5 的国家有 12 个（见表 6.5），其中 4 个国家高于 0.6，且仅有阿联酋超过中国人力资本水平 0.653。阿拉伯国家人力资本水平总体偏低，主要因地区内人力资本水平差异化严重所致；西亚国家的人力资本水平普遍高于北非国家；苏丹、毛里塔尼亚、也门等经济欠发达国家的人力资本水平不足 0.4，严重影响了阿拉伯地区整体人力资本水平。

[①] 《世行：人力资本投入决定未来，数字经济需更新税务体制》，第一财经网，https://www.yicai.com/news/100038465.html, 2018 年 10 月 12 日。

[②] 譬如，阿联酋 2020 年的人力资本指数为 0.673，说明 2038 年阿联酋新增 18 周岁成年人口中预计将实现 2/3 的可用劳动生产力。

上涨了52%，其中80%来自埃及、沙特和阿联酋。① 尽管目前阿拉伯地区的电子商务主要通过地区外部平台进行交易，② 但随着智能手机用户习惯逐渐转变，以及网上购物更加频繁，本地企业（如 Souq 和 Noon）都开始瞄准移动端业务，希望发展成为下一个亚马逊或淘宝，这无疑对推进阿拉伯地区的数字支付和数字包容性产生积极影响。

6.1.4 电子政务

数字经济是提高政务效率的捷径，电子政务也是赋能数字经济的最好手段。近些年数字经济催生了传统政府向"数字政府"的转变，各国开始关注本国电子政务基础支撑力的提升。联合国经济和社会事务部依据联合国193个成员国的电子政务发展状况，创建电子政务发展指数（EGDI）用以评估各国电子政务绩效水平，自2001年以来每两年发布一份调查报告，目前共发布了9份报告。各国的 EGDI 取值范围0~1，采用四个档次划分。高于0.75为极高分组，0.50~0.75为高分组，0.25~0.50为中等组，低于0.25为低分组。

随着全球范围内电子政务发展持续推进，世界平均电子政务发展指数（EGDI）水平不断上升，从2018年的0.55上升到2020年的0.6。《联合国电子政务调查报告2020》中阿拉伯国家的数据显示，阿拉伯地区有11个国家的电子政务发展指数水平达到高水平以上，占比52.38%（见表6.4）；8个国家的电子政务发展指数超过世界平均水平0.6，占比38.1%。值得一提的是，阿联酋、巴林和沙特超过了中国（0.795）；沙特、科威特、阿曼、埃及、阿尔及利亚等10个国家都因电子政务发展指数水平的提升而实现进阶；仅黎巴嫩的电子政务发展指数得分出现跌落，成为阿拉

---

① 《埃及推动了2020年中东北非地区电商发展》，商务部网站，http://www.mofcom.gov.cn/article/i/jyjl/k/202103/20210303047853.shtml，2021年8月10日。
② KPMG International,"The Truth about Online Consumers：2017 Global Online Consumer Report", https：//assets.kpmg/content/dam/kpmg/xx/pdf/2017/01/the-truth-about-online-consumers.pdf，2017-01-30。

续表

阿拉伯地区排名	国别	得分	世界排名	在线购物人数 占网民比例（%）	占人口比例（%）
7	约旦	54.7	76	9	7.1
8	突尼斯	54.6	77	11	4.7
9	阿尔及利亚	52.2	80	5	2.8
10	利比亚	49.7	85	20	14.6
11	摩洛哥	44.8	95	22	14.2
12	埃及	36.6	109	7	2.4
13	吉布提	27.7	125	—	—
14	伊拉克	25.4	129	16	8.6
15	苏丹	21.7	132	42	1.7
16	叙利亚	21.1	133	—	—
17	也门	18.5	138		
18	毛里塔尼亚	15	145	5	1.5
19	科摩罗	12	149		

资料来源：根据《联合国电子商务指数2020》（UNCTAD，"UNCTAD B2C E-commerce Index 2020"，https：//unctad.org/system/files/official-document/tn_unctad_ict4d17_en.pdf，2021年2月17日）整理。

2020年，新冠肺炎疫情的发生极大地刺激了阿拉伯地区的在线消费行为，普华永道《全球消费者洞察2020》①调查结果显示，中东地区有58%的受访者表示已经开始在线购物，49%表示自疫情之后还会大幅增加在线购物行为，因此成为该项调查结果中比例最高的地区。同期，全球在线支付解决方案提供商通过调查海合会国家以及埃及、约旦、巴基斯坦等中东国家的5000名消费者发现，有47%的消费者预期将在未来一年增加在线购物行为。② 2020年末，中东地区电子商务行业价值达220亿美元，

---

① "Global Consumer Insights Survey 2020：The Consumer Transformed"，https：//www.pwc.com/gx/en/consumer-markets/consumer-insights-survey/2020/pwc-consumer-insights-survey-2020.pdf，2020-07-07.

② "Seizing Opportunity in MENA and Pakistan (2020)"，https：//www.checkout.com/newsroom/news/connected-payments-seizing-opportunity-in-mena-and-pakistan-report-launch，2020-11-10.

续表

国别	男性	女性	基本技能	标准技能	高级技能
伊拉克	98.3	51.2	23.1	11.3	4.7
巴勒斯坦	72.3	68.9	—	—	—
苏丹	16.9	11.0	3.0	2.2	1.6
吉布提	59.9	51.6	15.8	12.6	4.5

注："—"数据不可得。
资料来源：根据国际电联《阿拉伯国家数字趋势2021》整理。

6.1.3 电子商务

电子商务是数字经济最活跃、最集中的表现形式之一，发展电子商务是发展数字经济的重要抓手。阿拉伯国家电子商务指数得分整体不高，其中阿联酋、沙特、卡塔尔三国的得分高于中国的70.1分，也是在全球152个调查对象中排名前50的阿拉伯国家（见表6.3）。作为阿拉伯地区电子商务水平最高的国家，阿联酋2017年在线购物人数超过本国网民人数的一半，但相较于同期中国网民在线购物率69%的水平，尚存在不小差距。另外，虽然苏丹的网民在线购物比例为42%，仅次于阿联酋，但受限于本地互联网渗透率低、网络连接水平低等因素，全民在线购物水平不足2%。总体上，阿拉伯国家的电子商务发展处于起步阶段，具有较大的发展潜力与空间。

表6.3 阿拉伯国家电子商务指数及网购情况

阿拉伯地区排名	国别	得分	世界排名	在线购物人数	
				占网民比例（%）	占人口比例（%）
1	阿联酋	78.2	37	54	49.6
2	沙特	72.3	49	30	24.9
3	卡塔尔	72.1	50	—	—
4	科威特	68.7	58	21	20.2
5	黎巴嫩	60.4	64	16	13.8
6	巴林	59.7	66	27	25.0

联网用户占女性总人口数的47.3%，略低于世界平均水平48.3%，但高于发展中国家平均水平40.4%。整体上，阿拉伯地区互联网用户存在性别鸿沟，女性通过网络获取知识的机会普遍少于男性，但在经济发展水平较高的海合会国家，互联网男女用户比例非常接近。一方面，这些国家因经济发展水平较高，在降低文盲率和提高教育水平尤其高等教育水平方面实力卓越，有助于缩小互联网使用中的性别差距；另一方面，在这些经济发达的阿拉伯国家中，女性手机用户比例非常高，移动电话作为网络访问最常用的手段，能够有效缩小网络使用上的性别鸿沟。

在用户技能层面上，各国在不同技能水平的用户比例上差距明显，但在不同技能水平的用户率上排名靠前的国家基本一致，其中包括阿曼、阿联酋、巴林、科威特、埃及、沙特、摩洛哥等国。另外一个差异是，即使同一国家在不同技能水平用户率上也存在较大差异，比如，阿曼的基本技能用户渗透率超过75%，但标准技能用户不到40%，高级技能用户则不足10%；相较而言，突尼斯的各项技能的用户比例最为均匀，基本保持在16%~20%的水平（见表6.2）。

表6.2　阿拉伯国家互联网用户性别、技能水平情况

单位：%

国别	男性	女性	基本技能	标准技能	高级技能
阿联酋	99.0	99.5	72.3	60.4	17.9
科威特	99.5	99.6	57.7	43.7	13.4
卡塔尔	100.0	99.3	44.8	30.1	5.1
阿曼	94.4	96.2	75.4	36.7	8.0
摩洛哥	78.6	70.2	36.6	27.8	9.3
突尼斯	72.5	61.1	20.0	17.1	16.1
沙特	96.5	94.6	56.7	49.6	13.8
巴林	99.9	99.3	60.8	42.0	18.1
阿尔及利亚	55.1	42.9	17.0	12.1	6.9
埃及	61.5	53.0	57.5	36.2	7.9

续表

维度	阿拉伯世界排名前五位国家	阿拉伯世界排名后五位国家	阿拉伯	中国
固定宽带渗透率	阿联酋（31.17）、沙特（19.85）、伊拉克（11.6）、阿曼（10.24）、突尼斯（10.2）	苏丹（0.08）、科摩罗（0.14）、毛里塔尼亚（0.24）、索马里（0.67）、也门（1.36）	7.7	31.34
可上网家庭比例	沙特（99.2）、阿曼（94.5）、黎巴嫩（84.4）、摩洛哥（80.8）、巴勒斯坦（79.6）	科摩罗（5.56）、也门（6.3）、毛里塔尼亚（14.3）、利比亚（23.7）、苏丹（33.6）	58.9	59.6

资料来源：根据国际电联《阿拉伯国家数字趋势2021》、国际电联《亚太地区的数字趋势2021》（International Telecommunication Union，"Digital Trends in Asia & the Pacific 2021"，https：//www.itu.int/en/myitu/Publications/2021/03/08/09/13/Digital-Trends-in-Asia-Pacific-2021，2021年3月8日）整理。

6.1.2 互联网应用

6.1.2.1 消费时长

据《数字2020：全球数字概览》[1]统计，阿拉伯地区每日手机上网时长2小时以上的用户比例为70%，超过10小时的用户比例为17%；每日电脑上网时长达2小时以上的用户比例为47%。智能手机已成为阿拉伯地区绝大多数互联网用户的首选设备，人均上网时长不断增长。

6.1.2.2 互联网用户

在用户年龄层面上，据国际电联（International Telecommunication Union）《衡量数字发展：事实与数据2020》[2]统计，阿拉伯地区青年（15～24岁）用户占该年龄阶段人口数量的67.2%，高于发展中国家平均水平65.6%，略低于世界平均水平69.4%。

在用户性别层面上，阿拉伯国家男性互联网用户占男性总人口数的61.3%，高于世界平均水平55.2%和发展中国家平均水平48.9%；女性互

---

[1] Digital 2020：Global Overview Report，https：//datareportal.com/reports/digital-2020-global-digital-overview。

[2] ITU，"Measuring Digital Development：Facts and Figures 2020"，https：//www.itu.int/en/ITU-D/Statistics/Documents/facts/FactsFigures2020.pdf，2020-11-30。

的关键因素。本书参考欧盟委员会发布的《数字经济与社会指数》报告中的维度分类,从网络联通性、互联网应用、电子商务、电子政务、人力资本五个方面评价阿拉伯国家数字经济现状。

6.1.1 网络联通性

数字基础设施为数字经济发展提供动力,网络联通性是衡量一国数字经济发展水平的首要表现。据国际电联《阿拉伯国家数字趋势 2021》[①],阿拉伯地区的互联网渗透率、可上网家庭比例与中国水平基本持平(见表6.1),尤其随着移动通信的高速发展,阿拉伯地区移动电话用户比例明显上升,甚至像突尼斯、叙利亚等经历动荡和战乱国家的移动电话渗透率都接近或者超过了中国,但其中约一半国家在各联通性指标上都落后于发展中国家平均水平。总体看来,阿拉伯国家网络联通水平持续改善但总体不佳,地区"数字鸿沟"明显。

表 6.1 阿拉伯国家网络联通水平及国际比较

单位:%

维度	阿拉伯世界排名前五位国家	阿拉伯世界排名后五位国家	阿拉伯	中国
互联网渗透率	巴林(99.7)、卡塔尔(99.65)、科威特(99.6)、阿联酋(98.5)、沙特(93.31)	索马里(2)、科摩罗(8.48)、毛里塔尼亚(20.8)、利比亚(21.76)、也门(26.72)	54.6	54.3
移动电话渗透率	阿联酋(200)、科威特(174)、卡塔尔(138)、阿曼(138)、摩洛哥(128)	吉布提(42)、索马里(51)、也门(54)、黎巴嫩(62)、科摩罗(67)	99	115.53
移动宽带渗透率	阿联酋(239.9)、科威特(131.8)、巴林(122.6)、卡塔尔(120)、沙特(116.9)	索马里(2.5)、也门(6)、科摩罗(9.5)、叙利亚(11.5)、巴勒斯坦(19.3)	62	96.7

---

① International Telecommunication Union (ITU), "Digital Trends in the Arab States Region 2021", https://www.itu.int/en/myitu/Publications/2021/04/07/12/19/Digital-Trends-in-the-Arab-States-region-2021, 2021-04-07.

第6章 中阿数字经济合作专题报告

阿拉伯国家是我国"一带一路"倡议的天然合作伙伴,在新冠肺炎疫情重创传统经济的情况下,数字经济的提速发展为全球经济社会注入了新动能,也为新发展格局下中阿数字经济合作带来新契机。中阿需要共同努力,推动数字经济合作成为双方高质量共建"一带一路"的实际路径与发展方向。

6.1 阿拉伯国家数字经济水平现状

作为新经济形态与社会经济活动深度融合,数字经济以信息通信技术为核心的技术手段,对社会经济的各个方面起着前所未有的促进作用[①],其"无边界、全球化、全天候泛在"的市场特征让各国的发展紧密联系在一起。近年来,一些西方发达国家限制高科技出口,我国数字经济企业的海外投资也屡遭限制与排斥,导致我国数字经济发展的国际环境日趋严峻。但以沙特、阿联酋等为代表的阿拉伯国家在高科技应用技术方面持务实态度,看重以5G为代表的新基建及其广阔的应用前景,反对西方大国的高科技垄断并顶住对方施加的政治压力,欢迎中国企业参与本国的5G基建。阿拉伯国家逐渐成为与我国数字经济合作的高地。

阿拉伯国家的数字经济发展现状是影响中阿数字经济合作层次与水平

---

① 裴长洪、倪江飞、李越:《数字经济的政治经济学分析》,《财贸经济》2018年第9期。

系",实现共同发展和互利共赢,努力携手打造面向新时代的中阿命运共同体,为推动构建人类命运共同体作出贡献。① 中阿目前正以合作共建"一带一路"为统领,进一步完善中阿合作论坛、中阿能源合作大会、中阿能源合作联盟等能源合作机制,不断夯实中阿在油气和新能源等领域战略合作的基础。② 2021 年 8 月召开的中阿能源合作高峰论坛上,国家能源局局长章建华在致辞中表示,中方在继续深化油气领域合作、加快推动能源低碳转型、共建高效通畅的合作平台等方面愿与阿方加强合作。他还表示中方愿与阿方一道,坚定不移地走能源转型之路,持续提升中阿能源合作水平。③ 中阿双方高层的政治引领为中阿关系打下了良好的政治基础,也是能源合作持续推进的长期优势,这在一定程度上有利于抵消地区地缘政治经济形势波动给有关合作带来的负面影响。

---

① 《中国—阿拉伯国家合作论坛第九届部长级会议安曼宣言》,中阿合作论坛网,http://www.chinaarabcf.org/chn/lthyjwx/bzjhywj/djjbzjhy/202008/t20200810_6836914.htm,2020 年 8 月 10 日。
② 《共建一带一路 深化中阿能源合作》,一带一路能源合作网,http://obor.nea.gov.cn/detail2/3098.html,2018 年 7 月 6 日。
③ 《中阿能源合作高峰论坛召开》,国家能源局网站,http://www.nea.gov.cn/2021-08/20/c_1310138987.htm,2021 年 8 月 20 日。

发生恶性竞争。此外，虽然伊核问题等地区热点有所降温，但巴勒斯坦问题并没有取得实质性进展，伊核协议前景难言明朗，造成问题的深层次矛盾并没有解决。阿拉伯国家内部如阿尔及利亚、苏丹等国，自2019年以来又发生一轮政治变动，余波至今未平。其他国家长期以来内部积累发展过程中的矛盾，在新冠肺炎疫情背景下也有再次爆发的可能性。地区政治安全形势对中阿合作造成的风险将长期存在。此轮地区形势缓和有利于为中阿开展能源合作提供良好的外部环境，但就长期趋势而言，目前宜持谨慎乐观态度。过去中国企业海外投资合作项目因所在国政治经济形势变化而遭受损失的案例并不鲜见，今后一段时间中阿双方开展能源合作时双方仍需坚持理性、务实原则，对开展合作项目的影响因素进行充分评估，避免卷入不必要的纷争，以求得共同利益的最大化。

5.4.3 良好的政治基础是中阿能源合作的长期优势

中阿之间没有悬而未决的历史纠葛，中国与阿拉伯乃至中东地区所有国家友好，双方也都有持续不断推动中阿各领域务实合作的强烈政治意愿。2018年习近平主席在中国—阿拉伯国家合作论坛第八届部长级会议开幕式上的讲话，为中阿开展能源合作指明了下一阶段的前进方向。习近平主席的讲话指出，要积极推动油气合作、低碳能源合作"双轮"转动，要继续推进"油气+"合作模式，深化石油、天然气勘探、开采、炼化、储运等全产业链合作，要顺应全球能源革命、绿色低碳产业蓬勃发展，加强和平利用核能、太阳能、风能、水电等领域合作，共同构建油气牵引、核能跟进、清洁能源提速的中阿能源合作格局，打造互惠互利、长期友好的中阿能源战略合作关系。[①]

《中国—阿拉伯国家合作论坛第九届部长级会议安曼宣言》强调，中阿双方将进一步加强"全面合作、共同发展、面向未来的中阿战略伙伴关

---

① 《携手推进新时代中阿战略伙伴关系——在中阿合作论坛第八届部长级会议开幕式上的讲话》，人民网，http://jhsjk.people.cn/article/30138530，2018年7月10日。

靠伙伴。① 中国拥有全球最大的新能源产能，是阿方理想的合作选择。在清洁能源领域，中国水电、风电、光伏装机容量和年发电量都处于全球领先地位，且相关技术发展趋于成熟，成本不断下降。② 与此同时，新能源代替传统化石能源还需要一定的时间，能源转型战略也难以在短期内完全实现，阿拉伯国家扩大油气产能需要投资，发展新能源需要更大的投资，这一时间差恰好是中阿深化能源合作的良好契机。可以预见，中阿传统能源合作的重要性在一段时间内不会轻易改变，能源转型对深化中阿能源合作而言蕴藏着巨大的机遇。

5.4.2 地区内外矛盾带来的政治经济风险始终存在

长期以来，中东地区热点问题不断，域外大国与中东国家之间以及本地区国家之间时有龃龉。2020 年以来，相关国家的政策有所调整，地区形势出现缓和迹象。2020 年 9 月 15 日，在美国大力推动下，阿联酋、巴林与以色列签署《亚伯拉罕协议》，阿以关系有所缓和。2021 年 1 月，卡塔尔埃米尔访问沙特并出席海合会首脑会议，标志着自 2017 年断交以来两国外交关系的恢复，卡塔尔与沙特等国的关系也走向改善。8 月 28 日，法国和伊拉克发起巴格达峰会，峰会期间伊朗与阿联酋和沙特都进行了外交接触，这是 2016 年以来的首次。③

但是，这些缓和迹象很有可能只是表面的、不稳定的，一些关键问题并没有真正触及，同时新的矛盾还在出现。2019 年 1 月 1 日卡塔尔退出欧佩克，成为欧佩克成立 58 年以来首个正式退出的中东国家。卡塔尔还宣布不受欧佩克减产限制，大幅提高石油产量。④ 长期以来，一些阿拉伯国家尤其是海湾国家之间经济发展模式相近，经济互补性较差，未来有可能

---

① 牛新春、陈晋文：《全球能源转型对中东政治的影响》，《现代国际关系》2021 年第 12 期。
② 中国人民大学国际能源战略研究中心：《中国能源国际合作报告 2017/2018》，中国人民大学出版社，2019，第 46 页。
③ 牛新春、陈晋文：《全球能源转型对中东政治的影响》，《现代国际关系》2021 年第 12 期。
④ 牛新春、陈晋文：《全球能源转型对中东政治的影响》，《现代国际关系》2021 年第 12 期。

目开工建设。该项目位于光照资源丰富的约旦南部沙漠地区,预计建设工期270天。项目建成后,中方公司还将负责两年的运营和维护。① 8月19日,中国能建葛洲坝集团与埃及孔雀能源公司线上签署埃及苏伊士湾120兆瓦风电建设工程承包项目框架合同协议,合同金额1.44亿美元。②

5.4 中阿能源合作的前景

5.4.1 能源转型:既是挑战也是机遇

能源转型是中阿双方共同面临的时代课题。传统的中阿能源合作关系建立在某种程度的油气相互依赖基础上。阿拉伯国家是中国最重要的油气供应来源,中国也是阿拉伯国家油气出口的重要市场。在能源转型背景下,中阿能源合作的领域和范围都有所扩大,从领域来看,能源合作从传统能源向风能、太阳能、水电、核能等领域扩展,从范围来看,能源合作从能源勘探、开采、贸易向全产业链合作拓展,从而形成油气和低碳能源"双轮"转动,"油气+"能源合作新局面。中阿能源合作要以构建中国与阿拉伯国家间可持续的能源伙伴关系为目标,探索发现新的合作潜力、合作路径,③ 打造中阿能源安全命运共同体。④

能源转型是双方的共同发展需求,中阿在新能源领域合作空间十分广阔。多个阿拉伯国家已经推出颇具雄心的新能源发展计划,要实现这些宏伟目标,需要庞大的新能源产能和投资,中国在这一方面具有明显优势。随着美国对中东能源依赖度降低,中国可成为阿拉伯国家发展新能源的可

---

① 《中企承建约旦光伏项目开工》,新华网,http://www.xinhuanet.com/fortune/2021-08/05/c_1127734842.htm,2021年8月5日。
② 《中企海外项目周报(2021.08.16-2021.08.22)》,中国一带一路网,https://www.yidaiyilu.gov.cn/qyfc/xmzb/184585.htm,2021年8月23日。
③ 孙霞:《中国与中东北非国家可持续能源合作关系探析》,《国际石油经济》2021年第10期。
④ 孙霞:《中国与中东北非国家可持续能源合作关系探析》,《国际石油经济》2021年第10期。

先进太阳能光伏发电技术的代表项目。项目位于阿联酋迪拜穆罕默德·本·拉希德·阿勒马克图姆太阳能公园，占地总面积为 10.17 平方公里。项目将分三期建设，一期工程建设 300 兆瓦及配套 132 千伏升压站。① 6 月 4 日，项目首次并网发电。②

4 月，中国能建广东火电通过视频会议方式，签约沙特拉比格 300 兆瓦光伏电站 EPC 项目合同，合同额折合人民币约 12 亿元。该项目建成后首年总发电量为 8.94 亿千瓦时，预计 25 年总发电量约 214 亿千瓦时。项目将为当地提供 900 个就业岗位，并为 4.53 万户家庭提供绿色清洁的电力供应。③

5 月，阳光电源签署了埃及康翁波神庙 200 兆瓦光伏项目订单。该项目位于埃及阿斯旺省康翁波神庙沙漠地区，夏季最高温度接近 60℃，高温、高沙尘的极端环境要求逆变设备具备超高可靠性。为此，该企业提供相关设备的整体解决方案，预计将有效提升电站发电量。④ 同月，中国化学中东公司与阿特拉斯工业有限责任公司在阿联酋阿布扎比举行 25 万吨/年生物质炼厂项目签约仪式。项目计划在阿布扎比哈里发工业区建设运营一座年产能力为 100 万吨/年的生物炼油工厂，总投资约 10 亿美元。项目计划分期进行，第一期规模为 25 万吨/年。该工厂将利用可持续植物油和生物质残留物生产绿色炼油，主要产品为绿色柴油、绿色航空燃油等。⑤

8 月，由中国电建所属山东电建三公司承建的约旦第仕 24 兆瓦光伏项

---

① 《中企海外项目周报（1.11-1.17）》，中国一带一路网，https：//mp.weixin.qq.com/s/zrIedNrLjuIpNNDH4ubTOw，2021 年 1 月 18 日。
② 《中国能建浙江火电承建迪拜五期 900 兆瓦光伏项目并网发电》，中国能源建设股份有限公司网站，http：//www.ceec.net.cn/art/2021/6/9/art_11019_2470332.html，2021 年 6 月 9 日。
③ 《中国能建广东火电签约沙特拉比格 300 兆瓦光伏电站 EPC 项目》，中国能源建设股份有限公司网站，http：//www.ceec.net.cn/art/2021/4/14/art_11016_2433125.html，2021 年 4 月 14 日。
④ 《北非最大！阳光电源签约埃及 200MW 项目》，阳光电源网站，https：//cn.sungrowpower.com/news/430.html，2021 年 5 月 7 日。
⑤ 《中东公司成功签署阿布扎比 25 万吨/年生物质炼厂项目》，中国化学工程集团中东公司，https：//mp.weixin.qq.com/s/PVUJVC6jYkq1hqEOvcvwHQ，2021 年 5 月 30 日。

现代化的能源体系，满足各国能源需求，增进政治互信，实现联动发展。①

2020年，中国—阿拉伯国家合作论坛第九届部长级会议制定的《中国—阿拉伯国家合作论坛2020年至2022年行动执行计划》声明，双方在加强石油天然气领域和电力领域合作之外，还将加强可再生能源领域的合作。双方计划加强在利用阿拉伯国家的光伏电池和光热能应用方面的合作，加强在相关领域的技术合作，鼓励开展联合项目；欢迎中阿双方共同推动中阿清洁能源培训中心工作，适时在一个或多个阿拉伯国家建立分中心；加强在作为综合性能源的垃圾转化能源领域合作，并为实现这一目标进行必要的能力、制度和立法建设；欢迎在中阿清洁能源培训中心框架下在华举办清洁能源领域培训班，并推动2021年或双方商定的时间继续举办培训班；加强绿氢供能的应用，通过开展研究和举办研修班借鉴中方在该领域的先进经验。该计划还提及将在能源效率领域和和平利用核能领域开展合作。②

2021年8月19～20日，以"面向未来：开创中阿能源合作新时代"为主题的中阿能源合作高峰论坛在银川举行。多个阿拉伯国家能源部门负责人和驻华使节，国际可再生能源署等国际组织、中阿能源和金融企业的400余名代表参加会议。与会各方均认为中阿能源合作前景广阔，并对双方在推动传统能源合作之外开展新能源合作表达了强烈意愿。论坛采取"线上线下相结合、以线上为主"的方式，探讨了碳达峰、碳中和背景下中阿能源合作面临的机遇，鼓励各方携手深化中阿能源发展。③

中阿在新能源领域也开展了卓有成效的项目合作。2021年1月8日，中国能建浙江火电承建、华东电力试研院参与调试的迪拜五期900兆瓦光伏项目正式开工。该工程为迪拜最大光伏电站项目，是目前中东地区使用

---

① 中国—阿拉伯国家博览会秘书处编《中阿经贸关系发展进程2019年度报告》，社会科学文献出版社，2020，第23页。
② 《中国—阿拉伯国家合作论坛2020年至2022年行动执行计划》，中阿合作论坛网，http://www.chinaarabcf.org/chn/lthyjwx/bzjhyw j/djjbzjhy/202008/t20200810_6836922.htm，2020年8月10日。
③ 《中阿能源合作高峰论坛在银川举行》，《宁夏日报》2021年8月20日第1版。

围内发展水电、光伏和风电。①

2021年10月以来，一些阿拉伯国家相继公布本国温室气体减排目标：沙特宣布将投资约1800亿美元，力争到2060年实现碳净零排放；阿联酋宣布要在2050年实现碳中和；巴林表示将在2060年前达到碳中和目标；卡塔尔则称到2030年本国将实现碳减排25%的目标。② 这表明了阿拉伯国家将加快推进能源转型，以及发展清洁能源的强烈意愿。

5.3.2 中阿新能源合作简况

2013年，中国提出共建"一带一路"合作倡议，为中阿合作创造了重要战略机遇，也为中阿合作论坛框架内的能源合作向纵深发展创造了有利的条件。中阿能源合作开始突破传统的油气贸易模式，并向产能合作以及非化石能源领域延伸拓展。

在原有的"和平、繁荣、开放、创新、文明之路"基础之上，中国还提出共建"一带一路"绿色之路，这为中国与阿拉伯国家共同应对气候变化、保护生态环境、促进可持续发展提供了新平台。2019年4月25日，"一带一路"能源合作伙伴关系在北京正式成立，各伙伴国在《合作原则与务实行动》指导下推进双多边能源合作向绿色、清洁、高效方向迈进，包括伊拉克、科威特、阿尔及利亚、苏丹等在内的阿拉伯国家成为首批"一带一路"能源合作伙伴国。③

当前，中阿双方正在按照"1+2+3"的合作格局，加强战略对接，改变对油气资源的高度依赖，以能源转型带动经济转型。中阿正充分利用阿拉伯国家区位优势，以阿拉伯国家能源互联网为平台，合作开发清洁能源，打造亚欧非清洁能源生产中心和贸易枢纽，形成能源生产清洁化、配置广域化、消费

---

① 郭艳：《低碳能源领域成为中阿合作新亮点》，《中国对外贸易》2021年第9期。
② 《海湾国家推动清洁能源建设》，人民网，http://env.people.com.cn/n1/2021/1216/c1010-32309595.html，2021年12月16日。
③ 余晓钟、罗霞：《"一带一路"能源合作伙伴关系内涵与推进策略》，《亚太经济》2020年第4期。

展新道路。习近平主席在第七十五届联合国大会一般性辩论上宣布,中国将提高国家自主贡献力度,采取更加有力的政策和措施,二氧化碳排放量力争于 2030 年前达到峰值,努力争取 2060 年前实现碳中和。①《中华人民共和国国民经济和社会发展第十四个五年规划和 2035 年远景目标纲要》指出,中国将在 2035 年建成现代化经济体系,并明确提出单位 GDP 能耗降低、单位 GDP 二氧化碳排放量降低等约束性指标。② 开展能源合作方面,《能源生产和消费革命战略(2016—2030)》提出:要按照立足长远、总体谋划、多元合作、互利共赢的方针,加强能源宽领域、多层次、全产业链合作,构筑连接中国与世界的能源合作网,打造能源合作的利益共同体和命运共同体。③

阿拉伯国家也加快制定能源转型规划,发展新能源产业。阿拉伯国家召开各种相关论坛和会议,并通过了《2010~2030 年泛阿拉伯地区可再生能源应用发展战略》(*Pan-Arab Strategy for the Development of Renewable Energy Applications*:*2010-2030*)。④ 阿联酋的能源发展战略规划预计到 2030 年,可再生能源发电量占阿联酋总发电量的比重将超过 10%。⑤ 2016 年,沙特发布"2030 愿景",并制定了阶段发展规划《2020 国家转型计划》。该文件提及,沙特拥有较丰富且尚未充分利用的太阳能风能资源,并据此制定了有雄心的可再生能源发展目标。⑥ 摩洛哥计划到 2024 年,将可再生能源发电比重提高至 52%。为了达到这一目标,摩洛哥正在全国范

---

① 《新时代的中国能源发展》白皮书,中华人民共和国国务院新闻办公室网站,http://www.scio.gov.cn/zfbps/32832/Document/1695117/1695117.htm,2020 年 12 月 21 日。
② 侯梅芳、潘松圻、刘翰林:《世界能源转型大势与中国油气可持续发展战略》,《天然气工业》2021 年第 12 期。
③ 《两部门印发〈能源生产和消费革命战略(2016—2030)〉》,中华人民共和国中央人民政府网站,http://www.gov.cn/xinwen/2017-04/25/content_5230568.htm,2017 年 4 月 25 日。
④ The International Renewable Energy Agency, League of Arab States, Pan Arab Renewable Energy 2030, 2014, p.38.
⑤ 《我国企业应密切关注阿联酋新能源领域的战略合作机会》,中恒远策网站,https://mp.weixin.qq.com/s/UIZoqgDbdpgpWkF6IAvBEQ,2018 年 8 月 14 日。
⑥ 刘辰、马鸢宇:《沙特阿拉伯新能源政策研究》,《长春师范大学学报》2021 年第 3 期。

互联项目签署一系列合作备忘录，埃及输电公司与沙特电力公司签署了埃及—沙特电力互联项目合同，其中中国能源建设股份有限公司、中国西电集团有限公司和埃及吉萨电缆工业公司组成的联合体，成功签约埃及—沙特±500千伏超高压直流输电线路EPC项目。①

12月13日，中国能建江苏电建一公司承建的埃及开罗西650兆瓦超临界热循环项目正式获得业主签发的移交接收证书（TOAC），标志着项目建设阶段圆满收官，进入质保期。该工程位于埃及开罗西北郊区，内容为建设一台650兆瓦超临界火力发电机组，采用油气混燃设计。项目投产后，预计年发电量约20亿千瓦时。② 12月20日上午，中国电力建设集团所属山东电建沙特吉赞项目PMCC-05、10、15正式签署机械完工证书，自此该项目四号机组全部PMCC（Partial Mechanical Completion Certificate即分部机械完工证书）完成签字并移交业主阿美石油公司。③

5.3 中阿新能源合作现状

5.3.1 中阿持续推进能源转型

进入21世纪以来，全球能源版图重塑，新一轮能源转型正在发生。能源转型意味着能源生产和消费结构发生变革。④ 本轮能源转型主要的方向是能源消费由化石能源转为核能、可再生能源等新能源和清洁能源。随着世界各国能源转型战略的推进，新能源将在人类的生活中起到越来越重要的作用。

中国积极参与全球能源治理，与各国一道寻求加快推进能源可持续发

---

① 《中企海外项目双周报（2021.9.27-2021.10.10）》，中国一带一路网，https://www.yidaiyilu.gov.cn/qyfc/xmzb/191063.htm，2021年10月15日。
② 《中企海外项目周报（2021.12.13-2021.12.19）》，中国一带一路网，https://www.yidaiyilu.gov.cn/qyfc/xmzb/208627.htm，2021年12月23日。
③ 《中企海外项目周报（2021.12.20-2021.12.26）》，中国一带一路网，https://www.yidaiyilu.gov.cn/qyfc/xmzb/210216.htm，2021年12月28日。
④ 吴磊、杨泽榆：《国际能源转型与中东石油》，《西亚非洲》2018年第5期。

5.2.3 其他能源基础设施项目合作

中阿在发电厂、变电站、输电线等能源基础设施建设方面也有着多项合作。2021年2月22日，中国西电集团总承包的埃及阿斯旺本班太阳能电场联网工程 Benban 500kV GIS 变电站竣工投运。该项目包含的14个间隔 500kV GIS 开关，10台 500/220kV 167MVA 单相电力变压器，以及 500kV 电容式电压互感器、避雷器等一系列超高压输变电设备，全部由中国西电集团生产制造。①

5月3日，由哈电国际总承包、中国能建所属天津电建承建的迪拜哈斯彦 4×600 兆瓦清洁燃煤电站项目 2 号机组首次并网一次成功。② 9月4日，项目 2 号机组正式投入商业运行。哈斯彦电站共配置 4 台单机容量 600 兆瓦的超超临界机组，总装机容量 2400 兆瓦，4 台机组将于 2023 年全部投入商业运行。其中，1 号机组已于 2020 年 7 月 20 日实现双燃料满负荷发电。作为中国"一带一路"建设的重大工程项目，哈斯彦电站建成后将是中东首个清洁燃煤电站。③

9月29日，由中国能源建设集团广东火电工程有限公司承建的约旦阿塔拉特油页岩电站 2 号发电机组并网成功。该项目为中约"一带一路"合作重点项目，共包括 2 台 235 兆瓦油页岩电站，预计建成后将成为约旦规模最大发电站。其中，1 号发电机组于 2021 年上半年成功并网，并于 7 月实现满负荷运行，达到具备稳定对外输电能力的阶段。④

10月5日，埃及电力和可再生能源部和沙特能源部在开罗就两国电力

---

① 《奋战开门红 | 集团公司总承包的埃及 Benban 500kV GIS 变电站成套工程竣工投运》，中国西电集团网站，https：//mp.weixin.qq.com/s/NtK8zjMCaDJwq8kQpRBRqw，2021年3月2日。
② 《中企海外项目周报 （2021.04.26－2021.05.09）》，中国一带一路网，https：//www.yidaiyilu.gov.cn/qyfc/xmzb/175331.htm，2021年5月10日。
③ 《中国能建设计承建迪拜哈斯彦项目2号机组投入商运》，中国能源建设股份有限公司网站，http：//www.ceec.net.cn/art/2021/9/7/art_11019_2512083.html，2021年9月7日。
④ 《中企承建约旦阿塔拉特油页岩电站并网成功》，新华网，http：//www.news.cn/silkroad/20211015/C99004C8CA30000175C2B38F16201A02/c.html，2021年9月29日。

田区块。原处理厂气处理量不能满足当地生产需要，该项目将对原处理厂进行升级改造。① 6月30日，中国石油工程建设中东地区公司与意大利埃尼（Eni）石油公司在伊拉克巴士拉签署祖拜尔油田脱气站扩建项目合同，合同额约6.9亿美元。② 该扩建项目于8月11日全面启动。项目建成后，祖拜尔油田产能将由目前的47万桶/天提升至70万桶/天（约3500万吨/年）。③

9月3日，中信建设签署伊拉克基尔库克炼油厂项目EPC工程总承包合同。基尔库克炼油厂位于伊拉克基尔库克省，项目规模为日处理7.5万桶原油（年处理量约350万吨原油），产品为符合欧五标准的汽油、柴油、航空煤油、燃料油、LPG、道路沥青等。项目EPC合同金额9.05亿美元，建设工期46个月。中信建设作为项目的EPC总承包商，将负责项目设计、采购、施工、调试等工作，并协助业主解决部分融资。④

11月9日，烟台杰瑞石油服务集团股份有限公司全资子公司杰瑞石油天然气工程有限公司收到科威特石油公司科威特北部侏罗纪生产设施5期项目授标函，合同金额超27亿元人民币。该项目位于科威特北部的侏罗纪气田，是科威特石油公司2022~2023年重点战略生产项目，旨在通过撬块化安装模式快速建设油、气、水生产设施，满足当地日益增长的天然气发电需求。⑤

---

① 《杰瑞油气工程签署阿尔及利亚天然气去瓶颈EPC项目》，烟台杰瑞石油服务集团股份有限公司，https://www.jereh.com/cn/news/press-release/news-detail-9653.htm，2021年6月2日。

② 《中企海外项目周报（2021.06.28-2021.07.04）》，中国一带一路网，https://www.yidaiyilu.gov.cn/qyfc/xmzb/179534.htm，2021年7月5日。

③ 《中企海外项目周报（2021.08.09-2021.08.15）》，中国一带一路网，https://www.yidaiyilu.gov.cn/qyfc/xmzb/183652.htm，2021年8月17日。

④ 《中信建设签署伊拉克基尔库克炼油厂项目总承包合同》，中信建设，https://www.cici.citic.com/content/details_39_2567.html，2021年9月6日。

⑤ 《重大捷报！杰瑞油气工程斩获27亿元科威特石油公司项目》，烟台杰瑞石油服务集团股份有限公司，https://www.jereh.com/cn/news/press-release/news-detail-9704.htm，2021年11月10日。

双方继续深化在油气生产方面的合作，一些中方企业在阿拉伯国家签约或继续推动又一批油气项目。2021年3月8日，中国化学工程集团有限公司所属中国化学工程第三建设有限公司中标沙特阿拉伯国家石油公司贝里增产项目AAP原油加工装置西区施工总承包工程。该项目位于沙特阿布阿里岛，合同额为15.57亿元人民币。项目对贝里油田阿布阿里炼油厂进行改扩建，将该炼油厂的阿拉伯轻质原油加工能力提高至每日50万桶。[①]

2021年4月，杰瑞油气工程与合作伙伴正式签署阿联酋杰贝阿里试点项目，该项目是阿联酋阿布扎比国家石油公司（ADNOC）2021年度重点生产项目。ADNOC计划评估位于阿布扎比东北部世界级气田杰贝阿里气田的地下天然气储藏潜力，为后续规模化开发作了充分准备。该项目工作范围是建设一套试点生产设施（PPF），将处理后的天然气输送到附近的外输管道。[②] 4月20日，大庆油田工程建设有限公司国际事业部收到来自中国石油工程建设有限公司伊拉克分公司的中标通知书，成功中标伊拉克哈法亚油田天然气处理厂工程项目，中标金额4.1亿元人民币。[③]

5月20日，中石化第五建设有限公司与意大利塞班公司（SAIPEM）举行沙特贝里油气处理项目线上签约仪式。该项目业主是沙特阿美石油公司，意大利塞班公司为项目EPC总承包商。项目主要内容是进行装置改扩建工程，处理每年增加的1100万吨阿拉伯轻质原油和每天4万桶含硫碳氢化合物。两个合同金额约2亿美元。[④]

6月，杰瑞油气工程获得阿尔及利亚天然气产能去瓶颈项目合同。该项目位于阿尔及利亚哈西梅萨乌德西南300公里撒哈拉沙漠中的BRN油

[①] 《三公司中标沙特贝里增产项目AAP原油加工装置西区施工总承包工程》，中国化学工程集团有限公司网站，https：//cncec.cn/articledetail/124491，2021年3月12日。

[②] 《中东市场再突破！杰瑞油气工程成功斩获阿联酋ADNOC试点生产设施项目》，烟台杰瑞石油服务集团股份有限公司网站，https：//www.jereh.com/cn/news/press-release/news-detail-9626.htm，2021年4月25日。

[③] 《中企海外项目周报（2021.04.19－2021.04.25）》，中国一带一路网，https：//www.yidaiyilu.gov.cn/qyfc/xmzb/175332.htm，2021年4月26日。

[④] 《中企海外项目周报（2021.05.17－2021.05.23）》，中国一带一路网，https：//www.yidaiyilu.gov.cn/qyfc/xmzb/175325.htm，2021年5月24日。

续表

	2017 年	2018 年	2019 年	2020 年	2021 年
埃及	5.61	18.24	18.55	6.43	131.20
沙特	123.12	212.14	199.36	97.57	75.91
阿尔及利亚	29.77	26.05	46.88	39.58	40.39
巴林	1.26	—	4.31	—	—

注："—"代表无该项数据。
资料来源：根据中华人民共和国海关总署"海关统计数据在线查询平台"中商品编码2711项下数据整理制作。

表 5.10 中国自阿拉伯国家进口天然气情况

单位：万吨

	2017 年	2018 年	2019 年	2020 年	2021 年
卡塔尔	748.23	923.97	831.96	814.45	898.01
阿曼	24.95	50.30	108.31	106.54	162.27
埃及	5.61	18.24	18.55	6.43	131.20
阿联酋	—	—	11.99	29.60	71.15
阿尔及利亚	5.66	6.79	6.16	12.24	24.38

注："—"代表无该项数据。
资料来源：根据中华人民共和国海关总署"海关统计数据在线查询平台"中商品编码271111、271121项下数据整理制作。表5.9商品编码2711范围涵盖本表所列271111、271121范围。

2021年3月22日，中国石油化工股份有限公司和卡塔尔石油公司签署了200万吨/年液化天然气（LNG）长期购销协议。从2022年起，卡塔尔石油公司将向中国石化每年供应200万吨LNG，为期10年。这是中国石化与卡塔尔石油公司首次签署LNG长期协议。该合作将进一步增强卡塔尔向中国市场的供货能力，满足中国市场不断增长的需求。[①]

5.2.2 油气生产项目合作

油气项目合作是中阿能源合作经营时间较长的领域。2021年，中阿

[①]《中国石化与卡塔尔石油公司签署200万吨/年LNG长期购销协议》，中阿合作论坛网，http：//www.chinaarabcf.org/chn/zagx/gjydyl/202103/t20210322_9155424.htm，2021年3月22日。

2021年,中国累计进口成品油2712万吨,其中自9个阿拉伯国家(阿联酋、阿尔及利亚、卡塔尔、埃及、科威特、伊拉克、沙特、巴林、阿曼)总计进口645.88万吨,约占23.82%。累计进口天然气12136万吨,其中卡塔尔是第五大进口来源国,自5个阿拉伯国家(卡塔尔、阿曼、埃及、阿联酋、阿尔及利亚)进口天然气1287.01万吨,约占进口总量的10.60%。除天然气外,中国还从阿拉伯国家进口液化丙烷、液化丁烷,以及液化乙烯、丙烯、丁烯及丁二烯等"石油气及其他烃类气"产品(见表5.8、表5.9、表5.10)。

表5.8 中国自阿拉伯国家进口成品油情况

单位:万吨

	2017年	2018年	2019年	2020年	2021年
阿联酋	110.24	243.20	184.79	146.59	282.77
阿尔及利亚	35.10	91.44	108.69	155.49	124.86
卡塔尔	24.07	32.91	90.00	88.71	121.50
埃及	2.66	15.62	10.96	48.01	45.23
科威特	22.33	12.13	2.92	5.50	29.80
伊拉克	—	12.18	14.78	5.57	21.75
沙特	52.88	31.64	18.38	60.13	12.64
巴林	10.00	0.66	5.65	18.79	7.32
阿曼	—	0.35	—	7.04	0.01

注:"—"代表无该项数据。
资料来源:根据中华人民共和国海关总署"海关统计数据在线查询平台"中商品编码2710项下数据整理制作。

表5.9 中国自阿拉伯国家进口石油气及其他烃类气情况

单位:万吨

	2017年	2018年	2019年	2020年	2021年
卡塔尔	1035.50	1235.33	1179.38	1117.51	1189.59
阿联酋	657.51	618.93	451.13	355.99	478.47
阿曼	24.95	50.30	311.89	342.68	472.04
科威特	121.42	223.74	226.03	132.56	137.77

表 5.7　中国自阿拉伯国家进口原油情况

单位：万吨

	2017 年	2018 年	2019 年	2020 年	2021 年
沙特	5217.95	5673.43	8332.96	8492.86	8756.71
伊拉克	3681.53	4505.07	5179.80	6011.41	5407.49
阿曼	3100.69	3290.18	3386.64	3787.77	4481.88
阿联酋	1015.77	1219.63	1527.96	3115.53	3194.15
科威特	1824.35	2321.22	2268.87	2749.75	3016.36
卡塔尔	101.41	134.77	85.83	619.91	785.01
利比亚	322.05	856.84	940.10	169.68	613.79
也门	156.69	124.55	175.52	182.51	94.34
埃及	208.42	208.69	79.52	132.33	49.00
阿尔及利亚	26.87	65.84	53.92	40.44	3.98
苏丹	72.09	44.42	63.12	16.00	—

注："—"代表无该项数据。

资料来源：根据中华人民共和国海关总署"海关统计数据在线查询平台"中商品编码 2709 项下数据整理制作。

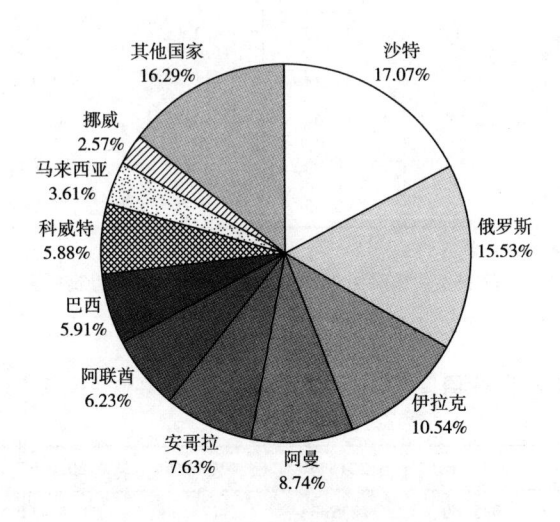

图 5.1　中国前十大原油进口来源国

沙特 17.07%
俄罗斯 15.53%
伊拉克 10.54%
阿曼 8.74%
安哥拉 7.63%
阿联酋 6.23%
巴西 5.91%
科威特 5.88%
马来西亚 3.61%
挪威 2.57%
其他国家 16.29%

资料来源：根据中华人民共和国海关总署"海关统计数据在线查询平台"中商品编码 2709 项下数据整理制作。

表 5.6 2020 年部分阿拉伯国家新能源发电量（不含水电）

单位：太瓦时

	风能	太阳能	其他能源	总计
伊拉克	—	0.377	—	0.377
科威特	0.018	0.153	—	0.171
阿曼	—	0.206	—	0.206
卡塔尔	—	0.008	0.115	0.123
沙特	—	1.038	—	1.038
阿联酋	—	5.553	0.006	5.559
阿尔及利亚	0.008	0.600	—	0.608
埃及	6.776	2.909	—	9.685
摩洛哥	5.390	1.581	—	6.971
世界总计	1591.20	855.70	700.10	3147.00

注："—"代表无该项数据。"其他能源"包括地热能、生物质能以及其他可再生能源的发电量（未逐项列出）。

资料来源：《BP 世界能源统计年鉴（2021 年版）》。

5.2 中阿传统能源合作现状

5.2.1 中阿油气贸易情况

油气贸易是中国与阿拉伯国家在能源领域的传统合作方式。阿拉伯国家是中国最重要的油气供应来源之一。根据中国海关总署的相关统计，2021 年中国累计进口原油 51298 万吨，排名前十的进口来源国分别为沙特、俄罗斯、伊拉克、阿曼、安哥拉、阿联酋、巴西、科威特、马来西亚、挪威。在十大原油进口来源国中，阿拉伯国家有五个（沙特、伊拉克、阿曼、阿联酋、科威特），占进口总量的 48.46%（见表 5.7、图 5.1）。

第5章 中阿能源合作专题报告

续表

	2016年 （十亿立方米）	2018年 （十亿立方米）	2020年 （十亿立方米）	2020年值 占比（%）
以上总计	562.0	586.8	574.0	14.89
世界总产量	3552.1	3852.9	3853.7	100.00

资料来源：《BP世界能源统计年鉴（2021年版）》。

5.1.2 阿拉伯国家其他能源资源开发利用情况

阿拉伯国家煤炭资源储量稀少。根据《BP世界能源统计年鉴（2021年版）》数据，全球煤炭已探明储量为10741.08亿吨，主要集中在以下少数几个国家：美国（23.18%）、俄罗斯（15.10%）、澳大利亚（13.99%）和中国（13.33%）。整个中东与非洲地区2020年底已探明储量仅为160.40亿吨，约占世界总储量的1.49%。

受水资源稀缺和沙漠、荒漠地貌广泛分布等自然条件限制，阿拉伯国家在水能利用方面先天不足。仅伊拉克、埃及等部分阿拉伯国家在摩苏尔、阿斯旺等地建成了水力发电设施。虽然阿拉伯国家水资源匮乏，但太阳能、风能资源比较丰富。大多数阿拉伯国家处于光照条件较好的地带，很少受海洋湿润气团的影响，当地太阳辐射强，其日照水平居世界首位。随着全球能源转型的推进，阿拉伯国家新能源的开发潜力将得以展现（见表5.5、表5.6）。

表5.5 2016~2020年部分阿拉伯国家水能发电量

单位：太瓦时

	2016年	2017年	2018年	2019年	2020年
伊拉克	3.37	2.18	1.82	2.48	2.46
阿尔及利亚	0.07	0.06	0.12	0.15	0.05
埃及	13.20	12.79	12.81	13.21	13.14
摩洛哥	1.26	1.18	1.69	1.26	1.15
世界总计	4018.70	4066.70	4176.70	4227.90	4296.80

资料来源：《BP世界能源统计年鉴（2021年版）》。

续表

	2016年（千桶/天）	2018年（千桶/天）	2020年（千桶/天）	2020年值占比（%）
埃及	567.0	544.1	507.3	0.62
利比亚	389.0	951.0	389.3	0.48
巴林	202.0	194.0	194.0	0.24
也门	24.2	94.0	95.0	0.12
苏丹	103.6	100.3	85.6	0.11
叙利亚	25.0	24.1	43.0	0.05
突尼斯	59.7	51.7	35.5	0.04
毛里塔尼亚	4.8	5.0	5.0	<0.01
摩洛哥	0.16	0.10	0.05	<0.01
约旦	0.01	0.02	0.02	<0.01
以上总计	24653.4	24873.7	21992.0	27.05
世界总产量	79955.8	87250.0	81292.0	100.00

注：突尼斯、叙利亚、卡塔尔、利比亚2020年值为估计值。
资料来源：Annual Statistical Report（2021），OAPEC。

表5.4 部分阿拉伯国家天然气产量

	2016年（十亿立方米）	2018年（十亿立方米）	2020年（十亿立方米）	2020年值占比（%）
卡塔尔	174.5	169.1	171.3	4.45
沙特	105.3	112.1	112.1	2.91
阿尔及利亚	91.4	93.8	81.5	2.11
埃及	40.3	58.6	58.5	1.52
阿联酋	59.5	58.0	55.4	1.44
阿曼	31.5	36.3	36.9	0.96
巴林	14.4	14.6	16.4	0.43
科威特	16.4	16.9	15.0	0.39
利比亚	14.8	13.2	13.3	0.35
伊拉克	9.9	10.6	10.5	0.27
叙利亚	3.5	3.5	3.0	0.08
也门	0.5	0.1	0.1	<0.01

续表

	2016年末（十亿立方米）	2018年末（十亿立方米）	2020年末（十亿立方米）	2020年末值占比（%）
伊拉克	3820	3820	3820	1.86
埃及	2221	2221	2209	1.07
科威特	1784	1784	1784	0.87
利比亚	1505	1505	1505	0.73
叙利亚	285	285	285	0.14
也门	266	265	266	0.13
阿曼	705	677	674	0.33
巴林	224	193	68	0.03
突尼斯	65	64	64	0.03
毛里塔尼亚	28	28	28	0.01
苏丹	25	25	25	0.01
约旦	6	6	6	<0.01
索马里	6	6	6	<0.01
摩洛哥	1	1	1	<0.01
以上总计	54227	54396	55244	26.87
世界总储量	195388	201651	205580	100.00

注：突尼斯、叙利亚、卡塔尔、利比亚2020年末值为估计值。
资料来源：Annual Statistical Report（2021），OAPEC。

表 5.3　部分阿拉伯国家原油产量

	2016年（千桶/天）	2018年（千桶/天）	2020年（千桶/天）	2020年值占比（%）
沙特	10488.8	10315.4	9213.2	11.33
伊拉克	4164.0	4410.0	3998.0	4.92
阿联酋	3088.2	3007.2	2780.4	3.42
科威特	2954.3	2736.2	2439.0	3.00
阿尔及利亚	1020.3	970.0	838.5	1.03
阿曼	908.6	870.0	765.0	0.94
卡塔尔	653.7	600.6	603.1	0.74

国家的油气产量也有所下降（见表5.3、表5.4）。

表5.1 部分阿拉伯国家已探明原油储量

	2016年末（十亿桶）	2018年末（十亿桶）	2020年末（十亿桶）	2020年末值占比（%）
沙特	266.21	267.03	261.60	19.58
伊拉克	148.40	148.40	148.40	11.11
阿联酋	97.80	97.80	107.00	8.01
科威特	101.50	101.50	101.50	7.60
利比亚	48.36	48.36	48.36	3.62
卡塔尔	25.24	25.24	25.24	1.89
阿尔及利亚	12.20	12.20	12.20	0.91
阿曼	4.74	4.74	4.79	0.36
埃及	3.39	3.19	3.11	0.23
也门	2.67	2.67	2.67	0.20
叙利亚	2.50	2.50	2.50	0.19
苏丹	1.50	1.50	1.50	0.11
突尼斯	0.43	0.43	0.43	0.03
巴林	0.12	0.09	0.09	<0.01
毛里塔尼亚	0.02	0.02	0.02	<0.01
以上总计	715.08	715.67	719.41	53.85
世界总储量	1242.60	1276.00	1336.00	100.00

注：突尼斯、叙利亚、卡塔尔、利比亚2020年末值为估计值。
资料来源：Annual Statistical Report (2021), OAPEC。

表5.2 部分阿拉伯国家已探明天然气储量

	2016年末（十亿立方米）	2018年末（十亿立方米）	2020年末（十亿立方米）	2020年末值占比（%）
卡塔尔	24073	23846	23831	11.59
沙特	8618	9074	8438	4.10
阿联酋	6091	6091	7730	3.76
阿尔及利亚	4504	4505	4504	2.19

第5章 中阿能源合作专题报告

阿拉伯国家能源资源丰富，是建设"一带一路"的重点区域。目前，中国已成为世界第一大能源消费国，能源因素在中国外交战略中的权重增加。中国与阿拉伯国家加强能源合作、共建能源丝路是"一带一路"建设的重要内容。

5.1 阿拉伯国家能源资源概况

5.1.1 阿拉伯国家油气资源储量与生产情况

阿拉伯国家所在地区原油储量丰富，目前探明原油储量占世界探明原油储量的比重超过50%，原油产量和出口量在世界市场的份额约为1/3［据《BP世界能源统计年鉴（2021年版）》］。相对该地区石油在世界上的重要地位而言，其天然气储量与生产方面在世界上的比重则要略低一些。沙特的原油储量和产量在阿拉伯国家中居首位，卡塔尔则在天然气的储量与产量上位于第一。

虽然从整体上看阿拉伯国家拥有丰富的油气资源，但其内部分布并不均衡。沙特、伊拉克、阿联酋、科威特四国的原油储量之和占全球总储量的比重达45%，而同为海湾国家的阿曼、巴林两国油气资源相对而言则并不充裕（见表5.1、表5.2）。部分国家如巴林的油气资源甚至已接近枯竭。受新冠肺炎疫情影响，全球能源需求和生产能力均受到制约，阿拉伯

派遣代表参与中阿博览会农业板块的活动，借助农业展会向阿方宣传企业的经营理念、专注方向和技术优势，也可主动邀请阿方代表进行实地考察。

概而言之，农业合作是增强中阿战略伙伴关系的重要抓手，也是落实全球发展倡议的主要方向，同时也受益于中阿战略伙伴关系的发展，促使农业和外交在中国和阿拉伯国家之间形成良性互动，引导变化中的中国和阿拉伯创造有助于彼此发展的战略机遇期。随着中阿农业合作的稳步推进，更多农业企业和农业研究机构将走向阿拉伯，开辟新市场，寻找新领域。中阿农业合作也将在多利益攸关方的共同推动下，取得更多合作成果并探索更多可资他国借鉴的合作经验，以期将农业合作打造成中阿关系的新亮点。

的互通有无和信息对称,从而协调配合,减缓卫生危机等突发扰动对粮食体系的冲击。同时,中国还可发挥基建优势,增加与阿拉伯国家在粮仓建设等方面的合作,助力阿拉伯国家提升粮食仓储能力。另一方面,随着数字科技的快速发展,中阿双方也应提升农业合作的数字化和智能化水平,以科技创新赋能农业合作。例如,中国可充分发挥在无人机方面的优势,提高其在阿拉伯国家民用领域的市场占有率,推动无人机走进阿拉伯的田间地头,通过无人机完成播种、除虫、撒药等农务,帮助阿拉伯国家提高农业耕种效率,提升农业现代化水平。

第三,在农业合作机制方面,中阿双方可考虑建立综合性农业合作机制。当前,中国已建立以农业农村部部长为召集人、以农业合作关联部门为参与方的对外农业合作部际联席会议制度,其主要目的是提高农业国际合作的综合绩效。这一机制可运用于中阿农业合作。这主要是因为农业发展不仅是农业单一领域的问题,还和气候、水源、交通运输、卫生、生物等领域相关,且这些领域中任一环节出现不稳定迹象,都将影响农业国际合作。这从新冠肺炎疫情引发的卫生危机和气候极端化加剧对农业体系的冲击便可管窥。对此,中国和阿拉伯国家可考虑以农业部门为中心,将外交、商务、卫生、生态环境、交通等与农业对外合作相关的部门纳入其中,构建综合性农业合作机制,并定期召开联席会议,以期形成合力,促进中阿农业可持续发展。此外,该机制的建立还有助于增强中阿农业体系的韧性,从而服务于中国粮食双循环发展格局的建立。

第四,在农业合作主体方面,地方政府和农企宜主动借力既有机制,积极配合国家对阿拉伯国家农业合作战略的实施,全面提升中阿农业合作水平。地方政府应依托自身农业优势,在了解阿拉伯国家农业生产现状的基础上,开拓合作领域,对接阿拉伯国家农业发展的需求,增强地方政府参与区域粮食安全治理和农业发展的能力,并以此为路径提升地方政府的国际影响力。同时,在中阿博览会框架下,宁夏回族自治区、各主题省市和主宾国可共同探索新领域、塑造新议题,以期找到利益聚合点,从而构建"小三边"合作,实现各自优势资源的最大使用价值。中国农业企业宜

彰显中阿合作论坛的机制优势，表明在中阿合作的机制化时期，双方的发展需求均得到满足，促使"既关心本国利益又关心对象国利益"成为内在接受且外在认可的行为方式。① 在中阿博览会框架下，农业已成为经贸合作重要板块之一，中阿双方不仅能扩展农业合作议题，也能开拓农业合作伙伴。在中阿技术转移中心框架下，农业是双方技术合作的主要方向，中国已在毛里塔尼亚、约旦、摩洛哥等国建立了农业技术转移中心，推动中国农业"走出去"，提升中阿农业科技合作的层次和规模。未来，为推动中阿农业合作朝着多层次、宽领域、立体化的方向发展，可考虑在风险防范、农业合作领域、农业合作机制、农业合作主体等四个方面综合施策。

第一，在风险防范方面，政府和民间应双管齐下，做好海外风险预防和管控。其一，中国驻外使领馆是保护海外农业利益的"桥头堡"。可考虑定期举办座谈会及时了解中国农企在阿拉伯国家的数量和经营状况，并帮助农企解决现实困境，切实发挥外交为民的作用。其二，农业农村部可考虑向埃及、苏丹、阿联酋、摩洛哥、阿尔及利亚、毛里塔尼亚等主要农业合作国派遣农业外交官，协调中阿农业合作事宜，帮助农企减少经济损失。其三，农企走出去之前应先参照商务部主持的有关阿拉伯国家的国别投资指南，了解合作对象国基本情况，而后有针对性地向国内高校和相关智库咨询专业问题，并派专家组赴阿拉伯国家调研，最后再制定农业合作规划。此外，农企也宜加强和阿拉伯国家地方政府和农企的沟通协调，可考虑让其加入中阿农业合作当中，以共赢的方式减少农企在当地的投资风险和阻力。

第二，在农业合作领域方面，中阿双方需加强在粮食危机预防领域和数字农业领域的合作。一方面，新冠肺炎疫情的暴发反映了中阿双方在粮食危机预防方面的合作仍存在短板。中国和阿拉伯国家的农业部门宜借助互联网平台，共建粮食舆情共享平台，及时更新本国及所掌握的域外国家的粮农信息，以便在重大危机发生时，中阿双方的农业部门能够保持政策

---

① 张帅、孙德刚：《论新时期中国特色的农业外交》，《宁夏社会科学》2019 年第 1 期。

业合作大会于 2021 年 8 月 20 日在宁夏召开。此次大会共筛选签约合作项目 36 个，总金额达 20 亿元。其中中阿合作"一带一路"框架下签署的"走出去"农业合作项目 4 个，农业新技术、新装备引进及贸易促进"引进来"农业合作项目 4 个，围绕农业特色优势产业签署农业投资贸易合作协议 28 个。① 约旦驻华大使胡萨姆·侯赛尼在大会上表示，中国利用现代技术和可再生技术实现了农业发展和现代化，欢迎中国在约旦设立农业技术研究和转让中心，期待与中国在农业领域开展更多合作。② 此外，在第五届中阿博览会举办期间，阿方向中国表达了联合举办技术培训和供需对话等活动的强烈意愿。对此，宁夏对外科技交流中心于 2021 年 12 月 15 日举办了"2021 面向'一带一路'国家现代农业节水技术线上培训班"，助力中阿博览会农业合作意向落地，并提升宁夏对外科技合作交流水平。③

4.3 中阿农业合作的前景展望

2021 年 9 月，习近平主席在第七十六届联合国大会一般性辩论上提出了全球发展倡议，粮食安全就是八大重点发展领域之一。④ 在"一带一路"框架下深化中阿多领域农业合作是落实全球发展倡议的重要抓手。当前，中阿双方已构建了中阿合作论坛、中阿博览会、中阿技术转移中心等合作机制，其中中阿合作论坛是"母体"，中阿博览会和中阿技术转移中心是"子体"，共同为农业合作提供机制保障。在中阿合作论坛框架下，农业已成为中阿双方进一步加强全面合作、共同发展、面向未来的战略伙伴关系的主要动力，服务于中阿命运共同体的建立。同时，中阿农业合作

---

① 《第五届中阿博览会现代农业合作大会签约农业合作项目 36 个》，新华网，http：//www.nx.xinhuanet.com/newscenter/2021-08/20/c_1127780209.htm，2021 年 8 月 20 日。
② 蔺紫鸥等：《科技合作为中阿交流注入新动力》，《光明日报》2021 年 8 月 21 日第 8 版。
③ 《2021 面向"一带一路"国家现代农业节水技术线上培训班成功举办》，中阿技术转移中心网站，https：//www.casttc.org/article/00001476.html，2021 年 12 月 16 日。
④ 《习近平出席第七十六届联合国大会一般性辩论并发表重要讲话》，《人民日报》2021 年 9 月 22 日第 1 版。

表 4.6　2021 年中国与阿拉伯国家的农产品贸易额

单位：万美元

国家名	出口额	排名	进口额	排名	贸易总额	排名
阿联酋	60622.73	1	64175.89	2	124798.62	1
苏丹	3929.54	13	73596.32	1	77525.86	2
埃及	26918.76	3	21963.36	3	48882.12	3
沙特	26853.25	4	4.38	13	26857.63	5
摩洛哥	30633.67	2	3203.83	5	33837.50	4
毛里塔尼亚	8476.48	8	14283.89	4	22760.37	6
伊拉克	16179.07	5	122.71	9	16301.78	8
阿尔及利亚	13231.46	6	8.39	12	13239.85	7
约旦	9473.73	7	19.67	11	9493.40	9
也门	7964.67	10	0	21	7964.67	11
黎巴嫩	4976.60	12	276.69	7	5253.29	12
阿曼	7980.04	9	0.96	15	7981.00	10
科威特	3626.01	14	0.16	17	3626.17	14
卡塔尔	3492.15	15	0.16	16	3492.31	15
利比亚	5226.96	11	0	20	5226.96	13
突尼斯	2476.45	18	146.55	8	2623.00	18
巴林	3022.02	17	3.80	14	3025.82	17
叙利亚	3335.45	16	42.57	10	3378.02	16
索马里	773.75	20	829.22	6	1602.97	20
吉布提	1605.72	19	0	19	1605.72	19
巴勒斯坦	434.28	21	0	22	434.28	21
科摩罗	215.51	22	0	18	215.51	22

资料来源：笔者根据联合国贸易数据库计算所得。UN Comtrade Database，https://comtrade.un.org/data。

4.2.2　中阿农业合作进展

除农产品贸易外，中阿农业合作在项目推进、协议签署和技术培训等方面也取得了新的进展。作为第五届中阿博览会的重要板块，中阿现代农

具体到22个阿拉伯国家，从表4.6中可以看出，2021年，农产品贸易总额排在前十的国家中，西亚阿拉伯国家和非洲阿拉伯国家各占一半，但中国与苏丹、埃及、摩洛哥、毛里塔尼亚和阿尔及利亚等非洲阿拉伯国家的农产品贸易总额（19.62亿美元）要高于与阿联酋、沙特、伊拉克、约旦和阿曼等西亚阿拉伯国家的贸易总额（18.54亿美元）。表4.6还显示出，从农产品进出口额的角度来看，中国与18个阿拉伯国家存在贸易顺差，和阿联酋、苏丹、毛里塔尼亚和索马里等4国处于贸易逆差，和2020年相比，贸易顺差国中减少了阿联酋和索马里。中国与阿联酋、苏丹、毛里塔尼亚和索马里等4个国家的农产品贸易逆差额分别为0.36亿美元、6.97亿美元、0.58亿美元和0.01亿美元。这主要是因为中国从阿联酋进口的"动、植物油、脂及其分解产品；精致的食用油脂；动、植物蜡"、"食品工业的残渣及废料；配制的动物饲料"和"糖及糖食"的数额要大于出口数额；从苏丹进口的"含油子仁及果实；杂项子仁及果实；工业用或药用植物；稻草、秸秆及饲料"、"动、植物油、脂及其分解产品；精致的食用油脂；动、植物蜡"、"食品工业的残渣及废料；配制的动物饲料"、"饮料、酒及醋"和"虫胶；树胶、树脂及其他植物液、汁"的数额要大于出口数额；从毛里塔尼亚进口的"动、植物油、脂及其分解产品；精致的食用油脂；动、植物蜡"、"食品工业的残渣及废料；配制的动物饲料"、"鱼、甲壳动物、软体动物及其他水生无脊椎动物"、"肉、鱼、甲壳动物、软体动物及其他水生无脊椎动物的制品"和"其他动物产品"的数额要大于出口数额；从索马里进口的"含油子仁及果实；杂项子仁及果实；工业用或药用植物；稻草、秸秆及饲料"、"鱼、甲壳动物、软体动物及其他水生无脊椎动物"和"虫胶；树胶、树脂及其他植物液、汁"的数额要大于出口数额。此外，从表4.6中还可以看出，2021年，中国从沙特、阿尔及利亚、阿曼、科威特、卡塔尔、巴林等国进口的农产品极少，进口额还不到10万美元，而中国与也门、利比亚、吉布提、科摩罗和巴勒斯坦没有农产品进口交易。

各农产品的进口额差距较大，有一半农产品的进口额还不到100万美元，进口规模有限。

表4.5 2021年中国从阿拉伯国家进口的农产品

单位：万美元

排名	农产品名称（代码）	进口额
1	含油子仁及果实；杂项子仁及果实；工业用或药用植物；稻草、秸秆及饲料（12）	67270.72
2	动、植物油、脂及其分解产品；精致的食用油脂；动、植物蜡（15）	42385.62
3	食品工业的残渣及废料；配制的动物饲料（23）	38265.81
4	食用水果及坚果；柑橘属水果或甜瓜的果皮（08）	12405.78
5	糖及糖食（17）	10860.38
6	鱼、甲壳动物、软体动物及其他水生无脊椎动物（03）	4090.30
7	虫胶；树胶、树脂及其他植物液、汁（13）	1117.74
8	烟草、烟草及烟草代用品的制品（24）	982.73
9	可可及可可制品（18）	343.76
10	咖啡、茶、马黛茶及调味香料（09）	301.59
11	杂项食品（21）	247.17
12	其他动物产品（05）	130.53
13	饮料、酒及醋（22）	74.08
14	活树及其他活植物；鳞茎、根及类似品；插花及装饰用簇叶（20）	50.25
15	谷物、粮食粉、淀粉或乳的制品；糕饼点心（19）	49.02
16	肉、鱼、甲壳动物、软体动物及其他水生无脊椎动物的制品（16）	43.13
17	编结用植物材料；其他植物产品（14）	31.40
18	乳品；蛋品；天然蜂蜜；其他食用动物产品（04）	14.70
19	活树及其他活植物；鳞茎、根及类似品；插花及装饰用簇叶（06）	11.34
20	食用蔬菜、根及块茎（07）	2.51
21	谷物（10）	0
22	肉及食用杂碎（02）	0
23	制粉工业产品；麦芽；淀粉；菊粉；面筋（11）	0
24	活动物（01）	0

资料来源：笔者根据联合国贸易数据库计算所得。UN Comtrade Database，https://comtrade.un.org/data。

续表

排名	农产品名称（代码）	出口额
8	杂项食品（21）	10160.81
9	烟草、烟草及烟草代用品的制品（24）	8676.39
10	鱼、甲壳动物、软体动物及其他水生无脊椎动物（03）	7746.03
11	糖及糖食（17）	7377.61
12	饮料、酒及醋（22）	3953.27
13	谷物、粮食粉、淀粉或乳的制品；糕饼点心（19）	2898.02
14	食品工业的残渣及废料；配制的动物饲料（23）	2268.17
15	虫胶；树胶、树脂及其他植物液、汁（13）	2066.01
16	可可及可可制品（18）	1924.46
17	其他动物产品（05）	1691.61
18	乳品；蛋品；天然蜂蜜；其他食用动物产品（04）	1447.05
19	活树及其他活植物；鳞茎、根及类似品；插花及装饰用簇叶（06）	1160.76
20	肉及食用杂碎（02）	1094.00
21	动、植物油、脂及其分解产品；精致的食用油脂；动、植物蜡（15）	762.87
22	制粉工业产品；麦芽；淀粉；菊粉；面筋（11）	505.05
23	编结用植物材料；其他植物产品（14）	190.04
24	活动物（01）	5.97

资料来源：笔者根据联合国贸易数据库计算所得。UN Comtrade Database, https://comtrade.un.org/data。

在进口方面，从表4.5中可见，2021年，中国从阿拉伯国家进口的农产品中，有3类农产品的进口额超过了2亿美元，这和2020年持平，其中"含油子仁及果实；杂项子仁及果实；工业用或药用植物；稻草、秸秆及饲料"和"食品工业的残渣及废料；配制的动物饲料"进口额有所增加，"动、植物油、脂及其分解产品；精致的食用油脂；动、植物蜡"的进口额有所下降。从各类农产品的进口额来看，相较2020年，2021年"食品工业的残渣及废料；配制的动物饲料"的增加额最大，增加了0.97亿美元，"动、植物油、脂及其分解产品；精致的食用油脂；动、植物蜡"的下降额最大，下降了2.63亿美元。整体来看，相比2020年，2021年中国对阿拉伯国家的农产品进口额有所下降。同时，从表4.5中可以看出，

续表

排名	农产品名称（代码）	贸易额
22	制粉工业产品；麦芽；淀粉；菊粉；面筋（11）	505.05
23	编结用植物材料；其他植物产品（14）	221.44
24	活动物（01）	5.97

注：农产品名称与编码参照海关总署报关员资格考试教材编写委员会编《进出口商品名称与编码》，中国海关出版社，2013。

资料来源：笔者根据联合国贸易数据库计算所得。UN Comtrade Database，https://comtrade.un.org/data。

在出口方面，从表4.4中可见，2021年，中国向阿拉伯国家出口的农产品中，仍有8类农产品的贸易额维持在1亿美元以上，这和2020年持平。其中"咖啡、茶、马黛茶及调味香料"、"含油子仁及果实；杂项子仁及果实；工业用或药用植物；稻草、秸秆及饲料"、"活树及其他活植物；鳞茎、根及类似品；插花及装饰用簇叶"和"食用蔬菜、根及块茎"的出口总额排名仍保持在前四，和2020年排名一致。但在具体贸易额方面，前4类农产品中，"咖啡、茶、马黛茶及调味香料"和"含油子仁及果实；杂项子仁及果实；工业用或药用植物；稻草、秸秆及饲料"的出口总额较2020年所有上升，剩余2类的出口总额有所下降。

表4.4 2021年中国向阿拉伯国家出口的农产品

单位：万美元

排名	农产品名称（代码）	出口额
1	咖啡、茶、马黛茶及调味香料（09）	57677.23
2	含油子仁及果实；杂项子仁及果实；工业用或药用植物；稻草、秸秆及饲料（12）	31357.72
3	活树及其他活植物；鳞茎、根及类似品；插花及装饰用簇叶（20）	30895.56
4	食用蔬菜、根及块茎（07）	23144.14
5	食用水果及坚果；柑橘属水果或甜瓜的果皮（08）	19098.85
6	谷物（10）	13801.51
7	肉、鱼、甲壳动物、软体动物及其他水生无脊椎动物的制品（16）	11116.82

"肉、鱼、甲壳动物、软体动物及其他水生无脊椎动物的制品"的贸易总额排名下降到了第 11 位，其他农产品的贸易总额排名虽有浮动，但仍处于前十之内。

表 4.3　2021 年中国与阿拉伯国家的农产品贸易

单位：万美元

排名	农产品名称（代码）	贸易额
1	含油子仁及果实；杂项子仁及果实；工业用或药用植物；稻草、秸秆及饲料（12）	98628.44
2	咖啡、茶、马黛茶及调味香料（09）	57978.82
3	动、植物油、脂及其分解产品；精致的食用油脂；动、植物蜡（15）	43148.49
4	食品工业的残渣及废料；配制的动物饲料（23）	40533.98
5	食用水果及坚果；柑橘属水果或甜瓜的果皮（08）	31504.63
6	蔬菜、水果、坚果或植物其他部分的制品（20）	30945.81
7	食用蔬菜、根及块茎（07）	23146.65
8	糖及糖食（17）	18237.99
9	谷物（10）	13801.51
10	鱼、甲壳动物、软体动物及其他水生无脊椎动物（03）	11836.33
11	肉、鱼、甲壳动物、软体动物及其他水生无脊椎动物的制品（16）	11159.95
12	杂项食品（21）	10407.98
13	烟草、烟草及烟草代用品的制品（24）	9659.12
14	饮料、酒及醋（22）	4027.35
15	虫胶；树胶、树脂及其他植物液、汁（13）	3183.75
16	谷物、粮食粉、淀粉或乳的制品；糕饼点心（19）	2947.04
17	可可及可可制品（18）	2268.22
18	其他动物产品（05）	1822.14
19	乳品；蛋品；天然蜂蜜；其他食用动物产品（04）	1461.75
20	活树及其他活植物；鳞茎、根及类似品；插花及装饰用簇叶（06）	1172.10
21	肉及食用杂碎（02）	1094.00

4.2 中阿农业合作情况

2017年，由农业农村部、国家发改委、商务部、外交部联合发布的《共同推进"一带一路"建设农业合作的愿景与行动》明确指出："农业发展仍然是'一带一路'沿线国家国民经济发展的重要基础……开展农业合作是沿线国家的共同诉求。在'一带一路'倡议下，农业国际合作成为沿线国家共建利益共同体和命运共同体的最佳结合点之一。"[①] 阿拉伯国家是中国共建"一带一路"的重要伙伴，农业合作是中阿推进"一带一路"发展的共同关切，这不仅体现在2016年中国政府发布的首份《中国对阿拉伯国家政策文件》之中，也反映在自2004年中阿合作论坛成立以来，中阿双方在论坛机制下所达成的合作共识之中。

4.2.1 中阿农产品贸易往来

综合来看，2021年，中阿农产品贸易总额为41.97亿美元（见表4.3），比2020年减少了0.12亿美元。其中中国向阿拉伯国家出口农产品总额为24.10亿美元（见表4.4），比2020年增加0.39亿美元；中国从阿拉伯国家进口农产品总额为17.87亿美元（见表4.5），比2020年减少0.51亿美元。2021年，中国对阿拉伯国家农产品贸易继续保持顺差状态，顺差额为6.23亿美元。

具体而言，从表4.3中可以看出，2021年，中阿农产品贸易额位于前十的农产品主要是药用植物、稻草、饲料、动植物油、咖啡、茶、香料、蔬菜、水果、坚果、水生动物、谷物、糖等。与2020年相比，贸易总额位于前十的农产品中，"含油子仁及果实；杂项子仁及果实；工业用或药用植物；稻草、秸秆及饲料"的贸易总额排名没有变动，仍处于第1位。

---

① 《共同推进"一带一路"建设农业合作的愿景与行动》，农业农村部网站，http://www.gjs.moa.gov.cn/ydylhzhhnyzcq/201904/t20190418_6184207.htm，2017年11月23日。

表 4.2 2020 年部分阿拉伯国家小麦进口状况

世界排名	国家	进口总额（亿美元）	进口变化幅度（%）
1	埃及	26.93	-10.9
7	阿尔及利亚	16.40	+11
10	摩洛哥	14.23	+48.2
21	也门	6.73	-1.8
25	苏丹	5.27	+10.5
30	突尼斯	4.66	+15
38	阿联酋	2.97	-12.5
44	利比亚	2.44	-7.1
48	约旦	2.15	+6.1
51	沙特	1.94	+57.2
55	毛里塔尼亚	1.82	+23.7
61	黎巴嫩	1.48	+20.5
62	阿曼	1.41	-10.5
68	科威特	1.26	-16.4

资料来源："Wheat Imports by Country", https://www.worldstopexports.com/wheat-imports-by-country/。

整体来看，农业发展缓慢和粮食不安全已在阿拉伯地区呈区域性聚集，地区内具有重要影响力的大国都不具备凝聚各方力量构建区域合作机制以解决地区内共有的发展和安全问题的能力。[1] 因此，对外农业合作成为阿拉伯国家集体应对农业和粮食安全的有效路径。中国是阿拉伯国家开展农业合作的重要伙伴，中阿农业交往既有历史积累又有现实基础，这为中阿共同推动全方位、多维度的农业合作创造了良好的氛围和有益的条件。

---

[1] 张帅:《中阿合作论坛框架下的农业合作：特征、动因与挑战》,《西亚非洲》2020 年第 6 期。

续表

国家	主要农作物及其耕种面积				
阿曼	椰枣 25630	新鲜蔬菜 12405	高粱 3674	西红柿 3504	玉米 3112
阿联酋	椰枣 38422	葱 1022	新鲜蔬菜 731	西红柿 684	黄瓜 683
约旦	橄榄 59761	大麦 43877	小麦 10926	西红柿 9140	土豆 5161
伊拉克	小麦 2143421	大麦 1132122	椰枣 245033	橙子 104221	稻米 101716
黎巴嫩	橄榄 62868	小麦 41000	土豆 22649	苹果 14787	大麦 14000
叙利亚	大麦 1502926	小麦 1350538	橄榄 696363	小扁豆 112657	鹰嘴豆 71864
也门	高粱 322408	小米 90000	小麦 57218	咖啡豆 37314	玉米 37000
索马里	玉米 100000	高粱 250000	干豆角 86202	芝麻籽 73769	籽棉 17901
巴勒斯坦	橄榄 54336	小麦 15147	大麦 7185	野豌豆 3403	葡萄 3200

注：表中统计的主要是各国耕种面积排前五的农作物，吉布提只有四种农作物被统计。
资料来源：笔者根据联合国粮农组织2021年12月21日发布的数据整理所得，https://www.fao.org/faostat/zh/#data/QCL。

进口粮食是阿拉伯国家解决粮食供不应求的主要路径。以小麦为例，从表4.2中可以看出，阿拉伯地区是全球主要的小麦进口地。2020年，全球小麦进口额最高的10个国家中，阿拉伯国家占3个，且在22个阿拉伯国家中，仅有8个国家的小麦进口额处于全球100名之外，其余14个国家均位于全球小麦进口国家前100名之内。此外，从表4.2中还可以看出，位于全球小麦进口前100名的阿拉伯国家，多数小麦进口量仍保持增长趋势，即便少数国家的小麦进口额相比上一年有所下降，其综合排名也依旧位居前列。可见，"高进口量"已经成为阿拉伯国家粮食贸易的主要特征。

亚阿拉伯国家；二是因为北非阿拉伯国家对小麦等谷物的需求量较高。此外，表4.1还反映了耕地面积不足是阿拉伯国家保障粮食安全的主要制约因素。

表4.1 2020年阿拉伯国家的主要农作物及其耕种面积

单位：公顷

国家	主要农作物及其耕种面积				
埃及	玉米 1458881	小麦 1370235	稻米 554205	甜菜 263543	土豆 178608
利比亚	橄榄 238759	小麦 168497	大麦 137084	带壳杏仁 60396	椰枣 32868
摩洛哥	小麦 2845290	带壳杏仁 209233	大麦 1495190	蚕豆 107408	橄榄 1068895
阿尔及利亚	小麦 1848083	大麦 978114	橄榄 438828	椰枣 170500	土豆 149465
突尼斯	小麦 606000	大麦 542000	橄榄 3642569	带壳杏仁 171385	椰枣 72205
毛里塔尼亚	高粱 205425	稻米 69256	干豆 36523	干豌豆 27972	干豇豆 22450
苏丹	高粱 5793609	芝麻籽 5173521	带壳花生 3197181	小米 2424630	干豇豆 853088
科摩罗	椰子 27957	稻米 23570	干豆 17033	木薯 11569	丁香 8130
吉布提	干豆角 7082	新鲜蔬菜 5010	干辣椒 317	玉米 9	—
沙特	椰枣 152705	小麦 86983	大麦 81520	高粱 55687	新鲜水果 41095
科威特	椰枣 3669	玉米 1259	新鲜蔬菜 1086	土豆 895	西红柿 803
巴林	椰枣 2470	新鲜水果 694	坚果 169	柠檬 94	香蕉 88
卡塔尔	椰枣 2216	新鲜蔬菜 473	西红柿 465	黄瓜 272	茄子 231

作为战略重点。① 此外，新冠肺炎疫情的暴发反映了阿拉伯国家在粮食仓储方面的不足，促使阿拉伯国家将粮食仓储作为粮农治理的重点关切。例如，阿联酋颁布法律，规范粮食战略储备监管；埃及进一步加大主粮战略储备；苏丹宣布建立应急粮食储备机制；等等。②

尽管农业已成为阿拉伯国家以变革促发展和以转型求自强的重要领域，但实现地区农业可持续发展仍面临耕地面积短缺、灌溉水源有限、土壤肥力下降、人口持续增长、贫困率居高不下、冲突频发等多重挑战，使得阿拉伯地区农业发展整体滞后，地区粮食安全形势尚未得到有效改善。据联合国粮农组织发布的《近东北非区域粮食安全和营养概述：数据和趋势》，2020年，近东北非地区营养不良人数约6900万人，比2019年增加480万人。此外，有近1.41亿阿拉伯人在2020年无法获得充足的粮食，较2019年增加了1000多万人，③ 其中叙利亚、苏丹、黎巴嫩、也门、索马里等国的粮食安全形势最为严峻。④

阿拉伯粮食安全问题突出表现为粮食供需矛盾尖锐，这与阿拉伯国家的农业耕种结构密切相关。如表4.1所示，阿拉伯国家种植面积排前五的农作物中，小麦、玉米和稻米等谷物占比相对较少，这主要是因为谷物创造的经济收益总体低于其他农作物。从保障国家粮食安全的角度来看，这种耕种结构无益于解决阿拉伯地区的粮食安全问题。从表4.1中还可以看出，北非阿拉伯国家的谷物耕种面积普遍高于西亚阿拉伯国家，这主要是由两方面原因所致。一是因为北非阿拉伯国家的农业自然资源总体优于西

---

① 《对外投资合作国别（地区）指南：约旦》，商务部网站，http://www.mofcom.gov.cn/dl/gbdqzn/upload/yuedan.pdf。
② 《境外涉农信息快报》（第64期、66期、67期），农业农村部网站，http://www.gjs.moa.gov.cn/。
③ FAO ed., *Near East and North Africa Regional Overview of Food Security and Nutrition: Statistics and Trends*, Cairo: FAO, 2021, p. v.
④ FAO and WFP, "Hunger Hotpots FAO-WFP Early Warnings on Acute Food Insecurity: February to May 2022 Outlook", FAO, https://www.fao.org/3/cb8376en/cb8376en.pdf#:~:text=The%20Food%20and%20Agricultu re%20Organization%20of%20the%20United, the%20outlook%20period%20from%20February%20to%20May%202022.

4.1 阿拉伯国家农业发展现状

农业对阿拉伯国家而言，不仅是经济问题，更是关系国家政权稳定的政治议题。事实上，2010年底开始席卷阿拉伯世界的"中东剧变"与2008~2009年世界粮食危机存在重要关联；① 2020~2021年，苏丹、叙利亚、黎巴嫩等国发生的"阿拉伯之春"第二波与这些国家面临的"面包危机"密切相关。② 历经中东剧变的阿拉伯国家比以往任何时候都重视农业发展和粮食安全，这从阿拉伯国家制定的愿景规划和发展战略中便可管窥。例如，沙特的"2030愿景"强调：将建立安全充足的粮食战略储备，以确保紧急时期的粮食供应；推动水产养殖业的发展，与拥有肥沃土壤和丰富水源的国家建立战略伙伴关系，水资源将优先用于农业生产；将加强与粮食消费者、生产者和分配者的合作，以减少资源浪费。③ 埃及《2030发展规划》制定了增加农作物种植面积、支持农业现代化、为战略性农作物建立分装和仓储设施、发展水产养殖、建立农业现代化中心、开发国家级家禽养殖项目等一系列农业发展规划。④ 约旦在《约旦2025：国家愿景和战略》框架下制定了《2020—2025年国家农业发展战略》，将推进农业结构调整、农业信息化、现代技术应用、提高生产力、发展战略性作物、发展物流经营链、改善农产品加工链、发展出口链、扩大林牧区等

---

① 张帅：《埃及粮食安全：困境与归因》，《西亚非洲》2018年第3期。
② "Syrian Capital Sees Worsening Bread Crisis", Asharq al-Awsat, https://english.aawsat.com/home/article/2623156/syrian-capital-sees-worsening-bread-crisis; "Lebanon Hikes Price of Bread by 50%", Asharq al-Awsat, https://english.aawsat.com/home/article/2736336/lebanon-hikes-price-bread-50; "Bread and Fuel Protests Continue Throughout Sudan", Dabanga, https://www.dabangasudan.org/en/all-news/article/bread-and-fuel-protests-continue-throughout-sudan.
③ "Kingdom of Saudi Arabia: Vision 2030", https://www.vision2030.gov.sa/media/rc0b5oy1/saudi_vision 203.pdf.
④ 《对外投资合作国别（地区）指南：埃及》，商务部网站，http://www.mofcom.gov.cn/dl/gbdqzn/upload/aiji.pdf。

第4章 中阿农业合作专题报告

当前,全球粮食体系正面临气候极端化、新冠肺炎疫情蔓延、局部冲突和战争、经济疲软等多重因素的叠加影响,全球粮食安全在供给、获取、有效利用和稳定性等四个层面均呈螺旋式恶化趋势,粮食危机越发严峻。联合国粮农组织、世界粮食计划署、国际农发基金等联合国机构联合发布的《2021年世界粮食安全和营养状况》显示,2020年,全球共有7.2亿至8.11亿人遭受饥饿,若取其中间值7.66亿,2020年饥饿人数较2019年增加约1.18亿,[①] 进一步加重了全球粮食安全治理的负担。

在全球粮食体系遭受冲击的背景下,加强对外农业合作、保障粮食安全、构建更具韧性和可持续性的粮食体系成为各国的普遍关切。中国作为农业大国,随着持续推进"一带一路"建设,加强与"一带一路"共建国家的农业合作,成为推动"一带一路"高质量发展的重要抓手。阿拉伯地区是"一带一路"的必经之地,农业是阿拉伯国家保民生、促发展的主要领域,农业合作日渐成为阿拉伯国家发展双、多边关系的核心议题。对农业和粮食安全的高度重视,促使农业合作成为中阿增进战略合作伙伴关系的主要路径。

---

① FAO et al., eds., *The State of Food Security and Nutrition in the World: Transforming Food Systems for Food Security, Improved Nutrition and Affordable Healthy Diets for All*, Rome: FAO, 2021, p. xii.

到了严峻挑战，导致吸引的外国直接投资全球占比较低，从而不能更好地从外国直接投资中获益。阿拉伯货币基金组织（AMF）报告指出，阿拉伯国家的经济自由度、政府治理和商业环境质量，是影响阿拉伯国家外国直接投资流入的关键因素。① 营商环境差限制了私营部门的发展，也影响了外资流入。疫情冲击下，一些阿拉伯国家财政吃紧，债台高筑，有可能出台过度保护本国企业的投资政策和法律法规，从而对中阿投资产生影响。

3.3.2.4 中国经济进入新发展阶段

新发展阶段，要求贯彻新发展理念、构建新发展格局、推动高质量发展。国内经济下行压力传导至金融体系，将给银行信贷需求、资产质量等带来负面影响，从而影响海外投资项目的融资空间和融资成本。国内企业由于预期投资收益下滑、现金流紧张，以及东道国经济收缩，也有可能放缓对外投资的步伐。

总之，中国进入"十四五"建设时期，中方将与阿拉伯国家一道，继续发扬合作精神，加强战略沟通，开展双边对话，以合作促发展，将高质量共建"一带一路"与地区国家规划相衔接，形成阿拉伯国家向东开放，中国向西拓展合作，双方优势互补、互利共赢的格局。② 正如习近平主席在致第五届中阿博览会贺信中所说，"中国愿同阿拉伯国家一道，合作应对挑战，共促和平发展，努力携手打造面向新时代的中阿命运共同体"③，这为中阿未来关系指明了前进的方向。

---

① AMF, *The Role of Economic Freedom, Governance, and Business Environment in Attracting Foreign Direct Investment in the Arab Region*, March 2022, p.5.
② 谢菲：《打造面向新时代的中阿命运共同体》，求是网，http://www.qstheory.cn/qshyjx/2021-08/21/c_1127782395.htm，2021年8月21日。
③ 《携手打造面向新时代的中阿命运共同体 推动中阿共建"一带一路"达到更高水平——第五届中国-阿拉伯国家博览会成功举办》，中华人民共和国商务部网站，http://www.mofcom.gov.cn/article/jiguanzx/202109/20210903195308.shtml，2021年9月6日。

3.3.2 中阿投资合作面临的新挑战

中阿投资合作总体环境利好,互补性强,双边需求强劲。然而,百年未有之大变局形势下,中阿投资合作仍面临许多风险和挑战。

3.3.2.1 全球经济面临不确定性

近年来,民粹主义和逆全球化思潮有所抬头,保护主义和单边主义对世界经济的负面影响逐步显现,霸权主义对世界和平与发展构成威胁,世界进入动荡变革期。新冠肺炎疫情对全球经济的影响仍在继续,国际货币基金组织和世界银行等国际机构均下调2022年全球经济增长预期。[①] 2021年全球外国直接投资流动大幅上涨77%,达到1.65万亿美元,超过疫情前的投资水平。流入西亚国家(包括土耳其)的直接投资大幅上涨49%,达到900亿美元,其中流入沙特的FDI增加了2倍,达到230亿美元,部分原因是跨境并购的增加。流入北非阿拉伯国家的直接投资却出现13%的降幅,降至90亿美元。[②] 新冠肺炎疫情全球冲击仍在延续,部分地区的地缘政治紧张局势升级,因此制造业和全球价值链的新增投资仍然处于低水平。疫苗接种率、基础设施投资、供应链瓶颈、能源价格和通胀将是决定未来全球投资的主要因素。

3.3.2.2 中东地区地缘政治风险高

战乱冲突和频频发生的暴恐事件,威胁阿拉伯国家中资企业人员及财产安全。一些西方大国出于自身利益对阿拉伯国家内政和外交横加干涉,甚至武力介入,逼迫阿拉伯国家在中美之间选边站队,成为中阿深化合作的潜在威胁。

3.3.2.3 阿拉伯国家总体投资环境较差

尽管该地区自然资源丰富,但阿拉伯国家在吸引外国直接投资方面遇

[①] 国际货币基金组织2022年4月的《世界经济展望报告》,预计2022年全球经济将增长3.6%,较此前1月的预测下调0.8个百分点。经济增长预期下调反映了新冠肺炎疫情反弹对经济的影响,以及俄乌冲突对全球经济的冲击。

[②] UNCTAD, *Investment Trends Monitor*, January 2022, p. 3.

近年来，谋和平求发展成为广大阿拉伯国家的共识，亟须国际经济合作。中阿真诚合作为阿拉伯国家的和平发展作出"中国贡献"，阿拉伯国家"向东看"趋势日益明显，双边合作领域不断拓展。第四，中国与阿拉伯国家互补性强，可以说，双方在转型发展、产业升级等方面高度契合，双方合作意愿强烈。第五，中阿都面临改革发展稳定的艰巨任务，双方在扩大青年就业、缩小收入差距、防范和化解重大风险、推进国家治理体系和能源现代化以及环境保护等方面都面临着相似的挑战和问题。[1]

3.3.1.3 中阿投资需求日益增大

阿拉伯国家，无论是石油进口国还是产油国，都在进行经济改革，促进多元化发展，都面临融资难和技术短缺问题。近年来，各国采取多种举措，改善投资环境以吸引外资，一些国家出台了新的投资法，给予外资各种优惠举措，欢迎来自中国的投资和技术。中国是全球第二大直接投资目的地和投资来源国，也是全球价值链的重要枢纽和制造中心。中国在"引进来"和"走出去"、发挥两个市场作用、利用好两种资源方面，获得了长足发展，成为双向投资大国。中阿投资空间大，前景广阔。

3.3.1.4 中阿投资合作领域出现新增长极

除了传统能源、基础设施和工程承包等领域，中国与阿拉伯国家在5G、大数据、人工智能、航空航天等高新技术领域的合作不断加强，携手应对气候变化和能源转型的交流方兴未艾，中国产品、中国技术、中国标准在阿拉伯世界的品牌效应不断显现。[2] 未来，中阿探索数字化转型合作加速，在传统能源合作的基础上，清洁能源与技术合作成为新的增长点，可再生能源、能源减贫与治理成为合作新亮点。未来中阿将拓展双方在数字经济、人工智能、新能源、现代农业等新兴领域的合作。

---

[1] 丛培影：《共建、共享"一带一路"谱写中阿合作新篇章》，http://fec.mofcom.gov.cn/article/fwydyl/zgzx/202109/20210903194173.shtml，2021年9月2日。

[2]《携手打造面向新时代的中阿命运共同体 推动中阿共建"一带一路"达到更高水平——第五届中国-阿拉伯国家博览会成功举办》，中华人民共和国商务部网站，http://www.mofcom.gov.cn/article/jiguanzx/202109/20210903195308.shtml，2021年9月6日。

3.3.1 中阿投资合作新机遇

"一带一路"推动中阿合作务实开展，中阿"1+2+3"合作格局逐渐升级换代。虽然受到全球疫情蔓延影响，但中阿合作和共建"一带一路"并未停滞，而是展现出强大韧性和旺盛活力，迎来投资合作新机遇。

3.3.1.1 高层引领推动"一带一路"高质量发展

近年来，中阿高层往来不断，习近平主席与多个阿拉伯国家领导人多次互通电话。2020年7月，中国—阿拉伯国家合作论坛第九届部长级会议成功举行，为新形势下的中阿战略伙伴关系开辟了更广阔前景。2021年4月6日，中阿合作论坛第九届企业家大会暨第七届投资研讨会在北京举办，以"携手推进面向未来的中阿经贸合作"为主题。6月22日，中阿合作论坛第十七次高官会和第六次高官级战略政治对话以视频连线方式举行，会议总结了论坛第九届部长级会议成果落实情况，讨论了中阿峰会筹备及下阶段工作计划，就双方共同关心的国际和地区问题交换了意见。7月，王毅国务委员兼外长访问埃及，并会见阿盟秘书长。

近年来，阿盟外长理事会连续作出对华关系决议，呼吁阿盟成员国积极发展同中国在各个领域的关系。2021年3月3日，第155届阿盟外长理事会会议通过决议，强调阿盟各成员国重视在"一带一路"倡议下加强同中国在各领域的关系，重申阿拉伯国家支持一个中国原则，重申欢迎沙特适时举办阿中峰会以拓宽阿中战略伙伴关系前景，服务于双方的共同利益，并赞赏阿中双方抗击新冠肺炎疫情方面所取得的合作成果。

3.3.1.2 中阿是共建"一带一路"的天然伙伴

第一，中国和阿拉伯国家的友好关系由来已久，双方在许多重大国际问题上立场相近，在国际舞台上相互尊重、相互支持。近年来，中阿双方在联合国改革、气候变化、多哈回合谈判等问题上保持着密切的协调与配合。第二，中阿双方在未来国家发展战略上高度契合。中国正在构建以国内大循环为主体、国内国际双循环相互促进的新发展格局。很多阿拉伯国家都迫切希望实现经济多元化发展战略，减轻对单一经济的依赖。第三，

光学产业制造基地项目二期动工奠基仪式在沙特朱拜勒举行，中沙产能合作迈上新台阶。在当天的动工仪式上，中国深工新能源有限公司、沙特基础工业公司等中沙企业间还完成了5项重点合作项目集中签约，签约总投资额达10亿美元，涵盖新材料、医疗器械、产业互联网、循环经济、绿色能源等领域。8月第五届中国—阿拉伯国家博览会以"数智云展·沟通无限"为主题，首次在线上举办，重点围绕分享发展战略新机遇、共享数字经济新成果、畅享云端丝路新未来三个方面实现数字赋能、双线融合。线上博览会充分运用数字化会议和展览手段，依托5G、人工智能、大数据、云计算等信息技术，通过搭建云展馆、云商城，开展云洽谈、云签约，积极引导国内外企业线上参会参展，吸引更多观众云逛展、云采购。

近年来，中阿北斗合作充满活力，越来越多的阿拉伯国家与中国开展了北斗应用领域的合作。北斗在阿联酋铁路建设、沙特精准农业、国土测绘等领域应用成果丰硕，积累了北斗建设应用发展经验。未来北斗在阿拉伯民用航空、石化能源、电力管理等行业领域的应用前景也令人期待。2021年12月8日，第三届中阿北斗合作论坛成功举办，为中阿北斗合作绘制新蓝图。

总之，在"一带一路"倡议推动下，中国与阿拉伯国家间各领域合作愈加密切深入，除传统能源领域和基础设施领域外，在清洁能源、数字经济、园区建设等领域也不断开拓创新，为双方合作注入新动力。

3.3 中阿投资合作新机遇和新挑战

尽管新冠肺炎疫情对全球经济影响深远，导致全球投资骤降，但国际投资监测机构仍然加大了对阿拉伯国家的关注，因为阿联酋、沙特、卡塔尔、埃及和阿曼等国具有巨大的投资潜力。作为共建"一带一路"天然伙伴的阿拉伯国家，投资活力和潜力都很大。中阿同处于百年未有之大变局之中，中阿投资合作迎来新机遇，但也面临新挑战。

仪式以"云签署"方式举行。根据合同,沙特基础工业公司与福建石化集团将成立一家合资企业,拟投资约400亿元人民币,在福建省古雷石化基地建设并运营一座世界级大型石化联合体——中沙古雷乙烯项目。该项目将建设一套年产150万吨乙烯的装置,同时配套建设一系列下游生产装置,采用多项全球先进技术,具有装置规模大、经济效益好、高端产品多、能耗排放少、下游带动强等特点。福建是海上丝绸之路的起点,沙特是最早的"一带一路"共建国家之一。这次双方合作的中沙古雷乙烯项目,对于推进共建"一带一路"同沙特"2030愿景"对接,进一步加深和巩固中沙长期合作与友谊,都具有重要意义。阿布扎比和中国的一些石油国企建立了战略合作伙伴关系,双方将携手探索在上游勘探开发、炼化产业和液化天然气等领域的合作机遇,未来十年两国的油气贸易有望继续增长。2021年6月28日,中国石油集团东方地球物理勘探有限责任公司(英文简称BGP)与科威特国家石油公司(英文简称KOC)通过跨国视频"云签约"的方式签订了科威特科西及穆特里巴三维勘探项目,进一步巩固了BGP在科威特乃至中东物探行业高端市场的龙头地位,标志着双方在"一带一路"油气合作上又取得了新成效。

3.2.3 数字化转型将成为中阿合作重点

中阿双方在数字经济、跨境电子商务等领域的合作为构建开放、公平、非歧视的数字营商环境创造了条件。中阿双方在科技含量更高领域的合作不仅提升了双方的合作水平,也为"一带一路"高质量发展注入新动力。中东多国纷纷出台数字化战略和相关政策,将发展数字经济作为加快推动经济多元化和产业转型升级的重要抓手。中国具备领先的数字技术优势,双方未来合作前景广阔。5G、大数据、人工智能等高新技术方面也有望成为双方合作的新增长极。中阿应抓住数字经济的机遇,加速数字产业化和产业数字化进程,推动经济转型和多元化,携手打造面向新时代的中阿命运共同体。

2021年7月1日,中沙合作高科技项目——深工沙特塑胶新材及电子

益于疫苗合作与充足产能，2020年迪拜世博会和2022年北京冬奥会筹备工作进展顺利，阿联酋和中国相互支持，正在共同努力改善国际健康和福祉，为各国人民和世界的和平与繁荣而努力。

3.2.2 面向未来，开创中阿能源合作新时代

中阿在新能源、清洁能源等领域的合作，实现"一带一路"绿色、低碳、可持续发展的理念。近年来，中阿双方加紧能源转型，在探索清洁能源利用领域加强合作。从中埃可再生能源国家联合实验室、卡塔尔绿色智能节水灌溉技术、阿联酋清洁煤炭项目到沙特红海综合智慧能源项目等，清洁能源建设成为中阿"一带一路"合作的重要领域和新亮点，积极推进"油气合作、低碳能源合作'双轮'转动"，重点推动清洁能源应用技术、低碳经济、能源转型等合作，开创中阿能源合作新时代。

2021年12月26日，中国潍柴集团同埃及吉时集团在开罗举行"油改气"、本地化生产以及天然气罐等合作项目签约仪式。埃及正致力于发展清洁和可再生能源，推动传统产业升级改造，努力实现可持续发展目标，欢迎更多中国企业来埃投资兴业，特别是参与埃及绿色合作和本地化生产项目，推动技术转移，助力埃及绿色转型，进一步拓展和深化中埃在各领域特别是清洁能源和本地化生产项目上的合作，推动中埃全面战略伙伴关系取得更大发展。2021年8月，伊拉克与中国电力建设股份有限公司（中国电建）签署了建设2000兆瓦光伏电站的协议，中国电建将首先建设750兆瓦的装机容量。同时，山东电力建设第三工程有限公司承建的约旦第仕24兆瓦光伏项目开工建设，这是中资企业在约旦承建的首个光伏电站项目。电站建成后，不仅将更好满足周边区域用电需求，还将大大缓解水厂用电压力，提升水厂供水能力，有助于降低当地用水价格。

在中阿传统能源合作领域，转型升级的步伐也不断加快。沙特阿美公司作为中国能源市场的重要供应商，与中国的大学和公司合作开发更清洁的发动机燃料系统和技术，以减少温室气体排放，双方还将开展更多新技术的开发合作。2021年8月，中沙古雷乙烯项目合资合同正式签约，签约

2021年8月，第五届中阿博览会经贸合作成果丰硕，共签约成果277个，计划投资和贸易总额1566.7亿元，其中投资类项目199个，投资额1539.2亿元；贸易类项目24个，贸易额27.5亿元；发布政策报告、签署备忘录协议54个。[①] 2021年4月中阿合作论坛第九届企业家大会暨第七届投资研讨会在北京以线上线下结合方式举办，会议以"携手推进面向未来的中阿经贸合作"为主题，就"加强经济融合，提升合作水平"和"共兴数字经济，实现共同发展"等议题进行深入讨论，聚焦"后疫情时代"中阿经贸合作新机遇。

3.2.1 携手共建人类卫生健康共同体

中方已向阿拉伯国家援助和出口大量中国疫苗，并与阿联酋、埃及等国开展疫苗联合灌装生产合作，有力支援了阿拉伯国家抗疫工作。后疫情时代，公共卫生合作将是中阿共建"一带一路"的重要领域，中阿将不断深化医疗物资采购、疫苗合作生产等卫生领域的投资合作，为阿拉伯国家战胜疫情、复苏经济提供强大助力，携手共建人类卫生健康共同体。

2021年3月，中国和阿联酋启动当地疫苗合作生产线。中国国务委员兼外长王毅于当地时间3月28日在阿布扎比同阿联酋外长阿卜杜拉举行会谈，双方共同出席中阿两国合作灌装中国新冠疫苗生产线项目的"云启动"仪式。阿联酋海湾制药厂Julphar将批量生产中国新冠疫苗，此次合作是中国新冠疫苗生产线首次在海外投产。阿联酋将成为海湾地区第一个拥有新冠疫苗生产基地的国家，整个中东地区的疫苗供应将得到较大改善。中方还分批向阿方提供了近1000万剂疫苗，助推阿跻身全球接种率最高国家行列。中国国药集团将与总部位于阿布扎比的G42公司成立合资公司，计划每年生产2亿剂新冠疫苗，助力阿联酋"疫苗枢纽计划"。得

---

① 《第五届中阿博览会成果丰硕》，宁夏新闻网，http：//www.nxnews.net/zt/2021/dwjzablh/dwjxwzx/202108/t20210823_7244891.html，2021年8月23日。

阿拉伯国家对华直接投资最大国，投资流量从 2019 年的 2141 万美元增加至 2802 万美元，约占当年阿拉伯国家对华投资总额的 71.6%。与此同时，沙特和科威特对华投资大幅下滑。2020 年，沙特对华投资额从 2019 年的 1170 万美元下降至仅为 97 万美元；科威特 2019 年对华投资额为 742 万美元，2020 年则没有对华投资。①

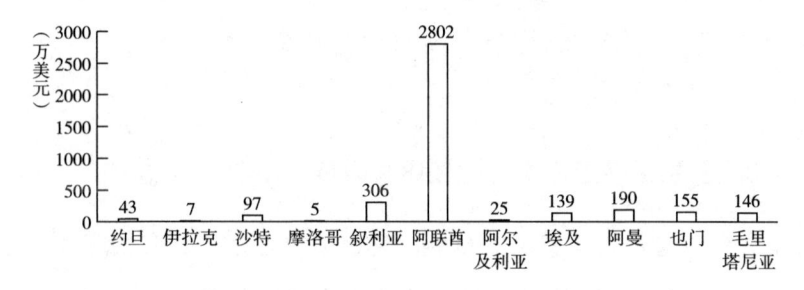

图 3.5　2020 年中国吸引阿拉伯国家直接投资流量

资料来源："国家数据"，国家统计局网站，https://data.stats.gov.cn/easyquery.htm?cn=C01，2022 年 4 月 6 日。

总之，2020 年，中阿双方同舟共济，合作领域不断拓展，为高质量共建"一带一路"提供坚强的物质基础，并在实践中探索有效的制度和理念支撑，向打造新时代中阿命运共同体迈出了坚实一步。

3.2　2021 年中阿投资新趋势

2021 年，中阿双方团结抗疫，贸易、投资和金融等领域的合作展现出强劲韧性和旺盛活力。事实上，从基础设施建设到产业园区扩增，从能源转型合作到跨境电商走红，从货物贸易交往到金融产业对接，得益于共建"一带一路"释放的政策红利，中阿合作已成功实现"换挡提速"，中阿投资呈现新特点和新趋势。

---

① "国家数据"，国家统计局网站，https://data.stats.gov.cn/easyquery.htm?cn=C01，2022 年 10 月 14 日。

表 3.1　2020 年中国对世界主要经济体直接投资情况

单位：亿美元

经济体	流量			存量	
	金额	同比（%）	比重（%）	金额	比重（%）
中国香港	891.46	-1.6	58.0	14385.31	55.7
东盟	160.63	23.3	10.4	1276.13	4.9
欧盟	100.99	5.2	6.6	830.16	3.2
美国	60.19	58.1	3.9	800.48	3.1
澳大利亚	11.99	-42.5	0.8	344.39	1.3
俄罗斯	5.70	—	0.4	120.71	0.5
阿拉伯国家	28.33	24.8	1.8	212.95	0.8
合计	1259.29	3.2	81.9	17970.13	69.5

资料来源：中华人民共和国商务部、国家统计局、国家外汇管理局编《2020 年度中国对外直接投资统计公报》，中国商务出版社，2021，第 33 页。

3.1.4　阿拉伯国家对华投资概况

海合会国家是阿拉伯国家对华投资主体。受疫情、低油价和全球经济衰退影响，2020 年阿拉伯国家对外投资流动也出现下降。阿联酋对外投资额从 2019 年的 201 亿美元下降至 190 亿美元；沙特对外投资额从 2019 年的 135 亿美元大幅下降至 49 亿美元，这是由于沙特公共投资基金（PIF）重新将重点放在国内投资上，以抵消疫情的负面经济影响以及外国直接投资放缓造成的影响。卡塔尔对外投资额从 2019 年的 45 亿美元下降至 27 亿美元。科威特对外投资仍大幅增加，到 2020 年达到 24 亿美元，这主要是因为科威特主权财富基金的新战略重点在海外股权和基础设施项目上，而不是投资组合。阿曼对外投资额也从 2019 年的 6 亿美元上升至 13 亿美元。[①] 受此影响，阿拉伯国家对华直接投资流量从 2019 年的 4448 万美元下降至 2020 年的 3915 万美元，同比下降 12%。如图 3.5 所示，阿联酋是 2020 年

---

① UNCTAD, *World Investment Report 2021*, June 2021, p.248.

占比仅为 0.8%。阿拉伯国家外国直接投资流入主要来源于欧洲、美国和阿拉伯地区内部，2020 年中国对阿拉伯国家直接投资流量占当年阿拉伯国家吸引直接投资总额（381.7 亿美元）的 7.4%。① 第四，中国对阿拉伯国家直接投资日益多元化。从投资主体来看，仍以国有企业为主，投资领域主要集中在能源、基础设施、建筑建材等。与此同时，民营企业走向阿拉伯国家的数量也呈较快上升态势，涉及信息业、制造业、建筑业、商贸服务业和生活服务业等。华为、中兴和阿里巴巴等企业已在阿拉伯开展通信设备、信息技术等服务。第五，合作领域不断拓宽，中阿"1+2+3"②的合作格局不断提质升级。在疫情防控期间，中阿双方跨境线上交流活动频繁，数字经济在双方交往合作中发挥了重要的作用。第六，打造健康丝绸之路，加强医疗卫生领域合作。在中国人民抗击疫情最困难的时刻，阿拉伯国家尽其所能积极支援。而在阿拉伯国家出现疫情后，中国政府也多次施以援手，生动体现了中阿之间的深厚友谊。

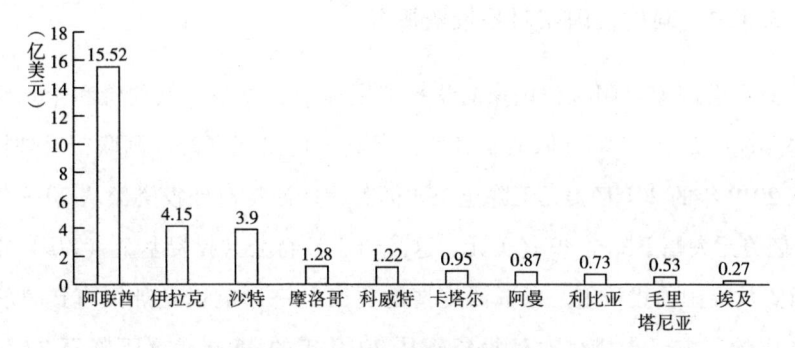

图 3.4　2020 年中国对阿拉伯国家直接投资流量前十位国家

资料来源：中华人民共和国商务部、国家统计局、国家外汇管理局编《2020 年度中国对外直接投资统计公报》，中国商务出版社，2021，第 50~70 页。

---

① 中华人民共和国商务部、国家统计局、国家外汇管理局编《2020 年度中国对外直接投资统计公报》，中国商务出版社，2021，第 3、50~70 页。
② "1"是以能源合作为主轴，"2"是以基础设施建设、贸易和投资便利化为两翼，"3"是以核能、航天卫星、新能源三大高新领域为突破口。

联酋哈利法港二期集装箱码头等一批重大投资项目,成为推动新时期中阿经贸合作转型升级的标志性工程。中阿基础设施合作正处于快速发展的"窗口期",双方合作的科技含量与装备水平不断提高。埃及新首都中央商务区、卡塔尔卢塞尔体育场等项目在疫情中持续推进,赢得了阿拉伯国家的赞誉。

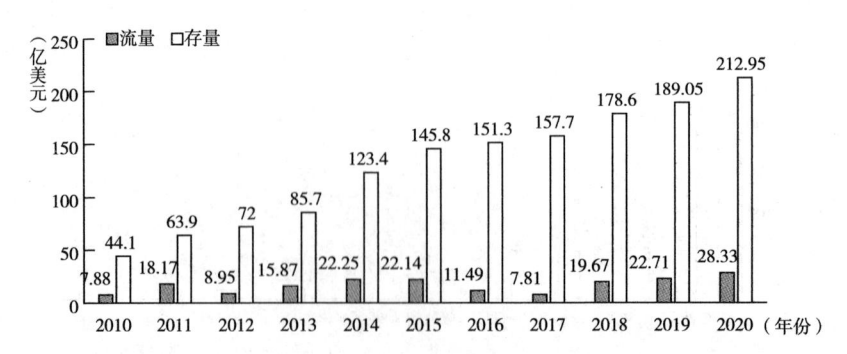

图 3.3　中国对阿拉伯国家直接投资流量和存量（2010~2020）

资料来源：中华人民共和国商务部、国家统计局、国家外汇管理局编《2020年度中国对外直接投资统计公报》,中国商务出版社,2021,第 3 页、第 50~70 页。

3.1.3　中国对阿拉伯国家直接投资特点

2020 年,中国和阿拉伯国家饱受疫情冲击,但中阿经贸合作经受住了疫情的冲击和考验,中阿全方位合作日益深化,成为南南合作的典范。2020 年中国对阿拉伯国家直接投资呈现以下特点。第一,中阿投资逆势增长,2020 年中国对阿拉伯国家直接投资流量同比上升 24.75%；投资存量同比上升 12.6%。第二,从投资国别来看,中国对阿拉伯国家投资集中度非常高。如图 3.4 所示,阿联酋、伊拉克和沙特位列投资目的地前三,仅阿联酋一国就占据投资总额的一半以上,在 2020 年中国对外直接投资流量前 20 位的国家中排名第 11 位。第三,中国对阿拉伯国家直接投资占比仍然很低。如表 3.1 所示,2020 年中国对阿拉伯国家直接投资流量占当年中国对外直接投资总额（1537.1 亿美元）的比例只有 1.8%,投资存量

资额增至 54.86 亿美元，增幅为 20%。黎巴嫩和阿曼的外国直接投资流入额分别上升至 30.67 亿美元和 40.93 亿美元。此外，埃及外资流入减至 58.52 亿美元，降幅为 35%，但埃及仍是非洲最大的外资接收国。[①] 尽管埃及努力促进外国直接投资多样化，自然资源部门仍是吸引外国直接投资的主要领域。同时，我们也应注意到，由于疫情的影响以及能源和初级商品价格低廉，阿拉伯国家绿地投资项目大幅减少。

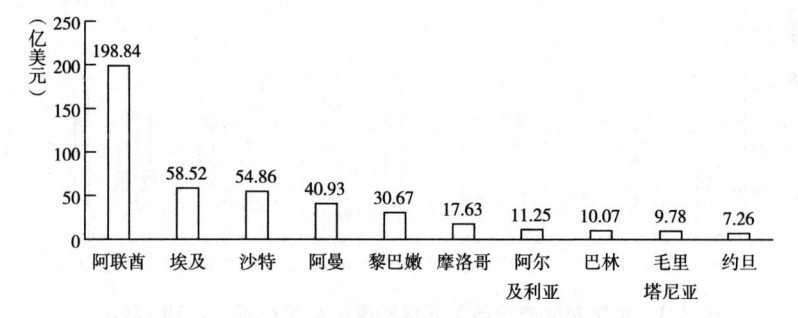

图 3.2　2020 年阿拉伯国家吸引 FDI 流入前十位国家

资料来源：UNCTAD，*World Investment Report 2021*，June 2021，pp. 248，250。

3.1.2　中国对阿拉伯国家直接投资规模

2020 年，尽管世界经济萎缩 3.3%，全球直接投资流动减少近四成，但中国仍是全球主要经济体中唯一实现经济正增长的。中国统筹推进境外企业项目人员疫情防控和对外投资发展，对外直接投资流量达 1537.1 亿美元[②]，同比增长 12.3%，首次位居全球第一。随着中阿共建"一带一路"合作日益深化，2020 年中国对阿拉伯国家直接投资流量达到 28.33 亿美元，直接投资存量达到 212.95 亿美元。[③] 埃及苏伊士经贸合作区、阿

---

① UNCTAD, *World Investment Report 2021*, June 2021, pp. 248, 250.
② 中华人民共和国商务部、国家统计局、国家外汇管理局编《2020 年度中国对外直接投资统计公报》，中国商务出版社，2021，第 3 页。
③ 中华人民共和国商务部、国家统计局、国家外汇管理局编《2020 年度中国对外直接投资统计公报》，中国商务出版社，2021，第 3 页、第 50~70 页。

等20大领域总共达成107项合作举措。

3.1.1 阿拉伯国家吸引外国直接投资规模

应对阿拉伯世界的投资挑战是提高生活水平、为年轻人创造就业机会和解决人口快速增长问题的关键因素。如图3.1所示，在2008年至2019年，阿拉伯地区的外国直接投资（FDI）出现了几次明显下降趋势。受新冠肺炎疫情影响，2020年全球外国直接投资下降了35%，降至1万亿美元，远低于10年前全球金融危机后的最低点。① 发展中国家的工业和基础设施项目的绿地投资受到的打击最为严重。阿拉伯国家吸引的外国直接投资流入额从上一年的389.8亿美元下降至381.7亿美元，同比下降2.1%。② 这个下降幅度低于全球投资流量和其他一些发展中国家及新兴经济体的降幅。

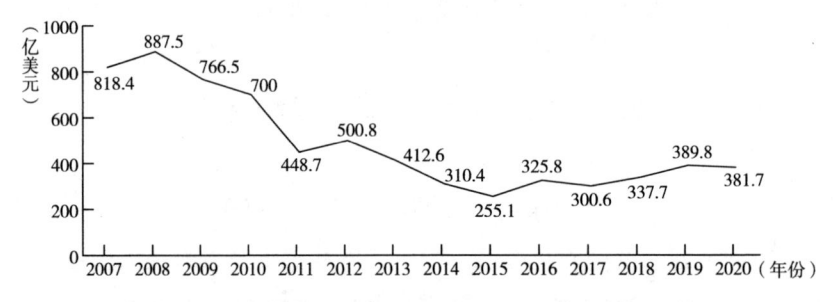

图3.1 阿拉伯国家FDI净流入（2007~2020）

资料来源：World Bank, Foreign direct investment, net inflows, https://data.worldbank.org/indicator/BX.KLT.DINV.CD.WD? locations=1A, March 12, 2022。

如图3.2，2020年阿拉伯国家吸引外国直接投资较多的国家是阿联酋、埃及和沙特。受能源部门收购活动的推动，阿联酋吸引的外国直接投资增至198.84亿美元，增幅为11%。沙特吸引的外国投资保持强劲，投

---

① 联合国贸发会议：《世界投资报告2021》，2021年6月，第5页。
② World Bank, Foreign direct investment, net inflows, https://data.worldbank.org/indicator/BX.KLT.DINV.CD.WD? locations=1A, March 12, 2022。

第3章　中阿投资合作专题报告

阿拉伯国家是中国"一带一路"倡议的天然伙伴,阿拉伯国家也是中国对外投资的重要目的地,投资主体、投资目的地和投资范围日益多元化。根据中国商务部数据,截至 2020 年底,中国对阿拉伯国家直接投资存量 201 亿美元,阿拉伯国家来华投资累计 38 亿美元。[①] 中阿双向投资涵盖油气、建筑、制造、物流、电力等众多领域,随着经贸合作深化和共建"一带一路"顺利稳步推进,未来将释放出更大潜力。

3.1　中阿直接投资规模和特点

2020 年,面对突如其来的新冠肺炎疫情,中阿守望相助、共克时艰,谱写了中阿命运与共的新篇章。习近平主席在致中国—阿拉伯国家合作论坛第九届部长级会议的贺信中指出:"新冠肺炎疫情发生以来,中国和阿拉伯国家风雨同舟、守望相助,坚定相互支持,开展密切合作,这是中阿命运与共的生动写照。"会议发布《中国和阿拉伯国家团结抗击新冠肺炎疫情联合声明》、《中国—阿拉伯国家合作论坛第九届部长级会议安曼宣言》和《中国—阿拉伯国家合作论坛 2020 年至 2022 年行动执行计划》三份成果文件。关于未来两年的"行动执行计划",中阿双方规划了务实合作、共同发展的前进路径,双方在政治、经济、能源、产能、科技、卫生

---

① 《商务部:中阿将拓展经贸合作新领域》,人民网,http://world.people.com.cn/n1/2021/0618/c1002-32134414.html,2021 年 6 月 18 日。

疫志》等内容，以文明互鉴促进民心相通。

随着中阿在服务贸易领域的交流合作不断加强，中国对阿服务贸易进口额不断上升。以阿联酋为例，阿联酋是重要的转口贸易所在地，许多中国企业把阿联酋作为进入中东和非洲的基地。中国与阿联酋自1984年建交以来，双边关系稳定发展，经贸往来不断密切。2020年我国与阿联酋双边贸易额为491.7亿美元，已连续多年成为阿联酋第一大贸易伙伴，阿联酋也连续多年成为我国在阿拉伯国家第一大出口市场。

中国的快速发展、国内消费的多样化以及中阿双方不断拓展经济互补性，是不断推动双边关系提质升级和取得诸多合作成果的动力所在。中阿友好交往与相互合作源远流长，基础深厚。长期以来，和平合作、开放包容、互学互鉴、互利共赢始终是中阿交往合作的主旋律。新时代的中阿合作，不仅为中阿两大民族实现复兴的进程注入了强大动力，让两大民族复兴之梦紧密相连，而且还为促进南南合作树立了典范，为推进地区治理与全球治理作出了重要贡献。

品，并与多个阿拉伯国家举办卫生专家视频会议分享经验。同时，阿拉伯国家也纷纷伸出援手，为中国抗击疫情提供力所能及的帮助。两国人民风雨同舟、相互支持、密切合作，用实际行动践行构建中阿命运共同体的郑重承诺，为新时代中阿战略伙伴关系注入新的强大动力。

在金融服务方面，中国—阿拉伯国家合作论坛第九届部长级会议于2020年7月6日通过视频连线方式召开，为发展全面合作、面向未来的中阿战略伙伴关系，会议特制定《中国—阿拉伯国家合作论坛2020年至2022年行动执行计划》。该文件提出在有关法律法规框架内，应加强双方金融业互利合作和有关监管部门合作，支持双方符合条件的金融机构互设分支机构，继续加强在亚洲基础设施投资银行框架下的合作。

中阿双方投资亮点纷呈。截至2020年底，中国对阿直接投资存量201亿美元，阿拉伯国家来华投资累计38亿美元，双方投资涵盖油气、建筑、制造、物流、电力等众多领域；埃及苏伊士经贸合作区、阿联酋哈利法港二期集装箱码头等一批重大投资项目成为推动新时期中阿经贸合作转型升级的标志性工程。教育服务方面，现代努瓦克肖特大学孔子学院于2020年12月进行汉语水平考试首考，这也是毛里塔尼亚境内第一次举办此类考试，当地汉语学习者不出国门就能够参加汉语水平考试和成绩认证。数字服务方面，疫情之下，联合国教科文组织提倡远程学习，并推荐了一份教育产品清单用于远程教学，中国企业网龙的远程教育平台位列其中；在埃及，网龙旗下产品被指定为全国远程学习平台，覆盖埃及2300万学生以及200万职业教育用户。旅游和文化交流方面，2020年1月11日，迪拜世博会阿联酋—广东精品展以"云展会+全球直播"的方式在广州举办，为充分利用迪拜世博会平台，帮助广东企业拓展国内国际市场，加速融入"双循环"新发展格局，主办方广东省贸促会组织动员300多家企业参展。2020年3月，位于摩洛哥的拉巴特中国文化中心以落实疫情防控为首要任务，积极探索文化交流新模式，利用中心旗下的Facebook（现为"Meta"）、YouTube等网络社交媒体平台开展文化旅游交流传播，推出"云·游中国——世界遗产在中国图片展"、"实用汉语小课堂"、《中国抗

表 2.12 2019 年中国从阿拉伯国家进口商品结构

单位：亿美元

产品编码	大类产品名称	2016年进口额	2017年进口额	2018年进口额	2019年进口额	2020年进口额
27—27	矿物燃料和矿物油	553.04	732.1	1128.52	1205.03	941.58
39—40	塑料和橡胶产品	57.09	75.4	98.08	91.24	83.98
28—38	化学产品	58.94	81.27	115.66	100.44	78.36
25—26	矿产品	18.18	22.11	26.09	26.73	20.75
72—83	金属产品	4.19	4.82	6.2	9.69	14.50
06—15	蔬菜	1.99	3.53	4.69	6.85	10.90
84—85	机械设备和电器产品	3.33	3.92	4.43	4.37	4.76
50—63	纺织和服装	2.92	3.48	4.19	4.17	3.82
16—24	食品	0.49	1.47	1.62	2.19	3.66
44—49	木及木制品	0.06	0.32	0.82	0.51	0.94
01—05	动物产品	0.28	0.23	0.35	2.16	0.65
68—71	矿石和玻璃	2.24	1.24	0.84	2.46	0.62
90—99	杂项制品	0.3	0.31	0.39	0.33	0.43
41—43	皮革和毛皮制品	0.3	0.44	0.42	0.39	0.28
86—89	运输设备	0.1	0.16	0.21	0.21	0.17
64—67	鞋靴类产品	0.11	0.04	0.05	0.05	0.04

注：以中国为报告国。
分类依据：HS3。
资料来源：根据联合国国际贸易数据库数据整理计算。

2.3.3 中国与阿拉伯国家服务贸易合作

面对百年未有之大变局与新冠肺炎疫情交织叠加的复杂局面，中阿经贸合作展现出强劲韧性和旺盛活力。中阿在共建"一带一路"中携手相伴，双方不断巩固政治互信、强化战略协调、深化务实合作，造福中阿人民。

在新冠肺炎疫情暴发后，中国为阿方提供疫苗、口罩等稀缺的医疗用

续表

产品编码	大类产品名称	2016年出口额	2017年出口额	2018年出口额	2019年出口额	2020年出口额
39-40	塑料和橡胶产品	57.59	59.15	65.34	76.63	79.47
86-89	运输设备	42.79	36.52	56.71	72.59	68.04
68-71	矿石和玻璃	48.22	42.06	44.12	57.65	54.52
28-38	化学制品	31.64	33.16	40.13	41.89	46.02
64-67	鞋靴类产品	34.05	32.71	30.22	37.68	32.92
44-49	木及木制品	27.74	25	26.22	29.25	27.85
06-15	蔬菜	11.6	11.56	11.82	14.34	14.84
41-43	皮革和毛皮制品	15.63	15.17	15.26	18.67	12.31
16-24	食品	7.88	8.5	8.61	9.34	8.50
27-27	矿物燃料和矿物油	7.28	6.9	14.55	9.93	6.28
25-26	矿产品	1.4	1.36	1.08	1.13	1.65
01-05	动物产品	1.89	2.14	1.67	2.14	1.04

注：以中国为报告国。
分类依据：HS3。
资料来源：根据联合国国际贸易数据库数据整理计算。

2020年中国从阿拉伯国家进口商品结构与2019年商品结构差别不大，总体发展趋势较为稳定。进口额排名第一的依然是矿物燃料和矿物油，为941.58亿美元，占中国从阿拉伯国家进口总额的80.79%，此类商品的进口额虽比2019年有所收窄，但是较2016年有较大提升，实现了自2016年起进口额的波动式增长。排名第二的是塑料和橡胶产品，进口额为83.98亿美元，较2019年的91.24亿美元有所收窄。排名第三的是化学产品，进口额为78.36亿美元。综上分析，进口额排名前三的大类产品较2019年均有所收窄。其他产品进口额皆有较大提升空间，所占比重也较低。这种贸易结构反映了阿拉伯国家普遍存在着产业单一、工业化程度低、现代化进程滞后、制造业发展薄弱等制约性障碍。

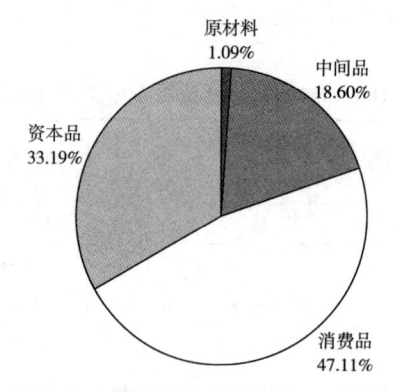

图 2.13　2020 年中国对阿拉伯国家出口四大类商品占比

分类依据：HS3。

资料来源：根据联合国国际贸易数据库数据整理计算。

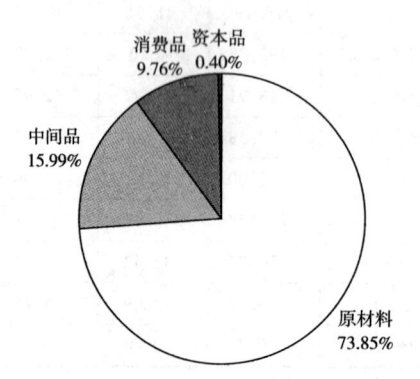

图 2.14　2020 年中国从阿拉伯国家进口四大类商品占比

分类依据：HS3。

资料来源：根据联合国国际贸易数据库数据整理计算。

表 2.11　2020 年中国对阿拉伯国家出口商品结构

单位：亿美元

产品编码	大类产品名称	2016 年出口额	2017 年出口额	2018 年出口额	2019 年出口额	2020 年出口额
84–85	机械设备和电气产品	312.02	319.16	344.74	368.35	387.76
50–63	纺织和服装	192.18	179.74	164.6	192.32	180.57
90–99	杂项制品	92.22	95.74	96.02	127.02	161.57
72–83	金属产品	122.61	117.85	132.02	146.26	144.64

可见中阿双边贸易结构相对稳定(见表2.10、图2.13、图2.14)。

表2.10 中国与阿拉伯国家大类商品贸易结构

UNCTAD 分类产品	贸易额和比重	2016年	2017年	2019年	2019年	2020年
原材料	出口额(亿美元)	11.52	11.69	10.56	13.15	13.22
	比重(%)	1.14	1.19	1.00	1.11	1.09
	进口额(亿美元)	494.82	644.81	994.81	1090.45	858.22
	比重(%)	70.33	69.27	71.44	74.94	73.85
中间品	出口额(亿美元)	194.60	191.86	221.13	236.02	224.92
	比重(%)	19.33	19.44	21.00	19.86	18.60
	进口额(亿美元)	127.95	170.30	226.78	207.85	185.84
	比重(%)	18.19	18.30	16.28	14.28	15.99
消费品	出口额(亿美元)	492.37	464.20	452.49	549.84	569.63
	比重(%)	48.91	47.04	42.97	46.27	47.11
	进口额(亿美元)	77.38	111.87	166.52	152.44	113.38
	比重(%)	11.00	12.02	11.96	10.48	9.76
资本品	出口额(亿美元)	299.58	310.08	354.47	389.39	401.29
	比重(%)	29.76	31.42	33.66	32.77	33.19
	进口额(亿美元)	3.24	3.69	4.28	4.35	4.68
	比重(%)	0.46	0.40	0.31	0.30	0.40

商品分类:根据联合国贸易和发展会议的分类整理计算。
注:以中国为报告国。
分类依据:HS3。
资料来源:根据联合国国际贸易数据库数据整理计算。

从更为具体的产品分类来看,2020年中国对阿主要出口产品是机械设备和电气产品、纺织和服装以及杂项制品,这些商品出口额占出口总额比重较高,分别达31.58%、14.7%和13.16%,上述三类产品占中国对阿出口总额的59.44%。此外,中国还向阿拉伯国家出口金属产品、塑料和橡胶产品、运输设备、矿石和玻璃以及化学制品等。与2019年相比,2020年出口结构变化较大,仅机械设备和电气产品、杂项制品、塑料和橡胶产品、化学制品、蔬菜、矿产品出口额增加,其余均出现收窄现象(见表2.11)。

海合会依然是中国在阿拉伯国家最大的区域性贸易合作伙伴。2020年，中国与海合会国家的双边贸易额为1614.06亿美元，占中阿贸易总额的67.44%，较2019年的1792.59亿美元减少9.96%（见图2.12）。

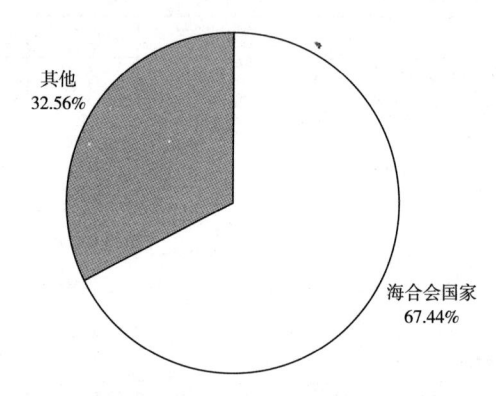

图2.12　2020年海合会国家进出口额占中阿贸易进出口总额比重
分类依据：HS3。
资料来源：根据联合国国际贸易数据库数据整理计算。

2.3.2　中阿双边贸易结构

根据联合国贸易和发展会议对贸易商品的分类方法，下面对2020年中阿双边贸易结构进行研究和相应分析。

2020年，中国对阿出口主要是消费品和资本品，出口额分别为569.63亿美元和401.29亿美元，这两大类出口商品总额为970.92亿美元，占中国对阿全部出口商品的80.30%，且较2019年增长3.37%。其中消费品出口增幅较大，较2019年增长3.60%。由此可见，中国对阿出口商品以制成品为主，原材料的出口额较低，表明中国对阿出口商品中制成品所占比例较大。

从进口看，中国从阿拉伯国家进口最多的商品是原材料，2020年进口额为858.22亿美元，较2019年收窄21.30%，占中国从阿进口总额的73.85%。其次为中间品，进口额为185.84亿美元，占比15.99%。中国从阿拉伯国家进口的消费品和资本品分别占全部进口额的9.76%和0.40%，表明中国从阿进口以原材料为主。2016~2019年中阿双边贸易结构基本状况也如上所述，

大变化,在这十个国家中,仅有阿联酋和科威特逆势而上,进出口总额增加,其余八个国家进出口总额均出现收窄。

表2.9　2020年中国与阿拉伯国家前十大贸易伙伴情况

序号	国家	金额(亿美元)			同比增长(%)		
		进出口	出口	进口	进出口	出口	进口
1	沙特	671.32	280.98	390.33	-14.13	17.45	-28.06
2	阿联酋	491.76	323.07	168.69	1.31	-3.42	11.81
3	伊拉克	301.77	109.24	192.53	-9.32	15.30	-19.12
4	阿曼	186.43	30.91	155.52	-17.07	2.36	-20.08
5	埃及	145.29	136.23	9.06	-15.90	252.84	-93.25
6	科威特	142.85	35.78	107.07	8.11	-70.71	973.92
7	卡塔尔	109.04	26.33	82.71	-1.75	9.28	-4.81
8	阿尔及利亚	65.94	55.97	9.97	-18.46	-19.42	-12.73
9	摩洛哥	47.64	41.73	5.91	-34.02	70.03	-87.60
10	约旦	36.07	31.82	4.26	-22.69	-21.05	-33.06

注:以中国为报告国。
分类依据:HS3。
资料来源:根据联合国国际贸易数据库数据整理计算。

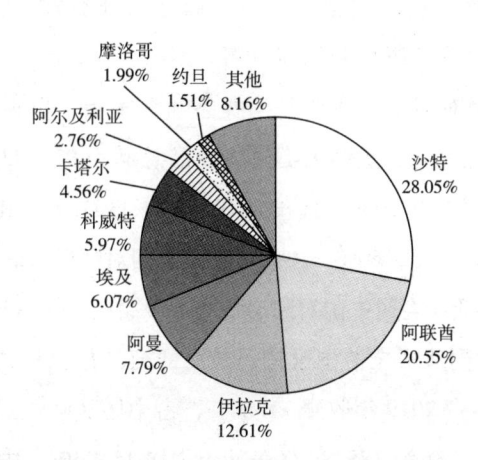

图2.11　2020年中阿前十大贸易伙伴进出口额占中阿贸易进出口总额比重
　　分类依据:HS3。
　　资料来源:根据联合国国际贸易数据库数据整理计算。

2.3 中国与阿拉伯国家贸易关系

2020年,阿拉伯国家与中国贸易合作稳步推进,贸易额占中国2020年对外贸易总额的5.29%,是中国的第七大贸易伙伴。

2.3.1 中国与阿拉伯国家主要贸易伙伴贸易基本状况

2020年,中国在阿拉伯国家的第一大贸易伙伴是沙特,总贸易额为671.32亿美元;第二是阿联酋,总贸易额为491.76亿美元。伊拉克、阿曼、埃及、科威特、卡塔尔、阿尔及利亚、摩洛哥和约旦分别位居第三位至第十位,其中伊拉克、阿曼、埃及、科威特和卡塔尔与中国的贸易总额均超过了100亿美元,贸易总额分别为301.77亿美元、186.43亿美元、145.29亿美元、142.85亿美元、109.04亿美元。在前十位贸易伙伴中,与中国贸易额增幅最大的是科威特,增幅达8.11%。

从出口来看,中国对阿联酋出口额最多,达到323.07亿美元,其次是沙特,达到280.98亿美元。埃及、伊拉克和阿尔及利亚紧随其后,分别为136.23亿美元、109.24亿美元、55.97亿美元。中国对这五个国家的出口占对阿出口总额的73.74%,在前十位贸易伙伴中,中国对埃及的贸易出口增幅最大,达252.84%。

从进口来看,中国在该地区最大的进口来源国是沙特,进口额为390.33亿美元。其次是伊拉克、阿联酋、阿曼和科威特,进口额分别达到192.53亿美元、168.69亿美元、155.52亿美元和107.07亿美元。中国从这五个国家的进口额占从阿拉伯国家进口总额的87.02%。在前十位贸易伙伴中,进口增幅最大的是科威特,达973.92%;进口跌幅最大的是埃及,下跌93.25%(见表2.9)。

总体来看,与2019年相比,2020年中国与阿拉伯国家排名前十的贸易伙伴并没有发生显著变化,只是约旦超越利比亚成为中国与阿拉伯国家排名前十的贸易伙伴。由于受到新冠肺炎疫情等影响,进出口增速发生较

续表

年份	进出口贸易额		进口贸易额		出口贸易额	
	总额（亿美元）	占比（%）	金额（亿美元）	占比（%）	金额（亿美元）	占比（%）
2018	1628.91	66.60	572.88	54.40	1056.03	75.83
2019	1792.59	67.34	681.5	38.02	1111.06	61.98
2020	1614.06	67.44	905.78	77.72	708.28	57.68

分类依据：HS3。

资料来源：根据联合国国际贸易数据库数据整理计算。

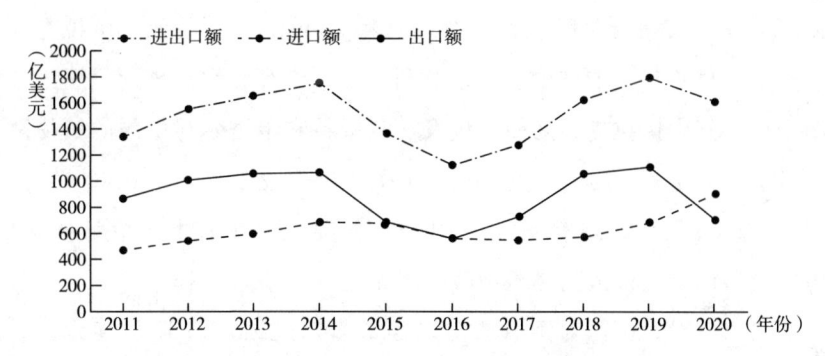

图 2.9　2011~2020 年海合会国家对中国贸易趋势

分类依据：HS3。

资料来源：根据联合国国际贸易数据库数据整理计算。

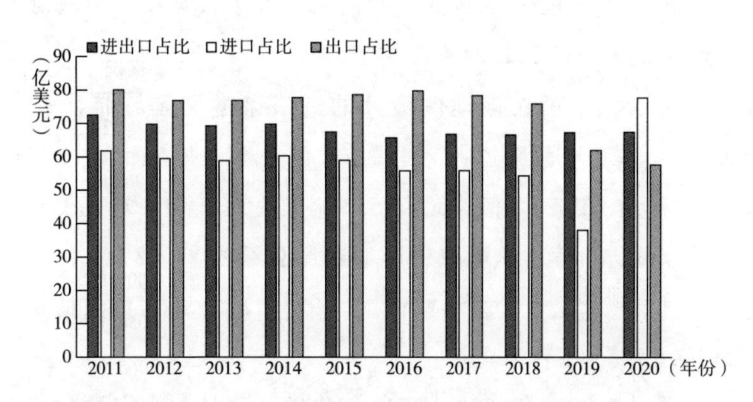

图 2.10　2011~2020 年海合会国家对中国贸易占阿中贸易比重

分类依据：HS3。

资料来源：根据联合国国际贸易数据库数据整理计算。

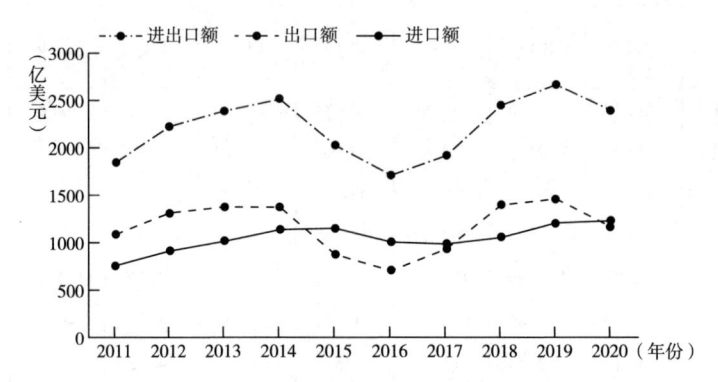

图 2.8　2011~2020 年阿拉伯国家对中国贸易趋势

分类依据：HS3。

资料来源：根据联合国国际贸易数据库数据整理计算。

　　海合会国家是中国在西亚北非地区重要的合作伙伴。2020 年，海合会国家与中国贸易进出口总额为 1614.06 亿美元，占中阿贸易进出口总额的 67.44%，其中海合会国家向中国出口 708.28 亿美元，占阿拉伯国家对中国出口的 57.68%，海合会国家从中国进口 905.78 亿美元，占阿拉伯国家从中国进口的 77.72%，可见，对于中阿贸易往来，海合会国家占据异常重要地位（见表 2.8、图 2.9、图 2.10）。

表 2.8　2011~2020 年海合会国家对中国贸易总体情况

年份	进出口贸易额		进口贸易额		出口贸易额	
	总额（亿美元）	占比（%）	金额（亿美元）	占比（%）	金额（亿美元）	占比（%）
2011	1337.14	72.53	468.68	61.78	868.46	80.05
2012	1551.12	69.74	543.3	59.52	1007.82	76.85
2013	1653.47	69.21	596.77	58.88	1056.70	76.83
2014	1751.83	69.78	685.90	60.30	1065.93	77.67
2015	1366.15	67.45	678.10	58.98	688.05	78.63
2016	1122.8	65.65	561.73	55.83	561.08	79.75
2017	1280.29	66.77	551.13	55.89	729.16	78.33

续表

国别	2013	2014	2015	2016	2017	2018	2019	2020
利比亚	84.72	74.56	46.58	28.83	—	—	62.67	—
毛里塔尼亚	9.99	9	6.41	6.05	—	—	—	8.45
摩洛哥	75.71	88.72	79.13	86.04	97.94	92.97	101.84	70.88
阿曼	97.98	100.14	102.14	99.46	—	—	—	55.39
卡塔尔	274.79	328.59	307.75	315.41	314.27	307.35	354.16	346.98
沙特	766.52	1005.45	880.36	702.67	768.18	554.77	749.73	538.83
索马里	10.17	12.24	13.28	13.35	14.52	14.78	—	—
苏丹	20.3	20.75	17.79	15.07	19.06	6.07	14.23	13.22
叙利亚	—	—	—	—	—	—	—	—
突尼斯	33.04	34	30.76	30.11	29.62	29.41	30.98	23.67
阿联酋	621.92	846.83	818.79	838.39	855	709.87	740.64	595.23
也门	22.72	27.43	12.75	—	—	—	—	—

注："—"代表数据缺失。
资料来源：根据WTO（世界贸易组织）网站数据整理计算。

2.2.3 阿拉伯国家对中国出口状况

受中阿关系和世界局势影响，近十年来阿拉伯国家与中国的贸易发展趋势呈波动状。2020年，中阿双边贸易额继连续三年显著增长后首次出现收窄，贸易总额为2393.43亿美元，较2019年2662.01亿美元下跌10.09%。2021年，中阿双边贸易总额实现强势增长，贸易总额首次突破3300亿美元，较2020年增加37.96%。

2020年阿拉伯国家对中国出口额为1165.44亿美元，较2019年1456.82亿美元下跌20.00%，是2016年以来的首次下跌。2020年阿拉伯国家对中国进口额为1227.99亿美元，较2019年1205.21亿美元上升1.89%。综上，整体表现为近十年阿拉伯国家对中国进口额在波动中稳步上升，而出口额变化幅度较大，不太稳定。2020年，阿拉伯国家对中国贸易逆差为62.55亿美元，贸易逆差大幅收窄，说明贸易结构持续优化（见图2.8）。

续表

国别	2013	2014	2015	2016	2017	2018	2019	2020
索马里	1.99	3.37	3.55	3.73	3.93	4.05	—	—
苏丹	12.58	15.68	17.27	15.45	15.17	14.86	13.68	12.30
叙利亚	—	—	—	—	—	—	—	—
突尼斯	48.31	47.34	32.94	32.49	32.60	36.43	42.73	22.75
阿联酋	212.39	583.25	607.76	655.96	704.97	708.78	734.65	621.38
也门	17.26	17.07	7.28	—	—	—	—	—

注："—"代表数据缺失。
资料来源：根据WTO（世界贸易组织）网站数据整理计算。

从服务贸易进口来看，2020年阿联酋位居第一，沙特居第二，卡塔尔位居第三，科威特和埃及分别位居第四和第五，其服务贸易进口额分别为595.23亿美元、538.83亿美元、346.98亿美元、189.92亿美元和181.99亿美元。其中，海合会依然是阿拉伯国家服务贸易进口总额占比最高的经济体，高达75.05%。2020年服务贸易进口额最少的国家为科摩罗，仅为0.97亿美元（见表2.7）。

表2.7 2013~2020年阿拉伯各国服务贸易进口额

单位：亿美元

国别	2013	2014	2015	2016	2017	2018	2019	2020
阿尔及利亚	107.95	118.03	110.77	108.81	115.99	104.52	—	80.03
巴林	70.51	67.64	65.92	75.3	76.42	79.39	80.83	92.63
科摩罗	1.09	0.99	0.83	—	—	—	—	0.97
吉布提	1.68	1.94	2.3	1.99	—	2.02	6.2	—
埃及	164.08	175.5	175.19	170.32	173.99	178.34	209.32	181.99
伊拉克	146.58	147.9	126.2	100.37	—	177.85	244.93	137.96
约旦	46.12	46.34	45.28	45.65	46.7	46.62	47.85	30.1
科威特	210.04	237.87	237.96	263.48	285.66	335.67	300.67	189.92
黎巴嫩	130.02	132.16	136.93	132.8	138.53	143.38	144.49	57.46

从阿拉伯国家服务贸易出口看，2020年服务贸易出口额位居前五位的国家依次是阿联酋、卡塔尔、埃及、摩洛哥、巴林。阿联酋是地区服务贸易出口规模最大的国家，出口额达到621.38亿美元，较2019年收窄15.42%；卡塔尔居第二位，排位相较2019年上升了三位，为194.29亿美元，较2019年增长1.83%；埃及位列第三，出口额150.53亿美元，较2019年降低28.09%；摩洛哥位列第四，出口额138.55亿美元，较2019年降低28.47%，埃及、摩洛哥的位次较2019年并未发生变化；巴林位居第五，出口额为114.68亿美元，较2019年降低0.95%。2020年，服务贸易出口最少的阿拉伯国家是科摩罗，出口额为0.68亿美元。以阿联酋为首的海合会国家在服务贸易出口方面增长速度较快，所占比重也较高，占阿拉伯国家服务贸易出口额比重达70.45%（见表2.6）。

表2.6　2013~2020年阿拉伯各国服务贸易出口额

单位：亿美元

国别	2013	2014	2015	2016	2017	2018	2019	2020
阿尔及利亚	37.73	35.44	34.55	34.33	32.61	30.40	—	32.00
巴林	85.01	85.71	91.13	109.98	111.30	119.15	115.78	114.68
科摩罗	0.80	0.85	0.84	—	—	—	—	0.68
吉布提	3.66	3.82	4.55	4.06	—	2.09	11.04	—
埃及	182.62	218.98	185.39	136.06	200.33	229.06	209.32	150.53
伊拉克	32.98	41.31	62.60	48.35	—	53.06	66.37	38.03
约旦	63.15	71.40	62.69	60.35	67.20	70.21	79.65	24.59
科威特	61.80	62.68	60.56	55.29	51.63	76.17	82.39	72.55
黎巴嫩	157.20	147.51	159.10	151.93	160.80	152.95	150.68	50.06
利比亚	1.80	0.79	4.83	0.86	—	—	1	—
毛里塔尼亚	1.86	2.79	2.46	2.70	—	—	—	1.83
摩洛哥	143.53	162.36	146.74	153.79	172.61	178.94	193.70	138.55
阿曼	29.55	31.30	33.79	36.04	—	—	—	18.30
卡塔尔	111.75	135.26	149.97	151.76	177.06	177.80	190.80	194.29
沙特	118.45	125.16	144.74	172.53	180.21	173.86	241.82	102.48

表 2.5 2011~2020 年阿拉伯国家服务贸易进出口额

年份	阿拉伯国家进出口		阿拉伯国家出口		阿拉伯国家进口		差额（亿美元）
	金额（亿美元）	同比（%）	金额（亿美元）	同比（%）	金额（亿美元）	同比（%）	
2011	3788.23	7.7	1222.52	-0.3	2565.72	12.0	-1343.20
2012	4077.73	7.6	1305.54	6.8	2772.19	8.0	-1466.65
2013	4220.32	3.5	1324.40	1.4	2895.92	4.5	-1571.52
2014	5268.17	24.8	1792.08	35.3	3476.09	20.0	-1684.00
2015	5029.84	-4.5	1812.73	1.2	3217.12	-7.5	-1404.39
2016	4859.74	-3.4	1825.64	0.7	3034.10	-5.7	-1208.46
2017	4846.27	-0.3	1910.41	4.6	2935.87	-3.2	-1025.46
2018	4810.82	-0.7	2027.81	6.1	2783.01	-5.2	-755.20
2019	5263.35	9.41	2174.80	7.25	3088.54	10.98	-913.74
2020	4018.71	-23.65	1595.00	-26.66	2423.71	-21.53	-828.71

资料来源：根据 WTO（世界贸易组织）网站数据整理计算。

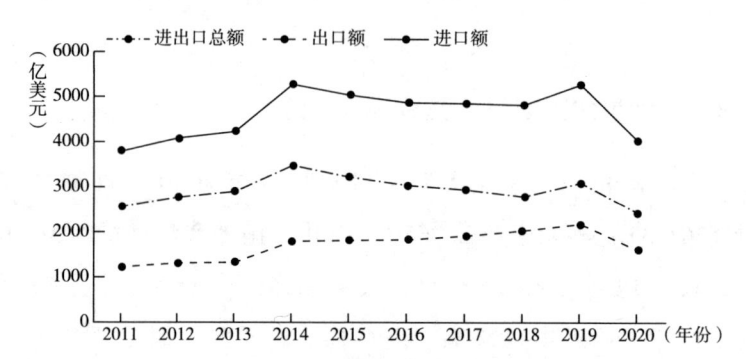

图 2.6 2011~2020 年阿拉伯国家服务贸易趋势

资料来源：根据 WTO（世界贸易组织）数据库数据整理计算。

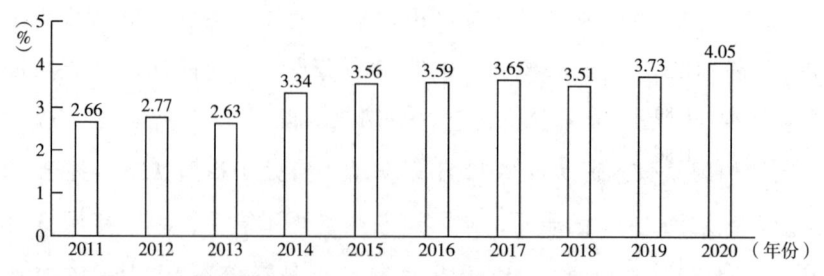

图 2.7 2011~2020 年阿拉伯国家服务贸易出口额占世界服务贸易出口总额比重

资料来源：根据 WTO（世界贸易组织）数据库数据整理计算。

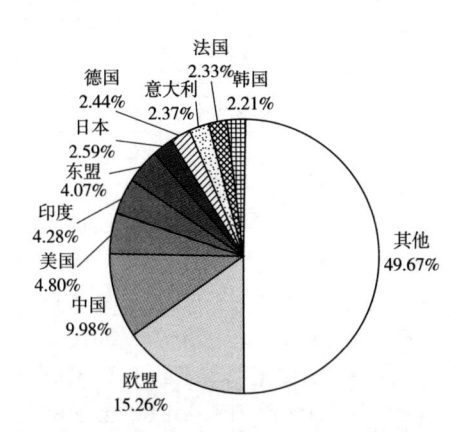

图 2.5 2020年阿拉伯国家对前十大贸易伙伴进出口总额占比
注：以阿拉伯国家为报告国。
分类依据：HS3。
资料来源：根据联合国国际贸易数据库数据整理计算。

2.2.2 阿拉伯国家服务贸易基本状况

2020年，阿拉伯国家服务贸易进出口总额为4018.71亿美元，较2019年5263.35亿美元收窄23.65%。其中，服务贸易进口额为2423.71亿美元，较2019年3088.54亿美元收窄21.53%，近六年来除2019年外均出现了贸易服务进出口总额、进口额收缩现象，服务贸易出口额为1595.00亿美元，较2019年2174.80亿美元收窄26.66%，为服务贸易出口额九年来首次出现收缩（见表2.5、图2.6）。

2020年，阿拉伯国家服务贸易出口额占世界服务贸易出口总额比重4.05%，较2019年的3.73%上升0.32个百分点，达到自2011年以来最高值，总体变化不大，基本保持稳定（见图2.7）。

阿拉伯国家服务贸易自2011年以来就一直处于逆差状态，且于2014年其逆差额达到1684亿美元，此后逆差基本逐年缩小，2020年服务贸易逆差额为828.71亿美元，较2019年服务贸易逆差额913.74亿美元收窄9.31%。

续表

年份	进出口贸易		出口贸易		进口贸易		贸易差额	
	总额（亿美元）	同比（%）	金额（亿美元）	同比（%）	金额（亿美元）	同比（%）	金额（亿美元）	同比（%）
2014	19208.59	-3.49	11205.41	-7.30	8003.18	2.40	3202.23	-25.05
2015	14392.32	-25.07	7091.00	-36.72	7301.32	-8.77	-210.33	-106.57
2016	13007.05	-9.63	6264.12	-11.66	6742.93	-7.65	-478.80	-127.64
2017	12838.43	-1.30	6744.69	7.67	6093.74	-9.63	650.95	235.95
2018	18598.23	44.86	9974.09	47.88	8624.14	41.52	1349.95	107.38
2019	14080.79	-24.29	7335.58	-26.45	6745.21	-21.79	590.37	-143.73
2020	11398.47	-19.05	5712.96	-22.12	5685.51	-15.71	27.45	-95.35

注：表中数据以阿拉伯国家为报告国。
分类依据：HS3。
资料来源：根据联合国国际贸易数据库数据整理计算。

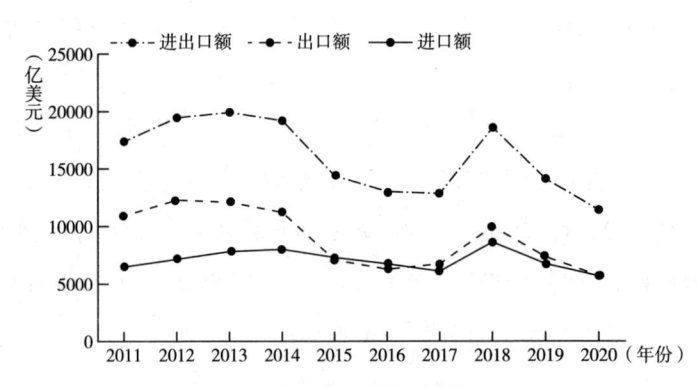

图 2.4　2011~2020 年阿拉伯国家贸易趋势

注：表中数据以阿拉伯国家为报告国。
分类依据：HS3。
资料来源：根据联合国国际贸易数据库数据整理计算。

2020 年，阿拉伯国家前四大贸易伙伴为欧盟、中国、美国、印度，进出口额分别占进出口总额的 15.26%、9.98%、4.80%、4.28%，合计占进出口总额的 34.32%（见图 2.5）。相比于 2019 年阿拉伯国家前四大贸易伙伴欧盟、中国、美国、印度，并无显著变化。

2.2 阿拉伯国家对中国贸易状况

2.2.1 阿拉伯国家对外贸易基本状况

2020 年，阿拉伯国家对世界贸易总额为 11398.47 亿美元，较 2019 年的 14080.79 亿美元下跌了 19.05%，下跌幅度较大。阿拉伯国家对外贸易额从 2011 年起，历经 2 年连续增长后，于 2013 年达到近 10 年的峰值 19903.86 亿美元。此后，石油价格下降、地区局势动荡等，导致其对外贸易额从 2014 年到 2017 年连续四年下跌（见表 2.4）。油价在持续数年走低后，于 2018 年出现复苏，而后又因复杂多变、动荡不安的局势以及新冠肺炎疫情等影响呈下跌趋势。

2020 年，阿拉伯国家对外贸易出口额为 5712.96 亿美元，较 2019 年 7335.58 亿美元下跌了 22.12%。2020 年，阿拉伯国家对外贸易进口额为 5685.51 亿美元，较 2019 年 6745.21 亿美元下跌了 15.71%。近六年阿拉伯国家对外贸易进口额除 2018 年实现了正增长，其他年份均为负增长（见图 2.4）。阿拉伯国家 2020 年贸易顺差为 27.45 亿美元，较 2019 年收窄了 95.35%。2011~2014 年，阿拉伯国家对外贸易为顺差，2015 年和 2016 年为逆差，2017~2020 年均为顺差。2011~2020 年阿拉伯国家对外贸易总体呈现不稳定、波动的状态（见表 2.4、图 2.4）。

表 2.4　2011~2020 年阿拉伯国家对外贸易额及增长速度

年份	进出口贸易		出口贸易		进口贸易		贸易差额	
	总额（亿美元）	同比（%）	金额（亿美元）	同比（%）	金额（亿美元）	同比（%）	金额（亿美元）	同比（%）
2011	17392.17	29.41	10906.28	37.01	6485.90	18.37	4420.38	78.17
2012	19446.23	11.81	12289.56	12.68	7156.67	10.34	5132.89	16.12
2013	19903.86	2.35	12088.30	-1.64	7815.56	9.21	4272.74	-16.76

续表

年份	进出口贸易		出口贸易		进口贸易		贸易差额	
	总额（亿美元）	同比（%）	金额（亿美元）	同比（%）	金额（亿美元）	同比（%）	金额（亿美元）	同比（%）
2016	1710.29	-15.56	1006.74	-12.49	703.56	-19.59	303.18	10.10
2017	1917.57	12.12	986.73	-1.99	930.84	32.30	55.89	-181.57
2018	2445.67	27.57	1053.10	6.70	1392.57	49.60	-339.47	-807.39
2019	2662.01	8.85	1205.21	14.44	1456.82	4.61	-251.61	-25.88
2020	2393.43	-10.09	1227.99	1.89	1165.44	-20.00	62.55	124.86
2021	3301.90	37.96	1473.12	19.96	1828.78	56.92	-355.66	-668.60

注：以中国为报告国。
分类依据：HS3。
资料来源：根据联合国国际贸易数据库数据整理计算。

2021年，中国对阿进出口贸易总额为3301.90亿美元，较2020年增加37.96%。其中，中国对阿进口总额为1828.78亿美元，较2020年增加56.92%。中国对阿出口总额为1473.12亿美元，较2020年增长19.96%。贸易逆差为355.66亿美元，较2020年收窄668.60%。如图2.3所示，中国对阿进出口总额、进口额、出口额均实现强势增长，中阿贸易关系日渐紧密。

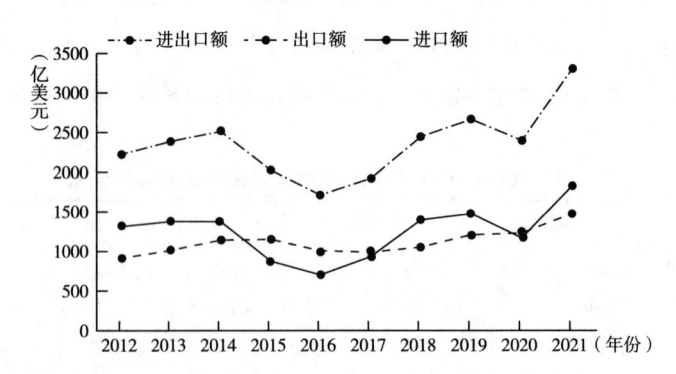

图2.3 2012~2021年中国与阿拉伯国家贸易趋势

注：以中国为报告国。
分类依据：HS3。
资料来源：根据联合国国际贸易数据库数据整理计算。

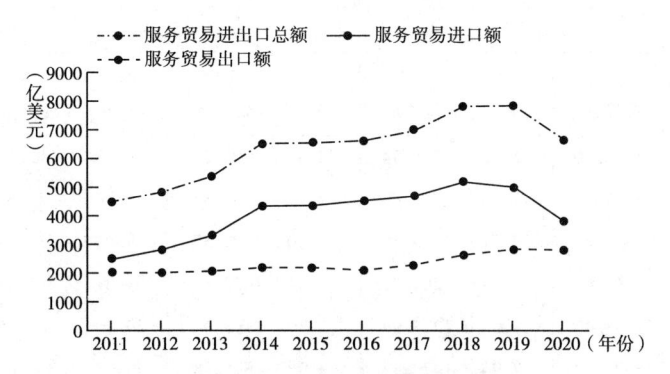

图 2.2　2011~2020 年中国服务贸易趋势

资料来源：根据 WTO（世界贸易组织）网站数据整理计算。

2.1.3　中国对阿拉伯国家出口基本状况

尽管受到新冠肺炎疫情的影响，2020 年中阿各自经济发展都受到一定冲击，但是总体来看，双边经贸合作的基本盘仍然相对稳固。

2020 年，中国对阿进出口贸易总额为 2393.43 亿美元，较 2019 年收窄 10.09%。其中，中国对阿进口总额为 1165.44 亿美元，较 2019 年收窄 20.00%。中国对阿出口总额为 1227.99 亿美元，较 2019 年增长 1.89%。贸易顺差为 62.55 亿美元，较 2019 年增长 124.86%（见表 2.3）。中国对阿进出口总额、进口额、出口额均实现波动式增长，中阿贸易往来日趋紧密（见图 2.3）。

表 2.3　2011~2021 年中国对阿拉伯国家贸易总体情况

年份	进出口贸易		出口贸易		进口贸易		贸易差额	
	总额（亿美元）	同比（%）	金额（亿美元）	同比（%）	金额（亿美元）	同比（%）	金额（亿美元）	同比（%）
2011	1843.58	34.71	758.61	20.53	1084.96	46.77	-326.35	197.14
2012	2224.20	20.65	912.79	20.32	1311.41	20.87	-398.62	22.14
2013	2388.97	7.41	1013.52	11.03	1375.45	4.88	-361.93	-9.20
2014	2510.51	5.09	1138.21	12.30	1372.30	-0.23	-234.09	-35.32
2015	2025.41	-19.32	1150.40	1.07	875.01	-36.24	275.38	117.64

上年收窄14.9%。其中，出口总额2806亿美元，同比上年收窄0.9%；进口总额3811亿美元，同比上年收窄23.9%。

根据表2.2可以看出，中国服务贸易呈现逆差状态。2011年逆差额为468亿美元，历经连续增长，2018年逆差额达到最大值2550亿美元，但2019年与2020年逆差额均有所收窄，2020年逆差额为1005亿美元。2012年以来，中国累计进口服务3.8万亿美元，年均增长4.6%，高于同期全球3.7%的平均水平，贡献全球服务进口增长的17.1%，对全球服务进口增长的贡献居全球前列。

表2.2 2011~2020年中国服务贸易进出口额

年份	中国进出口		中国出口		中国进口		差额（亿美元）
	金额（亿美元）	同比（%）	金额（亿美元）	同比（%）	金额（亿美元）	同比（%）	
2011	4489	20.8	2010	12.7	2478	28.2	-468
2012	4829	7.6	2016	0.3	2813	13.5	-797
2013	5376	11.3	2070	2.7	3306	17.5	-1236
2014	6520	21.3	2191	5.9	4329	30.9	-2137
2015	6542	0.3	2186	-0.2	4355	0.6	-2169
2016	6616	1.1	2095	-4.2	4521	3.8	-2426
2017	6957	5.0	2281	8.9	4676	3.4	-2395
2018	7821	12.4	2636	15.5	5186	10.9	-2550
2019	7839	0.2	2832	7.4	5007	-3.5	-2175
2020	6671	-14.9	2806	-0.9	3811	-23.9	-1005

资料来源：根据WTO（世界贸易组织）网站数据整理计算。

由图2.2可以得出，中国服务贸易进出口总额、出口总额、进口总额从2011年到2020年总体呈现波动变化趋势，服务贸易规模整体不断扩大。同时，图2.2也十分直观地描述了中国服务贸易从2011年到2020年一直处于逆差状态，服务贸易进口额远高于出口额，但近两年贸易逆差有所改善。

2020年

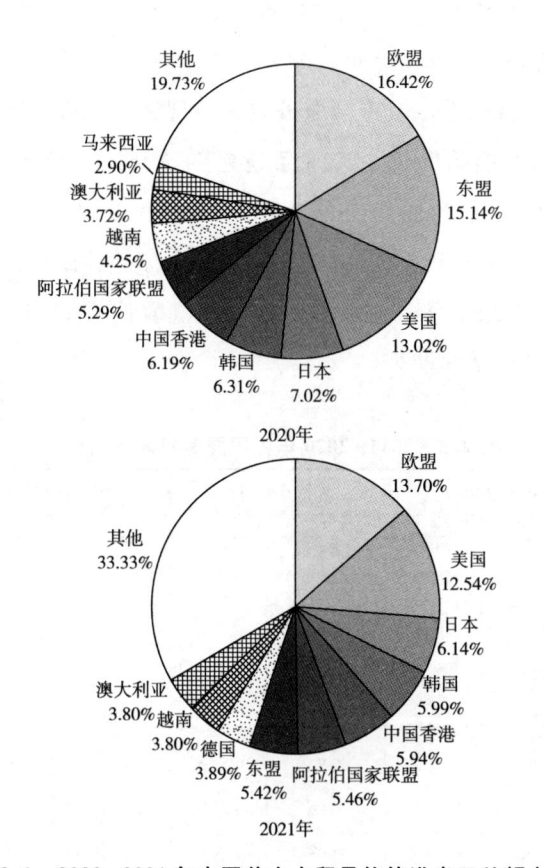

- 其他 19.73%
- 欧盟 16.42%
- 马来西亚 2.90%
- 澳大利亚 3.72%
- 越南 4.25%
- 阿拉伯国家联盟 5.29%
- 中国香港 6.19%
- 韩国 6.31%
- 日本 7.02%
- 美国 13.02%
- 东盟 15.14%

2021年

- 其他 33.33%
- 欧盟 13.70%
- 美国 12.54%
- 日本 6.14%
- 韩国 5.99%
- 中国香港 5.94%
- 阿拉伯国家联盟 5.46%
- 东盟 5.42%
- 德国 3.89%
- 越南 3.80%
- 澳大利亚 3.80%

图 2.1　2020~2021 年中国前十大贸易伙伴进出口总额占比

注：以中国为报告国。
分类依据：HS3。
资料来源：根据联合国国际贸易数据库数据整理计算。

2.1.2　中国对外服务贸易状况

2020 年，中国经济总体平稳、稳中求进，但是由于疫情等多方因素的影响，服务贸易自 2011 年以来首次出现收窄，进口与出口均呈下降趋势。同时，服务贸易差额收窄，服务贸易结构持续优化，高质量发展取得积极进展。

根据 WTO 数据，2020 年中国服务贸易进出口总额 6671 亿美元，同比

表 2.1　2011~2021 年中国对外贸易额及增长速度

年份	进出口贸易		出口贸易		进口贸易		贸易差额	
	总额（亿美元）	同比（%）	金额（亿美元）	同比（%）	金额（亿美元）	同比（%）	金额（亿美元）	同比（%）
2011	35191	22.75	18983.88	20.32	16207.80	25.73	2776.08	-3.82
2012	37240	5.82	20487.82	7.92	16752.69	3.36	3735.13	34.55
2013	40014	7.45	22090.07	7.82	17924.51	6.99	4165.56	11.52
2014	41566	3.88	23422.93	6.03	18143.54	1.22	5279.39	26.74
2015	38096	-8.35	22734.68	-2.94	15361.95	-15.33	7372.73	39.65
2016	36855	-3.26	20976.37	-7.73	15879.21	3.37	5097.16	-30.86
2017	39747	7.85	22633.71	7.90	17114.24	7.78	5519.47	8.29
2018	44828	12.78	24942.30	10.20	19886.01	16.20	5056.29	-8.39
2019	45675	1.89	24985.78	0.17	20689.50	4.04	4296.20	-15.03
2020	46462	1.72	25906.01	3.68	20555.91	-0.65	5350.10	24.53
2021	60467	30.14	33623.02	29.79	26843.63	30.59	6779.39	26.72

注：以中国为报告国。
分类依据：HS3。
资料来源：根据联合国国际贸易数据库数据整理计算。

2020 年，中国前四大贸易伙伴为欧盟、东盟、美国、日本，进出口额分别占进出口总额的 16.42%、15.14%、13.02%、7.02%，合计占进出口总额的 51.60%（见图 2.1）。与 2019 年相比，中国前四大贸易伙伴名次并未发生改变，进出口总额占比相较 2019 年有所增长。

如图 2.1 所示，2021 年，中国前四大贸易伙伴为欧盟、美国、日本、韩国，进出口额分别占进出口总额的 13.70%、12.54%、6.14%、5.99%，合计占进出口总额的 38.37%。尽管自 2020 年以来一直面临着复杂演变的国际局势和跌宕反复的新冠肺炎疫情，我国的对外贸易进出口业务展现出强劲韧性。

路"建设，在利用外资和扩大外贸方面取得了良好成效。尽管受到疫情严重冲击和全球经济整体低迷的影响，中阿互利共赢合作依然稳步推进，通过高质量共建"一带一路"，携手推动构建人类命运共同体。中阿复工复产、新闻合作、改革发展等合作梯次跟进，深入交流治国理政经验，不断充实和丰富中阿合作内涵。

2.1 中国对阿拉伯国家贸易状况

2.1.1 中国对外贸易基本状况

2020年全球经济不确定性和风险挑战显著增多，我国外贸发展面临的外部环境严峻复杂，经济增长持续放缓。据统计，2020年我国进出口总额46462亿美元，同比2019年增加1.72%。其中，出口总额25906.01亿美元，同比2019年增长3.68%；进口总额20555.91亿美元，同比2019年收窄0.65%；贸易顺差5350.1亿美元，同比2019年增加24.53%。2020年，我国对外贸易虽然实现了进出口总额、出口总额连续四年增长，但进口总额近三年来首次出现收窄（见表2.1）。

2021年，我国对外贸易发展面临的国内外形势依旧严峻复杂，但由于疫情带来的"出口替代"效应与进出口商品价格的上涨，我国进出口规模首次突破6万亿美元，创历史新高。根据联合国国际贸易数据库数据整理计算，2021年我国进出口总额60467亿美元，同比2020年增加30.14%。其中，出口总额33623.02亿美元，同比2020年增长29.79%；进口总额26843.63亿美元，同比2020年增加30.59%；贸易顺差6779.39亿美元，比2020年增加26.72%（见表2.1）。上述数据反映出我国出口的韧性较强，但也要看到，2021年的出口增长受临时性外需增加和价格因素影响较大。目前，由于疫情持续，世界经济复苏困难，再加上物流中断等原因，我国出口面临的挑战依旧较大。

第2章　中阿贸易合作专题报告

2020年是人类历史进程中具有分水岭意义的一年。突如其来的疫情引发全球性危机，各国人员往来按下了"暂停键"，世界经济增长挂上了"倒车挡"，强权政治、冷战思维沉渣泛起，单边主义、保护主义逆流横行，我国外贸发展面临不少风险和挑战。

近年来，中国贸易发展的风险挑战明显上升。国际上，中美贸易摩擦仍在继续；国内，城乡居民消费需求增长的市场驱动力不足。在当今世界处于百年未有之大变局下，我国始终坚持对外开放的基本国策，构建人类命运共同体，奉行互利共赢的开放政策。随着稳外贸措施落地发力，国家出台了一系列扩大开放、促进外贸稳定增长的政策。外贸结构不断优化、新旧动能转换加快，实现了量的稳定增长和质的同步提升，2020年，我国对外贸易总体平稳，并稳中求进。

2020年，中东地区形势跌宕起伏，为转移国内疫情矛盾和填补美国从地区战略收缩的"真空"，地区一些国家纷纷出场，或争夺地区事务主导权，或扩大影响力提升话语权。在此背景下，地区重新分化组合，出现阵营化、多元化、碎片化和"菜单式"合作。同时，为促进经济发展，阿拉伯国家采取各种措施摆脱单一经济模式，推动经济改革和多样化发展，寻求转型之路，允许私营部门发挥更大作用，实施财政和税收优惠以吸引外国直接投资，加大基础设施投融资和优化营商环境等，这些措施对阿拉伯国家经济发展起到了积极作用。

同时，阿拉伯国家谋求更加多元化的对外关系，纷纷融入"一带一

中阿战略伙伴关系在历经抗击新冠肺炎疫情共同考验后更加牢固深厚。未来应充分利用现有的合作机制，如在中阿合作论坛框架下利用卫生合作机制开展抗疫合作，深化协商与共享机制，继续保持密切沟通和配合，落实《中国—阿拉伯国家卫生合作2019北京倡议》，携手打造"健康丝绸之路"。创新合作方式与内容，如举办健康、医药主题论坛，加强交流，继续深化在公共卫生、传统医药、健康等各领域务实合作，促进"中国—阿拉伯国家医疗健康合作联盟"发展，为维护中阿人民的生命健康安全、实现中阿人民的共同福祉，进而构建人类卫生健康共同体携手努力。

1.4.4 共同开创中阿经贸合作新时代

气候变化与可持续发展问题已经成为全球社会经济发展的最重要议题。未来，如何应对绿色转型的能源挑战，需要中阿共同应对与通力合作。此外，发挥数字经济的推动作用，以科技创新和数字化变革催生新的发展动能，在拓展数字经济、清洁能源等新兴领域合作达成共识，解决数字经济给就业、税收以及社会弱势群体带来的挑战，弥合数字鸿沟，为中阿共谋合作发展，实现互利共赢，高质量共建"一带一路"创造了新机遇、新空间。

中国"一带一路"倡议与阿拉伯国家远景及发展规划将持续深化对接，共同高质量共建"一带一路"，扎实推进能源、投资、渔业、高新技术、人力资源等领域合作，实现优势互补、共同发展。中国正大力构建以国内大循环为主体、国内国际双循环相互促进的新发展格局，着力培育国内市场，全面扩大对外开放。在未来中阿经贸合作中，一方面，中国将继续扩大进口，与阿拉伯国家深化经贸合作；另一方面，更多的中国企业也将前往阿拉伯国家投资兴业，为阿拉伯国家的经济多元化发展作出贡献。疫情下，发展与民生问题成为中阿合作的重中之重。中阿应坚持共商、共建、共享原则，共建"一带一路"，巩固合作存量，拓展合作增量，推动中阿经贸合作结出丰硕成果，进一步充实中阿战略伙伴关系内涵，形成更加紧密的中阿命运共同体。

谈判，为中阿贸易往来提供便利，为双方企业提供更多贸易机会。截至2020年底，中国—阿曼（杜库姆）产业园已有入园企业6家，完成投资额8000万美元。①

1.4.2 推动高质量中阿经贸合作

世界经济数字化转型是大势所趋。加强绿色基建、绿色能源、绿色金融等领域与数字技术的融合和合作，努力建设更多环境友好型项目。数字能源技术的合作，将大力提高中阿经贸合作的质量；清洁发电、能源数字化、交通电动化、绿色ICT基础设施、综合智慧能源等将助力绿色低碳高质量发展。

中阿投资项目呈现综合化、专业化、大型化、创新化和高端化的特点，这对中国企业的产品创新能力、资源整合能力、高效管理能力及综合协调能力等提出了更高要求。未来随着中阿经贸合作的质量不断提升，企业在国际合作中也需不断提升自身竞争力，以配合中阿战略伙伴关系的更高要求。

1.4.3 深化拓展中阿经贸合作新领域

中阿从能源经济领域合作为主到全方位多领域合作是一个长期发展的过程，双方应继续稳定在能源经济领域合作的主基调，同时开展其他领域合作，重视中阿合作的长远性、稳定性和多层次性。近年来，阿拉伯国家为改变过度依赖油气产业的单一经济结构，全面推进经济多元化战略，大力招商引资，努力发展基建、制造、物流、旅游、渔业等非油气产业，鼓励和支持私营企业特别是中小企业在经济建设中发挥更大作用。未来应深挖中阿合作潜力，拓宽合作领域，培育新产品、新技术、新模式、新业态。科学合理定位，助力企业找到市场突破口，因地制宜开展推广营销，助力中企提升品牌知名度与影响力。例如帮助产业提高自身软实力，包括灵活产业合作、举办跨境电商大会、鼓励举办论坛、扩大开放政策等。

---

① 中国—阿拉伯国家博览会网站，https://cn.cas-expo.org.cn/index.html。

色优势农业"走出去"步伐。①

2020年12月21~25日,第十六届"一带一路"中阿技术转移与国际合作创新论坛系列分论坛以线上线下相结合方式召开,通过"中国技术""中国方案"给阿拉伯国家农业发展注入新的活力。

1.4 中阿经贸合作趋势展望

新冠肺炎疫情对中阿战略伙伴关系是挑战更是机遇。面对新冠肺炎疫情冲击,中阿关系逆势前行,继续焕发生机与活力。中阿企业携手复工复产,共战疫情,共胜困难。未来,双方需要互信互利,持续深化各领域友好交流和互利合作,共同推进国际抗疫合作,支持全球经济复苏,促进可持续发展,共同维护多边主义,推动中阿关系不断迈上新台阶。

1.4.1 落实经贸共识,稳固合作基础

中国与阿拉伯国家要继续坚定维护多边贸易体制,促进自由贸易,反对单边主义和保护主义,维护公平竞争。同时,在共建"一带一路"倡议引导下,利用好中阿合作论坛、海合会战略对话等多边对话与合作平台,继续推进中阿沟通机制常态化,保证双方战略互信。继续深化"一带一路"建设,积极推动"一带一路"与各国战略对接,共享双方在经济领域中的实际成果,凝聚共识,降低政治风险,加强合作,实现互利共赢。此外,中阿应继续通过搭建平台,建立更健全的服务企业保障机制,鼓励双方企业利用国家性活动,发展和扩大在两国的业务,助力更多企业实现更快更好发展。

落实《中国—阿拉伯国家合作论坛2020年至2022年行动执行计划》,加快中国—巴勒斯坦自由贸易区建设,尽早完成中国—海合会自由贸易区

---

① 景春梅:《宁夏是如何推动农业"走出去"的?》,中国农业外经外贸信息网,http://www.mczx.agri.cn/mybw/202012/t20201207_7572403.htm,2020年12月7日。

伙伴关系，共同推动沙特国家人工智能能力发展计划，帮助沙特实现数字化转型。①

在科技领域，中阿在无人机领域的合作成为中阿科技合作的亮点。沙特阿卜杜勒·阿齐兹科学技术中心（KACST）在阿联酋的 IDEX-2021 国防展览会上展示了与总部位于四川的中国公司腾盾科创（Tengoen Technology）共同开发的大型三引擎无人机 Al EQAB-1。

1.3.4 中阿农业合作稳步推进

农业是中国与阿拉伯国家经贸合作的重要领域。借助中阿合作论坛、中阿博览会、共建"一带一路"等平台，中阿不断加强农业贸易往来、深化农业技术合作，推动经济社会发展。中阿合作论坛框架下的农业合作是深化中阿多领域合作的重要路径，呈现出上下合作的联动性、议题设置的广泛性、整体个体的互动性、项目实施的阶段性、合作地域的均衡性等特征。②

中阿农业技术合作不断深化。中国自主研发的智能风光互补节水灌溉技术，取得了良好的经济和社会效益。中国宁夏自 2015 年被赋予"中国—阿拉伯国家农业技术转移中心"职能后，根据自身农业发展特点及对外开放需要，编制了宁夏农业对外开放规划，建立了由 16 个部门组成的农业对外合作厅际联席会议机制，制定了《中国—阿拉伯国家农业技术转移中心海外分中心建设管理办法（试行）》，不断巩固提升农业技术转移中心海外分中心建设水平，建立了 8 个中国—阿拉伯国家农业技术转移中心海外分中心，打造促进宁夏乃至全国农业对外交流合作的平台，加快特

---

① 《阿里云智能将为沙特提供云服务》，中华人民共和国驻吉达总领事馆经济商务处网站，http://jedda.mofcom.gov.cn/article/zxhz/202012/20201203027788.shtml，2020 年 12 月 31 日。

② 张帅：《中阿合作论坛框架下的农业合作：特征、动因与挑战》，《西亚非洲》2020 年第 6 期。

然环境、物资匮乏、交通困难、新冠肺炎疫情等难题，迎难而上，全力推进在阿拉伯国家的世界杯场馆、港口、机场等重大项目建设，赢得了阿拉伯国家和同行的高度评价和赞誉，为今后在阿承揽项目奠定坚实基础。

在通信技术领域，中国不仅鼓励中国企业积极参加阿拉伯国家经济社会建设，为阿数字经济、高科技等领域发展作出贡献，还支持进一步加强在通信技术应用、人才培养等领域的交流与合作，不断拓展中阿务实合作领域。如华为在中东地区重点打造"华为ICT学院""华为ICT大赛""华为未来种子计划"等公益培训类项目，培养了大量ICT人才，促进了信息通信领域的发展。2020年10月，第二届阿尔及利亚华为ICT大赛颁奖仪式暨第五届阿尔及利亚华为"未来种子计划"启动仪式顺利举办。

在金融合作领域，中阿加速金融科技和创新投资合作，中阿合作发展基金、跨境加密数字金融支付等"一带一路"项目成果引人关注。2020年9月的中国国际服务贸易交易会搭建了中阿相互了解的桥梁。如在阿布扎比国际金融中心展位展板上，多家阿布扎比大型企业、金融机构、创新机构、产业机构信息清晰陈列，它们当中很多在阿布扎比国际金融中心的促成下落地中国开拓市场，深度精准投资。2020年产业投资与国际金融合作论坛也为中阿金融合作搭建了新的平台，① 阿拉伯国家表示有充分条件和能力支持"一带一路"金融合作，借助新技术探索新的金融生态，全力实现可持续发展目标。

1.3.3 中阿科技合作成果丰硕

人工智能和大数据领域的合作成为亮点。2020年10月21~22日，沙特数据与人工智能局主办全球人工智能峰会，并与中国华为公司建立合作

---

① 《2020产业投资与国际金融合作论坛在沪举办》，中国对外贸易网，http：//www.ccpitcft.com/newsinfo/864438.html，2020年11月16日。

日中埃签署《中埃关于新冠病毒疫苗合作意向书》。2020年8月20日，国药集团中国生物与摩洛哥新型冠状病毒疫苗签约合作，推动了中国与阿拉伯马格里布地区的抗疫合作。此外，中国和阿尔及利亚也在积极商讨建设疫苗合作灌装生产线事宜。

此外，中国政府还援助阿尔及利亚、叙利亚等阿拉伯国家新冠疫苗，通过分享抗疫经验、提供医疗物资等方式有力地帮助抗击疫情。同时，阿拉伯国家普遍支持中国"春苗行动"接种点的设想，中国在阿拉伯国家的"春苗行动"顺利进行，如沙特、阿联酋、埃及、阿曼等国家积极参与并协助中国推进疫苗接种。

中国通过对阿拉伯国家的疫苗援助、捐赠等实际行动，减少了阿拉伯民众对中国参与阿拉伯国家投资的认知偏差和心理隔阂，加深了阿拉伯民众对中国的认识和了解，也为日后双方合作及项目的顺利落地奠定了良好的社会舆论基础。未来，中阿将继续发挥团结抗疫典范作用，积极考虑以多种形式向发展中国家提供疫苗，包括捐赠和无偿援助。

1.3.2 多领域合作促协同发展

中阿经贸合作得到多领域的支持与协作，各方积极响应"一带一路"倡议，利用平台为中阿经贸合作的发展提供支持。2020年11月24日，第四届中阿新闻合作论坛以线上形式举办。来自中国和阿盟成员国的新闻主管部门代表、主流媒体负责人等近60人围绕"新冠肺炎疫情下媒体在加强中阿共同发展中的责任"的主题进行了深入交流。中阿双方就加强新闻领域务实合作达成广泛共识，发表了《第四届中阿新闻合作论坛视频会议公报》。

2020年12月3日，中国贸促会会长高燕在京集体会见阿拉伯国家驻华使节，就进一步深化中阿工商界交流合作，推动中阿互利共赢发展等交换意见。① 中国企业发扬中国精神，重信守诺、攻坚克难，中企克服自

---

① 《中国贸促会会长高燕集体会见阿拉伯国家驻华使节》，中国国际贸易促进委员会网站，https://www.ccpit.org/a/20201204/20201204qcu3.html，2020年12月4日。

1.3 疫情下中阿经贸合作进展情况

1.3.1 疫苗合作彰显合作典范

面对新冠肺炎疫情，中阿风雨同舟，展现甘苦与共的友好情谊，诠释了中阿战略伙伴关系的真谛。新冠肺炎疫情全球大暴发伊始，中国各驻阿大使馆同各国卫生部、外交部等部门就疫情防控建立了密切联系，第一时间同阿方分享各类疫情防控数据材料。在阿中资企业协会在新冠肺炎疫情初期就号召会员单位为当地捐助医疗物资。各驻在国大使馆同在阿中资机构、侨团组织、留学生等代表进行视频连线，举行新冠肺炎疫情联防联控机制成立会议。

中阿抗疫理念相通，携手合作、共克时艰。疫苗合作凸显中阿高度信任，更加体现公平普惠，成为中阿全面战略伙伴关系发展的一大亮点。中国积极落实国家领导人关于将疫苗作为全球公共产品的郑重宣示，已向17个阿拉伯国家及阿盟援助和出口了7200多万剂疫苗。[①]

阿联酋是最先接受中国疫苗境外三期临床试验的阿拉伯国家。2020年6月23日，国药集团中国生物新冠灭活疫苗国际临床（Ⅲ期）阿联酋启动仪式以视频会议举办，为国际团结合作抗疫树立了典范。目前两国疫苗合作灌装生产线业已建成投产。对此，中国国务委员兼外交部部长王毅表示："创造了多国籍、大规模临床试验的全球纪录，推动了中国疫苗的国际认可，也为全球抗疫合作作出了重要贡献。"[②] 为帮助地区国家提升自主抗疫能力，共筑疫苗免疫防线，中国和埃及建成了非洲第一条拥有稳定产能的新冠疫苗联合生产线，首批100万剂量产，并于2021年1月1

[①] 《王毅：中方已向17个阿拉伯国家及阿盟援助和出口7200多万剂疫苗》，中国新闻网，https://www.chinanews.com.cn/gn/2021/07-22/9525868.shtml，2021年7月22日。

[②] 《王毅：中阿合作灌装中国疫苗为地区和全球抗疫作出新贡献》，中华人民共和国驻阿拉伯联合酋长国大使馆网站，http://ae.china-embassy.org/chn/xwdt/202103/t20210329_8910579.htm，2021年3月29日。

1.2.3 强化医疗健康卫生合作

团结抗疫是中阿合作的新亮点，其中疫苗合作成为中阿抗疫合作的核心。中阿共同推进包括疫苗研发在内的双边卫生医疗合作，一道推动构建中阿卫生健康共同体，不断充实中阿全面战略伙伴关系内涵。此外，中阿还就加强疫情防控物资采购国际合作进行多次交流，并且以中阿疫苗临床试验及疫苗合作为契机，进一步加深中阿在医药健康领域的合作。通过引入"互联网+医疗健康"，深化在传染病防控、医疗机构与技术研究等方面的合作。

中阿携手抗疫，通过达成《中国和阿拉伯国家团结抗击新冠肺炎疫情联合声明》等重要共识，落实《中国—阿拉伯国家卫生合作2019北京倡议》，共同将公共卫生合作打造成中阿合作新亮点，推动中阿医疗健康合作联盟的发展。

1.2.4 创新融合发展数字经济

在疫情影响下，阿拉伯国家开始注重如何有效应对流行病的影响。一些阿拉伯国家开始积极鼓励增加对数字经济的投资，重点是发展5G技术、人工智能、生物技术和绿色经济等先进技术领域，以促进经济复苏、转型和升级。在全球数字经济发展态势下，数字经济作为融合性经济，对推动中阿传统产业实现转型升级、优化资源配置、调整产业结构具有重要作用。中阿通过数字基础设施建设稳固数字经济基础。2020年，华为与奥瑞吉埃及公司在埃及合作建成了用于云计算服务的先进数据中心"商务云"。2020年6月，华为与沙特智慧城市解决方案签署关于智慧城市合作的协议。

中国与阿拉伯国家在数字化领域的合作不断深化，实现了中阿数字经济发展战略对接，为各国经济复苏增添了动力，尤其是中国的经验对加速阿拉伯国家的数字化转型起到了积极作用。

储量与 2019 年持平，即 7158 亿桶，主要集中在沙特（37.3%）、伊拉克（20.7%）、科威特（14.2%）、阿联酋（13.7%）和利比亚（6.8%）。[①] 中国从阿拉伯国家进口原油占中国同期进口一半，阿拉伯国家成为中国第一大原油进口来源地。其中，根据中国海关总署数据，2020 年中国从沙特进口的原油总量约 8493 万吨，约合 169 万桶/天，比 2019 年同期增长 1.92%，沙特继续保持中国最大的原油供应国地位。[②] 能源合作已经成为中阿合作的主要方向，"压舱石"作用更加牢固，全方位加强中阿能源合作，实现开放条件下的能源安全。

在双碳目标下，中阿以可再生能源行业为突破，能源供给结构加速优化。中国船舶集团和卡塔尔石油公司依托各自优势在能源运输、装备制造及全球化服务等领域开展广泛合作，为稳定全球能源产业发展、提振世界经济注入强劲动力。2020 年 4 月 22 日，中国船舶集团有限公司与卡塔尔石油公司在中国北京、上海及卡塔尔多哈三地以"云签约"方式联合签署《中国船舶—卡塔尔石油液化天然气（LNG）船建造项目》协议，所涉订单总金额超过 200 亿元人民币。这是卡塔尔天然气项目首批订单，也是中国船企迄今承接的金额最大的造船出口订单。

推广清洁能源，共享绿色发展，产业转型升级蹄疾步稳。中国与沙特共建智慧城市，资金引领中沙合作。例如延布作为沙特打造的首个智慧城市，多家中国企业对延布的持续发展作出重大贡献。其中，2020 年中沙宣布计划投资 56 亿美元，在沙特延布工业城合作兴建石化厂。目前，延布已发展为全球第三大炼油枢纽。此外，中国还与阿联酋、埃及等国就油气、新能源、核能等合作深入沟通，达成多项共识。

[①] 《阿拉伯国家天然气消费占全球总量的 11%》，中华人民共和国驻沙特阿拉伯王国大使馆经济商务处网站，http://sa.mofcom.gov.cn/article/jmxw/202201/20220103237389.shtml，2022 年 1 月 17 日。

[②] 2017 年，中国自沙特进口原油 5218 万吨。2018 年，中国自沙特进口原油 5673 万吨。2019 年，中国自沙特进口原油 8333 万吨（资料来源：中华人民共和国海关总署网站，http://dzs.customs.gov.cn/customs/index/index.html）。

2020年底，中埃·泰达苏伊士经贸合作区共吸引96家企业入驻，实际投资额超12.5亿美元，累计销售额超25亿美元，缴纳税费近1.76亿美元，直接解决约4000人就业，产业带动就业3.6万余人，成为"沙漠中的经济引擎"。① 中企承建的沙特城市地下隧道于2020年12月31日竣工通车。中国国家电网公司成功入股OETC后的首个大型基建项目"RABT"。② 中阿产能合作示范园，哈里法港码头和迪拜700兆瓦光热发电项目等"一带一路"项目稳步推进。

中阿实现绿色经济战略对接，共同践行绿色发展理念。2020年11月，中国宇通客车与卡塔尔国家运输公司签署协议，宇通客车向卡塔尔方面提供1002台世界杯专用车辆等公交运输支持。双方在卡塔尔自贸区建立电动客车组装厂签署了框架协议，以技术输出带动卡塔尔工业化水平，服务卡塔尔环保车辆转型战略，提升汽车产业配套能力、带动汽车产业集群发展，服务卡塔尔公交电动化战略。③ 此外，2020年，中国车企在沙特销量持续增长。长安汽车累计整车出口沙特近2万辆，同比增长近一倍，终端实销超过1.9万台；一汽奔腾出口2500辆，同比增长超2倍；上汽名爵销售1.8万辆，同比增长80%。④

1.2.2　聚焦绿色能源技术合作

能源合作是共建"一带一路"的重点领域，也是中阿合作的主轴和"压舱石"。虽然新冠肺炎疫情在全球蔓延，对全球能源生产和需求造成全面冲击，中阿能源合作依旧稳步前进。2020年，阿拉伯国家原油探明

---

① 《一晃5年，"沙漠新城"再升级》，"中东瞭望"公众号，2021年1月26日。
② 《阿曼OETC举行南北联网工程项目集体签约仪式》，中华人民共和国驻阿曼苏丹国大使馆经济商务处网站，http://om.mofcom.gov.cn/article/jmxw/202010/20201003010814.shtml，2020年10月26日。
③ 《周剑大使出席卡塔尔电动公交和充电站启用仪式》，中华人民共和国驻卡塔尔大使馆网站，http://qa.china-embassy.org/chn/zkgx/jmhz/202106/t20210630_8941420.htm，2021年6月30日。
④ 《中国乘用车开拓沙特市场成绩显著》，"中国驻吉达总领馆"公众号，2021年5月24日。

1.2 疫情下中阿经贸合作领域态势

在中阿合作论坛机制下，中阿加强抗疫合作与经验交流。2020年4月9日，疫情全球流行伊始，中国便同阿盟举行新冠肺炎疫情卫生专家视频会议，介绍中国抗击疫情的经验做法。阿盟秘书处和12个阿拉伯国家卫生部负责人以及专家、世界卫生组织应对新冠肺炎疫情特使等逾百人通过网络在线与会。2020年下半年，疫情有所缓和后，阿拉伯国家各领域蓄势待复工。2020年9月23日，中国同阿盟举行"中国应对新冠肺炎疫情对经济影响先进经验"视频研讨会，阿盟秘书处、阿拉伯劳工组织、阿拉伯农业发展组织、阿拉伯数字经济联盟、联合国贸发会议投资与项目部等机构代表近百人参会。中国就统筹推进疫情防控和经济社会发展工作相关经验上与阿方诚挚交流。9月29日，中国外交部会同卫生健康委、科技部与阿盟举行新冠肺炎疫情卫生专家视频会议，阿盟秘书处及10个阿拉伯国家卫生部门负责人和专家参加，双方重点就"新形势下的新冠肺炎疫情风险评估和分级防控"、"疫苗研发"和"新冠病毒毒性演化"等议题进行了深入探讨。

1.2.1 纵深发展经济产业合作

当前中阿关系正处于历史最好时期，中阿基础设施建设方兴未艾。在埃及的中资企业防疫保产双管齐下，承建项目未受太大影响。中国建筑埃及分公司承建的埃及新行政首都中央商务区项目一期工程标志塔主体结构已超过53层（约260米），8栋单体建筑主体结构封顶。中企承建的斋月十日城轻轨项目一期进展顺利，建成后将成为埃及第一条电气化轻轨线；500千伏输电线路工程项目也已基本完工，将成为埃及国家电力网络的大动脉。[①] 截至

---

① 《中国与埃及经贸务实合作疫情下稳中有升》，新华网，http://www.xinhuanet.com/silkroad/2021-01/14/c_1126981548.htm，2021年1月18日。

伯国家复工复产作出了积极贡献。中国电商平台在海湾六国互联网用户覆盖率已达80%。①"互联网+跨境电商"的优势互补使得阿拉伯电商发展空间潜力巨大。

1.1.3 中阿经贸合作机制持续优化

在新冠肺炎疫情全球大暴发的背景下，中阿经贸合作机制为两国企业开展经贸合作搭建了重要平台，对促进中阿贸易发展意义重大。中阿积极参加在对方国家举办的展览会、投资贸易洽谈会等活动。阿拉伯国家积极参加2020年中国第三届国际进口博览会。2020年7月15日，中国—阿联酋经济贸易数字展览会线上会议顺利召开。超过1000家中阿两国企业参展，展品涉及智慧城市、医疗产品、纺织时尚及文创、新农业及食品等多个类别。2020年10月20日，驻阿联酋大使倪坚应邀出席2020年迪拜世博会中国参展线上路演活动。2020年11月，中国—阿曼经贸联委会和阿商工投部联合举办的第九届会议以视频形式顺利召开。② 2020年3月4日，中国与叙利亚政府签署了《中华人民共和国政府和阿拉伯叙利亚共和国政府经济技术合作协定》。

1.1.4 新兴技术赋能中阿经贸合作

中阿积极分享并利用数字贸易和创新技术，推动科学抗疫。在能源领域，中国继续推动中阿在光伏、光热、风能等新能源、清洁能源领域的合作。人工智能和大数据领域的合作成为亮点。沙特国有企业沙特电信公司（STC）、阿里云和eWTP Arabia Capital基金将建立合作伙伴关系，为沙特提供高性能的公共云服务。③

---

① 《开启全球数字治理新篇章（和音）》，《人民日报》2021年3月30日第3版。
② 《中国—阿曼经贸联委会第九届会议顺利召开》，中阿合作论坛网站，http://www.chinaarabcf.org/chn/zagx/zajw/t1836073.htm，2020年11月27日。
③ 《阿里云智能将为沙特提供云服务》，中华人民共和国驻吉达总领事馆经济商务处网站，http://jedda.mofcom.gov.cn/article/zxhz/202012/20201203027788.shtml，2020年12月31日。

1.1.2 中阿经贸合作亮点纷呈

虽然全球疫情持续蔓延，但中阿经贸交流与合作的步伐并未停滞。面对疫情及严格的防控措施，中阿项目工程受到影响。但随着疫情缓解，中国同阿拉伯国家复工复产和务实合作也取得积极进展。中国政府援巴勒斯坦拉马拉市学校项目一期工程顺利完工；深圳开通中东非洲全货运航线；中方承建的卡塔尔超大型战略蓄水池完工并投入运营；中国政府在迪拜创建了第一所海外全日制学校——迪拜中国学校；[①] 埃及苏伊士经贸合作区、阿联酋哈利法港二期集装箱码头等一批重大投资项目，成为新时期中阿经贸合作转型升级的标志性工程。在全球经济低迷的大背景下，中阿在太阳能、铁路、机车等领域不断拓展新项目合作，推动中阿全面战略伙伴关系高水平运行。

在中阿经贸合作中，中国与海合会国家通过积极互动交流，经贸合作继续逆势而上，充分展现中阿双方经济的高度互利性和务实合作的韧性。原油贸易大幅增长30%以上，达到近1亿吨；新签工程承包项目总额增长14.5%，超过100亿美元。同时，中国全力支持阿联酋办好迪拜世博会；助力卡塔尔世界杯主体育场建设。中国铁建国际集团（中铁建）中标的卡塔尔2022年世界杯主体育场建设项目，于2020年完成主钢结构合龙，标志着中铁建承建的卡塔尔2022年世界杯足球赛主体育场项目主体钢结构施工完成。

在疫情全球大暴发的环境下，中阿数字经济合作成为亮点，电商产业成为中阿经贸合作新增长极，也成为共建"一带一路"新的合作空间。2020年7月，中阿合作论坛第九届部长级会议决定加强双方在互联网和数字经济发展领域的合作与互鉴。新冠肺炎疫情发生后，中国电商积极与阿方分享平台建设、物流管理等方面的技术和经验，为助力阿拉

---

① 《2020年12月10日外交部发言人华春莹主持例行记者会》，中华人民共和国外交部网站，https://www.mfa.gov.cn/web/wjdt_674879/fyrbt_674889/202012/t20201210_7816953.shtml，2020年12月10日。

1.1.1 中阿经贸合作总体健康发展

中阿在防控疫情的同时，继续推动共建"一带一路"高质量发展，加强宏观经济政策协调，统筹推进经济社会发展，保持贸易投资市场开放。2020年，中阿贸易总额为2393.43亿美元（见图1.1）。其中，中国对阿拉伯国家出口1277.99亿美元，在疫情影响下，仍实现了同比6.15%的增长，机电和高新技术产品占比达67.4%，同比分别增长6.1%和3.3%。中国稳居阿拉伯国家的第一大贸易伙伴国。截至2020年底，中国对阿拉伯国家直接投资存量201亿美元，阿拉伯国家来华投资累计38亿美元，双向投资涵盖油气、建筑、制造、物流、电力等领域。

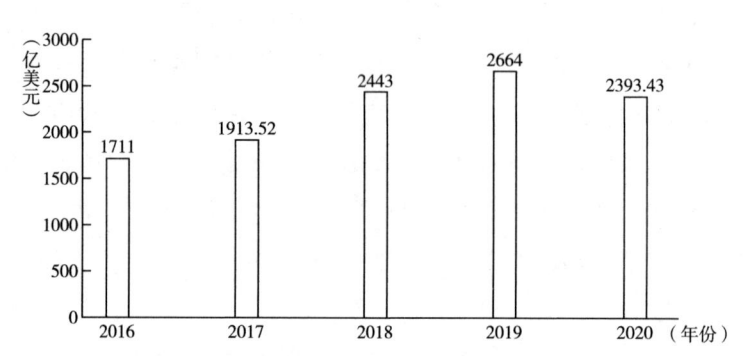

图1.1 2016~2020年中国与阿拉伯国家贸易总额统计数据
资料来源：中华人民共和国商务部。

2020年7月6日，中阿合作论坛第九届部长级会议以视频方式成功举行。双方签署了《中国和阿拉伯国家团结抗击新冠肺炎疫情联合声明》、《中国—阿拉伯国家合作论坛第九届部长级会议安曼宣言》和《中国—阿拉伯国家合作论坛2020年至2022年行动执行计划》三份重要成果文件。中阿双方在会上一致同意召开中阿峰会，并就打造中阿命运共同体、在涉及彼此核心利益问题上相互支持、推动共建"一带一路"、加强抗疫和复工复产合作等达成重要共识，为新形势下的中阿全面战略伙伴关系开辟了更广阔的前景。

第1章　疫情下中阿经贸合作总体形势

2020年是人类历史上极不平凡的一年，新冠肺炎疫情暴发深刻影响了国际格局和经济秩序，国际与地区形势更加复杂。在中国与阿拉伯国家元首的共同引领下，中阿高层互动频繁，中阿关系进一步巩固深化。中阿团结抗疫"闪亮全球"，各领域务实合作取得丰硕成果。中阿发表团结抗击新冠肺炎疫情联合声明，双方重申加强团结、促进合作、相互支持，携手抗击疫情，应对共同威胁和挑战。同时，中阿共同致力于疫后复苏和经济发展，维护双方人民福祉和经济社会可持续增长。中国国务委员兼外交部部长王毅积极评价疫情下的中阿关系，中阿患难与共，并肩战斗，团结互助，双方关系得到深化和升华。[①]

1.1　疫情下中阿经贸合作总体情况

2020年，在新冠肺炎疫情影响和全球经济低迷的不利环境下，中阿经贸合作受到一定冲击，但中阿战略伙伴关系并未受影响，尤其是中阿在抗疫合作中打造了更加紧密的中阿卫生健康共同体。在中阿团结抗疫的努力下，疫情不仅得到有效遏制，中阿开展合作的需求和机会也逐渐增多。中阿战略伙伴关系在疫情之下更加坚固，向世界显示了发展中国家团结的力量，为中阿共建命运共同体开辟了更加广阔的天地。

---

① 王毅：《加强抗疫合作，打造中阿命运共同体》，《人民日报》2020年7月3日第6版。

第5章 中阿能源合作专题报告 ·················· 073
- 5.1 阿拉伯国家能源资源概况 ·················· 073
- 5.2 中阿传统能源合作现状 ·················· 078
- 5.3 中阿新能源合作现状 ·················· 085
- 5.4 中阿能源合作的前景 ·················· 090

第6章 中阿数字经济合作专题报告 ·················· 094
- 6.1 阿拉伯国家数字经济水平现状 ·················· 094
- 6.2 中阿数字经济合作现状 ·················· 103
- 6.3 中阿数字经济合作前景 ·················· 108

第7章 中阿科技与生态环境治理合作专题报告 ·················· 112
- 7.1 中阿科技合作框架和传统领域 ·················· 112
- 7.2 中阿科技合作的重点领域 ·················· 114
- 7.3 中阿生态环境治理合作现状和前景 ·················· 121
- 7.4 中阿科技合作展望 ·················· 126

第8章 中阿卫生健康（抗疫）合作专题报告 ·················· 130
- 8.1 中阿抗疫合作的总体情况 ·················· 130
- 8.2 中阿抗疫合作的特点与意义 ·················· 140
- 8.3 中阿卫生健康合作展望 ·················· 143

第9章 宁夏对外开放专题报告 ·················· 147
- 9.1 宁夏与阿拉伯国家经贸合作总体情况 ·················· 147
- 9.2 前五届中阿博览会专题报告 ·················· 152

目 录

第1章 疫情下中阿经贸合作总体形势 …………………………………… 001
  1.1 疫情下中阿经贸合作总体情况 ………………………………… 001
  1.2 疫情下中阿经贸合作领域态势 ………………………………… 005
  1.3 疫情下中阿经贸合作进展情况 ………………………………… 009
  1.4 中阿经贸合作趋势展望 ………………………………………… 013

第2章 中阿贸易合作专题报告 …………………………………………… 016
  2.1 中国对阿拉伯国家贸易状况 …………………………………… 017
  2.2 阿拉伯国家对中国贸易状况 …………………………………… 023
  2.3 中国与阿拉伯国家贸易关系 …………………………………… 032

第3章 中阿投资合作专题报告 …………………………………………… 041
  3.1 中阿直接投资规模和特点 ……………………………………… 041
  3.2 2021年中阿投资新趋势 ………………………………………… 047
  3.3 中阿投资合作新机遇和新挑战 ………………………………… 051

第4章 中阿农业合作专题报告 …………………………………………… 056
  4.1 阿拉伯国家农业发展现状 ……………………………………… 057
  4.2 中阿农业合作情况 ……………………………………………… 062
  4.3 中阿农业合作的前景展望 ……………………………………… 069

《中阿经贸关系发展进程2021年度报告》课题组成员

顾问

朱威烈 （上海外国语大学教授、中阿改革发展研究中心专家委员会主任）

主编

王广大 （上海外国语大学教授、中阿改革发展研究中心执行主任）

统稿人

丁丽萍 （黄河出版传媒集团阳光出版社编辑）

章节撰写人员

孙德刚/武桐雨 （复旦大学国际问题研究院中东研究中心研究员/上海外国语大学中东研究所博士生）

杨韶艳 （宁夏大学经济管理学院教授）

姜英梅 （中国社会科学院西亚非洲研究所副研究员）

张　帅 （上海政法学院讲师）

潜旭明/张益森 （上海外国语大学中东研究副研究员/上海外国语大学中东研究博士生）

王晓宇 （上海外国语大学师资博士后、中阿改革发展研究中心讲师）

周　放 （上海外国语大学东方语学院副教授）

王广大/李雪婷 （上海外国语大学教授/中阿改革发展研究中心助理研究员）

杨子实/丁丽萍 （宁夏大学博士/黄河出版传媒集团阳光出版社编辑）

编写说明

本报告是在宁夏贸易促进委员会指导下，由上海外国语大学、中阿改革发展研究中心组织编写完成。课题组成员依托其在中阿经贸关系方面长期的知识积累，运用适当的分析工具描绘了中阿经贸关系的年度进程、特征和发展趋势。

本报告由王广大担任主编。丁丽萍对中文版进行了统稿。金蕊、王一涵等将中文版翻译为英文。

对所有人员在编写本报告过程中所付出的努力和所体现的专业精神，表示衷心的感谢。同时感谢宁夏贸易促进委员会对本报告给予的支持和帮助。

图书在版编目(CIP)数据

中阿经贸关系发展进程2021年度报告 / 宁夏贸易促进委员会编；王广大主编. -- 北京：社会科学文献出版社，2022.11
ISBN 978-7-5228-0840-6

Ⅰ.①中… Ⅱ.①宁… ②王… Ⅲ.①对外经济关系-研究报告-中国、阿拉伯半岛地区-2021 Ⅳ.①F125.537.1

中国版本图书馆CIP数据核字(2022)第186134号

中阿经贸关系发展进程2021年度报告

编　　者 / 宁夏贸易促进委员会
主　　编 / 王广大

出 版 人 / 王利民
组稿编辑 / 宋月华
责任编辑 / 周志静
责任印制 / 王京美

出　　版 / 社会科学文献出版社·人文分社(010)59367215
　　　　　　地址：北京市北三环中路甲29号院华龙大厦　邮编：100029
　　　　　　网址：www.ssap.com.cn
发　　行 / 社会科学文献出版社(010)59367028
印　　装 / 三河市龙林印务有限公司

规　　格 / 开本：787mm×1092mm　1/16
　　　　　　印张：22.5　字数：395千字
版　　次 / 2022年11月第1版　2022年11月第1次印刷
书　　号 / ISBN 978-7-5228-0840-6
定　　价 / 198.00元

读者服务电话：4008918866

版权所有 翻印必究

中国—阿拉伯国家博览会
معرض الصين والدول العربية
CHINA-ARAB STATES EXPO

中阿经贸关系发展进程 2021年度报告

宁夏贸易促进委员会 / 编
王广大 / 主编

The Development Process of
China-Arab States Economic and Trade
Relations Annual Report

—— 2021 ——

社会科学文献出版社
SOCIAL SCIENCES ACADEMIC PRESS (CHINA)